Information Systems
in Organizations

Information Systems in Organizations

ROBERT W. ZMUD

*The University of North Carolina
at Chapel Hill*

SCOTT, FORESMAN AND COMPANY

*Glenview, Illinois   Dallas, Texas   Oakland, New Jersey
Palo Alto, California   Tucker, Georgia   London, England*

Cover: 1964. Low-power, high-frequency (700 MHz) transistor. Made with planar technology, an important step in improving and simplifying the manufacturing process.

Acknowledgments

Photographs on cover and pp. 2, 84, 232, and 386 courtesy of Fairchild Camera and Instrument Corporation.

Zmud, Robert W., 1946–
   Information systems in organizations

   Includes index.
   1. Management information systems.   I. Title.
T58.6.Z578   1983   658.4'0388   82-20534

ISBN 0-673-15438-6

23456-RRC-87868584

Preface

Organizations have, over the last thirty years, expanded their ability to use computer technologies. For most of this period, computer specialists have been the key driving force. As a result of recent advances in computer hardware and software, however, end-users (workers, staff analysts, and managers) are now helping to decide when, where, and how computer-based information systems should be used to support organizational activities. Many organizations, in fact, depend on end-users to play a leading role in identifying and introducing new computer applications.

A primary objective of *Information Systems in Organizations* is to prepare future end-users (particularly staff analysts and managers) to fully participate in organizational efforts to implement computer-based information systems. This text is primarily intended to introduce advanced business students to (1) the ways computer technologies can be applied to perform or support organizational activities and (2) the tasks that must be undertaken and performed well if computer technologies are to be used successfully. While no experience with computer-related issues is assumed, students are expected to be familiar with the functional areas of business.

Information Systems in Organizations consists of four parts. Part 1 introduces basic computer and organizational issues. Part 2 offers a framework for viewing the major forms of computer-based support: transaction processing systems, information reporting systems, decision support systems, and programmed decision systems. Part 3 covers the activities normally associated with implementing computer-based information systems in organizations, emphasizing those that require extensive end-user participation: developing a master plan, selecting a project, performing a feasibility study, developing an implementation plan, determining requirements, and evaluating information systems already implemented. Factors contributing to organizational success or failure with information systems are also examined. In Part 4, two comprehensive cases challenge students to apply all the concepts they have learned to two complex, realistic situations. Finally, an appendix presents a variety of quantitative and qualitative methods for evaluating alternatives.

A number of features in this text are particularly suited to this end-user orientation. First, technical material is introduced on a managerial "need-to-know" basis, and the terminology and visual aids throughout have been made as nontechnical as possible. Second, a sociotechnical outlook is adopted that blends technical and organizational concerns.

Third, numerous examples from a variety of organizational contexts illustrate the concepts addressed. Fourth, each chapter concludes with a list of key issues, discussion questions, and brief cases that stress end-user decisions. Finally, Parts 1, 2, and 3 conclude with descriptions from *Information Systems News* of ways actual organizations approach the issues covered in the preceding chapters.

As with any other human endeavor, many individuals played roles in the development of this text. These too-brief acknowledgments (in chronological order, rather than order of importance) are my way of saying thanks to the many people (both end-users and computer specialists) from my days as a systems analyst who convinced me of the importance of adopting a sociotechnical approach when implementing computer-based information systems; to my students of the past five years, who, by suffering through a mismatch of course material and texts, enabled me to develop these materials; to my fellow teachers of information systems courses, who led me to most of the ideas in this book; to Bill Fischer, who got me thinking about writing the book; to Jim Sitlington, who enabled me to do so; to Jo Anne, Danny, and Jana, whose love and understanding helped me through the process; to Penny Kephart, who typed most of the manuscript; to my reviewers—Mike Ginzberg (New York University), Jim Wetherbe (University of Minnesota), John Schrage (Southern Illinois University, Edwardsville), Jeff Hoffer (Indiana University), Blake Ives (Dartmouth College), and Tom Athey (California State Polytechnic University), who provided valuable advice; and finally, to Diane Culhane, whose persistence and editing skills are both appreciated.

Bob Zmud

Overview

Contents

3 Organizational Concepts 53

Part 2
Choices 85

4 Introduction to Computer-Based Alternatives 87

5 Transaction Processing Systems 101

Part 3
Implementation 233

Appendix Evaluating Alternatives 425

Information Systems
in Organizations

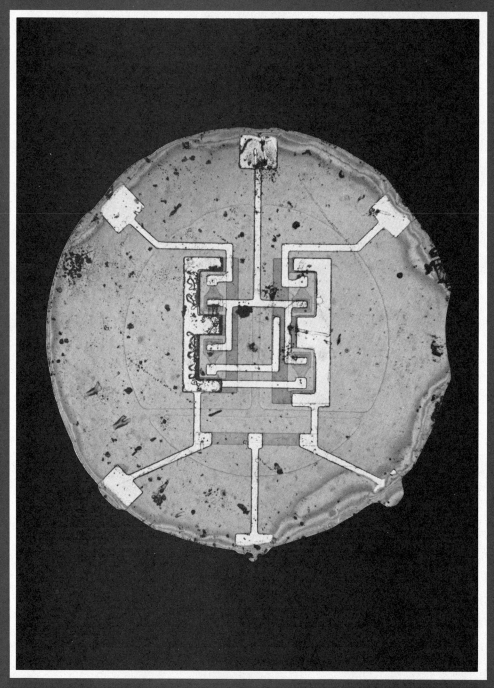

1961.
Dawn of the integrated circuit. The first integrated circuit available on a single chip was the resistor-transistor logic (RTL) device. This reset/set flip-flop is the fundamental memory storage cell in computers.

Concepts 1

Information, Computers, and Organizations 1

IT IS GENERALLY accepted that we are experiencing a knowledge explosion. Researchers in all fields continue to examine our world, producing an ever-expanding mass of data, facts, theories, and laws to help us better understand and cope with our environment. As shown in Figure 1.1, fifty years elapsed before the amount of knowledge available in 1800 doubled. The information available in 1950 doubled in ten years, and in 1970, in only five years.

This growing body of knowledge is but one information-related factor affecting the modern organization and its economic-political environment. As will be explored in more depth in Chapter 3, information has become a critical resource of modern organizations. To survive, organizations must gather, filter, store, and use vast quantities of information; to prosper, organizations must perform these tasks better than competing organizations. While other concerns predominated in earlier decades (1940s—production, 1950s–60s—marketing, 1970s—finance), the information function is likely to become the critical corporate function, as well as a major competitive tool, in the 1980s and beyond.[1] For certain industries (e.g., the airline, insurance, and banking industries), the information function is already dominant.

Why are organizations becoming so dependent on an ability to process information? As mentioned earlier, the knowledge explosion is one factor. Other factors include the size and complexity of modern organizations, their increasing interdependence, organizational specialization and diversification, the technological complexity of modern society, and growing scarcities of natural resources, as well as increasing rates of technical and environmental change. These factors require that organizations not only process vast quantities of information, but be more responsive and forward-looking in doing so.

FIGURE 1.1
The Knowledge Explosion

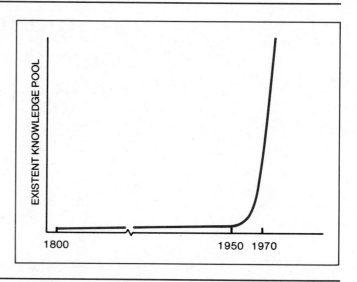

These information demands on organizations have led some to term the U.S. economy an information economy.[2] The information sector of our economy, those industries involved in the direct sale of information (such as education, banking, publishing, advertising, research, consulting, and data processing), will soon account for half of the U.S. gross national product. When general information functions necessary in all organizations (such as planning, administrative, and clerical) are included, the information sector already employs almost half of the U.S. labor force.

THE INFORMATION REVOLUTION

Another explosion has been occurring over the last few decades—one that Herbert Simon has referred to as the third information revolution (following the emergence of written language and the invention of the printing press).[3] The performance improvements and cost reductions that have occurred in information processing technology (computers, telecommunication, mass copying equipment, mass storage devices, display systems, etc.) have enabled many organizations not only to keep up with the information economy, but to exploit it. Just as many organizations, however, have *not* capitalized well on information-processing technologies.

The technological advances in information technologies over the last twenty years have been nothing less than phenomenal, and the gains to be seen over the next twenty years are expected to be at least as significant.[4-7] Since 1960 processor speeds have increased by a factor of 200, while costs per function have dropped by the same amount, main memory costs have dropped by a factor of 200, and disk storage costs have dropped by a factor of 100. Such gains can be attributed primarily to the miniaturization of electronic components.

Obvious explanations for the dramatic performance (at a given price) gains achieved through electronics miniaturization are the employment of mass production processes and a reduction in the number of discrete steps required to manufacture a product. Less obvious factors include the following:

- Increases in processing speeds, since electrons travel shorter distances when flowing through circuits,
- Increases in reliability, since fewer components must be connected,
- Decreases in the materials requirements associated with wiring, housing, etc.,
- Decreases in air-conditioning requirements, since less heat is being generated.

However, these gains apply to *purely electronic* components. The performance gains associated with electromechanical components have been substantially less.

Two specific examples might provide some insights into the technological improvements being experienced. First, today's microprocessor, a single chip, has the computational power of the giant computers of 1950. Such a device didn't exist in 1974, cost four hundred dollars in 1975, thirty dollars in 1976, and three dollars in 1977![8] Second, IBM's most powerful processor in 1979 could perform 5 million instructions a second and occupied a cubic yard of space; IBM forecasts that by the late 1980s it will have six-inch-cubic processors that perform 70 million instructions a second.[9]

It is particularly relevant that these productivity gains have been occurring at a time when *U.S. labor productivity* has experienced only slight gains. If only straightforward, well-defined clerical tasks are considered, the break-even point for converting the performance of such tasks from humans to computers has been reached for most organizations.[10]

ORGANIZATIONAL COMPUTERIZATION

As illustrated in Figure 1.2, the number of computers used in organizations has been steadily increasing, with the most rapid gains occurring in minicomputers.[11] The influx of minicomputers is expected to continue, with an annual growth rate estimated by one source at 33 percent a year![12] These figures do *not* include microcomputers, which did not exist prior to 1970 but are expected to top 10 million units by 1985. (The distinctions between micro-, mini-, and larger computer systems will be brought out in Chapter 2.)

Even with such increases in the number of computers being used by organizations, organizational investments in information resources tend to be comparatively low. Studies indicate that the data processing budgets of many organizations represent only 1–2 percent of their total budgets.[13,14] While these figures are probably low (many information-related functions, such as computer-aided manufacturing, typing pools, and library services, are likely buried in other resource budgets, particularly those for manual functions), they are fairly representative.

Organizations are just beginning to feel the impact of information resources on their budgets. It is widely accepted that by the year 2000— and possibly by 1990—the portion of the organizational budget represented by information resources will approach and perhaps exceed 40 percent! For example, the current investment in information technology of $5,000 per white-collar worker will probably increase to $20,000 by 1990.[15] The impact this will have on the thinking of top management and hence on organizational policies, plans, and politics will undoubtedly increase the importance given to the information resource and to individuals who manage it.

No aspect of organizations is immune from computerization. Factories are automated, computer-aided design is a reality, and point-of-sales terminals collect and process transactional data as organizational activities transpire. A large portion of the *increased investment* in information, however, is expected to occur in four major areas:

- *Elimination of paper.* Much human labor and great financial resources are currently spent by organizations on the creation, storage, retrieval, copying, transmittal, and transformation of paper documents. The use of information technologies to substantially reduce organizational dependence on paper technology is expected to have a profound impact on all organizational levels.
- *Internal organizational interfaces.* Technological improvements are resulting in the development of truly integrated information systems, enabling organizational activities dependent on one another to be kept informed of each other's activities and status.

FIGURE 1.2
U.S. Computer Usage

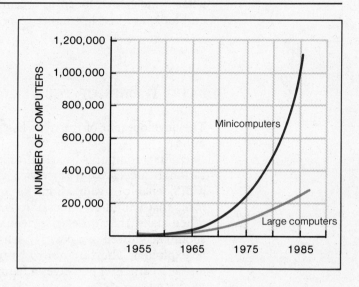

- *Management support.* While the support of managerial planning, control, and decision making has traditionally been recognized as an information function, few organizations have truly been successful at it. Recent technological advances that increase capabilities to economically maintain and rapidly access vast amounts of data and to use problem-oriented modeling aids should make meaningful managerial support a reality.
- *External organizational interfaces.* The information explosion is creating a requirement that all organizations establish closer linkages with other organizations (e.g., clients, vendors, and government agencies). Recent improvements in telecommunication technologies not only make such external linkages possible, but provide opportunities for organizations to attain some control of their environments.

While organizational computerization over the next decade is certainly not limited to these four areas, these are expected to be areas of growth for all organizations.

Taken together, these developments indicate a *technological convergence* in the automated communication process in organizations (i.e., data processing, information processing, word processing, library services, message transmission, and visual presentation material preparation). The advantages arising from viewing such activities as an integral whole, and hence locating organizational responsibility under a single umbrella, are just beginning to be recognized.

BASIC THEMES OF THE TEXT

The development of this text has proceeded with three major themes in mind.

First, computer-based information systems are necessary for organizational success and survival. Computer-based information systems (CBIS) enable organizations to more economically accomplish many tasks that would be impossible with available resources, and to perform other tasks that otherwise would be utterly impossible. Thus, CBIS should be viewed in a *positive* sense. They are not to be overcome, but to be exploited. They are not to be revered, but to be considered as a tool, just as a carpenter perceives a hammer. They are not an end, but a means to an end.

Second, computer-based information systems strongly affect organizations and organizational members. While CBIS are simply a means of accomplishing or otherwise supporting organizational activities, their *direct* influences on work systems can be significant: certain activities are taken over by CBIS, others are eliminated, still others are created. Because of possible shifts in resource, product, or service flows, departmental boundaries and responsibilities are often redefined. The *indirect* influence of CBIS can be just as demanding. An organization heavily exploiting information technology must concern itself with issues such as privacy, computer crime, organizational impersonalization (and its effect on employees, clients, customers, and suppliers), and organizational dependence on information technology. Thus, CBIS must be viewed in a *holistic* sense. Planned applications must be viewed from multiple perspectives, and intended outcomes must be traced beyond their immediate spatial and temporal impacts.

Third, computer-based information systems must be directed by all organizational members so all intended benefits are attained. These systems must not be viewed as belonging or responding to a limited constituency. Each member of an organization should develop an understanding of how his or her work behaviors are and can be affected by CBIS and what his or her own responsibilities are with regard to ensuring effective use of CBIS. Thus, CBIS must be viewed in a *personal* sense. The information resource will be fully exploited only when organizational members are alert to all the possibilities that exist for improving organizational activities and are aware of various means of implementing these notions.

OBJECTIVES OF THE TEXT

This text is intended for the ultimate users of CBIS, particularly those who perform managerial or staff roles in organizations. On completing the text, the reader should

- Be aware of the ways in which CBIS support organizational activities,
- Be able to compare the benefits and limitations of CBIS support and of alternative CBIS designs,
- Be able to project and assign an order to a portfolio of CBIS applications relevant to organizational success,
- Be able to communicate effectively with computer specialists when participating in a CBIS implementation effort,
- Be aware of the contributions of the CBIS user to an implementation effort and be able to contribute to such an effort,
- Be aware of problems that often arise in CBIS implementation and of steps organizations can take to avoid such problems,
- Be aware of steps organizations can take to increase the likelihood that the information resource can be fully exploited.

It is also hoped that the reader will incorporate the three themes of the text—that CBIS should be perceived as positive, holistic, and personal.

PLAN OF THIS PART

The remaining chapters in this part will examine computer concepts and organizational concepts in some detail.

Chapter 2 provides technical material on computers that is necessary for readers to understand later text material, particularly that touching on CBIS capabilities, limitations, benefits, and costs. The emphasis is on issues that influence analyses performed when acquiring information resources, examining the feasibility of a CBIS application, planning a CBIS implementation effort, planning future CBIS projects, and evaluating CBIS success. The chapter begins with discussions of the status of the hardware (electronic and electromechanical equipment), software (sets of instructions that drive the hardware), and people (personnel who develop, operate, and manage CBIS applications) that, along with data, comprise the information resource. The chapter concludes with three topics of managerial importance: distinctions among the major types of computer systems (microcomputers, minicomputers, small computers, and large computers), alternatives available to organizations regarding the acquisition of computer resources, and factors to be considered when acquiring computer hardware and software.

Chapter 3 provides an overview of the information processing nature of organizations. The perspective developed emphasizes the role played by information systems in enabling people to cope with their environment. The chapter concludes with an introduction to systems modeling, its basic ideas and its relevance to organizational understanding.

KEY ISSUES

Microelectronics, the miniaturization of electronic components, has brought about a third information revolution (following the invention of the written word and the printing press). The impact of this revolution on industry and society is just beginning to be felt.

While the performance gains and costs reductions associated with computer components have been phenomenal, both are expected to accelerate through the 1980s.

The breakeven point has been reached in the replacement of human labor by computer resources for straightforward, routine tasks.

The U.S. economy is fast becoming an information economy.

That portion of organizational resources represented by information resources is expected to expand from today's level of approximately 2 percent to over 40 percent by the year 2000.

Information resources are becoming strategic tools for many organizations.

Ripe application areas for organizations through the 1980s include reduction in paper flow (office automation and support of knowledgeable workers), interorganizational linkages, management support, and intraorganizational linkages.

DISCUSSION QUESTIONS

1. Why must today's organizations rely on their information processing capabilities much more than organizations did twenty years ago?
2. What types of organizations compose the "information sector" of the U.S. economy?
3. Give some examples of "information handling" positions (job assignments) in manufacturing organizations, in investment firms, and in hospitals.
4. Many information-related costs are "buried" in organizations today. Illustrate this phenomenon.
5. What is meant by the "technological convergence" of automated communication processes? Give some examples.
6. Provide some illustrations of how information resources can play strategic roles in organizations.
7. Why are organizations attempting to integrate their information systems?
8. Are any disadvantages associated with "organizational computerization"?

BRIEF CASES

1. *Southside Auto Parts*
   Sam Hellick, the owner-manager of Southside Auto Parts, had just finished playing eighteen holes with his firm's insurance agent, Bob Tomes. Bob was describing the minicomputer that had recently been installed at the re-

---

gional sales office. Not only did this system handle most of the paperwork associated with the office's normal work flows, but since it was connected to corporate headquarters, the exchange of sales reports and market information among offices had greatly improved. While Sam was a little envious, he saw no way he could use a computer system in his little company.

Should Sam investigate the use of a computer system? How might his business be aided by enhanced information processing?

2. *Greco Components*
Rose Leary, sales manager for Greco Components, a manufacturing firm specializing in packaging equipment for the cosmetics industry, had just been visited by the new head of the system analysis section of the company's Information Systems Division. While the young man had been very pleasant and obviously knew his stuff, he clearly knew little about managing a diverse group of forty-three individuals. Numbers just cannot provide the kind of "people" information needed to motivate a sales force.

How can information resources be used to manage a sales force? What type of data can be collected? What type of reports can be generated?

NOTES

1. F. Petro and G. Lion, "Systems Planning in the 1980s," in *Information Systems in the 1980s* (Cambridge, Mass.: Arthur D. Little, Inc., 1979), pp. 35–46.

2. C. Bell, "The Social Framework of the Information Society," in M. L. Dertouzos and J. Moses (eds.), *The Computer Age: A Twenty-Year View* (Cambridge, Mass.: MIT Press, 1979), pp. 163–211.

3. H. A. Simon, "What Computers Mean for Man and Society," *Science* 195(1977): 1186–1191.

4. C. Weitzman, *Distributed Micro/Minicomputer Systems* (Englewood Cliffs, N.J.: Prentice-Hall, 1980).

5. J. Moses, "The Computer in the Home," in Dertouzos and Moses (1979), pp. 3–20.

6. J. W. Cortada, *EDP Costs and Charges* (Englewood Cliffs, N.J.: Prentice-Hall, 1980).

7. M. V. Lines and Boeing Computer Services Company, *Minicomputer Systems* (Cambridge, Mass.: Winthrop Publishers, 1980).

8. D. M. Smith, "Data Processing in the 1980s," in A. E. Westley (ed.), *Convergence: Computers, Communications and Office Automation*, Vol. 2 (Maidenhead, Berkshire, England: Infotech International, 1979).

9. D. L. Stein, "Price/Performance, Semiconductors and the Future," *Datamation* 25(1979):14–20.

10. Smith, 1979.

11. T. A. Dolotta, M. I. Bernstein, R. S. Dickson, Jr., N. A. France, S. A. Rosenblatt, D. M. Smith, and T. B. Steel, Jr., *Data Processing in 1980–1985* (New York: Wiley-Interscience, 1976).

12. *Information Systems News* (1980).

13. P. H. Dorn, "1979 Budget Survey," *Datamation* 25(1979):162–70.

14. Cortada (1980).

15. "Solving a Computer Mismatch in Management, *Business Week*, April 2, 1979, pp. 73–76.

Computer Concepts 2

IT IS DIFFICULT to appreciate CBIS without first understanding their underlying technology. The intent here is to introduce those issues that significantly affect assessments of the overall performance characteristics of information systems. These concerns, because they reflect the inherent capabilities of alternative computer configurations, are most relevant to decisions to acquire and use information resources.

The chapter begins with an overview of the elements comprising modern computer systems. Then selected hardware, software, personnel, and management topics are addressed. Specifically covered are the following:

- Hardware issues and trends,
- Software issues and trends,
- Personnel issues and trends,
- Computer system configurations,
- Alternatives for acquiring information services, and
- The information resource acquisition process.

COMPUTER SYSTEMS OVERVIEW

Regardless of the form of computer-based support provided, a basic set of processing functions are invariably involved. These functions, shown in Figure 2.1, can be defined as follows:

Input	Capturing and entering input items,
Transmission	Sending items from one component to another without changing the items' intrinsic form,
Transformation	Changing the intrinsic form of items,
Storage	Retaining items to permit timely, repeated retrieval without reentry,
Output	Disseminating output items to their point of use.

FIGURE 2.1
Basic Processing
Functions

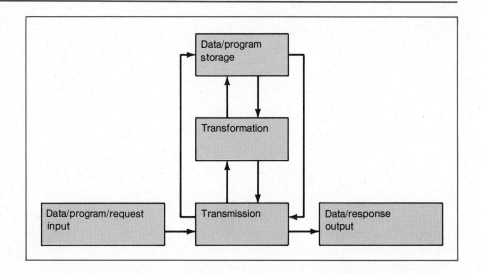

These processing functions correspond closely to the electronic and electromechanical devices that comprise what are collectively referred to as computer *hardware*. Figure 2.2 illustrates the relations among selected hardware devices.

An additional basic processing function derives from the desirability that *all* processing be error free. Some *validation* activity, thus, is necessary within each processing function.

Note that hardware simply *permits* these processing functions to transpire. For processing to occur, hardware must be directed by software—sets of instructions generally referred to as *programs*. Two categories of software are required with modern computer systems. *Applications software* refers to programs that directly support organizational activities (e.g., a payroll, sales analysis, or inventory control program). *Systems software* create information resource environments that enhance the performance capabilities of computer systems and personnel.

Three classifications of computer personnel are typically employed: operations, software development, and administrators. *Operations personnel* refers to those who execute already implemented CBIS applications. Normally, this involves manual procedures associated with entering data, disseminating output, readying secondary storage devices, and monitoring the processing units. *Software development personnel* are those who design, develop, and maintain programs. *Administrative personnel* refers to those who manage an organization's investment in information resources.

FIGURE 2.2
Selected Hardware Devices

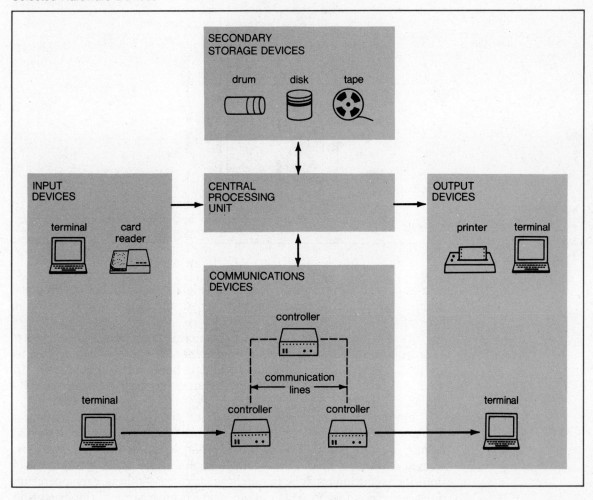

HARDWARE ISSUES

Central Processing Unit

A large portion of the productivity gains being realized with information resources can be traced to the computer's *central processing unit* (CPU),

FIGURE 2.3
Central Processing Unit

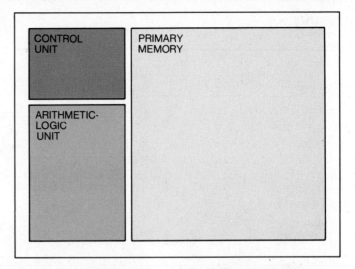

as it is a purely electronic device. To appreciate the implications of these developments, a brief excursion into the technical realm of the CPU is beneficial.

As shown in Figure 2.3, the CPU contains three major components: a *control unit* (CU), an *arithmetic-logic unit* (ALU), and a *primary memory* (PM). Programs being executed and data being manipulated reside in the PM. The ALU contains circuitry that manipulates data, while the CU contains circuitry that directs ALU processing.

Programs are executed one instruction at a time, with each instruction consisting of two segments: an *operator code* denoting which ALU circuit is to be activated, and an *operand* denoting the PM locations, termed *addresses*, holding the data to be manipulated. Program instructions for execution must be in *machine language*—that is, each operation must correspond to an ALU circuit. Viewed most simply, the execution of a single instruction involves the following steps:

1. The instruction to be executed is loaded into an appropriate CU storage area,
2. Activation of a CU circuit "decodes" the instruction into its operator and operand segments,
3. The CU readies the appropriate ALU circuit,
4. Needed data items are copied by the CU from PM to appropriate ALU storage areas,
5. The ALU circuit is activated,

6. The manipulated data items are copied by the CU from the ALU to their PM locations.

An overview is provided in Figure 2.4, with the numbers referring to the above operations.

Modern CPUs possess a limited number of electronic circuits providing data manipulation capabilities. A computer's *instruction set,* the operation repertoire available to programmers, can be expanded through *microcode*—instructions permanently maintained in (read only) PM—that initiate the predefined, ordered execution of specific ALU circuits. The computational power of any computer thus depends on the number and versatility of the hardwired circuits in its ALU and its microcoded instruction set. Larger, more expensive computers have both faster circuitry and more comprehensive instruction sets. It is possible, nonetheless, to perform many CBIS applications with computer systems possessing quite limited instruction sets—it simply takes longer to accomplish each task.

A second architectural feature worthy of note is a computer's *word size,* the number of *bits* that can be referenced as a unit. A bit is a storage area that can represent one of two values, "0" or "1". Typical word sizes are 8, 16, and 32 bits, though larger word sizes also exist. As word size increases, the production costs of a computer increase in a greater-than-linear fashion. Two major advantages, however, accrue with larger word size: higher-precision mathematics and an ability to reference a larger PM.

The benefits of the second advantage are subtle. As all data manipulation by a CPU involves transfers of program instruction and data to and from PM, CU storage areas must represent the addresses in PM of needed program instructions or data. With an 8-bit word, the largest address possibly represented is 256; with a 16-bit word, the largest address is 16,536. Consequently, a computer's word size can severely limit the amount of PM that can be accessed. This, in turn, drastically limits the capabilities of a computer system because only small programs can be loaded into PM. Such limitations can be circumvented through hardware or software, but this adds to the complexity and cost of the computer system.

Storage Devices

Storage devices are generally classified as belonging to three storage levels: primary, secondary, and archival. *Primary* storage (memory) is normally used to hold data or programs currently being processed, *secondary* to hold data or programs that are regularly exercised, and *archival* to maintain data less regularly or only rarely referenced. Why three storage

FIGURE 2.4
CPU Program
Instruction Execution

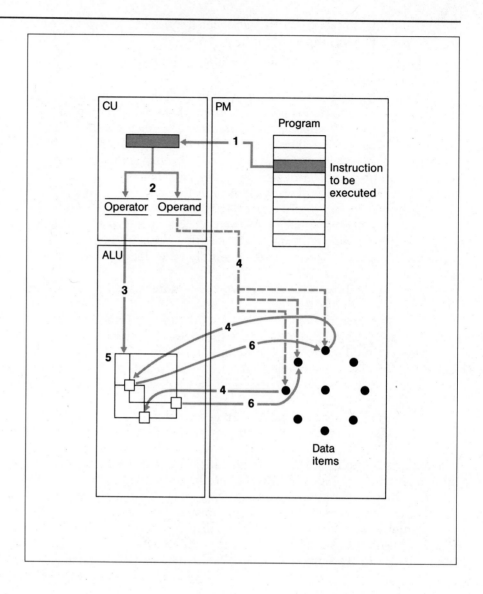

Part 1 / Concepts

levels are maintained will be explained below. Table 2.1 provides relative comparisons of the performance characteristics of the three storage levels, as well as individual devices.[1-4] *Access time* refers to the amount of time required to store or retrieve one piece of data. The cost figure represents the expense of storing one bit of data for one year.

With secondary storage devices, two important distinctions are necessary. First, *on-line* and *off-line* refer to whether the storage *medium*, (i.e., the magnetic recording material), is (on-line) or is not (off-line) directly accessible by the CPU at a given time. If a tape reel or disk pack is off-line, it must be loaded onto an appropriate read/write unit (i.e., the storage device) prior to being accessed. Second, drums and disks are *direct-access* devices: any storage location can be immediately accessed. Tapes are a *sequential* device: the tape reel must be searched from its beginning to locate a particular storage location. Mass storage devices (of which there are numerous types) provide a compromise between direct-access and sequential devices by providing direct access to a large number of short sequential devices, e.g., ten thousand strips of tape, each a foot long.

Archival storage devices may also be used as secondary storage devices. While it is quite easy to produce computer-output microfilm (COM), it is currently quite expensive to input data from microfilm to the CPU. Consequently, humans must typically read data that has been

TABLE 2.1
Storage Device Performance Characteristics

Level	Device	Access Time (seconds)	Cost per Bit per Year[a] (cents)
Primary storage	High performance	10^{-8}	10^1
	Main	10^{-7}	10^{-1}
	Low performance	10^{-5}	10^{-2}
Secondary storage	Drum	10^{-2}	10^{-2}
	On-line disk	5×10^{-2}	10^{-3}
	Off-line disk	10^2	10^{-5}
	Mass storage	10^1	10^{-6}
	On-line tape	5×10^1	10^{-3}
	Off-line tape	10^2	10^{-6}
Archival storage	Computer output microfilm	10^1	10^{-6}
	Laser	10^{-3}	10^{-7}

[a]At full utilization.

stored on microfilm. Lasers are used to store data by etching patterns in silicon materials; such etching, however, is irreversible.

Computer systems have been designed with a number of storage levels to meet two conflicting objectives:

1. It is desirable to maintain data and program elements on inexpensive storage devices. Generally, however, less expensive devices have low data transfer rates (the speed with which data flow from one device to another).
2. Data and program elements are constantly being transmitted between hardware devices. When transmission is between two devices that vary markedly in speed, the faster device must operate at the speed of the slower. To use fast, expensive components at their engineered performance levels, data and program elements should be maintained on fast, and hence expensive, storage devices.

Two strategies are taken to resolve this conflict. First, extensive use is made of *storage hierarchies* that minimize speed discrepancies between devices. This is illustrated in Figure 2.5 for a data file update application. To take advantage of the low costs of off-line magnetic tape storage, the data file is maintained on tape between update runs. (Historical volumes of this data file would be maintained on COM.) Just before processing, the tape file is copied onto a disk file. While off-line disk storage is slightly more expensive than off-line tape storage, on-line disk storage is comparable in cost to and faster than on-line tape storage. During processing, data items are brought into the ALU via a series of transfers: from disk to a low-performance, low-cost form of PM; from low-performance PM to main PM; from main PM to a high-performance, high-cost form of PM; and from the high-performance PM to the ALU. With the second strategy, rather than require all data processing to be performed in the CPU, certain functions (normally set-up or validation activities) are accomplished by using small, limited capability, slower, and less expensive processing units incorporated within other hardware components. As a result, these selected processing functions occur at speeds and costs more compatible with the devices involved, and the CPU is used for its particular engineered advantages.

Input Devices

Input devices can be grouped into three performance categories: those used for source data capture (immediate input without human intervention), those used in on-line data entry (immediate input via a human

FIGURE 2.5
A Storage Hierarchy

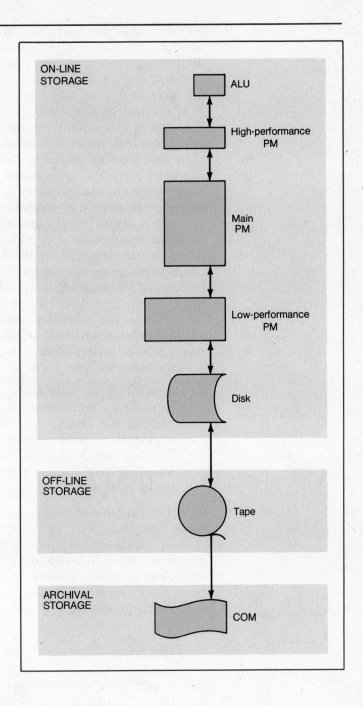

operator), and those used for off-line data entry (conversion of input items to a form more amenable to computer processing). As one moves from off-line data entry to on-line data entry to source data capture, the timeliness and accuracy of data input improve. There is generally a corresponding increase in cost, which is often balanced by a capability to handle large volumes of data, thus actually reducing unit cost.

Source data capture devices make use of pattern recognition to interpret original, preprinted, or imprinted items. A wide diversity of devices have been developed in response to the varied environmental demands of particular applications. Optical character readers (OCR) can examine handwritten or preprinted characters, may require that printed characters be written in magnetic ink (MICR), and can be fixed or portable, such as wands or light guns. Optical mark readers (OMR) may examine printed materials (e.g., coded answer sheets or universal product codes) or permanently imprinted items (e.g., badge readers). Developments in computerized speech recognition are making voice input a viable alternative in certain situations, such as those requiring limited vocabularies.

With on-line data entry, a human operator captures the input items and then submits them to the computer system through some terminal. Again, a wide variety of devices exist. Possible ways of distinguishing between terminal types include

- Primarily input only (such as point-of-sales terminals or key-entry data terminals on a shop floor) versus the human operator being able to receive prompts and responses,
- Typewritten versus screen (CRT) printing,
- Graphics or color graphics capability,
- Key-entry versus more "natural" forms such as that made possible by light pens and touch-sensitive screens.

A readily available and inexpensive "terminal" increasingly used is the touch-tone phone!

Off-line data entry finds a human operator capturing data from a source document and recording it on an intermediary storage medium for later input to a computer system. While the traditional medium of such intermediate storage has been punched cards, most organizations with large data volumes are now using cassettes and diskettes.

Output Devices

Output devices are perhaps best categorized in terms of performance by their interactiveness. Interactive devices such as terminals or telephones allow for a dialogue between the end-user and the program being executed. Noninteractive devices, such as printers, plotters, and computer-output microfilm, generally are more cost efficient for large quantities of output, but lack the user-friendliness (flexibility, convenience, and pleasant physical environment) of interactive devices.

Output devices increasing in use include terminals with color graphic capabilities because of the rich opportunities to provide visual information, nonimpact printers (e.g., xerography, thermal printing, and ink jets) because of their speed, quietness, versatility, and increasing price competitiveness, and computer-output microfilm because of its cost-effectiveness and ease of handling, and because of the availability of portable, inexpensive readers.

Communications Devices

Data communication is accomplished by linking hardware devices through communication lines and equipment. Communication lines vary in capacity and cost. Narrow-band lines (e.g., teletype) transmit 150–300 bits a second and are relatively inexpensive. Voice-grade lines (e.g., telephone) transmit 4,800–9,600 bits a second and are moderate in cost. Broad-band lines (e.g., microwaves) transmit 19,200–230,400 bits a second and are relatively expensive. As an organization's data volumes increase so that a higher capacity line can be *fully* utilized, it becomes economically attractive to do so.

Communication lines can be public or private. A public network is available to anyone, whereas a private line is leased for the sole use of one organization. While private lines tend to be of better quality and permit access to be tightly controlled, public lines have the advantage of readily available backup, as well as flexibility and ease of operation. As a general rule, private lines are advantageous when a concentrated terminal population exists at one location and when line activity is high. Many types of subscription plans are available, and all alternatives should be carefully examined in deciding on a line strategy.

Extremely important communications devices encountered when communication networks are being configured are the control units that handle much of the actual processing associated with data communications. Front-end processors (located at the computer end of a communications network) relieve the CPU of much of the processing required when communicating from remote sites to the computer system. This processing, which might otherwise exhaust a significant amount of a CPU's capabilities, is performed with communications-oriented circuitry and hence becomes more cost effective. At remote sites, communication processors are directed toward enabling a number of input/output (I/O) devices to transmit over a few lines, thus increasing line use and lowering overall communications costs. Examples are concentrators, which enable a cluster of I/O devices to compete for a single line, and multiplexors, which enable a cluster of I/O devices to concurrently share a single line.

Hardware Trends

Future improvements in microelectronics are expected to sustain existing trends toward ever greater performance at less cost. With smaller CPUs gaining increased capabilities, processor specialization will dominate computer architecture—rather than having a single large CPU computer, systems will possess a number of small CPUs, each designed for particular processing functions. As primary storage costs decline, primary storage may become competitive with most other storage alternatives. When this occurs, information resource costs will decline even more drastically as much software overhead can be eliminated. Increased capabilities of small CPUs will also foster current trends toward developing "intelligent" hardware components.

Secondary storage and input and output devices, as they are electromechanical in nature, will not experience the full benefit of microelectronic performance improvements. Nevertheless, gains are expected to occur, particularly with devices designed for minicomputers and microcomputers. Existing hardware support for small computer systems lags behind that for large systems, primarily because of the more severe environments allowed and the relatively recent emergence of small systems capable of providing a full range of processing support.

The increasing availability of satellites and conversions to fiber optic lines should greatly expand communications possibilities for all organizations. While cost declines will not be so large as those associated with microelectronic equipment, comprehensive communication capabilities will become economically viable for even small organizations. Of special importance are the information services—technical literature, consumer/industry data, financial/investment data, news services, training aids, etc.—being offered in increasing numbers by telecommunications linkages.

SOFTWARE ISSUES

Software is the communication medium by which people (end-users, analysts, programmers, etc.) interact with or direct computer hardware for productive purposes. Figure 2.6 illustrates that a number of software "layers" exist, with each successive layer permitting a more natural mode of hardware–human communication. While all processing must ultimately

FIGURE 2.6
Software as a Communications Medium

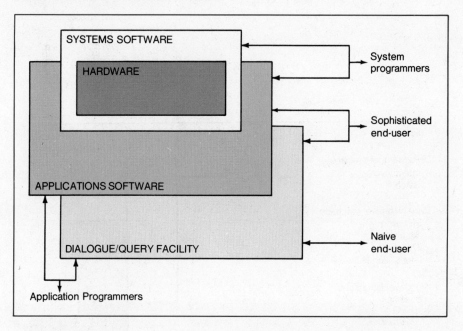

be performed in terms of the specific instruction set of a CPU (i.e., the program must be in *machine language* form), human interaction is typically well cushioned from this inner level of processing. Figure 2.7 provides an overview of the numerous "language" forms available, along with the classes of operators who normally work at each language level.

Applications Software

The ultimate objective with applications software is to support organizational functioning as effectively as possible. This leads to three basic requirements:

- Design and processing interactions should be performed by individuals who understand organizational functioning,
- The development of applications should occur rapidly so benefits can be quickly realized,
- Applications should not be affected by subsequent hardware expansions or modifications.

FIGURE 2.7

Hardware–Human Communication Levels

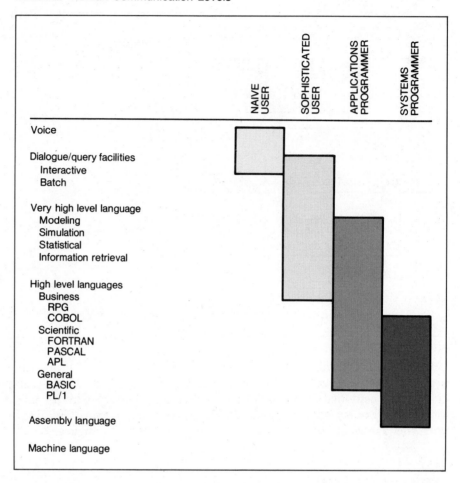

It is consequently advantageous for applications software to be written in higher-level language forms.

As will be discussed in depth later (Chapter 9), software development tends to be expensive and time consuming. While each organizational context is unique, great similarity exists in the information processing undertaken within all organizations. Applications such as those related to payroll, accounts payable, and inventory control, for example, are often structured very similarly in quite different organizations. As a result, a great variety of *applications packages* can be acquired—often with little or no modification—for far less than it would cost to develop an equivalent program from scratch.

The advantages of acquiring, rather than developing, applications software can be significant. Just as important as cost are the following:

- Fewer requirements for in-house programmers,
- Faster realization of benefits,
- Fewer problems, as they have been discovered in previous implementations of the package,
- Likelihood that the program design is better because of the package's specialized designers and developers.

It is not always possible to locate suitable packages: an organization's needs may truly be unique, too much modification of a package may be required to fit it within an organization, or an organization's hardware may not be compatible with available packages. Nonetheless, the advantages of using software packages are so great that these packages should always be considered.

Systems Software

Systems software plays two major roles in CBIS. First, it frees higher-level language (communication) forms from the need to understand the technical details of the hardware devices being employed. Consequently, applications software can be written in a general manner, which is then "translated" via systems software to run on the existing hardware configuration. Second, and more important, systems software can dramatically expand the inherent capabilities of a hardware configuration. Each of these roles will be made clear as the various types of systems software are introduced.

Operating System.   The collection of programs that direct and control what transpires within a computer system are collectively referred to as the *operating system*. Operating systems enable other programs to be scheduled and executed, allocate processing resources between executing programs, and handle the flow of data through executing programs and between hardware devices. Without a sophisticated operating system, these functions would need to be done within applications software, thereby drastically increasing their complexity, development time, and cost.

The most significant benefits to accrue from operating systems, however, are the varied processing environments they provide, which greatly enhance a computer system's capabilities and convenience. Early computer systems, as they possessed minimal operating systems, were difficult to use and inefficient. Modern operating systems have resolved these, as well as other, problems. The major processing environments created by operating systems are briefly examined.

Multiprogramming.   The first computing systems executed only one program at a time. As a result, most hardware devices were underutilized. Consider, for example, a program needing to read data off a tape. While the required data were flowing from tape to primary memory, all remaining hardware—including the CPU—was idle. As the data transfer rate of input/output and secondary storage devices is extremely slow compared to a CPU's speed, programs requiring extensive input/output—such as most business data processing—ran inefficiently.

Multiprogramming operating systems enable multiple programs to share a computer system's resources at one time through concurrent use of the CPU. *Concurrent use* means that while only one program is actually using the CPU at any moment, other programs can be having their input/output needs serviced. Smaller processors, termed *channels*, which are limited in their circuitry to input/output processing functions, actually perform all input/output. Multiprogramming not only results in greater hardware utilization, but enables more programs to be processed through a computer system in a given period.

Multiprocessing.   Another way of increasing the effective workload through a computer system is to have the operating system coordinate the functioning of two or more CPUs. Multiprocessing (i.e., the use of multiple processors) may take the form of a "host-slave" relationship, where a small CPU handles much of the "administrative" processing in workload scheduling and in allocating processing resources to programs and a large CPU handles computational tasks, or it may involve the simultaneous use of multiple, equally powerful CPUs.

Interactive Processing.   Interactive processing enables end-users to enter or receive items (data, programs, commands, responses, etc.) directly from terminals. Such processing activities involve sophisticated communications flows that, if not supported through the operating system, would severely hinder the development of applications programs.

Real-time Processing.   Real-time processing enables a computer system to *immediately* respond to high-priority processing requests. A common multiprogramming strategy that economically provides real-time capability is a *foreground/background* environment. Here a critical application program—say, inventory control—is continuously maintained in PM as a high-priority (i.e., foreground) task. Whenever an inventory movement is communicated to the computer system, the inventory control program obtains control of the CPU and adjusts the inventory file appropriately. When no inventory movements need to be processed, other application programs (i.e., the background workload) can be run through the computer system.

Time-sharing Systems.   A common use of computer systems finds programmers or sophisticated end-users developing programs or creating command streams (dialogues associated with very high level applications software) at an interactive terminal and then executing these programs and command streams. If extensive use is made of previously stored data, programs, and command streams, relatively little terminal input and output are required.

In such situations, the speed differential between a CPU and a human operator (composing or keying input or reading or interpreting output) enables literally hundreds of individuals to simultaneously (or so it seems) make use of the computer system. A time-sharing operating system provides such an environment.

Virtual Systems.   The necessity to maintain all executing programs in PM created severe problems. Very large programs either had to be run at specific times (e.g., 3:00 A.M.) or required the programmer to break a program into segments and control the execution so one segment at a time was loaded into PM and run. The first alternative was inconvenient, and the second required highly skilled programmers. *Virtual operating systems* eliminate such concerns by exploiting the fact that at any point in time only a very small part of each executing program needs to be in PM. Under a virtual operating system, *all* programs are broken into small segments, most of which are maintained in secondary storage by the operating system and brought into PM as needed. Thus, programming is simplified and many organizations can increase their workloads without acquiring additional, and expensive, PM. Virtual operating systems, however, are very complex themselves and require a large amount of PM. (The paradox thus arises that, to create an environment in which PM size is unimportant, a computer systems must possess a PM large enough to hold a virtual operating system.)

Language Translators.   As discussed earlier, programs must be expressed in a machine language form when executed. Programming at this level (i.e., assembly language) is undesirable for a number of reasons:

- The programmer needs a detailed understanding of the hardware,
- Programming is more complex and less productive,
- The resultant program can be executed only on that CPU,
- The resultant program is hard for other programmers to understand, and thus difficult to modify.

FIGURE 2.8
Translation of a High-Level Language

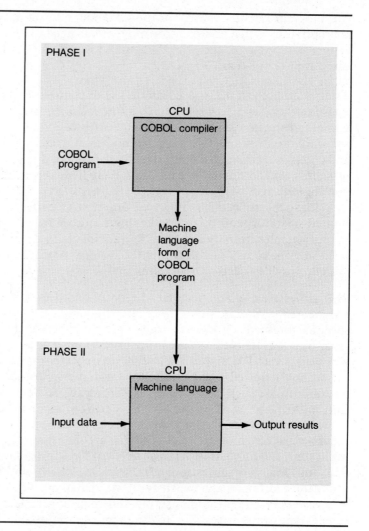

Most programming, consequently, is done in higher level languages, which are then translated to machine language form prior to execution. Compilers are systems software that accomplish this translation, as illustrated in Figure 2.8. This two-phase process may occur whenever the program is executed, or the machine language form of the program may be stored and used directly.

Library Programs.   Most vendors provide as system software numerous programs of general use. Common examples are mathematical and statistical routines, programs that sort and merge data files, and programs that copy disk files onto tape files. Also available is a librarian program to manage these programs and all others that are acquired or developed.

Special Purpose Systems Software.   A interesting phenomenon with modern computer systems is that, to provide the levels of computer system responsiveness, accessibility, and ease of use desired by most organizations, substantially more complex software is required. If this increase in complexity were accomplished by in-house applications software, few organizations could hire the programmers required to exploit recent advances in information technologies. This situation is avoided through specialized system software packages, such as data base management and telecommunications systems.

Software Trends

While systems software greatly enhances the capabilities of a computer system, it is expensive and often requires substantial computer resources (e.g., extensive PM as well as high-performance secondary-storage devices). Three interrelated developments, however, make possible the implementation of sophisticated systems software on smaller computers: hardware performance price improvements, improved computer architectures that enable processing functions to be performed quicker while using less memory, and the use of firmware (software instructions permanently stored in primary memory as microcode), which again enables functions to be performed quicker while using less memory.

Quality application packages, often designed for a specific industry segment, are becoming more available. Thus, many organizations can obtain computer-based support without expensive software development efforts. Often these packages are "parameterized" so they can be easily customized to meet the particular requirements of an organization.

An opposing trend with application software is the consideration of more complex organizational functions as candidates for computer-based support. Software development costs usually increase in a nonlinear fashion with application complexity. Furthermore, these complex applications are often not of a general nature and, hence, are likely not available as a software package.

COMPUTER PERSONNEL ISSUES AND TRENDS

Operations Personnel

Operations personnel typically include computer operators, program/ data file librarians, data entry personnel, and their supervisors. With today's sophisticated operating systems, fewer operations personnel are required. This is most evident in smaller computer systems, which often require no operations personnel; employees with clerical skills and minimal training more than adequately "run" the computer.

Software Development Personnel

Software development personnel are those individuals who design and develop software. The general classification commonly employed is: systems analysts, who determine the requirements to be met by a program; systems designers, who arrive at hardware/software composites that meet stated requirements; and programmers, who design, code, and test sets of program instructions that reflect particular designs. Often the same individual performs two or all three of these activities.

A major problem facing the computer industry today is the scarcity of analysts and programmers. Many reasons have been offered to explain this situation, the two most common being that vendors continue to produce more products at lower costs for an ever-widening spectrum of organizations, and that educational programs cannot staff faculties large enough to produce enough computer science or information systems graduates to meet the demand. With the increasing availability of standardized software packages, it is generally believed that the demand for programmers will eventually level off or even decrease. Despite such projections, however, demand remains high. No decline has been forecast for systems analysts, however, as their tasks must be performed, regardless of how software is acquired.

One solution to the scarcity of software development personnel lies in automating the software development process. Considerable effort is currently being devoted toward this end. The day is not too far away when end-users will be able to interact with a computer system to produce most applications software.

Administrative Personnel

Administrative personnel are those individuals who manage an organization's investment in information resources. Two trends have been increasing the number of administrative positions associated with the information resource. First, as more organizational functions receive computer-based support, the scope of the information system function necessarily enlarges, requiring more administrative personnel. Second, an increased organizational awareness of the importance of information has resulted in the creation of management roles that focus on defining the scope of information in an organization, and in an elevation in the organizational hierarchy of the chief information executive (with a resulting increase in middle-management positions). Both movements are expected to intensify. Interestingly, many of these administrative positions require individuals whose prime assets are organizational, thereby permitting much needed cross-fertilization between the information systems function and the rest of the organization.

COMPUTER SYSTEM CONFIGURATIONS

Continuing developments in microelectronic technologies are constantly readjusting the boundaries used to classify computer systems. The industry is in such a state of flux that it is almost impossible to categorize computer configurations in ways that are not quickly outdated. This situation obviously hinders communication between organizational members wishing to increase their understanding of computer-based technology and computer vendors, consultants, and specialists.

Rather than attempt to provide a current classification of computer configurations, two separate classifications are given: one representative of the late 1970s, the other a prediction for the late 1980s.[5,6] A comparison of these two classifications indicates what is available in today's computer marketplace, and what should be available in tomorrow's.

Table 2.2 categorizes the major classes of computer systems of the late 1970s, and Table 2.3 suggests likely hardware configurations representative of each class. With a microcomputer, the entire CPU is imprinted on a single "chip"—a microprocessor. With the remaining computer system classes, the CPU results from a combination of multiple

TABLE 2.2
Computer System Classification: Late 1970s

Characteristic	Large Computer System	Medium Computer System	Small Computer System	Minicomputer System	Microcomputer System
Purchase price ($)	1–12 million	.2–1 million	50–250,000	2–100,000	1–10,000
Processing speed	Very fast	Fast	Moderate	Fast	Moderate
PM size (bytes)[a]	1–8 million	.1–1 million	8–100,000	4–64,000	Limited
Operating system	Sophisticated	Sophisticated	Fair	Fair	None
Application versatility	Extensive	Extensive	Fair	Limited	None
Device versatility	Excellent	Excellent	Good	Fair	Poor

[a]A byte represents eight bits and can store one character of data.

TABLE 2.3
Illustrative Computer Configurations: Late 1970s

Large Computer System	Medium Computer System	Small Computer System	Minicomputer System	Microcomputer System
CPU	CPU	CPU	CPU	CPU
Consoles (terminal)	Console (terminal)	Console (terminal)	CRT	CRT
Extra PM devices	Printers	Printer	Printer (small)	Diskette device
Printers	Card reader/punch	Card reader/punch	Diskette device	
Card reader/punch	CRTs	CRTs	Cassette device	
CRTs	Magnetic disk devices	Magnetic disk devices	Magnetic disk device	
Magnetic disk devices	Magnetic tape devices	Diskette device		
Magnetic tape devices	Other I/O devices			
Mass storage device	Communications devices			
Other I/O devices				
Communications devices				

TABLE 2.4
Computer System Configurations: Late 1980s

Characteristic	Super Computer System	Multi-minicomputer System	Minicomputer System	Microcomputer System
Purchase price ($)	5–12 million	.1–1 million	5,000–50,000	500–1,000
Processing speed	Very fast	Fast	Fast	Fast
PM size (bytes)	2–10 million	1–4 million	.5–1 million	32,000–100,000
Operating system	Sophisticated	Sophisticated	Sophisticated	Fair
Application versatility	Extensive	Extensive	Good	Fair
Device versatility	Excellent	Excellent	Excellent	Good

chips, each of which provides particular circuitry or storage elements. A minicomputer differs from larger computer systems in three prime ways: durability, dedication to a fairly narrow functional capability, and limitations in both the performance and availability of hardware to attach to the CPU. The three classes of general-purpose computer systems represent fairly distinct market segments in terms of the processing requirements of organizations acquiring information resources.

Table 2.4 provides a glimpse of the computer configurations likely available in the near future. Essentially two architectures are evolving: supercomputers (very large, very fast processors) and variations on minicomputers. The boundary between microcomputers and minicomputers is becoming very hazy, with most computer systems being networks of minicomputers and microcomputers linked together for particular market segments. The consumer to a large extent is dictating the type of computer systems being configured and, as a result, should be able to closely match organizational information processing requirements with acquired computer hardware. Performance differences across configurations are tending to center on processing speed, rather than application or device versatility.

ALTERNATIVE MEANS OF ACQUIRING INFORMATION RESOURCES

Organizations obtain computer-based support for their activities in many ways. Each way provides unique opportunities, so most organizations should be able to maximize the return from their computer investments by employing more than one way.

One decision is whether to provide an in-house computer facility or to make use of a service center. Table 2.5 presents the advantages and disadvantages of the service center alternative.

Service Centers

Some organizations make their computer systems available at a price to others. Such a service is termed *time-sharing* if the system can be accessed from a remote terminal at the client's location; otherwise it is

TABLE 2.5
Service Center Advantages and Disadvantages

Advantages	Disadvantages

Avoidance of overhead associated with in-house capabilities
  Physical plant
  Staff
	Service center profit margin
	Loss of control
	  Operations
	  Security

Avoidance of risk of overcapacity in in-house capabilities	Inability to integrate CBIS
Avoidance of large front-end investments in information resources	Possibility that available software is not appropriate
Likelihood that information resources available through service center are of higher quality than those initially acquired for in-house capability	Risk of service center becoming unavailable or insolvent
	Risk of becoming dependent on hardware or software not easily brought in house
	Reduction in organizational learning associated with information resource

termed a *service bureau*. Providing the service may be the purveyor's main business, or it may be a response to excess computer capacity, such as a bank has during the evening or night. Often the cost may be lower and contracts simpler when one deals with an organization whose main sources of revenue derive from activities other than providing computer services. The risk exists, however, that the excess capacity may cease to be made available.

Service centers typically provide a full range of computer-related services: access to processors, specific data files, storage devices, and input/output devices; application software; programming support; data entry operations; and others. Often the service center specializes in a particular industry segment, such as physician or lawyer client-billing, wholesale/retail inventory control, or savings and loan institutions.

Many organizations use service centers. Most savings and loan institutions, for example, handle all their information processing in this fashion. Also, many organizations with in-house computer systems use service centers when their internal capabilities are exceeded or for specified, often analytic, needs. Some common justifications for using a service center are as follows:

- A first-time computer user is leery of sinking funds into a technology not understood very well,
- An application requires a large amount of computer resources but runs only occasionally,
- A service center already has the required application software,
- A one-time application arises,
- Short-term in-house capabilities are inadequate.

A subtle risk of using a service center is the tendency not to reevaluate the decision. Eventually it might be less expensive to acquire or expand in-house capabilities.

In-house Computer Services

Three basic alternatives are available in obtaining in-house computer capabilities: use of a systems house, employment of a facilities management company, or establishment of an in-house staff to handle the acquisition and provision of information services. Table 2.6 summarizes the advantages and disadvantages of each option.

Systems House. Some vendors provide complete (usually small) computer systems for specific (usually limited) application environments. These vendors deal directly with computer manufacturers and acquire or develop software to meet client needs. Little if any in-house staffing is

TABLE 2.6
In-house Alternatives

Alternative	Advantages	Disadvantages
Systems house	Minimal in-house staffing required	Limited to relatively unsophisticated, common applications
	System house personnel evaluate organizational information processing needs and design appropriate computer system	Needs assessed by individuals not intimately related with organization
		Difficulty in evaluating system house recommendations
Facilities management	No recruitment, development, or evaluation of technical staff required	High cost of facilities management services
	Information resource costs known in advance	Technical staff may not be familiar with organization
		Technical staff not committed to organization
In-house staff	Technical staff more knowledgeable about organization and more committed to organization	Recruitment, development, and evaluation of technical staff required
	Information resource "learning" remains within organization	

required by organizations acquiring computer systems through system houses.

System houses can play a valuable role for the new computer user who intends to provide computer-based support for a limited and well-defined set of organizational functions. While most system houses are extremely capable, the naivety of many clients has attracted a few disreputable and incompetent individuals to this segment of the computer industry. All claims should be closely checked and references of other clients required.

Facilities Management. A facilities management firm completely takes over the management and operation of information resources for its clients. While the technical staff are employees of the facility management firm, all information resources are the property of client organizations. Many organizations find this an attractive option, particularly when the organization's investment in computer resources is perceived to be poorly managed by an in-house staff. A common strategy of a facilities management firm is to offer to provide a similar level of service at a lower overall cost than that being experienced by the organization. The disadvantages that accompany facility management services—a loss in internal control over a large investment, the need to expose sensitive information to outsiders, a lack of organizational commitment on the part of computer professionals, the potential problems encountered when changing back to in-house staffing, etc.—have prevented this alternative from being enthusiastically adopted by many organizations.

Facilities management services tend to be best received in areas where *industry* information processing needs are standardized or tightly regulated (e.g., hospitals and insurance companies). Such services also seem most appropriate for medium-size firms.

In-house Staff.   While in-house staffing undoubtedly provides the greatest potential for exploiting the information resource, the problems associated with recruiting, developing, and maintaining a competent technical staff cannot be minimized. The demand for qualified personnel exceeds the supply, particularly when individuals experienced in particular technical or functional areas are needed.

It is possible to maintain a relatively small in-house staff and supplement the capabilities of these individuals through service centers, systems houses, software houses, and consultants. This practice should be encouraged because of the knowledge, objectivity, and "freshness" of outside perspectives. However, as an organization's CBIS applications become more pervasive and interdependent, the desire to maintain total control over information resources and to internalize the benefits of organizational learning about information resources leads organizations to emphasize in-house servicing.

INFORMATION RESOURCE ACQUISITION

Acquiring Computer Hardware

When acquiring hardware, three financial options are available: renting, leasing, and purchasing. Table 2.7 lists the advantages and disadvantages of each. The prime distinctions are as follows: a rental arrangement can be negated in a relatively short time (30–180 days); a lease arrangement is less expensive (up to 30 percent less than rental), but involves a longer contractual period (1–10 years); and a purchase arrangement is irreversible but generally least expensive if the computer is held for more than four years. (By "flexibility" in Table 2.7 is meant being able to take advantage of technological developments as they occur or being able to react to organizational changes requiring additional, or more sophisticated, information resources.)

A consideration that tends to differ with each situation involves maintenance services. While a maintenance contract is separately negotiated when renting or purchasing, leases often include maintenance. The service *response* may vary, however, with vendors tending to provide bet-

TABLE 2.7
Hardware Financing Alternatives

Alternative	Advantages	Disadvantages
Rental	Least financial commitment Greatest flexibility	Most expensive Least security (vendor *can* terminate agreement)
Lease	Less expensive than rental Commitment shorter than purchase Little risk of technological obsolescence Controllable costs Low risk of being oversold No risk of relying on residual value of hardware (drops roughly 10 percent a year) No capital investment Often purchase option Often no extra shift charges	May be more expensive than purchase Cash flow is expense and cannot be leveraged Risk of undercapacity
Purchase	Least cost over long term Residual value to owner (residual value high relative to other capital investments) Favorable cash flows Investment tax credit No extra shift charges Often very flexible terms Profitable use of investment funds	Greatest commitment Greatest risk of technological obsolescence Must have access to capital Must thoroughly understand information needs

ter service to rental clients to build goodwill (and to justify the higher expense).

A related issue involves the decision to acquire hardware from multiple vendors or to use a single vendor's equipment. It generally is possible to purchase a CPU from one vendor and compatible, and often better, storage or input/output devices from other vendors while saving 15–40 percent in hardware costs. While attractive, these lower costs must be balanced against the need for separate maintenance contracts with each vendor. Management of maintenance services and organizational leverage with vendors regarding service response could become problems.

Acquiring Computer Software

There are three basic means by which organizations can obtain software: acquiring an existing package, having one's own analysts and programmers develop the program, or having a consultant develop the program specifically for one's organization. The objective in all situations is to acquire software that will meet organizational requirements at the most reasonable cost.

As software development is labor intensive, it tends to be very costly, particularly when the application involved is complex or highly specialized. As discussed earlier, it is generally far less expensive to locate existing software packages than to develop programs from scratch. Such software packages are available from numerous sources: computer manufacturers, software houses, system houses, computer user groups, other organizations, and the public domain (federal government). Sometimes usable programs can be located whose sole cost is to cover copying and distribution expenses.

A number of problems often materialize, however, that prohibit this alternative:

- No software may be available that meets the organization's needs,
- The effort to modify an available package so it meets the organization's needs is excessive,
- Software is available but is incompatible with the organization's CPU or operating system.

In these situations, which are becoming less frequent, software must be developed in house or contracted out to consultants.

Again, the decision revolves around cost. If personnel with the required capabilities are available in house, it is not cost effective to use a consultant. If needed skills are not available internally but are expected to be needed for an extended time, it is normally desirable to hire the required personnel and develop the software in house. However, it may be less expensive and more effective to use consultants if, for example,

- The consultant possesses skills or experience not readily available,
- The desired skills, or just manpower, will be needed for only a limited time,
- All in-house personnel are unavailable, given a project's time constraints, and the organization does not wish to hire more personnel.

The obvious danger of using consultants is that once the assignment is completed, the consultant (and hence knowledge of the software) leaves.

The Computer Resource Acquisition Process

Many similarities exist, regardless of whether an organization is acquiring hardware, software, or consultant resources. The following sequence of activities is normally followed:

1. Requirements determination,
2. Proposal preparation,
3. Bid solicitation,
4. Bid evaluation,
5. Contract negotiation.

Each will be covered below except for the quantitative and qualitative techniques associated with bid evaluation. As these methods are applied under many CBIS circumstances, they are separately covered in the appendix.

Requirements Determination.   The first step is to carefully analyze the purpose behind the acquisition effort: the organizational activities supported, the objectives sought, and the means by which these objectives will be attained. Only after such analysis can hardware (speeds, capacities, efficiencies, volumes, etc.) or software (functions performed, outputs produced, etc.) performance characteristics be realized.

Proposal Preparation.   A formal document should be prepared that clearly defines why resources are being sought, lists all criteria considered important in the resource being sought, and explains how the final selection of a supplier will proceed. The aim is to provide enough information that vendors can evaluate the extent to which their products or services meet the criteria to be used in bid selection. Thus, in addition to performance attributes, *all* relevant evaluation criteria must be stipulated. Criteria commonly employed include the following:

- Hardware performance (speed, access time, capacities, etc.)
- Software performance (functions, input-output volume and medium, timeliness, etc.)
- Cost, efficiency
- Compatibility with existing hardware and software
- Ease of use
- Documentation (extent, cost)
- Training (extent, cost)
- In-house skills required
- Expandability, modifiability, flexibility
- Vendor experience (application, industry)
- Vendor financial solvency
- Vendor prior performance (product claims, installation support, postinstallation support).

Bid Solicitation.   One of the most difficult tasks in acquiring hardware and software, particularly for the first-time user, is identifying likely vendors. The more vendors located, the greater the likelihood of obtaining a suitable product at a reasonable cost. A common error is to examine the offerings of only one vendor.

Among the means by which organizations can locate vendors are the phone book, industry associations, other organizations in the industry or region, contacts through professional groups, trade periodicals, computer industry periodicals, and consultants. Additionally, organizations exist whose major service is to channel information about hardware and software products/services to interested parties. Among such organizations are the following:

Auerbach Publishers, Inc.
6560 North Park Drive
Pennsauken, NJ 08109

Applied Computer Research
Suite 298
8808 North Central Avenue
Phoenix, AZ 85020

Canning Publications, Inc.
925 Anza Avenue
Vista, CA 92083

Computer Software Management
  Information Center
112 Barrow Hall
University of Georgia
Athens, GA 30602

Datapro Research Corp.
1805 Underwood Blvd.
Delran, NJ 08075

International Computer
  Programs, Inc.
1119 Keystone Way
Carmel, IN 46032

Management Information Corp.
140 Barclay Center
Cherry Hill, NJ 08034

Minicomputer Data Services
20 Coventry Lane
Riverside, CT 06878

Bid Evaluation. Bid evaluation includes a preliminary task: bid validation. Bid validation includes all efforts to ensure that claims made by vendors are valid. Common steps that can be taken to evaluate vendor product claims are given below. As mentioned earlier, specific methods to use in evaluating and selecting among alternative bids are discussed and illustrated in the appendix.

The four procedures typically employed to assess vendor claims are references, trial periods, benchmark testing, and simulation modeling. Vendors should always be asked for names of organizations currently using their products. Probably only satisfied clients will be made available, but even satisfied customers experience problems. Additionally, it is often possible to identify additional clients when talking with those identified by the vendor.

Second, vendors sometimes allow potential clients to try out their products. As this is the best way to validate vendor claims, it should be investigated. Some costs (e.g., transportation and installation), may be incurred that, even if allowed, make direct testing inappropriate.

A third approach is to develop a sample of the workload (termed a *benchmark*) to be processed by a vendor's product, take this workload sample to an installation where the vendor's product is being used, and obtain actual measures of how well the product handles the workload. By using this one benchmark with the products offered by competing vendors, one can make relative comparisons of performance. Factors to consider in benchmark testing are the expense and difficulty required to arrive at a representative benchmark and the programming required to run a benchmark.

A final option is to develop a simulation model of current operations, introduce performance attributes believed to represent a vendor's product into this model, and examine the extent to which overall operations are improved, as disclosed by simulated outputs. Special skills are obviously required to use this means of validating vendors' claims. However, some consulting firms have developed generalized simulation models that allow such experimentation at a reasonable cost to their clients.

A final issue regarding bid validation involves evaluating products currently under development. As true validation is impossible, the risk associated with decision making increases. It is possible to gauge the degree of risk somewhat by examining vendors' past performances with similar products. Many vendors will discount their prices to initial customers, recognizing that problems may arise. In any case, the decision to select an untested product must ultimately depend on the costs to be incurred by the organization if the product does not perform as expected or is unavailable for an extended period of time.

Contract Negotiation.   An oversight committed by many organizations involves treating vendor-provided preprinted contracts as inviolate. A computer-related contract should never be signed before legal counsel (preferably counsel experienced with computer product/service contracting) has been consulted.

Points to be negotiated and made clear in a contract include delivery, testing, acceptance, installation, support during and after installation, and termination, *along with penalties to be associated with unmet conditions.* Two especially critical factors to be considered in contracts are backup provisions (in case the product becomes inoperable) and client rights regarding future product modifications or enhancements. The more specific and comprehensive a contract is, the less likely it is that contractual problems will arise.

CONCLUSION

This introduction to computer concepts has had three aims. The first aim was to provide the reader with an elementary vocabulary that will be used throughout the text and that should enable him or her to interact comfortably with computer specialists and vendors. This introduction is simply that—an introduction. Numerous alternative sources are available to those who want more explicit and detailed treatments of these and related subjects. The second objective was to expose the reader to the variety of computer-related services and to the procedures normally followed when acquiring information resources. The computer industry *is* rich in alternative means of acquiring computer-based capabilities. The third aim was to illustrate the dynamic nature of the computer industry. Technological advances are regularly felt throughout all facets of the industry, so what was too expensive or complex yesterday may be feasible today.

Organizations cannot expect to successfully exploit the information resource by relying on external sources, such as consultants and vendors, to provide information on technological opportunities. Internal sources must be cultivated that identify emerging information products and services in terms of the organization's unique perspective. Lack of such internal information sources (individuals or groups) might explain much of the inappropriate use, or nonuse, of information resources.

KEY ISSUES

Hardware consists of the electronic and electromechanical components used to process (input, transmit, transform, store, and output) data.

Software consists of the instructions that direct the hardware in its processing of data.

Data can be rapidly and economically transmitted along communication lines. These lines might link remote devices to a central processor or might link two or more processors together.

Applications software programs, used to directly support or perform organizational activities, are becoming more available in the form of generalized software packages.

Systems software programs, used to enhance the capabilities and ease of use of computer systems, are becoming increasingly sophisticated for all computers.

A computer's power is represented by its speed, its amount of addressable primary memory, the variety of peripheral devices to be attached to it, and the availability of software packages to be run on it.

Performance gains from microelectronics are greatest with purely electronic components.

Software costs are increasing rapidly, and currently exceed hardware costs for most organizations.

Personnel costs associated with information resources are increasing even more rapidly.

Storage costs can be reduced greatly if effective use is made of storage hierarchies.

Managing communication costs is becoming an important activity in most organizations.

Generally, it is less expensive to buy software when available packages are appropriate and require only moderate changes.

The demand for analysts and programmers far exceeds the supply.

Most computer vendors are beginning to produce "families" of computer systems to meet particular market segments.

A variety of means exist for acquiring computer resources. All of these must be assessed whenever new requirements for information processing arise.

Vendors' claims must be validated.

Computer contracts should never be casually glanced over, but should be examined by knowledgeable individuals.

All organizations should develop in-house expertise in relevant information system products and services.

DISCUSSION QUESTIONS

1. What is maintained within a computer's primary memory when a program is executed?
2. What is the function of the CPU's control unit? What is the function of its arithmetic-logical unit?
3. What is meant by the phrase "storage hierarchy"? What is the reason for employing storage hierarchies?
4. Explain the "on-line" and "off-line" distinction with regard to secondary storage devices.
5. What is gained by using "source data capture" techniques?
6. What are the functions of communication control units?
7. How does a "very high level" programming language differ from a "high level"?
8. Illustrate how an operating system can extend the capabilities of a computer system.
9. Some experts say the role of the programmer may soon disappear. How might this come about?
10. When might an organization with an internal information systems staff make effective use of a "service center"?
11. When might an organization use the services of a facilities management firm?
12. What are some dangers associated with being one of the first organizations to use a hardware (or software) vendor's product? of using the products of a recently established vendor?
13. Provide some examples of penalty clauses that might be inserted into a contract for computer hardware and for computer software.

BRIEF CASES

1. *East Coast Business School*

   Tom Tiles, the MBA program director for East Coast Business School, was beginning to feel like the shoemaker who could not keep his own children in shoes. His small staff had just barely gotten through another year of processing over 2500 applications and selecting 150 applicants for the coming year. It seemed obvious to Tom that many, if not most, of the staff's activities could be automated.

   After talking with a colleague whose area of expertise involved computer-based information systems, Tom was beginning to feel that the task of automating his staff was not as easy as he had initially believed. Would it be best to use the university's mainframe computer or to buy a microcomputer for use solely by the MBA program staff? How should applicant information be entered into a computer system? What type of storage media should be used? Should any more sophisticated types of applications be run?

   What should Tom do now?

2. *Woodstock Heaters*

Woodstock Heaters was a eighty-seven-year-old company in southern Vermont that specialized in home energy products. The company had recently started producing solar water heaters and had run into a pleasant (for the moment, at least) problem—its sales were outrunning the manufacturing department's ability to produce heaters and components. The firm's management was beginning to worry about the long-term implications of the growing frequency of production delays. One solution would seem to be to invest funds in a standard manufacturing control system.

Woodstock Heaters owned a small business computer that was used mainly to process sales, financial, and accounting information. It had sufficient excess capacity on this machine to implement a manufacturing control system. The internal systems staff (analyst/programmer, programmer, and operator), however, had no experience with manufacturing systems.

The question was whether to purchase a software package, to develop the needed programs internally, or to hire a consultant to develop the programs. Fortunately, the small business computer was a popular model for which much software had been developed.

What specific information would have to be collected to make an appropriate decision about acquiring manufacturing control software? Given that the decision is to buy a software package, what criteria should be applied to the selection decision?

3. *Mercy Hospital*

Susan Horowitz was the only employee of Mercy Hospital who had an MBA. Susan had started at Mercy as a staff accountant after obtaining her BS in accounting. She then won a scholarship to attend graduate school, and completed a respected two-year MBA program while on leave from Mercy. On her return, she was appointed the financial staff assistant to the hospital's director.

Like many large urban hospitals, Mercy used sophisticated computer-based information systems to support patient care activities, but was rather deficient in supporting administrative functions with computer-based means. Susan took this as an opportunity to demonstrate her recently gained prowess. Given recent advances in financial modeling and the importance of financial planning to any hospital's success, it seemed to be a low-risk move to introduce the hospital's administrators to interactive financial modeling.

Once Susan began to explore the marketplace, however, she began to doubt her ability to implement an appropriate financial modeling system. A rather casual investigation of products uncovered almost one hundred different systems—some offered by time-sharing firms, some that ran on mainframes, and others that ran on microcomputers. Additionally, little help was available from the hospital's internal information systems group, which had not heard of many of the vendors and reluctantly admitted that little excess capacity remained on the hospital's two computers. Susan, however, had committed herself to this project. It was too late to gracefully back away.

What does Susan need to determine to make an appropriate decision?

NOTES

1. J. E. Gessford, *Modern Information Systems* (Reading, Mass.: Addison-Wesley, 1980).

2. L. D. Hemmerich, "Streaming Revives 1/2-in. Tape Market," *Mini-MicroSystems* 13(1980):173–78.

3. D. M. Smith, "Data Processing in the 1980s," in *Convergence: Computers, Communications and Office Automation*, Vol. 2 (Maidenhead, Berkshire, England: Infotech International, 1979).

4. J. T. Soma, *The Computer Industry* (Lexington, Mass.: Lexington Books, 1976).

5. S. L. Mandell, *Computers and Data Processing* (St. Paul, Minn.: West, 1979).

6. N. Weizer, "Distributed Systems of the 1980s," in *Information Systems in the 1980s* (Cambridge, Mass.: Arthur D. Little, 1979), pp. 9–20.

Organizational Concepts 3

ORGANIZATIONS ARISE when people realize that certain objectives can best be attained through cooperation and specialization. As roles become formally defined and objectives take on a long-term nature, the group acquires the sense of impersonality and permanence that characterizes an *organization*. While the perspective adopted here emphasizes the formal nature of organizations, this clearly represents only the skeleton of the living organism encountered when interacting with an organization. Very similar organizational "skeletons" (i.e., formal, permanent arrangements of roles, facilities, and resources) take on quite varied personalities once an organization's members are engaged.

This chapter begins with a functional view of organizations that stresses the role of information in organizations. Then, as a means of introducing the reader to organizational information processing systems, the human information processing system is discussed. The chapter concludes with a discussion of systems modeling that emphasizes the construction of organizational systems models as one means of understanding organizational functioning and, hence, information needs.

ORGANIZATIONS: A FUNCTIONAL PERSPECTIVE

An organization can be viewed as a collection of work units, each of which performs functional roles related to organization-wide objectives.[1,2] Each work unit comprises organizational resources (human, financial, materials, facilities) bound together through a complex of responsibilities reflecting degrees of authority over resources.[3] To understand an organization or organizational segment, it is valuable to identify each functional work unit and to uncover the organizational role(s) performed by each work unit. Once this is accomplished, concern shifts to describing the relationships among work units.

Identification of Work Units

The organizational responsibility centers identified as work units can be characterized along two dimensions: *horizontal*, or related directly to operations performed by the organization in providing products or services, and *vertical*, related to the management of organizational resources. The horizontal dimension is representative of what Mintzberg refers to as the *operating core*.[4] These responsibilities involve *mainstream activities*, such as securing resources, converting resources into products or services, securing clients or customers, and distributing products or services, as well as *supportive activities*, such as personnel, maintenance, and administration. Table 3.1 describes common mainstream functions for a variety of organizations to illustrate the universality of this perspective. Supportive activities, such as the need to hire and develop employees, are more generally recognized as being relevant in all organizations.

The vertical dimension includes the hierarchical structures used to facilitate effort associated with setting objectives, devising plans, allocating resources, directing activities, and evaluating the degree to which plans are attained.[5] Again using Mintzberg's terminology, one can identify three major vertical zones of responsibility: *operating managers*, who have direct supervisory responsibilities within the operating core; the *strategic apex*, who direct the organization as a whole; and the *middle line*, who link the strategic apex with the operating core.

Figure 3.1 provides a visual interpretation of the way these horizontal and vertical dimensions merge in defining the centers of responsibili-

TABLE 3.1
Mainstream Activities

Activity	Organizational Contexts				
	Manufacturing	Retail	Banking	Health	Public Safety
Marketing	Identifying products Securing orders	Identifying products Securing customers	Identifying service Securing customers	Identifying service Identifying client	Identifying service Handling complaints
Resource acquisition	Purchasing raw materials and procured components	Purchasing retail goods	Purchasing equipment and supplies	Purchasing equipment and supplies	Purchasing equipment and supplies
Operations	Manufacturing	Presenting product	Providing financial services	Providing medical treatment	Providing public safety services
Distribution	Shipping	Delivery	Transmitting funds	Providing out-patient care	Delivery to judiciary

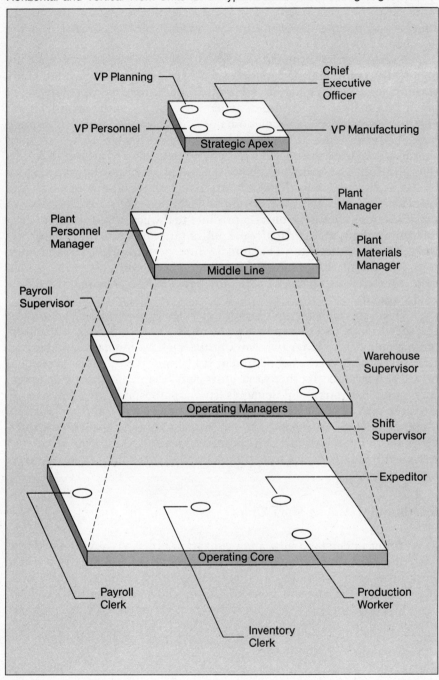

ties referred to as work units. Here individuals responsible for work unit performance represent each work unit. The functions performed by the operating core, operating managers, and strategic apex are generally quite clear, but this is often not the case with the middle line. Stated simply, the middle line performs an information function within the organization.

A small organization is composed of only a few work units, typically broadly defined operating core units and a small strategic apex. For many reasons (some associated with strategies for attaining an expanding set of organizational objectives, others reflecting changes in the organization's environment), organizational domains increase over time in variety, complexity, and interdependence. As a domain expands, additional *horizontal* work units are formed to benefit from economies of scale and specialization. Specialization, however, implies increased functional differentiation between work units, even though the operating core's overall functional characteristics may remain relatively constant. As many of these differentiated work units contribute to the accomplishment of joint functions, additional *vertical* work units must be formed to coordinate their interdependencies. The middle line performs this coordination role—the channeling of information among work units, between the strategic apex and the operating core, and between the organization and its environment.

Means in addition to information flows can be used to coordinate the activities of interdependent work units. Inventories and queues are often employed to buffer two work units, such as purchasing and manufacturing, that operate under different time frames. Work units dependent on the performance of other work units (such as manufacturing on inventory) or on environmental demands (such as a hospital emergency room) are often provided slack resources to handle stressful situations. Furthermore, organizational redesign efforts aimed at reducing work unit interdependence by identifying self-contained tasks (e.g., a social service department handling *all* the needs of a certain client group) can be observed.

Relationships Among Work Units

One cannot understand how an organization functions simply by identifying its work units. The crucial task involves recognizing how these work units are related. Schematic representations of simple sets of linkages between organizational work units are shown in Figures 3.2 and 3.3.

It is possible, however, to categorize work unit relations fairly simply by focusing on the basis for each relationship:

- Exchanges of resources,

FIGURE 3.2
Horizontal Work Unit Relationships

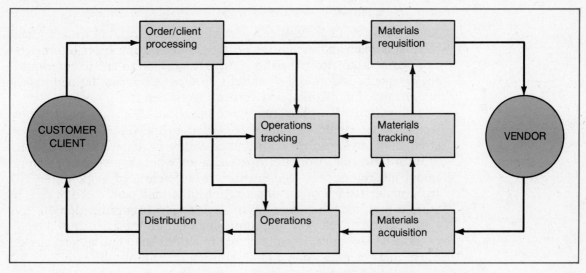

FIGURE 3.3
Vertical Work Unit Relationships

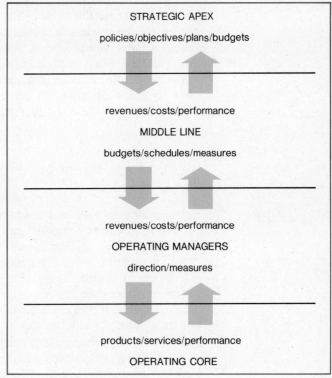

- Flows of work in process or clients through successive manufacturing or service operations,
- Exchanges of information (plans, budgets, directives, statuses, rates, performance measures, procedures, and policies).

Resource, work in process, and client flows are associated with (horizontal) mainstream and supportive activities in an organization. Information flows arise from efforts by the vertical dimension to create order out of the diverse behaviors and potentially different, even conflicting interests of specialized (horizontal and vertical) work units.

In summary, organizations accomplish tasks, and hence attain objectives, that would be impossible if left to individuals. The inherent strength of any organization lies in its ability to achieve both functional differentiation (i.e., work unit specialization where appropriate) and functional integration (i.e., coordination of differentiated work units).[6] To truly understand how an organization functions (and this is precisely what is required when computer-based support of organizational activities is explored), relevant work units and their interrelationships must be examined. As critical organizational functions may not be formally defined, their identification and description often prove difficult.

Prior to examining organizational information systems (i.e., channels permitting the flow of information between work units), we shall examine the notion of human information processing. Most concepts, mechanisms, and problems associated with human information processing can be applied to organizational information processing. Since we all experience the "human information processing system," we should more readily grasp information processing concepts, mechanisms, and problems when we view them from a human perspective.

HUMAN INFORMATION PROCESSING

The world we inhabit is complex. Consider the simple act of driving a car in a residential area and the resultant pool of data captured by your five senses: sight provides constantly changing images of your environment; hearing provides a continuous stream of sounds; touch, smell, and taste provide multiple sensations regarding the "feel" of the ride, the condition of the car, the immediate environment, and your own physical condition. Some of these data are critical if your ride is not to end in tragedy, some are enjoyable, but many are irrelevant. How do you make sense of a mass of data? The answer lies in the most sophisticated information system known—the *human information processing system (HIPS)*.

Through evolution, we have developed an internal means of directing environmental searches for relevant data, of filtering the data sensed,

FIGURE 3.4
A Model of the Human Information Processing System

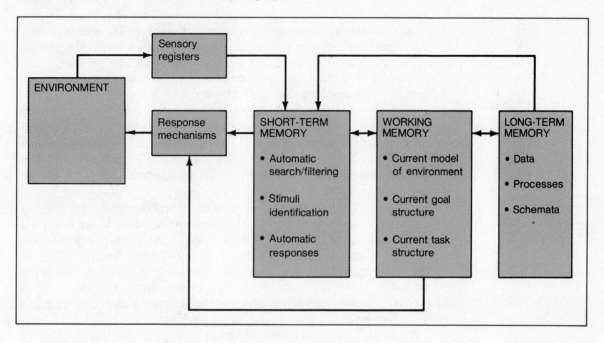

of establishing and maintaining representations of our environment, and of transmitting responses back to our environment. This "means" is the elaborate data capture, analysis, storage, and response system referred to as the HIPS.

While many scientists have developed models and theories to explain human–environmental interaction, the ideas of cognitive psychologists will perhaps be most meaningful to our eventual study of organizational information systems. Figure 3.4 shows one way of representing the functioning and components of the HIPS.[7,8]

Environmental stimuli enter the HIPS through sensory registers (eyes, ears, nose, etc.). A limited number of these stimuli are actively attended to in *short-term memory*, where they are identified and readied for further processing. As short-term memory is characterized by extremely short retention (around one second) and relatively small capacity, most of this processing must be automatic, i.e., predetermined as to what is expected and how it is to be handled. Stimuli not actively attended to are lost.

When too many stimuli are directed toward the HIPS, compensating behaviors are often invoked to overcome short-term memory limitations. These behaviors normally take the form of filtering processes in which less relevant stimuli are ignored and other stimuli are only partially captured. In this way an "abstracted" representation of reality is maintained. The likelihood of errors occurring during information processing, while always high, clearly would increase during information overload.

When automated processes cannot be applied but stimuli are judged important, the stimuli are brought into *working memory* for controlled processing, i.e., analysis, problem solving, decision making, comparison with existing models of reality, etc. Working memory is believed to possess limited storage capacities and to be characterized by a retention period of ten to thirty minutes. Responses back to the environment can thus be transmitted automatically from short-term memory or consciously from working memory.

Because of the limited storage capacity of working memory, entities (problems, solution strategies, tasks, algorithms, models, heuristics, etc.) are often maintained as "chunks" consisting of mental tags representing more detailed representations of some components. Problem solving, for example, commonly involves breaking a problem into parts and working on one part at a time to build an overall solution. By maintaining most of the problem in the form of chunks, one can examine each part in depth without losing the context of the larger problem.

The models of reality used in working memory are the results of a lifetime of experience and learning organized in *long-term memory* and composed of interrelated sets of data (facts and experience), processes (skills, rules, and procedures), and higher-order entities (concepts, goals, and values). Long-term memory is believed to possess a vast storage capacity and a limitless retention period. However, while items are not lost, they can be "misplaced" in that mechanisms for retrieval can be forgotten. An example is the common experience of having an answer at the "tip of your tongue" but not being able to verbalize it.

Long-term memory is organized as complex, often subconscious relationships among stored entities. As the associations between entities reflect an individual's unique set of life experiences, quite varied associations are likely to exist for any two people for even a small number of entities. That the same "trigger" may result in different entities' being retrieved from long-term memory should not be surprising.

Finally, cognitive frameworks referred to as *schemata* are believed to reflect the organization of long-term memory and, hence, to direct the HIPS. Each schema represents *weltansicht*, a world view representing an individual's unique perception of reality. Schemata encode both the automated processes of short-term memory and the models employed in working memory. Many schemata exist: some provide a universal context for behavior, while others account for situations that repeatedly arise. A critical factor in the functioning of the HIPS is the appropriateness of existing schemata to a given situation. When discrepancies arise, a new schema must be activated or, as is more likely, the active schema must be modified. The all-important role of schemata is aptly put by Rumelhart in describing the human organism: "It perceives what it expects to, it understands in terms of what it has experienced, and it remembers just what fits with what it knows."[9]

In summary, the purpose of the HIPS is threefold. First, *communication* with the environment is provided through the reception of stimuli and emission of responses. Second, *guides for action* (some automated, others merely suggested and controlled by the individual) make it possible to deal with repetitious or similar situations. Third, and most important, a cognitive *context* is provided with which to interpret and react to environmental stimuli. It is such contexts that enable one to quickly assess a new or changing situation and activate appropriate schemata. Without this ability, humans would be unable to distinguish relevant from irrelevant stimuli, resulting in a state of perpetual chaos.

A final point must be introduced regarding the HIPS. Schemata evolve over time from individual experiences and individual learning. As these tend to be unique experiences, each individual's schemata are unique. The perceptions and behaviors of any two people encountering the same situation may differ significantly because of dissimilarities in the schemata activated by each (other factors, such as a person's mood or the degree of attention given the situation, add further distortions). It should not be surprising, then, that people from different experiential, educational, social, or cultural backgrounds often have difficulty communicating with one another. Similarly, the error in expecting uniform behaviors from a heterogeneous group of individuals should also be clear.

ORGANIZATIONAL INFORMATION SYSTEMS

The handling of information flows is as important for organizations as for individuals. Organizations, like humans, must facilitate exchanges of information with their environment. This implies the establishment of linkages (i.e., sensory registers) with key organizations and key individuals in the organization's environment. The captured stimuli must be interpreted, evaluated as to importance, reacted to, and stored for later retrieval. Responses (products, services, requests for resources, etc.) must flow back to the environment. Finally, models of reality, guides for action, values, and objectives must all be maintained to guide these information processing tasks.

The HIPS operates within a single processing unit—the individual. Organizational information systems (OIS) must enable multiple processing units—vertical and horizontal work units—to interact in coping with an environment. Consequently, information flows *among* work units must be handled as well as those linking work units with the environment. This layered aspect of OIS becomes even more complex as one recognizes that individual work units develop their own OIS, just as each organizational member evolves a unique HIPS. The desirability of establishing organization-wide schemata that influence the functioning of all these OIS and HIPS should be obvious.

Even without the problems accompanying a consideration of individuals, OIS still take a variety of forms. A major difference among OIS is a formal–informal distinction. A formal OIS is designed and controlled by the organization. In other words, it is developed by organizational members to serve a definite purpose associated with the attainment of organizational objectives, and it is modified by these or other individuals over time to reflect shifts in objectives and organizational or environmental changes. An informal OIS develops spontaneously to respond to a previously unforeseen situation or to enable individuals to transmit unofficial information (rumors, tentative plans, secrets, etc.) within and between organizations. Table 3.2 provides examples of common formal and informal OIS.

Observations of individuals in organizations indicate that much of the information they require to perform their duties derives from informal information channels.[10] As the focus moves up the organizational hierarchy, this reliance on informal channels increases. It often represents more than 70 percent of the information used by top managers. Three questions naturally arise. Why is informal information more useful than formal? What can organizations do to improve the flow of informal information? Finally, what is the role of formal information systems in organizations?

TABLE 3.2
Common Organizational Information Systems

Formal	Informal
Scheduled meetings	Grapevine
Memorandums	Conversation
Reports	Observation
Policies/procedures manuals	Public and private information sources (newspapers, trade journals, magazines, TV, etc.)
Planning/control systems	
Evaluation/reward systems	

Importance of Informal Information

Organizational behavior, particularly that of managers, is often characterized by brevity, variety, and fragmentation. Specific problems and tasks can be attended to for only short time segments over a long period of time, and many problems and tasks are often attended to in a single period. It is difficult in such circumstances for organizational members to know in advance where their attention will be focused at any time. Thus, formal information is often *too limited* (with its emphasis on economic and quantitative data), *too general* (as it is not situation specific), *too late* (reflecting time delays inherent in many data collection procedures), and *unreliable* (because of an orientation toward quantifying organizational realities and errors often encountered in data collection).

Informal information is typically better able to match the situation-specific information needs of many organizational members. One caution, however, should be noted. As informal information is channeled through individuals, the HIPS must be extensively relied upon. If the schemata, models, and processes employed in interpersonal communication are similar and relevant, no problems arise. The potential for miscommunication, however, is real.

Design of Informal Information Systems

Organizations exert some influence on the informal information channels available for use by organizational members.[11,12] Great latitude exists in the manner work units can be formed. For example, they may be designed to facilitate specialization, economies of scale, or workflow interdependencies. The last objective touches on the design of informal OIS through the creation of organizational roles whose primary purpose is to channel information into, within, and from work units.

The information processing requirements of organizations are directly related to the uncertainties facing organizational members. As work-related uncertainty increases, so does the need for increased amounts of information. A close examination of any organization will disclose that certain positions involve searching for or filtering information to be disseminated informally and formally throughout the organization. Examples include task forces, steering committees, client councils, and liaison roles (internal or external relations).

It is becoming possible, with evolving information technologies, to provide computer-based support for certain informal information processing needs of organizational members. Such efforts, however, require the adoption of a fresh approach to CBIS design, where primary consideration is placed on individual and situational concerns.[13]

Functions of Formal Information Systems

As with the HIPS, formal OIS serve three major purposes in organizations. First, they provide (by plans, budgets, reward systems, etc.) organizational schemata that reduce the need for organizational members to continuously monitor their environments. Through a process of organizational socialization, these schemata become assimilated into each individual's HIPS, thus avoiding what would otherwise be an exhaustive HIPS effort. Second, they provide (by policies, procedures, rules, controls, etc.) guides informing organizational members of when and how to act. Third, they provide (by plans, budgets, resource statuses, activity statuses, etc.) a means of coordinating interdependent work units. All three purposes reduce the information processing loads of organizational members by focusing attention on specific areas and by automatically providing relevant information.

While many benefits can accrue from formal OIS, if too much reliance is placed on them the information system itself may dictate the behavior of organizational members. As stated earlier, formal information tends to be limited in scope, general in nature, untimely, and unreliable. It should provide a broad context for behavior, it should not direct behavior! If organizational reward systems are closely tied to formal OIS, these information systems will naturally begin to direct organizational functioning. Information that is easily measured tends to permeate formal OIS; information difficult to measure is not used. Whether or not measurable information is meaningful is obviously situation dependent. A more important concern may be the relevance of unmeasurable information.

As formal OIS are designed by individuals, design assumptions and intentions will reflect the designers' HIPS. As a result, incompatibilities may arise between a formal OIS and organizational members expected to make use of it. The more divergent are the schemata employed by designers and users, the greater is the likelihood such problems will arise.

Information as a Source of Power

Regardless of whether the information is informal or formal, ownership of information is a source of power for organizational members. Ownership implies control of information: an ability to influence its production and to limit who has access to it. Consequently, when organizational structures are being designed, organizational roles defined, or OIS developed, organizational power relationships may be affected. This facet of the information resource is too often ignored. What compounds the problem is that no standard means of guiding or preventing such power shifts exist. Recognizing that such changes occur, however, is a large step toward coping with such disturbances in organizational authority and social structures.

SYSTEMS MODELING

The systems approach is based on the premise that nothing—no organization, person, problem, or crisis—can be understood on its own; *everything* is influenced by the larger environment, to which it is inextricably tied.[14] Our world is complex. Any attempt to fully understand even a minute aspect of its reality is doomed to failure. A systems modeler, admittedly an optimist, strives to approximate reality to the extent he or she can recognize its most relevant facets.

Any attempt at system modeling ultimately results in a series of trade-offs between the goals of *comprehensiveness* and *relevancy*. If one segment of reality depends on all other segments, then one's focus must broaden as analysis continues. For a model of a segment of reality to truly capture reality's essence, the model should be as complex (in number of components, attributes, goals, functions, etc.) as reality. Modeling efforts, however, are invariably undertaken for a specific purpose. Given that purpose, it is clear that some segments of reality are more important than others and that the marginal returns from added complexity soon decrease. Deciding whether a particular segment is relevant or irrelevant and deciding at what complexity level to stop at are precisely where the *skill* of systems modeling leaves off and the *art* begins. Such decisions need to be reassessed over time: reality itself continually changes, as does our purpose in modeling reality.

This introduction to systems modeling is not meant to be complete, but simply to provide a basic understanding of its use. Additional systems concepts will be introduced later.

Basic Systems Concepts

A *system* is any interacting set of elements acting toward a common goal. Relationships between system elements are the links that bind the elements together in the joint accomplishment of some purpose. Anything can be modeled as a system. Abstract entities, such as organizations, often prove more difficult than physical entities, such as biological organisms.

Every system must have a boundary that distinguishes between those elements composing the system and all other elements, i.e., the system's *environment*. Many relationships exist between a system and its environment (such as exchanges of resources, energy, and information; constraints; and goals). As a group, however, these relationships tend to be fewer and weaker than those among the system's internal elements.

A system accomplishes its purpose by transforming *inputs* into *outputs*. Inputs are received from the environment, and outputs are returned to the environment. Specifically, input elements are consumed or transformed by system operation while output elements are created. In performing their various functions, system elements either convert inputs into outputs or support this conversion process. System elements can be further categorized as *processors* and *controllers*. Processors actually perform input–output conversions, while controllers direct and monitor processor activities. An overview of these relationships is provided in Figure 3.5.

Systems are *open* or *closed*. Elements within an open system have many relationships with environmental elements, while elements within a closed system have no relationships with environmental elements. This concept is purely an abstraction, as there are no totally closed systems. However, systems being modeled can generally be placed at discrete points along a hypothetical open–closed continuum.

FIGURE 3.5
A Simple System
Model

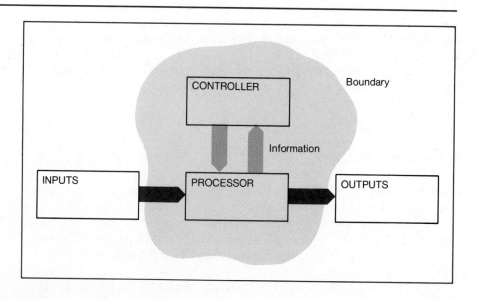

The open–closed concept is important because it introduces the notion of *entropy*. Without sufficient environmental exchanges, systems would slowly decay as energy and required resources were exhausted during system operation.

Systems belong to hierarchical families. Every system is composed of elemental subsets called *subsystems*. A subsystem is totally contained within its system, but may also belong to other systems. Every system is a subsystem of larger systems, i.e., *suprasystems*. Thus, a subsystem has horizontal relationships with other subsystems and with certain environmental systems, and vertical relationships within its system in both upward and downward directions.

All points of contact, formal and informal, between systems or between a system and its subsystems are called *interfaces*. Interfaces are crucial to system behavior, as they may facilitate or impede system performance. The design of appropriate interfaces is especially important when the interacting systems are striving to attain different, possibly conflicting goals or when coordination of behaviors among the systems is difficult to achieve.

MODELING ORGANIZATIONS AS SYSTEMS

Organizations are modeled as systems for three major reasons. First, systems modeling is a *mechanism* by which an organization can be better understood. The questions raised in building a systems model (isolating and then relating elements, identifying goals and processes, categorizing inputs and outputs, etc.) address issues basic to the existence, composition, and functioning of all organizations. Second, a system model can serve as a common *frame of reference* to enhance communication among individuals working together to accomplish organizational tasks. Without a single model that all understand, each individual would employ a unique organizational representation, that maintained in his or her own HIPS. As these representations might be very different, the potential for misunderstanding would loom large. Third, as presented earlier in this chapter, an *appealing view* of an organization holds that the information flowing among organizational elements and between environmental and organizational elements is a major force linking these elements together. Adopting this view implies that organizational design must follow an intensive effort directed at understanding the organization, its components, and the information linkages among these components. Such an effort is greatly aided by the construction of a systems model of the organization. In addition to these three reasons, the systems approach possesses other attributes well suited for modeling organizations: it is goal oriented, it is qualitative rather than quantitative, and it benefits from the adoption of broad perspectives in analyzing organizational functioning.

Organizations are open systems whose processors are horizontal work units and whose controllers are vertical work units. These work units, or organizational subsystems, are best identified in terms of the functions performed. A systems model of an organization seldom parallels the formal organizational structure. Remember, the objective is not simply to *describe* the organization, but to *understand* it.

Work units are related to each other and to environmental elements through exchanges of resources that enable the organization to perform its functions and thereby accomplish its goals. These goals typically reflect social needs, customer or client needs, product or service attributes, and organizational survival.[15]

To illustrate how an organization can be modeled as a system, an independent, owner-operated retail shoe store in a neighborhood shopping center will be used. Figure 3.6 depicts our hypothetical enterprise.

A likely goal for our shoe store is to provide a reasonable return on the owner's investment. Such a goal could probably be achieved by offering an appealing assortment of shoe styles at attractive prices and by keeping resource utilizations (labor, on-hand stock, flow space, utilities, etc.) at appropriate levels. A representative set of functional work units are as follows:

Merchandising	Selecting shoe styles to offer customers,
Inventory	Maintaining an adequate supply of on-hand stock,
Advertising	Enticing potential customers into the retail location,
Sales	Convincing customers to purchase an on-hand style,
Accounting	Tracking resource flows through the above functional work units.

Clearly, these functional work units are linked by customer and shoe movements, as well as by resource (such as labor and cash) flows.

An organization's environment can be broken into two segments: the general environment and the specific environment.[16] The general environment refers to the cultural, economic, educational, and sociopolitical milieu that surrounds an organization. Out of this general environment emerges a specific set of organizations (and individuals) with which the organization must directly interact to attain its goals, including customers, clients, competitors, vendors, parent organizations, and regulatory agencies. For our shoe store, critical components of the specific environment are a certain segment of the buying public, competing shoe

FIGURE 3.6
A Retail Shoe Outlet

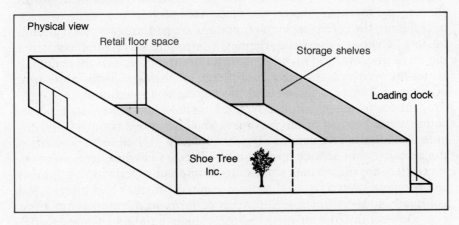

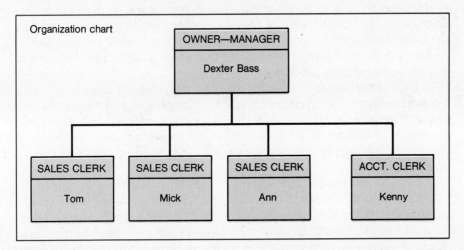

stores, shoe manufacturers, and local advertising media (newspapers, radio, television, etc.).

The organizational boundary might be drawn in two ways. It could be defined in terms of resources used (such as capital, labor, materials, and facilities), or in terms of the organization's *domain*[17] (such as population served, functions performed, and products or services rendered). While employing both is best, more attention should be given to explanations of domain, as it is here that much misunderstanding arises.

It should be easy, for example, to list the resources used by our shoe store—similar sets of resources would likely be used by all shoe stores. It is each store's domain, however, that differentiates it from other stores: the targeted market segment, the specialized services (e.g., precise fitting of children), the extent to which functions are performed by store personnel (e.g., creating advertising themes, composing advertising, constructing retail displays, and identifying customer trends). Until these domain issues are resolved, it would be difficult to distinguish this store from others and, hence, to understand its purpose and functioning.

Inputs to organizational systems include raw materials, procured components, product or service orders, and clients or customers, and outputs include the products or services provided as well as byproducts of the production or service operation. As discussed earlier, processors and controllers are the various work units (comprising facilities, equipment, and personnel interrelated through a complex of tasks and hierarchical, political, and social relationships) that perform organizational functions.

One common error made by individuals building systems models for the first time is to confuse inputs and processors. In the case of our shoe store, customers (needing shoes) and shoes are obvious inputs, with the directly related outputs being customers (with and without shoes) and shoes (returned to the manufacturer or sold to a discounter). Labor is *not* an input—it is a processor!

Each organization is a part of many suprasystems. Examples include a parent company, a government, and a geographic region. Suprasystems of our shoe store might include the shopping center, chamber of commerce, and shoe retailers' association. An important consideration in conceptualizing system hierarchies is that a subsystem must be totally within its system(s).

System interfaces exist where systems or subsystems exchange resources, products, clients, or information. These may occur horizontally (a vendor sends a shipment to the organization, manufacturing takes parts out of inventory, or two competitors exchange information on a third) or vertically (a supervisor receives an order from the department manager, corporate headquarters issues new budgets to operating units, or a report on employee absenteeism is sent from a plant manager to the corporate personnel director). What is most interesting about system interfaces is that most organizational problems arise at these points of contact. Important interfaces for our shoe store would include both horizontal points of contact (with customers, advertisers, etc.) and vertical ones (between Dexter and his employees).

The discussions about our shoe store illustrate a *verbal* systems model. To more clearly show the relationships among systems elements, it is useful as well to construct a *pictorial* systems model. This is shown as Figure 3.7 for our shoe store. The results of two additional hypothetical

FIGURE 3.7
Pictorial Systems Model of Shoe Tree, Inc.

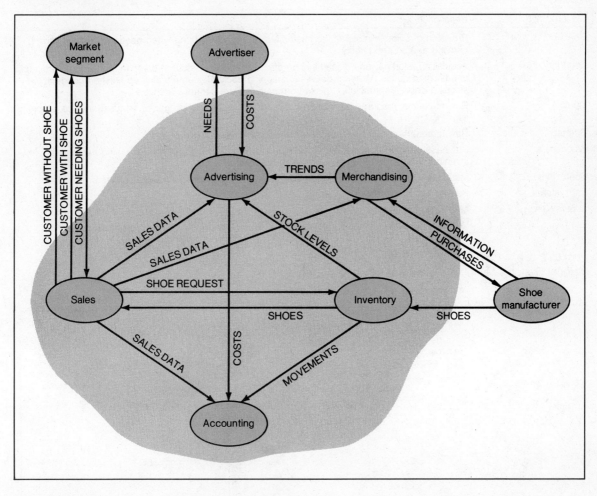

modeling efforts are provided: Table 3.3 and Figure 3.8 depict the materials management function in a manufacturing plant, and Table 3.4 and Figure 3.9 depict a hospital emergency room.

One final comment must be raised regarding the construction of an organizational systems model. There is no such thing as one correct model. In this case beauty *is* in the eye of the beholder. Systems do not exist, they are manufactured (as abstractions) by people. A system has been *chosen* by a person to be regarded as an entity; the system's proper-

TABLE 3.3
Verbal Systems Model of a Materials Management Work Unit

System Entity	Description
Goal	Provision of suitable materials to customers and manufacturing when needed while minimizing carrying and ordering costs
Boundary	Acquisition, storage, and dissemination of raw materials, procured components, work-in-process, and finished goods. Vendors deliver to shipping dock. Customers pick up finished goods at shipping dock. Manufacturing picks up materials from central warehouse.
Inputs	Raw materials, procured components, work-in-process, finished goods, request, invoice, shipping list
Outputs	Raw materials, procured components, work-in-process, finished goods
Processors	Purchase agents, receiving clerks, inventory clerks, packing personnel, loading personnel, inventory bins, loading equipment, inventory tracking system
Controllers	Materials manager, shipping supervisor, inventory manager, purchasing manager
Subsystems	Purchasing, receiving, inventory, packing, shipping
Suprasystem	Manufacturing plant
Interfacing systems	Vendors, customers, manufacturing work units, marketing work units, plant management

FIGURE 3.8
Pictorial Systems Model of a Materials Management Work Unit

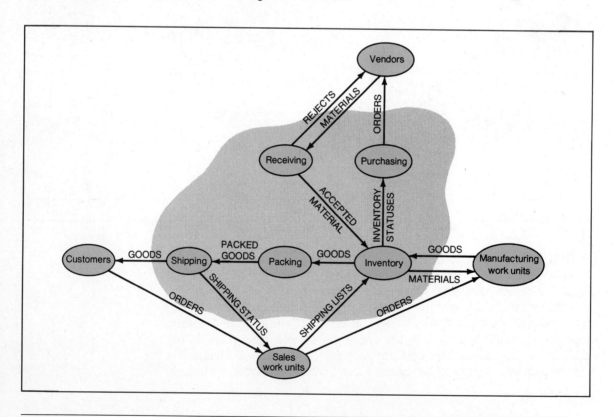

TABLE 3.4
Verbal Systems Model of a Hospital Emergency Room

System Entity	Description
Goal	Provide appropriate and timely care to patients entering facility
Boundary	Diagnosis and short-term treatment; no specialized facilities (x-ray, laboratory, etc.); patients must enter facility to receive treatment
Inputs	Injured or sick patients, supplies, specialists from other hospital work units
Outputs	Treated patients, waste
Processors	Emergency room staff, facilities, equipment, procedures
Controllers	Nursing supervisor, medical supervisor, emergency room administrator, admissions supervisor
Subsystems	Triage, treatment units, admissions, emergency room store, accounting
Suprasystems	Hospital, regional emergency care system
Interfacing systems	Ambulance service, police, hospital clinics, hospital central store, accounting, admissions, pharmacy, morgue, wards, hospital administration, regional emergency authority

FIGURE 3.9
Pictorial Systems Model of a Hospital Emergency Room

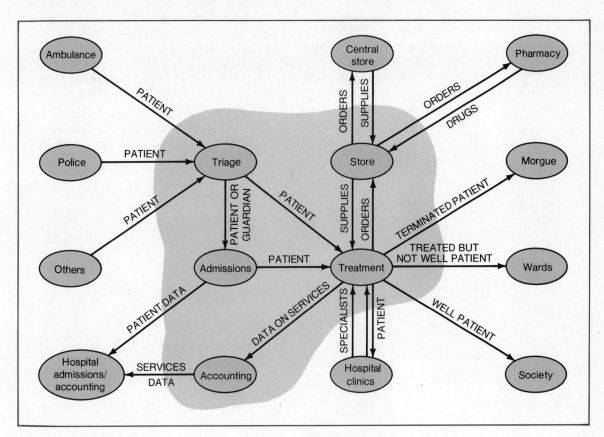

ties and functions have been *selected* as relevant by a person. Thus, if the individuals who develop a model are satisfied the model represents the essence of the organization, it is appropriate. A new perspective raised regarding the organization may later result in revisions in the system model, and two models of the same organization may well differ substantially, given the backgrounds and objectives of two sets of developers. A general observation with systems modeling is that better models can be developed when modelers possess different backgrounds, perspectives, interests, and skills. Getting such a group to communicate effectively with one another is a different matter!

CONCLUSION

Organizations can be modeled in many ways. The notions introduced in this chapter have emphasized an information processing view of organizations because this perspective has proven particularly useful in investigations of how information resources can be used to support organizational functioning. Other modeling frameworks (e.g., sociological, economic, psychological, and political) should be used in any effort to understand organizations and their members. The more perspectives that are adopted when organizations are studied, the greater is the likelihood that the understanding achieved will approach reality.

This chapter has excluded any discussion of computer-based information systems so preconceived notions about information systems might be overcome. A variety of information systems exist in organizations. Effective exploitation of the information resource requires that all be recognized and evaluated in terms of their potential for computer-based support.

KEY ISSUES

Organizations are comprised of horizontally and vertically related responsibility centers or work units.

To understand an organization, it is necessary to identify its work units and to describe their functions and interrelationships.

Work unit interaction invariably involves resource, material, product, client, or data flows.

The human information processing system (HIPS) provides people with a means to communicate with their environment, guides to action, and cognitive contexts in which to interpret environmental stimuli.

Organizational information systems (OIS) give organizations a means to communicate with their environment, a means for work units to communicate with one another, and guides for actions and behavioral contexts, which focus the attention of organizational members and reduce their individual information processing loads.

Formal OIS are most useful in providing generalized, relatively stable action guides and behavioral contexts.

Informal OIS are most useful in providing information specific to an emerging situation.

Control of information represents a source of power for individuals in organizations.

Modeling organizations as systems serves three main purposes: a means of better understanding an organization, a common reference frame for individuals working together to resolve a problem or exploit an opportunity, and a vehicle for representing resource, material, product, client, or data (information) flows when OIS are being designed.

The more perspectives there are among individuals constructing a systems model of an organization, the greater is the likelihood that a valid representation of the organization will be obtained.

DISCUSSION QUESTIONS

1. What is a "responsibility center"? Give examples of responsibility centers in a police department and in a department store.
2. An early forecast about computer-based information systems was that their introduction into organizations would greatly reduce the number of middle-management positions in organizations. Has this been borne out?
3. One popular view of managers holds that they primarily serve as organizational information processing nodes. Discuss this notion, giving examples of the various information processing roles managers play.

4. Give examples from your own experiences of the following aspects of the HIPS: chunking, filtering, automatic responses, and schemata.

5. Suggest steps an organization might take to improve the flow of informal information among its members.

6. Given the many disadvantages associated with formal OIS, why are they so common in organizations?

7. Provide an example from your own experience of how control of information can become a source of power.

8. Why is it important to precisely define organizational boundaries when constructing system models?

9. How are relationships among elements represented in a systems model of an organization?

10. Why do problems frequently arise at system boundaries?

BRIEF CASES

1. *Hickory Manufacturing Company*

   The corporate planning group at Hickory Manufacturing Company was beginning to assess how it might exploit the technologies associated with the "automated office." The first step in this assessment effort was to analyze the existing information flows to, from, and within the corporate planning group as it worked toward devising long-term and annual plans. Hickory Manufacturing Company was one of the leading office furniture makers in the country.

   Suggest some formal and informal OIS that might be identified as the analysis proceeds.

2. *Big Apple Promotions*

   Big Apple Promotions, a major New York advertising firm, decided to expand its computer-based support mechanisms to include its "lifeblood" activity—creating innovative and effective advertising campaigns for its clients. Some efforts involved included understanding the clients' products and values, identifying consumer desires regarding these products, and creating and then implementing campaign themes.

   The initial meeting between the firm's senior computer analyst (with an MS in computer science) and the firm's senior account executive (with a double BA in journalism and the fine arts) was a disaster. They simply could not communicate with one another. Both left feeling frustrated and not very confident that anything close to an information system would ever come about.

   What might have led to this situation? What would you do next if it was your responsibility to get these two individuals to work together successfully?

3. *East Coast Business School*

   The dean of East Coast Business School felt very strongly that one of the best ways to assess the effectiveness of any organization was to examine its inputs, outputs, and objectives, paying particular attention to the value added by the organization. It consequently was not surprising when she announced that precisely this type of study was to be undertaken in evaluating the school's MBA program.

Using your own understanding of MBA programs, construct a systems model of a hypothetical MBA program and then attempt the analysis specified above by the dean.

NOTES

1. M. L. Tushman and D. A. Nadler, "Information Processing as an Integrating Concept in Organization Design," *Academy of Management Review* 3(1978):613–24.

2. M. S. Poole, "An Information-Task Approach to Organizational Communication," *Academy of Management Review* 3(1978):493–504.

3. J. Pfeffer, *Organizational Design* (Arlington Heights, Ill: AHM Publishing, 1978).

4. H. Mintzberg, *The Structuring of Organizations: A Synthesis of the Research* (Englewood Cliffs, N.J.: Prentice-Hall, 1979).

5. R. N. Anthony, *Planning and Control Systems: A Framework for Analysis* (Cambridge, Mass.: Harvard University School of Business Administration, 1965).

6. P. R. Lawrence and J. W. Lorsch, *Organization and Environment* (Cambridge, Mass.: Harvard University School Of Business Administration, 1967).

7. R. E. Mayer, *Thinking and Problem Solving: An Introduction to Human Cognition and Learning* (Glenview, Ill: Scott, Foresman, 1977).

8. D. E. Rumelhart, *Human Information Processing* (New York: Wiley, 1977).

9. Rumelhart (1977), p. 213.

10. H. Mintzberg, *Impediments to the Use of Management Information* (New York: National Association of Accountants, 1975).

11. J. Galbraith, *Organizational Design* (Reading, Mass.: Addison-Wesley, 1977).

12. Tushman and Nadler (1978).

13. P. G. W. Keen and M. S. Scott Morton, *Decision Support Systems: An Organizational Perspective* (Reading, Mass.: Addison-Wesley, 1978).

14. C. W. Churchman, *The Systems Approach and Its Enemies* (New York: Basic Books, 1979).

15. C. Perrow, *Organizational Analysis: A Sociological View* (Belmont, Calif.: Brooks-Cole, 1970).

16. R. N. Osborn, J. G. Hunt, and L. R. Jaunch, *Organization Theory: An Integrated Approach* (New York: Wiley, 1980).

17. J. D. Thompson, *Organizations in Action* (New York: McGraw-Hill, 1967).

MIS STRATEGIES

The first MIS Strategy describes the approach taken by Equitable Life, a nationwide insurance company, to introduce word processing technology into the firm's many operating units. The second Strategy discusses some of the information resource policies adopted by the Emhart Corporation, a multinational manufacturing conglomerate, to permit intraorganizational information flows in an environment consisting of many types of computer systems. While these two organizational sketches may at first glance appear quite different, a second reading should disclose three key similarities—similarities that reflect some of the major issues brought out in the preceding chapters:

1. Inter- and intraorganizational communication flows are growing increasingly dependent on information technologies.
2. The economics of computing are changing, leading to a proliferation of information technologies that the organization must control if it is to make effective use of the information resource.
3. End-users, along with an organization's information specialists, are actively involved in charting organizational paths for information resource use.

Equitable Profits by Tackling Spread of WP

Uncontrolled proliferation of diverse and increasingly numerous word processing systems at all organizational levels is one of the latest headaches corporate MIS departments have been called upon by top management to remedy.

At Equitable Life, the cure was obvious: "We decided to become the dragger rather than the draggee," says Robert Madan, the computer services department's planning and control bureau chief. He is responsible for the New York City–based insurance company's office automation effort, and adds that the treatment of the widespread malady requires specific, saleable solutions.

Saleable?

"In effect, we became salesmen for our solution," notes Madan, an assistant vice president in the corporation's staff-level department. The computer services department had to sell its prognosis not only to top management, but to users at both corporate and divisional MIS levels.

"We formed a strategy about a year and a half ago, and an office automation group (OAG) about a year ago," Madan says. "The policy of OAG is to find solutions and make recommendations that are, first of all, good for the corporation, then for the user and, finally, good for the department of computer services—in that order."

What OAG is selling is a Wang VS system solution to divisions where each user had the authority to buy any system it wanted.

"At Equitable Life," he observes, "we're rapidly going in the direction of decentralized, distributed data processing. With 750 leaseholds around the U.S., if everyone were building separate word processing solutions, we'd be hard pressed to achieve management objectives."

The department had some options, however, in how to approach the problem. One was to allow systems to proliferate, or "let things go, but consolidate later on. And that approach was almost immediately discounted." Madan explained: "As hardware purchase prices rapidly decreased, it became accessible to areas of the corporation where the level of authority had not been sufficient before to authorize purchase of word processing or distributed processing equipment, because the cost was above the level they were allowed to okay," Madan says.

Thus, WP equipment of all types began cropping up around the corporation. "It became evident that if we allowed that to continue, we'd have gotten an increase in productivity with no consistency, control, or cross-communications between users— things that corporate management wants to maintain, even though it is willing to disperse the authority and responsibility."

The second option was to choose a solution and form "a strong mandate for that system. But that wouldn't work with the organization as currently constituted," Madan says, "Everyone wants to become controller of his own bottom lines."

The final option—ultimately chosen—was "to get in front of OA and become its spokespeople, offering assistance and support so that later on, we wouldn't have to fight.

"The matrix management setup here gives the user greater authority to choose his own path in office technology and in other areas as well. We serve as a clearing house, to make sure they know what they're getting into."

Having chosen its path, Madan said, the OAG spent "six to eight months explaining our strategies to users." Those strategies included the MIS objectives of gaining a good entry price into word processing systems that would offer the function needed by the user then and in the future.

Also, the solution would have to be one that could be easily supported in the field, offer productivity improvements, and meet the corporate objectives of consistency, control, and cross-communication.

"I feel in going with Wang we got the best available now, and got a good entry price through centralized purchasing," Madan says. Equitable is both an A and B test site for the Massachusetts-based equipment vendor. So far, the firm has spent about $2.5 million on Wang equipment, and has about $6 million on order. Sources indicate that the total may run as high as $16 million before the project is finished.

Perhaps most important, however, Equitable is purchasing a system solution that encompasses both word processing and distributed data processing, Madan says.

"There are really two important considerations here," he continues. "First, office automation needs a strategy, one that is applicable today to fill the users' needs. Second, office automation includes distributed data processing and should be treated as such."

So the word processing networks planned for corporate affairs, insurance affairs, and investment affairs—the three main business operating groups at Equitable—are all part of distributed systems.

They also allow for flexibility. For example, systems planned for three of the complex operations carried out by investment affairs—pensions, realty, and securities—include distributed solutions from Prime Computer and Digital Equipment Corp.

"We'll build bridges where we need them," Madan notes.

While he is convinced that Wang systems are the solution at Equitable for distributed data word processing, Madan admits there are problems.

"Granted, communications is a problem," he said. "The biggest problem is that there is no 'Wangnet'—no network architecture. All the different pieces are there, and they can be hooked up under SNA [IBM's Systems Network Architecture] the way we've been doing, but it could be a lot simpler."

So far, the OAG has installed about 50 Wang VS sites, including 31 in individual insurance operations. The number will be doubled by the end of 1980, with the entire individual insurance system to be completed by the end of 1981.

The OAG has also created a corporate "laboratory"—a Wang VS system for on-site testing and development, that also measures its own usefulness and resulting productivity gains. "The strategy is very important here," Madan observes. "Vendors try to sell everybody at all levels of an organization when it comes to office automation. Users come to expect too much and associate the vendor's failures with the concept behind the machinery.

"We obviously can't afford that in our situation," Madan explains. "So the lab offers us a check. If vendors oversell and over-enlarge user expectations, we can check their veracity in the lab before any damage is done."

The OAG, Madan notes, is particularly geared toward helping the user make decisions on office automation equipment. So far, its 20-person staff has established the ability to train users, install systems, and resolve user problems. User groups have been formed, and generic/utility program development—such as diagnostics that can be utilized across all user environments—is under way.

Madan emphasizes that the strategies will "grow and bend," and that each operations are looks to the VS systems for different reasons.

In individual insurance operations, for example, agents are most interested in word processing functions like report generation; regional management is concerned more with how the system will assist in the maintaining and creating of policies; top management sees it as an enhancement to communications. And each operations area has different needs.

But whatever the reasons the user chooses the VS systems, the decision will come from the actual user, not corporate management—if only because technology is evolving toward the user.

"Data processing, when it was a new technology, produced high productivity gains at a high price. Because of this and because it was extremely specialized, it could support a large staff.

"With office automation," Madan says, "you've got to get 'friendly' equipment, because large office automation staffs can't be justified the way DP staffs were."

How friendly? Madan goes by this motto: "If you can't explain it to the user, you're wrong!"

From *Information Systems News*, August 11, 1980. Copyright © 1980 by CMP Publications, Inc. Reprinted by permission.

Multinational Firm Favors Decentralized DP

Mention a multinational operation around an MIS manager and visions of complex reporting systems and intricate communications networking schemes begin to appear.

Yet at Emhart Corp., a medium-sized diversified manufacturing company with 50 percent of its operations overseas, simplicity is the rule rather than the exception.

"Management style here dictates concern over whether or not the local proprietor is doing his job," comments Charles Margeson, director of data processing for the Hartford, Conn., firm. That autonomous philosophy also extends into the MIS operations, he adds.

Margeson's corporate data processing department administers budgets, planning, policy, and standards for the two major operating groups in the company, namely, machinery and nonmachinery operations. Each group is headed by an executive vice president.

Seven divisional presidents report to the group level, representing shoe, glass, and general machinery in the machinery group, and electrical, industrial fastener, hardware, and chemical products in the nonmachinery group. A specialized store equipment product operation reports separately.

About 150 manufacturing and warehousing presidents and managing directors worldwide report at the division level. These geographically dispersed operations demand that corporate headquarters position itself to allow for their differing product and marketing needs.

Decentralized DP grew as the company went through an acquisition phase during the '70s that culminated with a merger with USM Corp. in 1976. "All of a sudden we had a billion-dollar company on our hands," Margeson remembers.

"Both merging companys had been advocates of competitive bidding for computers and use of mixed vendors," he adds, "so we were faced with a wide array of computer manufacturers, equipment sizes, models, and types in the operating units." These included (as they do today) IBM, Sperry Univac, ICL Ltd., Burroughs Corp., NCR Corp., and Siemens AG mainframes, as well as Data General Corp., Hewlett-Packard Co., and other minicomputers. All told, there are about 61 different computers in place internationally at Emhart locations.

What has evolved at Emhart is a strategy that maintains centralized control over the company's far-flung and diverse operations through budgetary reviews and the creation of policies and standards, while at the same time accenting service to the users.

Experiments with regional data centers are one reason for this evolution. "We don't get a great benefit from them," Margeson said, commenting that two remaining data centers, one in Massachusetts and the other in Connecticut, were being phased out.

"Computer sharing just didn't work," he goes on. "Units have eventually gone to their own machines in order to have control over their own resources. While corporate management, I believe, does give fair and evenhanded treatment to users of data centers, users do tend to resent it when corporate comes 'crashing through' for a priority on computer time.

"We're finding out—to our surprise—that the 'economy of scale' we had 10 years ago doesn't exist anymore, due to the plunging cost of computer hardware," Margeson says. "We can break up our regional centers at relatively low cost now."

Another factor weighing against a data center is that it is only in use in American operations. "Overseas, there is a very bad situation—particularly in Europe—for the data center," due to government regulation and laws in different countries, he adds.

"But we're not closing the door," Margeson says. "There may turn out to be an economy of scale in software as time goes on and if software costs keep rising." He mentioned that one division with multinational locations and similar product lines but with different computer makes was considering standardized software across the board for its information needs. "But that will take a couple of years, if it ever happens," he observes.

Standardization of equipment, however, has become an important thrust of corporate DP. "Since the merger, we've said that proliferation will eventually kill us. So we've announced to units worldwide that, in new proposals for equipment, they're limited to three vendors."

Although Margeson notes that there is room for exceptions, he doesn't feel there's much. "Some users seem to be painting themselves into a software corner," not leaving themselves many options for growth. As a result, tighter controls have been established on equipment selection.

Despite the diversity of equipment at Emhart, Margeson is keen to standardize systems wherever possible. Since financial reporting is a common thread across all lines, standardized management information reports (MIRs) are pulled together monthly by the units, transmitted by Telex, and consolidated at corporate headquarters. A uniform system of accounts will be installed worldwide next year to simplify the process, and a Four-Phase Inc. minicomputer system is being considered to replace the Harris on-line terminal system running under RJE that currently does the consolidations.

These simple answers to problems may not satisfy those who crave state-of-the-art solutions, but they do have one thing going for them—they work. And often the simple answers produce surprising and beneficial results, Margeson says.

"Several years ago, one of our operating units wanted to upgrade from its IBM 1440 to a 360. I found a 360/40 for them on the used computer market," he says, which headed off a recommendation from IBM that the unit purchase a 370/135.

"Last year the company acquired a satellite plant and wanted to upgrade. I found a 360/50 on the used market, and by simply pulling the 40 boards out and putting the 50 boards into the mainframe and adding a Paradyne Inc. RJE terminal at the satellite plant, we got them what they needed. Plus, the next time they upgrade, it will probably be to a 4300-type computer, and they will have skipped the 370 series computers entirely."

From *Information Systems News*, December 15, 1980. Copyright © 1980 by CMP Publications, Inc. Reprinted by permission.

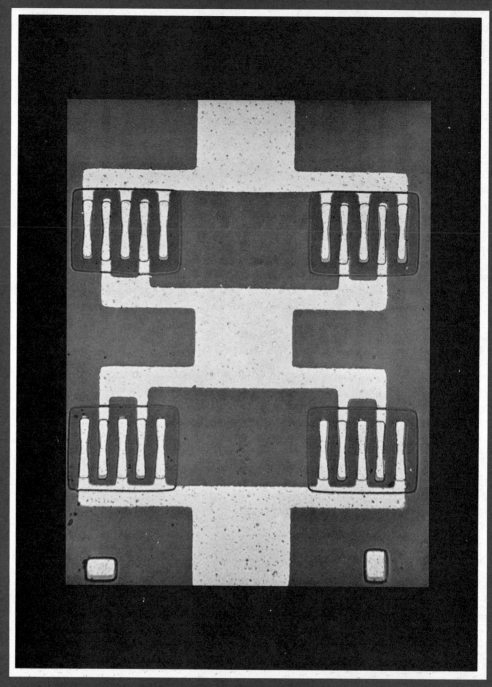

1964.
Radio frequency power transistor. A 1-watt, 300-MHz device
used in small radio transistors.

Choices 2

Introduction to Computer-Based Alternatives

4

COMPUTER-BASED INFORMATION SYSTEMS (CBIS) offer a variety of capabilities that can be used to accomplish organizational objectives. In Part 2 we shall examine those capabilities to illustrate the vast potential of the information resource.

We shall begin this chapter by analyzing the most basic tasks that comprise organizational activity. Next, the comparative advantages of using humans and computer systems to perform these tasks will be examined. Then a practical CBIS taxonomy will be introduced that describes how computers can be used by organizations. Finally, brief introductions to the four remaining chapters of Part 2 will be provided.

THE POTENTIAL FOR COMPUTER-BASED SUPPORT

Figure 4.1 presents the basic model of organizational activity developed in Chapter 3: actions on or with the materials or clients processed by a work unit, the resources provided a work unit, or data describing materials, clients, or tasks. Viewed simply, these activities can be classified as involving *procedural* or *decisional* tasks. Procedures represent physical or mental effort requiring no choices between alternative actions, and decisions represent efforts that involve the exercise of choice.

While even simple activities probably require a sequence of discrete procedural or decisional tasks of varying duration, most activities can be categorized as procedural or decisional. If rules are formally or informally defined to be followed without error, then the activity is a procedure. If predefined "error-free" rules do not exist, then the activity should be classified as a decision.

FIGURE 4.1
Organizational Activity Domains

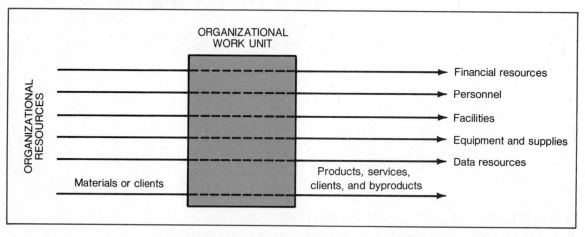

Generally, then, four types of computer-based support of organizational activities can be identified. A CBIS may perform a procedural task, perform a decisional task, support human performance of a procedural task, or support human performance of a decisional task. *Performance* of a task results in the CBIS directly accomplishing an organizational activity (such as the printing of an invoice, the issuance of a purchase order, or the denial of a loan application). *Support* of a task finds the CBIS aiding organizational members in their performance of procedures by remembering and providing data (e.g., order descriptions and work schedules) and in making decisions by remembering, providing, and transforming data (e.g., order status and work rates).

Whether an organizational activity should be performed or supported by a CBIS depends in part on the comparative advantages of both computers and humans and on the characteristics of the activity. Overall assessments of computer and human attributes as they relate to task accomplishment are provided in Tables 4.1 and 4.2, respectively. In summary, computers tend to excel in unambiguous situations benefiting from speed, accuracy, and reliability, while humans tend to excel in situations requiring flexibility, adaptability, creativity, and judgement.

Table 4.3 lists a number of task characteristics in terms of their potential for CBIS support. While most of these characteristics are readily recognizable, a few may not be. A structured task is one whose crucial elements are well understood; an unstructured task is one whose crucial

TABLE 4.1
Computer Attributes

Contributions	Limitations
Speed	Actions controlled by predefined rules
Reliability	Access to data limited to that previously stored
Consistency	Storage limited to data that are easily captured
Accuracy	and represented in computer-readable forms
Storage of large amounts of data	
Quick retrieval of stored data	
Quick search through stored data	
Complex processing tasks	

TABLE 4.2
Human Attributes

Contributions	Limitations
Storage-related	Storage-related
Vast capacity	Retrieval time
Sophisticated retrieval mechanisms	Forgetfulness
Input-related	Input-related
Multiple sources	Limited capacity
Assessment of data relevance	Limited attention
Location of missing data	Multiple filters
Pattern recognition	
Processing-related	Processing-related
Subjective probability estimation	Slowness
Judgment and valuation	Inconsistency
Goal and constraint modification	Unreliability
Alternative identification	Inaccuracy
Hypothesis development	Emotional bias
Synthesis generalization	Lack of completeness
Side-effect forecasts and evaluation	Low capacity
	Conservatism
	Hesitancy
	Resistance to change
	Primacy and recency effects
	Difficulty in probabilistic tasks
Output-related	Output-related
Spoken language	Low capacity
Body language	

TABLE 4.3
Assessing Task Characteristics

Favorable to Computer Processing		Favorable to Human Processing
Structured task		Unstructured task
Goal clarity		Goal ambiguity
Known inputs		Unknown inputs
Known actions		Unknown actions
Certain outcomes		Uncertain outcomes
Data available		Data not available
Internal sources		External sources
Quantitative measures		Qualitative measures
Already captured data		Nonexistent data
	Miscellaneous	
Stable environment		Dynamic environment
Repetitious event		One-time event
Independent activities		Interdependent activities
Complex calculations		Simple calculations
Many calculations		Few calculations
Many data		Few data
More accuracy		Less accuracy
More reliability		Less reliability
More consistency		Less consistency
Quick response		Slow response

elements are poorly understood, if understood at all. The "data availability" entry reflects concern for the difficulties often encountered in measuring and capturing desired data elements. "Task stability" refers to the length of time the current understanding of a task will remain appropriate; the longer this period, the more stable the task. "Task independence" reflects the extent to which a task is linked to the accomplishment (sequential or simultaneous) of other tasks; an independent task is self-contained.

By contrasting the characteristics of the tasks comprising a particular organizational activity with those listed in Table 4.3, one can make an initial assessment of the viability of computer-based support. It is important to recognize that an activity can be partially computerized in that only certain tasks are actively supported by a CBIS, and that a decision to computerize might hinge on only a few task characteristics critical to activity accomplishment. Of course, other factors—the benefits and costs involved, organization computer capabilities, the readiness of organizational members to accept computer technology, etc.—remain to be examined in making a meaningful decision. The ability to spot potential targets for computer-based support nonetheless is a valuable skill to be developed by all organizational members.

A CBIS TAXONOMY

The Need for a Taxonomy

Many terms are used to characterize the different types of CBIS used in organizations: data processing system, management information system, decision support system, etc. Of these, the phrase "management information system" is the most used and misused. The taxonomy to be presented distinguishes among CBIS forms on the basis of the types of support provided to organizations through information technologies.

The traditional way of differentiating among CBIS is to distinguish between data processing systems and management information systems. A *data processing system* (DPS) manipulates entered data to accomplish clerical tasks and then stores the data for future processing. The outputs are most often simply listings of the entered data (providing a printed reference) or documents facilitating organizational operations (invoices, purchase orders, shipping labels, paychecks, etc.). As a general rule, the data being output vary little from that input. A *management information system* (MIS), on the other hand, enables organizational members to access and transform stored data to produce reports that support such management activities as planning, organizing, directing, and controlling. Thus, the following major distinctions between a data processing system and a management information system can be made:

A DPS is data oriented.	An MIS is report oriented.
A DPS is concerned with data collection.	An MIS works with data already collected.
A DPS is procedure oriented.	An MIS is decision oriented.

(Unfortunately, the acronym MIS is often used to encompass both CBIS classifications.)

While this distinction is simple, it has not proved satisfactory in practice. The view of a DPS as procedure oriented may unduly restrict its data collection role. Without broadening this role, much needed data will simply not be made available. The description of an MIS does not convey the variety of ways the selective reporting of information can support organizational functioning. An MIS, for example, supports more than just managers. Clerical and blue-collar personnel, staff specialists, and customers or clients can all be aided through an MIS in the following ways:

- Simple retrieval of data, requiring all "meaning" to be added by the decision-maker,
- Operations on data to produce predictions and inferences regarding future conditions and their impact on organizational activities,

- Incorporation of values and choice criteria into these predictions and inferences to generate recommendations for actions,
- Actual selection of the action to take, thus relieving the organizational member of a decision task (but not the responsibility for the task).[1]

By not clearly differentiating among these MIS capabilities, one cannot fully appreciate the benefits, difficulties, and dangers associated with computer-based technologies.

A More Precise Taxonomy

The taxonomy to be employed here elaborates on an existing classification scheme that has not received general usage.[2] Four CBIS classifications are defined:

- Transaction processing systems (TPS),
- Information reporting systems (IRS),
- Decision support systems (DSS),
- Programmed decision systems (PDS).

Essentially, the TPS classification is an expansion of the earlier described DPS, and the IRS, DSS, and PDS classifications represent refinements of the MIS concept.

The primary role of a TPS is the collection, storage, and processing of data describing *transactions* within the organization so these data can be used to guide the "procedural" actions of organizational members, to produce necessary clerical documents, and to be "remembered" for later use in an IRS, DSS, or PDS. Additionally, a TPS often supports the collection and storage of data originating from sources *external* to the organization.

The acronym IRS refers to the production of *predefined* information reports, generated by operations on data previously captured and stored, that are delivered to organizational members. No restrictions are placed on the nature of these reports, the frequency with which they are received, or the "triggers" that cause their dissemination. For example, these reports may be tables of data or graphs indicating trends; on paper or a CRT screen; detailed or summarized; received hourly, daily, weekly, or monthly; and received on a regular basis, on demand, or by exception.

The key distinction in classifying a CBIS as an IRS is the *interaction* that occurs between an organizational member and the CBIS. There is *no true interaction* with an IRS: the user has prespecified what is desired and only this is obtained. Any change necessitates a formal respecification by the user and subsequent modification of the software elements affected by the new specification. Generally, such efforts involve considerable delay and the aid of a computer analyst or programmer.

An IRS provides *passive* support of decision making. While useful in indicating a need for action, in suggesting actions to consider, or in providing background material, an IRS is rather limited in its ability to significantly support decision-makers in the day-to-day situations they face. Decision needs vary considerably from situation to situation, even when the same task is involved. As an IRS must be prespecified, it is not flexible enough to meet all the information needs of many, if not most, organizational decision-makers.

The *active* support of decision making is the aim of a DSS. Flexibility is attained by enabling decision-makers to specify their needs when a decision task is addressed. The aim is the joining of decision-maker and CBIS in a decision-making team, with the CBIS allowing the decision-maker to quickly retrieve and analyze (by predefined rules) vast quantities of data and the decision-maker contributing creativity, experience, intuition, and judgement.

There is currently some confusion concerning DSS. Since the phrase includes "decision support," almost any CBIS could be so designated, and the phrase *is* employed by many people in a much broader scope than used here. Here a DSS is defined as providing situational support for organizational members throughout the decision process.

Finally, a PDS actually makes a decision previously handled by a human decision-maker. Rules are specified and incorporated into software so that when certain input conditions arise, a specific action is instigated by the computer system. With both IRS and DSS, the act of decision making is accomplished by the human decision-maker; with PDS, it is accomplished by the CBIS. Responsibility for the consequences of such actions, however, remains with the human.

Another means of illustrating the differences between IRS, DDS, and PDS, the three CBIS alternatives for supporting decision tasks, follows from the concept of *task structure.* This concept refers to the extent to which the decision-maker has defined a situation in terms of required information, decision criteria and objectives, model variables and parameters, possible actions, resultant outcomes, and probabilities relating actions to outcomes. The more complete and certain the description of a situation, the more structured is the task.

Task structure greatly influences the types of CBIS that can be effectively applied. In poorly structured situations, no rules exist for a PDS, nor are there general procedures to employ with a DSS. The only support possible is the use of an IRS to provide background material that creates a context to guide action. In semistructured situations, the definitive rules required in a PDS are again nonexistent. Enough is known about the decision, however, to enable the decision-maker to interact with a DSS to arrive at a better understanding (and eventually resolution) of the situation. Finally, in well-structured situations, it is possible to have a PDS resolve the situation and initiate action.

Figure 4.2 illustrates the four types of CBIS described. The dotted line from external data to the organization's store of data indicates that data may be acquired directly from external sources. Table 4.4 suggests applications frequently handled with each CBIS form. The TPS are the most common CBIS, representing the vast majority of computer applications in most organizations. The IRS typically represent the remaining applications, with an increasing number of PDS being used. *True* DSS are seldom encountered because of their relatively recent emergence. How-

FIGURE 4.2
CBIS Forms

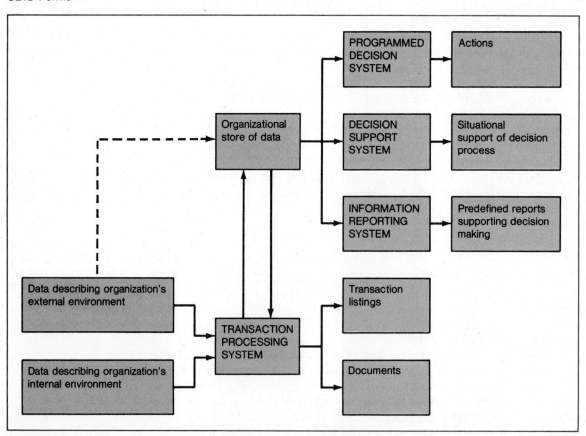

TABLE 4.4
Application Examples for the CBIS Types

Organizational Function	TPS	IRS	DSS	PDS
Materials management	Tracking of inventory movements	Report giving turnover and profit contribution of inventory items	Reorganization of where items are kept in inventory to improve efficiency in handling movements	Reordering
Personnel	Payroll	Report contrasting training expenses of departments	Analysis of wage/benefits package alternatives for labor negotiation	Skills location
Marketing	Order entry	Report showing regional sales performances	Advertising media selection decision for a campaign	Notification to customer of when to expect shipment
Finance	General ledger	Report projecting liquidity position over next 6 months	Analysis of various long-term debt alternatives	Short-term cash management

ever, the non-TPS portion of the CBIS portfolio of all organizations will gradually increase as organizations provide structure to more tasks and are better able to use computer-based technology.

PLAN OF THIS PART

The remaining four chapters in Part 2 focus on more detailed descriptions of the four CBIS forms, along with discussions of technical issues crucial to each form. Chapter 5 examines TPS, Chapter 6 introduces some important technical topics, Chapter 7 examines IRS, and Chapter 8 examines DSS and PDS.

The organizations of Chapters 5, 7, and 8 are similar. First, the organization functions being supported are explored in more depth. Second, CBIS design features crucial to implementation success are described to make clear the need for user contributions. Finally, directions indicating future trends, guidelines for use in selecting potential applications, and descriptions of the major difficulties typically encountered are provided.

More and more, TPS are being used for two basic purposes: to perform clerical activities surrounding the production of documents needed to accomplish organizational objectives, and to collect and store data for later use by the organization. As the success of the first purpose hinges on the second, these two processing functions are the primary concern of

Chapter 5. Specific topics addressed include the meaning of organizational data; the steps involved in data collection; design criteria associated with data entry, input controls, and data file organization, access, and maintenance; and the variety of processing environments that can be established. Issues of current interest introduced because of their growing impact on both data capture and day-to-day organizational activities are *electronic funds transfer* and *office automation*.

Two of the more important technological CBIS developments (at least from the standpoint of increasing organizational support capabilities) have been the *data base concept* and *distributed processing*. While their current benefits are most closely linked to TPS applications, both developments will have a far greater impact on IRS and DSS applications because of the end-user services made possible. Each topic is introduced in Chapter 6, with emphasis given to organizational implications. Then the areas of *computer security* and *computer auditing* are addressed. The growing sophistication of CBIS, while offering many opportunities, is increasing the likelihood that computer-related disasters will occur if proper controls are not installed. Ways of reducing the risk of such disasters are discussed.

An IRS is usually used to provide organizational members with a general context indicating what needs to be done, what has and has not been done, and which organizational and environmental factors must be closely monitored if organizational objectives are to be attained. This type of support generally takes the form of computer-based aids supporting planning and control. The central focus of Chapter 7 relates to planning and control. Specific topics addressed include organization efficiency and effectiveness, planning and control concepts and processes, the meaning and characteristics of organizational information, report design, and the influence of organizational and individual characteristics on IRS design.

As noted in Chapter 8, DSS and PDS are directed, respectively, at supporting and performing decision tasks. The primary concern of this chapter, consequently, is decision making. Specific topics addressed include the structure of decisions, the decision-making process, decision-making activities, and joint computer-human decision making. Topics of current interest introduced because of their growing impact on DSS developments are *the manager's work station, group decision support,* and the *support of human intuition in decision making*.

KEY ISSUES

Organizational activities can be viewed as efforts to accomplish procedural (no action choices) and decisional (action choices) tasks.

Computer-based support of organizational activities can take one of four forms: performing procedural tasks, performing decisional tasks, supporting human performance of procedural tasks, and supporting human performance of decisional tasks.

Computers generally outperform humans when tasks stress speed, accuracy, and reliability, when the task situation is structured, stable, and repetitious, and when the required data items are easily measured or already captured.

Humans generally outperform computers when tasks stress adaptability, creativity, and inventiveness, when the task situation is less structured, dynamic, and infrequently encountered, and when the required data items are difficult to measure or capture.

Transaction processing systems (TPS) collect, store, and process data describing organizational transactions to produce clerical documents, to guide organizational members in performing procedural tasks, and to be used later.

Information reporting systems (IRS) operate on previously collected data to produce predefined reports delivered to organizational members in support of decisional tasks.

Decision support systems (DSS) join together a human and a computer system as a decision-making team to effectively respond to situational demands.

Programmed decision systems (PDS) incorporate within their software decision rules that enable appropriate decisions to be made when particular data items have been input.

DISCUSSION QUESTIONS

1. Give examples of procedural and decisional tasks associated with the purchasing function in an organization.
2. It should be fairly easy to envision how a computer might perform a procedural task (such as handling accounts receivable or accounts payable). However, can a computer really perform a decisional task? Can computers exercise choice?
3. How can a computer help a human perform a procedural task, such as helping a salesperson determine what price to place on a special order? How can a computer help a human perform a decisional task, such as helping a plant manager decide on next year's staffing needs?
4. How might a human overcome the computer limitations listed in Table 4.1? How might a computer overcome the human limitations listed in Table 4.2?

5. Distinguish between a TPS and a PDS. Use the inventory control activity as a discussion context.
6. Distinguish between an IRS and a DSS. Use the retail shelf allocation decision as a discussion context.
7. How can IRS be used in poorly structured tasks when such information systems involve prespecified inputs, processes, and outputs?
8. Give one example each of TPS, IRS, DSS, and PDS applications that might be observed in a police dispatch operation.

BRIEF CASES

1. *Mercy Hospital*

   Following the efforts of Susan Horowitz, one of the "fast trackers" on the hospital's management team, Mercy Hospital implemented a number of computer-based information systems to support clerical and administrative functions. These included budgeting, admissions, billing, and inventory (supplies, drugs, and equipment) management. Along with basic patient care information systems, which already existed, these new information systems made Mercy Hospital one of the most advanced hospitals in the state.

   One area of the hospital that was still not making much use of computers, however, was the emergency room. Dr. Joseph Banks, Director of Emergency Services, doubted the practicality of supporting emergency room activities with computers. His doubts were reinforced whenever he attended the hospital's computer policy committee meetings, as the information systems representatives never suggested emergency room projects. Still, at the last convention Dr. Banks had attended, a daylong series of panel discussions was held on emergency room computer applications. He later reflected that he should have attended at least one of them.

   Can you identify any possible computer applications in the emergency room?

2. *Bennison Construction Company*

   Bennison Construction Company was a small but successful heavy construction (roads, bridges, dams, airport runways, etc.) firm in the Midwest. Its reputation had been built on a combination of quality work and honest contracting. However, the budgetary pressures being felt by state and federal governments, Bennison's major customers, were beginning to worry the firm's executive committee. Contracts were placing increasingly tight control on costs to minimize overruns, and companies with histories of overruns (such as Bennison) were not being treated favorably.

   Currently Bennison was using computers for only standard accounting applications. The executive committee believed that computer-based information systems just might enable it to better cope with this new business environment. For example, implementing project costing, scheduling, and control applications should have a significant impact on Bennison's history of cost overruns.

As a result, the executive committee approved an expansion of the company's information systems staff, including the appointing of a new information systems head.

You are being considered for this position and are paying an initial visit to the company tomorrow. It seems safe to assume that you will be asked the same question repeatedly as you talk with the firm's management team: What type of applications would be emphasized if you were hired?

Identify some TPS, IRS, DSS and PDS applications that might be appropriate.

NOTES

1. R. O. Mason, "Basic Concepts for Designing Management Information Systems," in R. O. Mason and E. B. Swanson (eds.), *Measurement for Management Decision* (Reading, Mass.: Addison-Wesley, 1981), pp. 81–94.

2. G. W. Dickson and J. K. Simmons, "The Behavioral Side of MIS," *Business Horizons* 13(1970):59–71.

Transaction Processing Systems 5

WHEN ANALYZED, an organization's mainstream functions are invariably found to involve actions on materials or clients being processed *or* on organizational resources that permit or facilitate such processing. Materials, client, and resource flows through a hypothetical work unit were illustrated in Figure 4.1.

Each discrete action on or with materials, clients, and resources is referred to here as a *transaction*. This definition is much broader than that typically associated with an "accounting" transaction. Included as transactions, for example, are sales, employee terminations, receipts of material into inventory, purchases, and receipts of client complaints.

As transactions collectively represent an organization's efforts to accomplish its primary purposes, they need to be "remembered" so they can later be reconstructed, usually in an abbreviated form. Such processing might be undertaken for a number of reasons: to bill a customer or client, to enable management to assess what has been done, to report on organization activities to external bodies such as stockholders or government agencies, or to provide a historical basis on which to forecast the future.

The CBIS support referred to as a *transaction processing system* (TPS) can most simply be viewed as a computer-based means of capturing these transactions so they can be recreated. Figure 5.1 illustrates this concept and lists the three main outputs of a TPS: a corporate memory holding transaction representations, documents needed by the organization to fulfill its mainstream purposes (invoices, production orders, shipping orders, purchase orders, mailing lists, paychecks, work orders, etc.), and listings of transactions that have occurred over a period of time (for confirmation or reference).

FIGURE 5.1
Transaction Processing Tasks

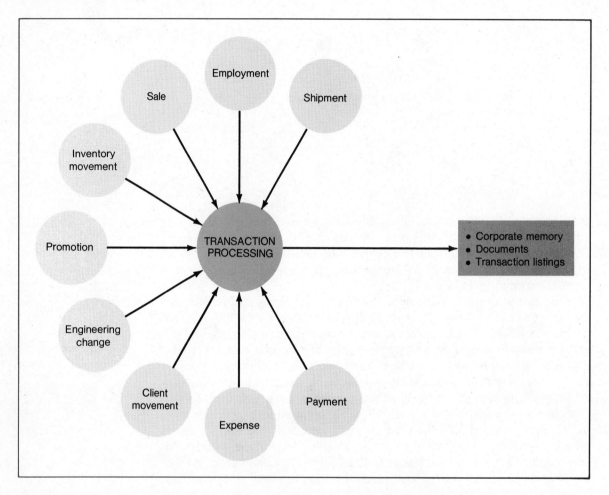

Transactions are captured by collecting data items that describe particular transactional attributes. Such transactions can be later recreated by retrieving the stored attributes and piecing them together. In deciding which data items to collect, one must consider *all* potential future references to the transaction. It usually is impossible to go back later and collect data items initially overlooked. Table 5.1 lists data items likely to be collected to represent the sale of an appliance by a department store. It might not be necessary to collect all these data at the time of the transaction if reference can be made to earlier stored data items. For example, by knowing stock number one should be able to obtain the price, and by knowing the customer account number for a credit sale one can often access the customer name and address.

It is practically and economically impossible to completely recreate each transaction that has occurred. Thus, key issues addressed in designing a TPS include deciding which transactions to capture, what attributes to focus on with each transaction, how to best represent each attribute (i.e., data item form), what procedures to employ in collecting data items, and when to collect data items. Such design issues depend on the ultimate uses of the transaction recreations, as well as on economic realities. The cost of collecting, storing, and processing transactional data must not exceed the organizational benefits attained.

In this chapter we shall introduce the objectives, constraints, and technologies associated with transaction processing. The basic activities of transaction processing (data entry, storage, and output), as well as the processing environments most typically encountered (batch entry and batch processing, on-line entry and batch processing, and on-line entry and immediate processing), will be discussed. Then two TPS contexts receiving considerable coverage in the popular and management press, *electronics funds transfer systems* and *office automation*, will be described in depth.

DATA ENTRY

While the steps involved in data entry (shown in Figure 5.2) may be fully automated, the initial steps are often handled manually. Examples of manual procedures include filling out forms to be used as *source documents* (such as a sales form, personnel change form, purchase order form,

---

TABLE 5.1
Relations Among Data Items and Their Potential Uses

Data Item	Potential Use
Stock number	Shipping, inventory, sales analysis
Date of sale	Accounting, sales analysis, commission
Type of sale (cash or credit)	Accounting, cash flow, accounts receivable
Amount of sale	Accounting, cash flow, commission, accounts receivable
Customer account number	Accounts receivable
Customer address	Shipping, sales analysis
Shipping date	Shipping, inventory
Salesperson number	Commission, performance evaluation

FIGURE 5.2
Steps in the Data Entry Process

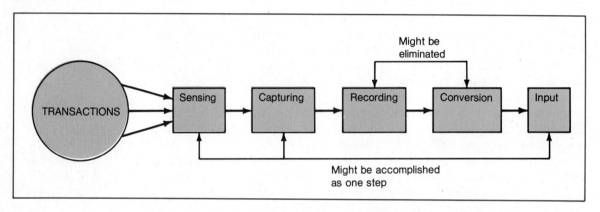

or inventory request form) and keying data onto computer-readable media or directly into a processing unit. The primary aim in this section is to compare the advantages of manual and automated data entry operations.

Sensing means detecting that a transaction has occurred; this is the "trigger" that initiates data entry for a transactional event. *Capturing* refers to the measurement or categorization activities that assign values to data items representing transaction attributes. This assignment of values may result in precise, quantitative representations or, through some coding scheme, merely some qualitative representation. These alternatives are summarized in Figure 5.3. Coding greatly eases data entry, storage, and retrieval, and often makes data more easily recognized and manipulated by organizational members. *Recording* refers to the initial act of placing assigned data values on some medium from which they can be later read by human, electronic, or electromechanical means. *Conversion* refers to the copying of data values from one medium to another. Typically this involves a transfer from a noncomputer-readable medium (such as a sales form) to one that is computer readable (such as punch cards) or from one computer-readable medium (such as punched cards) to another (such as magnetic tape) to enhance processing efficiency. *Input* refers to actual entry of data into the CPU of a computer system.

As indicated in Figure 5.2, all these steps may not be present in every situation. By employing a point-of-sale terminal with a sensor that reads universal product codes (imprinted earlier) at a cashier station, a system can sense and input a customer's purchase in one step. If a customer representative takes sales orders over a telephone and enters them di-

FIGURE 5.3
"Capturing" a Transaction

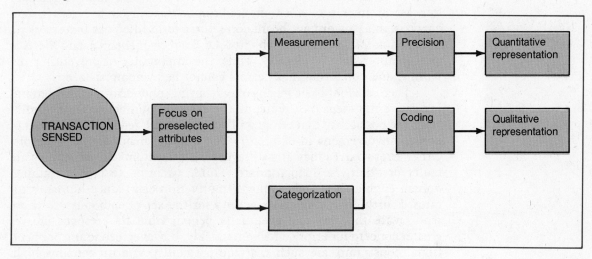

rectly through a CRT, sensing and capturing can occur together, followed by a single recording and input step. In other situations, all the steps are evident: an admissions clerk greets an arriving hospital patient; by questioning the person, the clerk obtains the information to complete an admission form; the form is eventually sent to a keypuncher, who transfers the data onto punched cards; the data are then copied onto magnetic tape, from which they are finally read into the computer for processing.

The objective in data entry is to collect required data in a cost-effective, error-free, timely, and unobtrusive way. While the first three criteria are clear, the last may not be. Unobtrusive procedures do not overly burden organizational members with data entry tasks. The more convenient and less visible are data entry procedures, the greater is the likelihood the procedures will be carried out as intended and the less disruption of organizational activities there should be.

As might be expected, however, efforts to enhance the accuracy, timeliness, and unobtrusiveness of data entry invariably result in higher costs. In most situations it is *impractical* to provide precise data measurements or total unobtrusiveness. Moreover, it is *impossible* to be truly current, as some time must transpire between the occurrence of a transaction, its sensing by a TPS, and its entry into a computer system. The key, thus, is to determine acceptable levels of accuracy, timeliness, and unobtrusiveness that make possible realization of CBIS benefits without imposing excessive costs in hardware, software, or human labor.

Error Control

Most errors associated with CBIS (incorrect billing, lost shipments, a poor forecast, an inventory stockout, etc.) can be traced back to errors in data entry, such as a word not heard correctly, a form filled out incorrectly, a transaction lost, or a keypunch error. Once an error *enters* a data file, it is almost impossible to identify. Thus, the importance of preventing, detecting, and correcting input errors cannot be overemphasized.

There are four basic means of *preventing* input errors. First, combining data entry steps (i.e., reducing the absolute number of steps) diminishes the possibility that errors will occur. Second, reducing the extent of human involvement in data entry controls the major source of errors. Other error sources may arise, however, if the automated procedures are faulty or otherwise inappropriate. Third, attention to proper training, human engineering, and employee motivation can reduce human error rates. Fourth, assigning responsibility for the act of data entry to those who create the data and eventually benefit from its presence creates greater concern for error control. Invariably, however, economic or operational constraints are such that the possibility of error remains high.

The primary deterrent to input errors, thus, is *detecting* data errors before they are processed and stored. A number of error detection mechanisms are listed in Table 5.2. These fall into two groups: process controls, which directly relate to the data entry process, and program controls, which are program statements that assess the reasonableness of data after

TABLE 5.2
Data Entry Error Detection Mechanisms

Process Controls	Program Controls
Visual verification—Visual inspection of source documents, CRT screens, transaction listings, etc., for data correctness and completeness and for missing or out-of-sequence items	*Logical checks*—Decision statements that check the reasonableness (completeness, value types, and value ranges) and consistency (a transaction often results in a series of data items that can occur together in a limited number of ways) of entered data
Repetition—Performance of an operation twice (having a manual procedure performed twice by different individuals, transmitting a message or data stream more than once, etc.) and then checking the results of the two operations for equivalence	*Arithmetic checks*—Operations with sequence numbers, hash totals, transaction counts, check digits, etc.
Recording of "extra" data—Inclusion as input data of sequence numbers, hash totals (the sum of a series of transactional data items), transaction counts, and check digits (a digit that is appended to a number so its validity can be assessed; the original number is operated on by some algorithm that produces the check digit as a result)	*Echo check*—An entered data item that is "bounced" back to an operator for visual verification

it has been read but before it has been processed. The cost of recording extra data, repeating steps, manually checking transactions and inserting program checks into programs, and then correcting detected errors cannot be ignored.

Economic Considerations

Figure 5.4 illustrates some pertinent economic relationships associated with the design of data entry procedures. The rather large initial investment required with automation generally prohibits the use of such designs with low transaction volumes. (Of course, strict accuracy or time requirements may necessitate such designs even when transaction volumes are low.) As transaction volume increases, however, per-unit analyses begin to favor automation. Two facts that suggest automation will become even more economically viable over time are: (1) indirect costs associated with manual processing (error occurrence) tend to increase at a greater than linear rate with transaction volume, and (2) the direct costs (salaries) associated with manual processing will invariably increase.

FIGURE 5.4
Economic Considerations in Data Entry

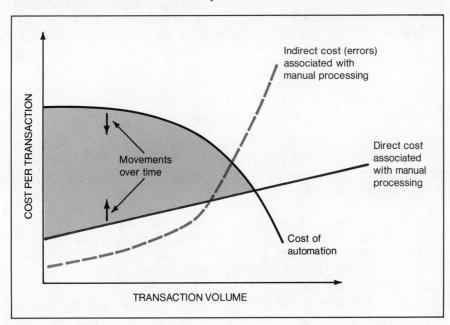

Forms Design

An important but often overlooked facet of data entry design are the source documents on which many transactions are initially captured. The expense of designing, purchasing, and handling these forms can become exorbitant, particularly when data are collected on multiple forms, when collected data are already held in storage, or when the collected data are never used. By including form design as an integral element of data entry design, and thus eliminating redundancy, one can realize considerable cost savings. Additionally, concern with human engineering in the design of forms can significantly reduce recording errors. Wording, layout, color, coding schemes, form size, and preprinting all offer opportunities for *preventing* errors in data entry.

DATA STORAGE

As discussed earlier, an important TPS function involves storing transactional data so they can be referenced later. The traditional objectives associated with data storage have emphasized cost effectiveness, i.e., maintaining data on the least expensive medium while allowing efficient processing of the data by application programs. Recent trends in the computer industry (falling hardware costs, rising software development costs, and more attention to the end-user) have increased the need for flexibility in data storage. The following discussion of data storage will adopt the more traditional perspective; current trends in data storage will be covered in the next chapter when the *data base* concept is introduced.

File Structure

Early TPS applications tended to address straightforward and relatively narrow independent business activities such as payroll, accounts receivable, inventory control, accounts payable, and sales analysis. Transactional data, and thus the storage of these data, were closely tied to each application. Certain sets of data were seen to naturally fit together because of their associated uses: a payroll application required data on personnel, accounts receivable required data on customers and sales, accounts payable required data on vendors and inventory purchases, inventory control required data on inventory status, and sales analysis needed data on sales and customers. As a result, most organizations kept collections of *data files*, with each file directly tied to at least one application and each application accessing a limited number of files (often one). Table 5.3 lists common data files and their associated uses.

TABLE 5.3
Common Data Files

Data File	Uses
Personnel	Payroll, performance appraisal, skill location
Customer	Accounts receivable, sales analysis, advertising
Vendor	Purchasing, accounts payable
Product	Production planning, engineering
Sales	Sales analysis, market planning, sales management
General ledger	Financial statements, standard costs, budgeting

It is necessary to distinguish between *logical* and *physical* file structures. A logical structure is what is maintained in the mind of the applications programmer (or end-user) and, hence, is reflected in the "logic" of the applications program. The physical structure refers to the way the data set is actually maintained on the storage medium. For any application, the logical or physical file structures may or may not be the same. When a disparity exists, the transformations from one form to the other are usually handled by systems software.

A logical file is composed of a collection of *records*, each of which describes a unique entity of the type being represented by the file. The inventory file in Figure 5.5 consists of a collection of inventory records, each of which contains data on one part in a parts inventory. The individual data items describing individual attributes of all parts are *fields*. The forms of each record in a file are similar, but the contents of the record fields differ with the differences in the parts. (Record forms may differ if multiple entries are allowed for some fields. With the file in Figure 5.5, for example, the existence of "purchase date" fields containing dates purchase orders had been issued for each part would reflect the varying occurrences of purchase orders.)

One record field must uniquely identify each record. It is through this field, known as the *identifier key*, that access to individual records in a file is gained. With the file shown in Figure 5.5, field 1 (part number) would be a suitable identifier key, as each part has a unique part number. *Secondary keys* can also be defined to facilitate the selective retrieval of predefined subsets of the records in a file.

While many physical file structures are in use, only three will be discussed: the sequential, random, and indexed sequential structures. Most operating systems provide the means to implement these three structures. With the *sequential* structure, the records of a data file are placed contiguously on the storage medium in the sequential (ascending or descending) order of their identifier keys. The *random* structure places

FIGURE 5.5

Logical Structure of an Inventory File

FIELD 1	FIELD 2	FIELD 3	FIELD 4	FIELD 5	FIELD 6
•	•	•	•	•	•
•	•	•	•	•	•
•	•	•	•	•	•
1238	3-INCH FLANGE (BOX)	A125	25	10	C
1239	5-INCH FLANGE (BOX)	A125	50	20	C
•	•	•	•	•	•
•	•	•	•	•	•
•	•	•	•	•	•
3285	ROTATOR DISK (UNIT)	C256	1205	400	A
•	•	•	•	•	•
•	•	•	•	•	•
•	•	•	•	•	•

FIELD 1 — PART NUMBER
FIELD 2 — DESCRIPTION
FIELD 3 — VENDOR CODE
FIELD 4 — QUANTITY ON HAND
FIELD 5 — REORDER POINT
FIELD 6 — REORDER CODE

records randomly throughout a storage medium based on an algorithm designed to minimize the time to access an individual record, given an acceptable amount of allocated storage space. The *indexed sequential* structure stores two sets of items on the storage medium: the records contiguously in the sequential order of their identifier keys and an index that allows "identifier key/physical storage location" references for each record. Figure 5.6 illustrates the three structures.

Other physical file structures have proved useful for certain applications, particularly applications that require sophisticated search and retrieval capabilities. Two interesting structures are *linked* and *inverted lists*. With a linked list, predefined record subsets are linked together through "pointer" fields. A field in one record holds the physical storage location of the next member record in the subset. A complete "ring" can be formed for this subset so any member record can be reached from any other member record by following the pointer linkages. By maintaining an index that provides for each predefined list a reference to the physical location of one member record, one can directly access the entire list. Such a list could be used to locate personnel skills or vendors for raw

FIGURE 5.6
Sequential, Random, and Indexed Sequential File Structures

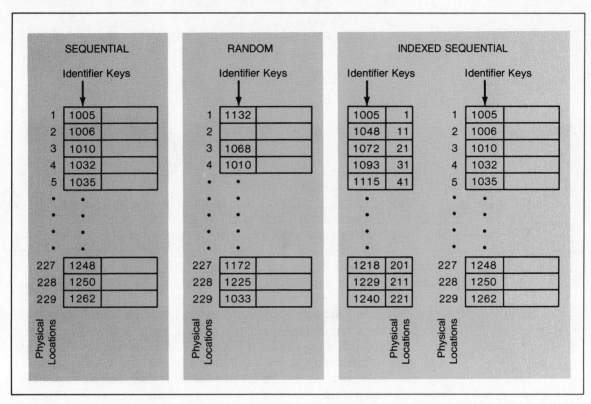

materials and procured components. With an inverted list structure, the index used to refer to each list holds the physical storage location for all member records, rather than for a single member record. Thus, member records can be accessed directly from the index, and pointer fields are no longer required.

File Access Methods

Data files are accessed primarily for two reasons. First, files are *updated* with transactional data so they represent current organizational realities. Update activity typically involves changing fields in records, adding records to a file, and deleting records from a file. Second, data maintained in record fields are *retrieved* for use by organizational members through

TABLE 5.4
File Access Information Needs

Activity	Information
Update	Operation code (change, add, delete)
	Record identifier key
	Field identifiers (possibly)
	Data values (if relevant)
Retrieval	Record identifier key
	Secondary keys (possibly)
	Field identifiers (possibly)

application programs. Table 5.4 indicates the basic information needed to perform update or retrieval activities.

Viewed most simply, records in files can be accessed *sequentially* or *directly*. With sequential access methods, one locates a record by initially accessing the first record in a sequentially structured file and examining its record identifier key. If the identifier key of the accessed record matches that desired, the search is completed. If no match occurs, succeeding records are accessed until the correct one is read or the end of the file is reached (an error condition).

Things become considerably more complex with direct access, as the objective is to read a record from storage into the CPU without having to read in any other records (as is the case with sequential access). This can be accomplished if one can determine solely from a record's identifier key exactly where the record is located on the storage device. For a number of reasons (primarily avoiding waste of primary or secondary storage), it is impractical in most situations to provide "pure" direct access. What has proved effective in many situations is an "approximated" form of direct access whereby records are randomly assigned to physical storage locations by application of an algorithm to the identifier key and location of the record when access is desired by reapplication of the algorithm. To minimize the amount of wasted secondary storage space, most such schemes allow for record overflows—two or more records being assigned to the same physical location. In such instances the first record assigned is placed there and succeeding records assigned to the same location are placed elsewhere ("overflowed") according to some decision rule. This same decision rule is then applied when these overflowed records are accessed. Because of this overflow problem, most "direct access" methods do not actually provide direct access. However, most methods can locate a record in a limited number (say, three to five) of accesses.

Generally, decisions to employ sequential or direct access hinge on processing cost and on response time constraints imposed by the application. For the sake of simplicity, processing cost can be viewed as the total number of accesses to a storage device (i.e., read operations) required to process an application. Response time is reflected in the time it takes to locate and access a record. Obviously, the time to access a single record is much less with direct access than with sequential access.

The critical characteristic of an application in selecting an access method is the proportion of records in a file that *must* be accessed during processing. This is termed *file activity*. One application characterized by high file activity is payroll: access to all the records in the personnel file is required. An application characterized by low file activity is the handling of customer billing complaints by a clerk personally interacting with a customer: only a single record from the customer file is desired. A general rule to follow regarding employing sequential or direct access is the following:

- Use sequential access for high file activity.
- Use direct access for low file activity.

An illustration of this principle is presented in Table 5.5. (The "access costs" in this example do not accurately reflect reality: steps can be taken when reading data files to greatly improve efficiency. The example merely suggests the type of trade-off that exists.) Clearly, as the file activity exceeds 20 percent, it becomes desirable to use sequential processing to minimize processing costs. Such an analysis may be voided if the application's response time requirements dictate the use of direct access.

The most commonly used access method is neither sequential nor direct, but the *indexed sequential access method* (ISAM), which makes

TABLE 5.5
Relationships Between Access Method and File Activity

Number of Records in File	File Activity	Expected Number of Accesses with Sequential Access Method[a]	Expected Number of Accesses with Direct Access Method[b]
1000	.001	500	5
1000	.01	1000	50
1000	.1	1000	500
1000	.2	1000	1000
1000	.5	1000	2500
1000	1.0	1000	5000

[a]Assumes desired records are distributed randomly throughout file.
[b]Assumes average of 5 disk accesses are required to locate desired record.

use of the indexed sequential file structure. If an indexed sequential file structure is used, both sequential and direct access of a file are possible. With sequential access, the index is referenced to determine the location of the first record. After this record is accessed, the remainder are accessed as with a sequential structure. With direct access, the index is searched to determine the location of the desired record. Then this area of the storage device is examined to locate and access the record. While both sequential and direct accessing are possible, processing performance will be poorer than that observed with a sequential or random file structure.

The reason ISAM is the most commonly employed access method is that most data files are used with multiple applications, some of which are characterized by high file activity and others by low file activity. It would be desirable, for example, to access an inventory file sequentially when performing a biweekly analysis of stock levels, but to access the file directly when checking the availability of a particular item in response to a customer inquiry. With the ISAM access method, appropriate performance levels can be achieved for both applications at a reasonable cost (i.e., only one form of the data file is required).

These three file access methods are compared in Table 5.6.

DATA OUTPUT

Aside from storing captured transactional data, TPS also output these data in performing and supporting organizational functions. As indicated earlier, these outputs are of two types: documents produced by a computer rather than manually because it is more economical, timely, or

TABLE 5.6
Comparison of Standard Access Methods

Access Method	File Structure	Storage Device	Advantages	Disadvantages
Sequential	Sequential	Tape or disk	Simple software Economical storage (tape) Best for high file activity	Only sequential access Poor response time Worst for low file activity
Direct	Random	Disk	Quick response time Best for low file activity	Complex software Wasted secondary storage Worst for high file activity
ISAM	Indexed sequential	Disk	Both sequential and direct	Complex software Wasted secondary storage Slight performance impairment

reliable to do so, and simple reports (i.e., transaction listings) that indicate the occurrence of certain events.

Documents are used to provoke or promote organizational and environmental actions and to facilitate an action and then facilitate the capture of responses to the action (i.e., a *turnaround* document). Transaction listings likewise serve two purposes: a "hardcopy" confirmation that required activities have transpired, and a reference source readily accessible to organizational members. Table 5.7 provides examples of these output types.

The objective in data output is to provide the required material in usable form and at a reasonable cost. Important criteria to be considered when deciding the best way to produce a particular output include the following:

Document characteristics	Simple report characteristics
Cost per unit	Volume of output
Rate of output	Detailed vs. summary
Physical form required	Complete vs. exceptions
Accessibility by end-user	Frequency
	Accessibility by end-user

While most TPS output has traditionally been paper based, technological advances in areas such as audio output, micrographics, and telecommunications are enabling many organizations to significantly increase their productivity in performing these functions. For example, by printing its sales manuals on microfiche rather than paper, an insurance company reduced its production costs, as well as the expense and inconvenience of modifying the sales manuals. Its $90,000 investment was recovered in

---

TABLE 5.7
Typical TPS Outputs

Output Type	Function	Example
Document	Action	Invoice, purchase order, shipping order, paycheck, service order
	Turnaround	Time card, billing card, production trailer
Simple report (transaction listing)	Confirmation	Shipments, purchases, clients served, deliveries, completed production stops
	Reference	Orders, complaints, errors, expenses, changes

---

two years in postage alone! By employing audio output to handle some clients' inquiries regarding yields and prices, an investment firm claims to have obtained a $500,000 annual savings in staff.[1]

It is clearly advantageous for organizations to examine the media used with their existing TPS. The potential for significant gains from a minimal investment does exist.

PROCESSING ENVIRONMENTS

A TPS can be implemented in a variety of ways, resulting in significant performance differences. Basically, three processing environments can be described that together capture the essence of most TPS implementations. These environments are *batch entry, batch processing, on-line entry, batch processing,* and *on-line entry, immediate processing.*

The major performance differences among these three revolve around the accuracy and currentness of stored data. Inaccuracy within data files can usually be traced to problems associated with one or more data entry steps: sensing, capture, recording, conversion, and input. As pointed out earlier, efforts can be made to prevent or to detect and correct such errors. A data file's currentness can be viewed as a function of three time delays:

Recognition   The time between when a transaction occurs and when it is sensed by the TPS.

Update   The time between processing runs to update a data file.

Processing   The time it takes to complete a processing run to update a data file.

A single application will be used to describe the differences among the three processing environments. One activity common to all organizations is the maintenance of a personnel file (i.e., the processing of changes to a file of employee data). Events that might result in change transactions include hiring an employee (adding a record to the personnel file), terminating an employee (deleting a record from the personnel file), promoting an employee (modifying a field in an existing record), and completing a training course (adding to a multiple-entry field in an existing record).

Batch Entry, Batch Processing

Whenever a personnel transaction occurs, it is noted on a personnel change form and sent to a personnel clerk. The clerk logs in receipt of the transaction, checks it for errors, and places the form in a "suspense" file, usually a folder on the clerk's desk. After a set period (say, two weeks), all accumulated forms are sent to keypunch. This period is the *batching cycle*, or update interval. At keypunch, the transaction data are copied onto punched cards, which are then processed to produce a *sorted* transaction file on magnetic tape. The transaction file is then run against the current personnel file to produce an updated personnel file.

Figure 5.7 suggests how a sequential file update operation might take place using magnetic tape storage. By sorting the transaction records according to the personnel file's record identifier key (i.e., employee number), so they follow the order in which the personnel records are stored on the personnel "master" file, the processing operation becomes quite sim-

FIGURE 5.7
Sequentially Updating a Master File

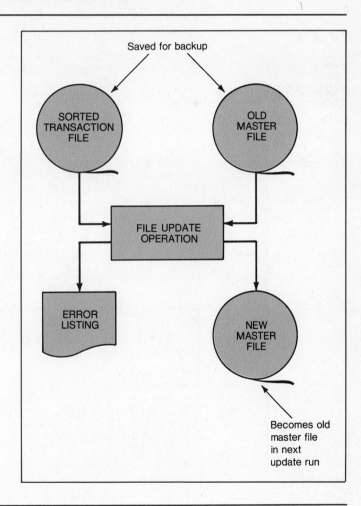

ple. Note that a new master file is physically created, and becomes the file to be updated in the next batching cycle. At the conclusion of a processing run, the transaction file and old master file can be kept as backups in case the new master file is destroyed, damaged, or lost.

An overview of the manner in which this personnel file is updated with batch processing is shown in Figure 5.8. Errors can arise in numerous ways:

- Error in initial filling out of change form,
- Form lost or damaged when sent to personnel clerk,
- Error by personnel clerk when handling form,
- Form lost or damaged while in external suspense file,
- Form lost or damaged while being sent to keypunch,
- Error in punching cards,
- Cards lost or damaged,

FIGURE 5.8
Updating a Personnel File by Batch Entry, Batch Processing

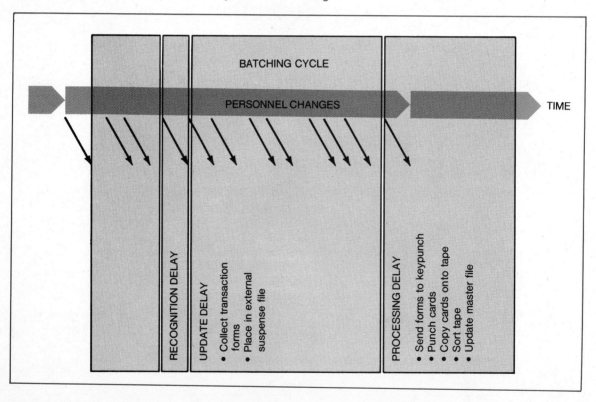

- Error in converting cards to sorted transaction tape,
- Error when reading transaction tape during sequential updating of personnel master file.

As detailed in Figure 5.9, delays occur throughout the handling of the transaction:

Recognition   Time is lost capturing the change on the change form and sending it to the personnel clerk.

Update   On average, the update delay is half the batching cycle.

Processing   Considerable time can be taken sending the transaction forms to keypunch, punching cards, converting cards to tape, and updating the master file.

FIGURE 5.9
Delays in Batch Entry, Batch Processing of Personnel Changes

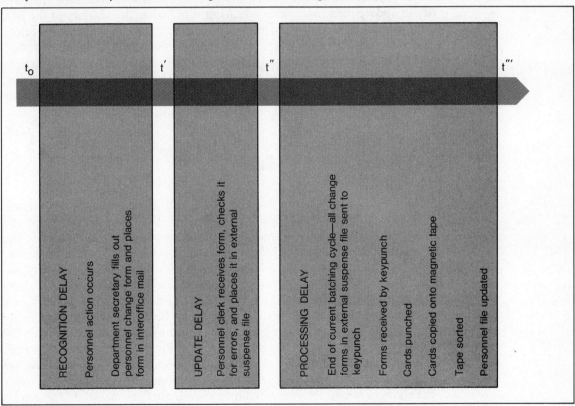

Given these potential accuracy and currentness deficiencies, one might reasonably question why batch processing is used as much as it is. The answer is fourfold. First, the manual procedures and software required are relatively unsophisticated. Most organizations have or can hire the personnel needed to develop or acquire a TPS and to perform the required activities. Second, the processing can be handled by relatively inexpensive computer equipment. Third, error controls can often be employed to attain enough accuracy. Finally, for many applications the inevitable delays present no problem. In this personnel example, how current need the personnel file be kept? For applications that occur regularly, such as payroll, activities can be scheduled far enough in advance to compensate for delays in the process.

An important design issue with any *batch processing* TPS is the length of the batching cycle. Two often conflicting points must be resolved in reaching a decision on this issue. First, how current must the data file be? If it is imperative to know which clients were serviced yesterday, it makes little sense to update a client service file on a weekly basis. Second, batch processing involves sequentially accessing the data file in update runs. As discussed earlier, the higher the activity of the file, the more efficient is the process. The longer the batching cycle, the more likely it is that a higher portion of the records of a file will require updating. Also, short batching cycles result in more frequent, smaller processing runs, which are usually less cost efficient than fewer, larger runs. Clearly, both organizational needs (currentness demands) and processing costs must be analyzed in selecting a batch cycle.

On-line Entry, Batch Processing

With on-line entry, batch processing, personnel change forms are again filled out when necessary and sent to the personnel clerk. On receipt of a form, the clerk keys the transaction into a "smart" terminal linked to the computer system. Error checking is usually facilitated by prompts generated by a data editing program. Edited transactions are transmitted directly to the computer system, where they are stored in a tape- or disk-based internal suspense file. At the end of a batching cycle, one of two operations begins. The personnel file may be updated sequentially by sorting this suspense file, which then becomes the transaction file used to update the master (personnel) file. Alternatively, the suspense file may be used in its existing state to update the personnel file by a direct access procedure. In the latter case, the master (personnel) file is stored on a disk and changes are directly inserted into this single file—no "old" file can be kept as a backup, as with sequential processing. Such protection could be

FIGURE 5.10
Updating a Personnel File by On-line Entry, Batch Processing

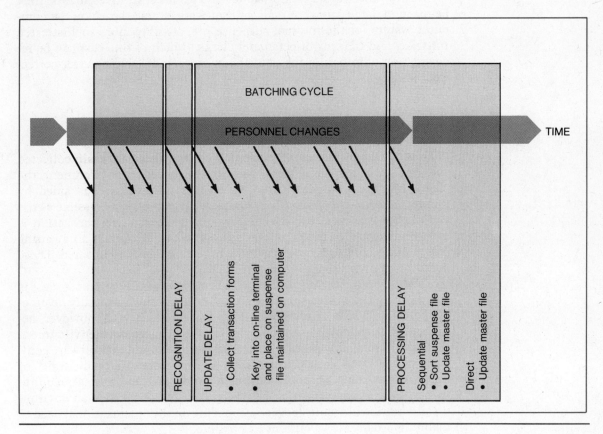

BATCHING CYCLE

PERSONNEL CHANGES

TIME

RECOGNITION DELAY

UPDATE DELAY
• Collect transaction forms
• Key into on-line terminal and place on suspense file maintained on computer

PROCESSING DELAY

Sequential
• Sort suspense file
• Update master file

Direct
• Update master file

achieved, however, by copying the updated personnel file at the end of the run. An overview of this updating process is shown in Figure 5.10.

The major advantage of employing on-line entry with batch processing lies in the potential improvements in *accuracy*. Once a form is received by the personnel clerk, the likelihood of errors occurring should significantly diminish for the following reasons:

- An editing program can help detect errors.
- The suspense file is stored in the computer system.
- There are fewer conversion steps.
- Human involvement is greatly reduced, as no human interaction is required once the personnel clerk has keyed in the transaction.

While no reduction is likely in recognition or update delay, much improvement is seen with processing delay.

These advantages are not achieved without cost. Investments must be made in data entry terminals and software, storage space on the computer system for the internal suspense file, possibly more sophisticated software, and training of personnel clerks. (Much of this cost can be recovered by eliminating the conversion steps and reducing error-correction activity.)

On-line Entry, Immediate Processing

With the third environment, personnel change forms are again collected and sent to the personnel clerk. As with the preceding environment, the clerk keys the transaction into an on-line terminal and is aided by prompts in error checking. More complete error control is possible as the clerk can now access the affected personnel record. The transaction is then transmitted to the computer system, where it triggers an awaiting processing program and the personnel file is *immediately* updated. These activities are represented in Figure 5.11.

While only a slight improvement is made in accuracy, currentness is significantly enhanced as there is no update delay and essentially no processing delay. The cost of obtaining these benefits is high, however, because of the expense of establishing an operating system environment that can immediately process entered transactions and the software complexity associated with direct access. Furthermore, no "audit trail" of transactions exists without additional processing and storage requirements. Careful analysis must be undertaken to justify such an environment, with the ultimate decision depending on the organizational need to maintain a data file as current as possible.

Summary of the Three TPS Processing Environments

A summary of the preceding discussions is provided in Table 5.8. While advances in both hardware and software technology are resulting in on-line data entry's becoming an appropriate design in more situations, the sophistication and expense of immediate processing remain prohibitive unless the need for data files to reflect current organizational realities is extreme. Such an environment *can* be approximated by using very short batching cycles (such as hourly), along with on-line data entry.

Maintaining data files on direct access storage devices, as is required in immediate processing and as is usually the case with on-line entry, results in the ability to update almost simultaneously all data files af-

FIGURE 5.11
Updating a Personnel File by On-line Entry, Immediate Processing

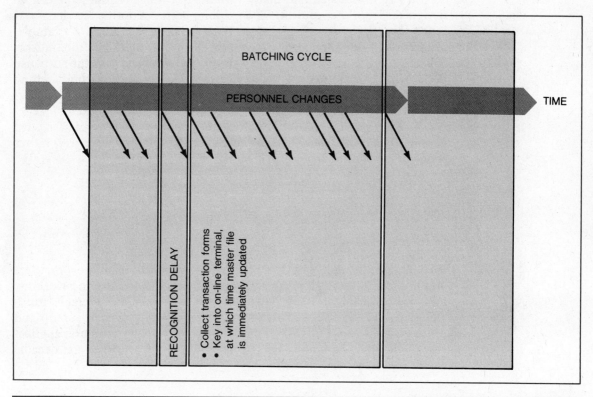

TABLE 5.8
Overview of TPS Processing Environments

TPS Environment	Advantages	Disadvantages
Batch entry, batch processing	Simple software Backup automatically provided Use of low-cost storage (tape) Suitability for many applications	Error potential high Master file always out-of-date
On-line entry, batch processing	Significant accuracy improvements Some improvement in currentness of master file	Hardware expense Software expense Personnel training
On-line entry, immediate processing	Significant improvement in currentness of master file Some improvement in accuracy	Significant increase in software expense

fected by a transaction. This results in greater currentness and consistency in data files.

As mentioned earlier, many variants of these environments can be designed. Often the resulting TPS exhibits better performance characteristics than those described above. With batch processing, for example, accuracy can be enhanced by having the personnel clerk key the transactions into a stand-alone data entry station, which results in the suspense file's being maintained on a cassette tape. At the end of the batching cycle, the cassette tape is delivered to the computer center and the processing sequence is begun. With all three processing environments, recognition delay can be reduced by providing departmental secretaries with data entry terminals and making them responsible for data entry, rather than the personnel clerk.

EMERGING TRENDS IN TRANSACTION PROCESSING

The increasing sophistication and decreasing costs of microcomputers and minicomputers, along with improvements in computer networking, have led the popular and professional presses to pay considerable attention to the TPS application areas of *electronic funds transfer systems* and *office automation*. The CBIS implications of these two computer applications will likely be among those most widely felt over the next decade.

Electronic Funds Transfer Systems

Advocates of the "paperless society" have long argued the advantages of basing the U.S. payments system on digital impulses, rather than on cash and checks: costs would be reduced for financial institutions (elimination of check processing expenses and floats), business organizations (guaranteed payment and immediate use of funds), and the public (less financial expenses, no need to carry cash), and greater accuracy and freedom from fraud would be observed. While a number of *electronic funds transfer systems* (EFTS) applications are in place today (see Table 5.9 for examples), the "paperless society" has not arrived. For the most part, what exists today is a greatly improved paper-based financial system.[2]

That this is so is not surprising. Consumers hesitate to accept EFTS because of their reluctance to adopt new behavioral patterns and their unfavorable experiences reconciling billing errors under the present payment system. If consumers are inconvenienced or dissatisfied under the current payment system with its *visible* audit trail, it is not surprising

TABLE 5.9
Common EFTS Applications

Application	Example
National bank card networks	Visa, Mastercharge
Preauthorized procedures	Direct payment of recurrent expenses Telephone bill payment
Automatic banking	Automatic tellers Credit and check authorizations
Automated clearinghouses	Direct deposit
Point-of-sale-terminals	Credit and debit cards

they are reluctant to accept a payments system with an invisible audit trail.[3] What may not be so easily comprehended is that bankers, as a group, are also not pro-EFTS.[4] Reasons for this lack of enthusiasm by the financial community include the following:

- The economics of EFTS remain to be proven.
- The competitive implications for both large and small institutions are unknown.
- Many legal and legislative snarls exist.
- There is increased potential for infrequent but high-loss incidents.

In general, both consumers and financial institutions are satisfied with the present system, which can handle existing (and projected) transaction flows.

Small changes will probably move us incrementally toward a "paperless society." A recent survey of EFTS services in thirty-five institutions reveals that most growth in this area involves an expansion of existing services, with the institutions' clients, after prolonged exposure, exhibiting increased acceptance.[5] Two events likely to accelerate the growth of EFTS are NOW accounts (accompanied by a passing on to consumers of the *actual* cost of processing checks) and the impending deregulation of the banking industry (accompanied by an exploitation of EFTS for marketing purposes).

Office Automation

The attention of industrial and governmental information policymakers is increasingly being drawn to automating office work—those clerical

TABLE 5.10
Office Functions

Domain	Document-Oriented	Data-Oriented	Task-Oriented
Clerical	Type, modify, file, copy, dictate, sort, retrieve, mail	Perform simple calculations, organize for presentation, insert into documents	Locate
Administrative	Locate, trace, retrieve, review	Locate, retrieve, review, summarize	Monitor, evaluate, schedule

and administrative activities that maintain the flow of paper necessary to support organizational efforts to produce products or provide services. An overview of the many functions included in office work is given in Table 5.10.[6,7]

Automating the office has become an area of concern because of three converging forces. First, the financial impact of an outdated office environment is being increasingly felt by organizations.[8] Office workers comprise about one fourth of the U.S. labor force, but represent almost one half of corporate costs—a situation reflective of both concern for manufacturing productivity (a 90 percent increase over the last decade) and *lack* of concern for office productivity (a 4 percent increase over the last decade). Second, manufacturers of office products have begun to take advantage of microelectronics, thereby greatly increasing the capabilities of their equipment. Finally, computer manufacturers have realized there is a vast market to be exploited.

Examination of the office environment, however, revealed that the real potential in automating office functions lay with nonclerical personnel. Clerical and secretarial costs represent only around one third of office costs; the remaining two thirds are associated with management and professional employees.[9] Managers and professionals, for example, spend one fourth of their time in clerical activities[10] (looking for reports, proofreading, checking the status of an activity or document, preparing correspondence, trying to reach people, etc.) and find that about 40 percent of their time involves processing mail, handling telephone calls, and traveling.[11] Automating these activities becomes even more desirable when one realizes that much of the time involved is totally unproductive, wasted on busy or misdirected phone calls, junk mail, last-minute cancellations, and meetings held up because of late attendees.

The technology used to automate the office combines telecommunications (video, voice, and digital), data processing (stored programs used in processing and analyzing data), word processing (text generation and editing), and information retrieval (data and document) capabilities. The ultimate aim of designers of office systems is to tie together the following four elements, which may be individually automated today but are most often linked by manual processes:

Administrative support center	Support of office management functions through document storage and retrieval and activity tracking
Word processing center	Automated typing pool
Data processing center	Traditional TPS activities
Graphics arts service center	Creation and duplication of presentation and report materials[12]

Additional nodes most likely to be linked to such an interorganizational communications network are satellite word processors and on-line terminals, satellite small business systems, electronic mail terminals, and "smart" copiers (devices that produce document copies from originals in mass storage).

While many office automation systems today are quite limited in scope, some manufacturers are beginning to offer integrated systems moving toward the ideal described above. Some recently introduced products are Xerox's STAR system, Wang's Integrated Information System, Datapoint's Integrated Electronic Office, and Primes' Office Automation System.[13] Functions typically being provided include electronic message systems, calendar systems, authorship tools, and access to external information services. These and other common automated office functions are listed in Table 5.11.

TABLE 5.11
Common Office Automation Implementations

Category	Description	Functions
Word processor	Automated text production by individuals	Text editor Grammar and spelling aids Computation and graphics aids
Message systems	Enhanced communication flow among individuals	Message banks Electronic mail
Activity management	Monitoring and scheduling of individual and organizational activities	Calendars Electronic ticklers Project management
Computer conferencing	Multi-media, multiple-location group interaction	Message switching Analysis and synthesis tools Group memory

Many benefits can arise from automation of the office. Most visible are productivity improvements arising from replacing human labor with electronic technology: increased speed, lower costs, and greater accuracy. Less visible are the gains realized from enabling organizational members to make better use of their time (less interruption of work, less "set-up" time, 24-hour availability and geographic independence of information, extension of the workday or week), and from improvements in the quality of work life (employees can choose work times and locations). Most subtle of all—but perhaps of greatest potential benefit—is the recognition that it will likely be through office automation that microcomputers or computer terminals initially enter professional and executive offices.

As with other computer-based applications, decisions to implement office systems must follow careful analysis of the benefits to be attained and the problems that might arise. Office automation is an expensive investment, with the most common figure cited for an automated office being around $20,000 per office employee. While this figure appears high compared to the $2,000 currently invested per U.S. office worker, it compares favorably with the average investment in manufacturing employees—$25,000.[14] Nonetheless, considerable capital will be required to finance the automated office. Technological limitations exist, despite the advances that have occurred. Of particular concern to office automation are the following:

- Information retrieval capabilities for *documents* lag far behind those for *data*,
- Techniques to capture oral information are just approaching economic viability,
- Automated means of capturing much externally created printed material are almost nonexistent.

The last two limitations discourage many potential uses of office automation. Finally, considerable resistance has been observed to efforts to automate offices. Earlier technologies to improve office productivity (e.g., the electric typewriter) did not require behavioral changes in the office environment. Office automation does! Office processes become less personal and job descriptions often change in both activity and responsibility. Thus, the behavioral implications of office automation become as important as the economic and technical aspects.

CONCLUSION

Transaction processing systems perform two major functions in organizations. *First*, they provide a low-cost, quick, and more accurate alternative to human labor in handling many clerical activities (data or document gathering, generation, organizing, storage, retrieval, and transmission) associated with providing an organization's products or services. Activities that typically benefit from such computerization are characterized by high volume, repetition, vast storage requirements, need for quick retrieval of stored data, fast response times, and stringent accuracy, and sizable, complex calculations.

Second, these systems collect data describing those transactions that, taken together, present a historical view of the organization and of particularly relevant environmental elements. Typically this involves tracking work and resource flows whenever the benefits from referencing the captured data exceed the cost of data collection and storage. Transactions that represent continuing operating problems (such as work flow bottlenecks, under- or overutilized facilities, excessive costs, and customer or client complaints) and those that provide for multiple uses are ideal candidates for TPS support. As technological advances decrease the cost of computer hardware and as application software packages become even more available, computer-based applications should become cost effective even for organizations lacking in financial or human resources. Thus, an ever-increasing number of organizations will be able to exploit the information resource.

It is crucial, however, that the following major concerns associated with TPS be understood:

- Concern for accuracy in data entry,
- Concern for security as organizational CBIS dependence grows,
- Concern for the potential alienation of customers, clients, vendors, and employees because of the impersonality, inconvenience, and change that often accompany CBIS implementation.

By recognizing these potential difficulties and resolving them through an open dialogue among all affected parties, one can overcome them. Too often, however, these and related problems are ignored until a crisis arises. What results then are costly corrections and the sowing of seeds of distrust regarding CBIS among an organization's members.

KEY ISSUES

An organization's captured transactions, when reconstructed, provide a means of "remembering" what has occurred in the organization's past.

A TPS has three main purposes: to construct a corporate memory of past events and actions, to produce clerical documents that accompany organizational efforts to produce products or provide services, and to produce simple reports that identify recent events and actions.

Data entry may involve a series of discrete steps (sensing, capturing, recording, converting, and data input) or a single step (source data automation).

The objective in data entry is to collect required data in a cost-effective, error-free, timely, and unobtrusive manner.

It is extremely difficult to prevent data entry errors. Numerous techniques exist, however, to detect such errors.

The objective in data storage is to maintain data in the least expensive manner possible while still providing timely data retrieval, given the needs of the data applications.

Sequential access is often used when highly active files are processed on a periodic basis. Direct access is often used when extremely quick data retrieval is required or when file activity is low. Indexed sequential access provides a means of obtaining both sequential and direct access.

The objective in data output is to provide required materials in usable form at a reasonable cost.

The three major processing environments (batch entry, batch processing; on-line entry, batch processing; and on-line entry, immediate processing) differ primarily in the accuracy and currentness of maintained data files.

The major gain in moving from batch entry to on-line entry involves accuracy. The major gain in moving from on-line entry, batch processing to on-line entry, immediate processing involves currentness.

Incremental adoptions of the various components of electronic funds transfer systems (EFTS) are slowly moving the U.S. payment system to a dependence on digital impulses, rather than on cash and checks.

While most current office automation implementations focus on automating clerical activities in organizations, the real potential for this technology lies in supporting professionals and executives.

Efforts to implement TPS can greatly affect the task and social relationships that bind an organization's members into productive work units.

DISCUSSION QUESTIONS

1. Provide examples of some transactions common to both a hospital and a manufacturing firm. Provide examples of transactions that would be observed in one but not the other.

2. For the examples given in question 1, list some data items that might be captured to describe the transaction. Then illustrate how these data might be used in the future.

3. Describe some documents that might be produced by a TPS in a wholesale lumber firm, as well as some transaction listings that might be produced within the same firm.

4. Data entry operations can be greatly improved by eliminating some data entry steps. Consider, for example, the following accounts payable operation: invoices received from vendors are collected throughout the month in a file cabinet; at the end of the month, these invoices are copied onto coding sheets and then keypunched; the punched cards are copied onto magnetic tape, which is then used as an input file to the accounts payable program. Describe alternative data entry operations that might provide greater accuracy or timeliness.

5. Provide an example of an unobtrusive data entry procedure.

6. An electrical supply wholesaler might well have a vendor file on its computer system. Describe some applications that might use sequential access in retrieving data from this file, as well as applications that might use direct access.

7. What is the "overflow" problem associated with direct access methods? A similar problem arises when "volatile" sequential or ISAM files are stored on disks. (A volatile file is one that experiences a high rate of record addition or deletion.) Propose a strategy for handling this second type of overflow.

8. What is a "turnaround" document? Give some examples.

9. State employment agencies match the unemployed with employers who need workers. An important data file for such an organization would be the "open job" file. Describe procedures for updating this file for each of the three processing environments: batch entry, batch processing; on-line entry, batch processing; and on-line entry, immediate processing.

10. What is "recognition delay"? Using the example of a state employment agency, how might recognition delay be reduced for the open job file?

11. For each of the processing environments described in question 9, identify where data entry errors are likely to occur.

12. Would EFTS tend to be favored by large or small financial institutions? Why?

13. Why might the potential for high-loss incidents increase with EFTS?

14. Why is attention suddenly being paid to the office worker after years of neglect?

15. What impact do you think office automation will have on the role of the personal secretary?

16. Recent experiences indicate that many professionals and executives who have access to electronic mail systems do not use them. Others, however, use them extensively. Why is the reaction so mixed?

BRIEF CASES

1. *The State Motor Pool*

   Among the largest expenses of many state governments are those associated with providing state vehicles for government employees to use in performing their duties. In one midwestern state, rapid rises in oil prices and car maintenance costs led to an average annual increase of 27 percent in the State Motor Pool budget for the years 1976–80. To get a better handle on exactly where these rises were occurring, the state's information systems group was assigned to work with the State Motor Pool to design a vehicle information system. The purpose of the VIS was to collect data on operation and maintenance costs for each state-owned vehicle, store these data on the central computer facility, and produce appropriate management reports.

   Suggest a plausible data entry scheme for the VIS.

2. *Morningside Cereals*

   Toni Sellek had been a product manager at Morningside Cereals for over three years. Morningside was a rapidly growing manufacturer of natural foods specializing in breakfast and snack foods. Toni's current responsibilities centered on the firm's latest line of snack foods—products made from yogurt and cereals. While this line had just been introduced, it was being closely watched. The firm was in a minor cash squeeze and could not risk carrying a product that might take a year or two to take off.

   Two of Toni's concerns involved tracking the sales performance of these fifteen products across the firm's twenty-eight marketing regions and tracking the effectiveness of the various marketing programs directed toward these products. Toni had recently convinced her boss to allocate funds to develop information systems to support her department. Her first meeting with the systems analyst assigned to these projects ended with the analyst's saying that before their next meeting a week later, Toni should consider which type of processing environment (batch, on-line, or immediate) might be required with these two information systems.

   What environment should Toni choose?

3. *Hickory Manufacturing Company*

   Saul Rosen, production manager at Hickory Manufacturing Company, had worked his way up through the ranks over thirty-three years. While getting an industrial engineering degree at night over an eight-year period certainly did not hurt his career, the secret to his rise was tied to his willingness to roll up his sleeves and work on the shop floor whenever problems arose.

   Saul had just returned from a three-hour meeting of the firm's executive committee. The corporate planning group had given a presentation on the productivity gains that had been experienced since the installation of an office information system. The president had been impressed by the fact that the group had turned the corporate five-year plan around in six days when in the past this task had taken about three weeks. Each member of the committee had been told to investigate the potential for his or her own group to use office technologies. It was clear to Saul why the corporate planning group had been successful: its tasks consisted of examining the firm's costs and revenues, analyzing industry trends and competitors' moves, and writing reports. Office automation, however, seemed to have little to offer a work group such as Saul's, which was concerned with production schedules, inventory stockouts and excesses, machine breakdowns, and productivity on the shop floor.

Is Saul correct?

4. *Power King Tools*

Power King Tools was a large manufacturer of power tools for the home hobbyist. One of its major worries was undiscovered manufacturing defects. Even though its internal inspection effort was stringent, the potential for hazardous defects always exists. For this reason, the firm had recently approved a project to develop a customer quality assurance information system. The aim of this information system was to capture information on consumer injuries so major defects could be discovered early in any of their products (currently numbering 264).

This customer quality assurance program was supported by a clever marketing scheme in which customers reporting hazards received rebate coupons. Reports could be sent through the mail (forms were included in the product packings), made over a "hot line," or given to the dealer who sold the product (in this case the dealer would complete and send in a form). The volume of reports was quite erratic. On good weeks only twenty-five forms might be received by the marketing department, but on bad weeks 200 or more forms might be received. Luckily, the good weeks outnumbered the bad by a 10-to-1 margin.

One major design decision regarding this information system involved the length of the batching cycle (i.e., how frequently should the product defects file be updated). What might be an appropriate batching cycle?

NOTES

1. *MIS Week*, May 21, 1980.

2. K. L. Kraemer and K. W. Colton, "Policy, Values and EFT Research: Anatomy of a Research Agenda," *Communications of the ACM* 22(1979):660–71.

3. T. D. Sterling, "Consumer Difficulties with Computerized Transactions: An Empirical Investigation," *Communications of the ACM* 22(1979):283–89.

4. R. H. Long, "Public Protection and Education with EFT," *Communications of the ACM* 22(1979):648–54.

5. W. Schatz, "EFT Is Alive and Well," *Datamation* 27(1981):76.

6. R. P. Uhlig, D. J. Farber, and J. H. Bair, *The Office of the Future* (New York: North-Holland, 1979).

7. L. C. Bracker and B. R. Konsynski, "A Specification Methodology for Office Processes," working paper, Department of MIS, University of Arizona, 1980.

8. C. D. Sadleir, "Office of the Future—New Challenges for Operational Research," *OMEGA* 8(1980):21–28.

9. Uhlig *et al.* (1979).

10. H. L. Poppel, "The Automated Office Moves In," *Datamation* 25(1979):73–77.

11. Sadleir (1980).

12. J. C. Burns, "The Office in the 1980s," in *Information Systems in the 1980s* (Cambridge, Mass.: Arthur D. Little, 1978), pp. 21–34.

13. R. R. Panko, "Integration in Office Automation," *Proceedings of the 14th Hawaii International Conference in Systems Science* (Western Periodicals Co., 1981), pp. 685–89.

14. Sadleir (1980).

Emerging Information Resource Environments 6

THE DRAMATIC GAINS being experienced with information resources (decreasing hardware costs, increased availability of quality software packages, and improved ability to integrate CBIS within and among organizations) are causing major shifts in the way TPS are being used to perform and support organizational activities. The more visible of these trends include the following:

- Reducing the number of paper-based transactions,
- Capturing data as close as possible to their source,
- Mirroring the interdependent nature of organizational activities, and
- Having end-users rather than computer personnel accept responsibility for data entry.

So these developments can be better understood and managed, two key concepts—*data bases* and *distributed processing*—will be discussed.

While the opportunities provided by these technological developments most directly affect TPS, their potential is realized only when viewed from the perspective of IRS and DSS applications. For this reason this chapter serves as a bridge between Chapter 5, which discussed TPS issues, and Chapters 7 and 8, which will discuss IRS and DSS.

While the enhanced information environments provided through technological advances such as data bases and distributed processing have much to offer organizations, organizational risks increase unless steps are taken (1) to counter threats to data integrity brought about by growing accessibility of data files and programs, lack of visible audit trails, and dispersal of information resource responsibilities, and (2) to protect the organization from a deepening dependence on computer-based technologies. A number of related topics involving *computer security* and *EDP auditing* suggest steps that can be taken to reduce these risks.

THE DATA BASE CONCEPT

The link between application programs and data files has historically been extremely tight. Each application typically accessed its own set of data files, with each data file being unique but related in context to others. Many data items, consequently, resided on multiple data files. Because of differing batching cycles associated with the applications, it was common for a data item to vary in value at one time across the numerous data files on which the item was maintained.

It is easy to see how such a situation arose. Consider the implementation of a new inventory application that requires transactional data previously not captured. To add these data to an existent inventory file would require modifying all the programs that used this file. As an organization's applications begin to share data, such modifications become time consuming and costly and allow errors to creep into previously correct programs.

Storing data across numerous files and tying the physical structure of data directly to its logical structure, however, presents numerous difficulties, the more important of which relate to storage cost, data file maintenance, and program modification. Clearly, maintaining multiple copies of data items increases the total amount of data to be stored and the associated costs: more volumes (disk packs, tape reels, etc.), more physical space to store the volumes, and management of the file inventory. Less obvious but just as troublesome are the difficulties that arise in efforts to maintain consistency across data files, many of which hold different versions of the same data item. Finally, if the physical and logical structures of data must exactly match, changes in either data structure or program structure are likely to require that the other be modified accordingly.

Advantages of the Data Base Approach

The *data base concept* evolved as a means of overcoming these problems. When stored data are organized in a data base, ideally only one copy of each data item is maintained in storage. Each item is treated as a unique entity, which is associated with other data items through sets of *relations*. Each relation reflects the logical structure of a set of data expected in a particular application program. Consequently, it is through these relations, which must also be maintained in the data base, that application programs access individual data items and, hence, data files. What is desired is a *state of independence between data and programs*. When achieved, this independence should provide a store of organizational data that is shareable, accessible, easily enlarged, and of high quality, and a

TABLE 6.1
Advantages of Adopting the Data Base Concept

Data	Programs	Operations
Shareability	Less maintenance	Shorter set-up time
Easier access	Easier, faster maintenance	Less human intervention
Sophisticated access	Easier, faster development	Fewer scheduling delays
Easier to maintain		
Consistency		
Integrity		
Security		
Flexibility		
Fewer storage devices		

software environment in which it is relatively easy to modify or enhance application programs. These and other advantages of adopting the data base concept are listed in Table 6.1.

Data Base Technology

These benefits are made possible by advances in software technology that provide an additional level of software between the operating system and application programs. The role of this software interface, referred to as a *data base management system* (DBMS), is pictured in Figure 6.1. The data item relationships must be formally defined and are maintained in a *data dictionary*, which also describes other attributes of each data item (such as name, current usage, access limits, storage media, format, legal values, and retention period) and is extremely useful as a reference aid disclosing what data are available for use. Most DBMS provide a *data description language* (DDL) through which the data dictionary is established. Some DDL are so convenient and easy to use that end-users can directly establish the data dictionary. The DBMS itself performs most of the processing necessary in creating, maintaining, and securing the data base and in accessing individual data items or sets of related data items. These complex procedures, consequently, are for the most part invisible to both application programmers and end-users. Programmers interact with the DBMS through a *data manipulation language,* while end-users interact through a *query language* or a *report writer*.

As might be expected, DBMS tend to be very sophisticated. Their popularity, however, has led many vendors to develop software packages that are readily available in the marketplace. Because of the one-to-one

FIGURE 6.1
The Data Base Environment

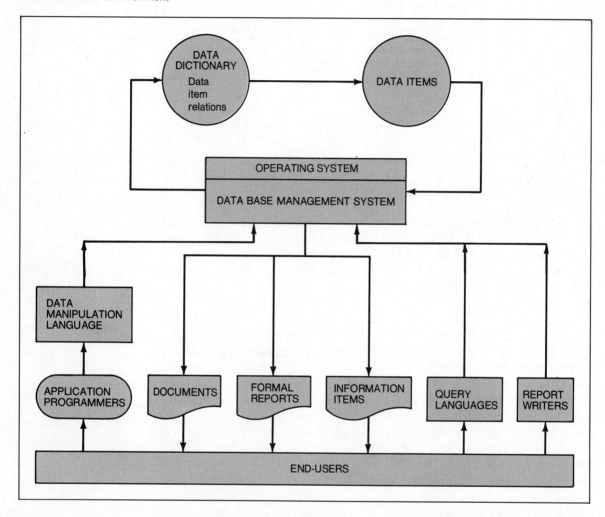

relationship between a DBMS and a computer's operating system, organizations with less popular mainframes will have fewer DBMS to choose among. Organizations using minicomputers, small business computers, or microcomputers will also have difficulty locating DBMS offering a full range of capabilities because of primary memory limitations. The cost disparity in DBMS is quite large, as packages are available for purchase prices from under $1,000 to over $200,000.[1] The cost differences primarily reflect differences in DBMS characteristics, the more important of which are shown in Table 6.2. A wide variance can also be observed in the extent to which data–program independence is actually achieved.[2]

Data Administration

Simply acquiring a DBMS, however, does not result in adoption of the data base concept. A DBMS is simply a tool, which to be truly effective should follow a policy decision to treat data as a valuable resource to be shared throughout an organization. When this occurs, the individuals and departments traditionally responsible for managing data (i.e., those who collected the data) can no longer exercise control.[3] What results is the emergence of a new organizational function—*data base administration*. Control of data is given to the *data base administrator*, whose responsibilities include defining data, defining and creating a data base, maintaining the data base, selecting a DBMS, ensuring data security, handling end-user interface concerns, and monitoring data base activity. What is most interesting about this position is that the incumbent needs to understand organizational issues as well as technical issues, and in many instances the individual selected has emerged from a managerial rather than computer-related segment of the organization.

While many organizations claim to have adopted the data base concept, few have truly reoriented their policies toward the data resource. One recent study, for example, found that only 28 percent of the firms studied had created a data base administration function, that even with these firms the data base administrator's role was primarily technical, and that, while most firms surveyed had acquired a DBMS, the packages were not extensively used.[4]

TABLE 6.2
Data Base Management System Characteristics

Hardware/Software/Service	Performance
Computer systems on which package runs	Number of storage devices handled
Operating systems on which package runs	Types of storage devices handled
Software maintenance agreement	Number of terminals handled
Hardware/software backup agreement	Batch, on-line, or immediate processing
Active user group	Types of file structures handled
Types of documentation provided	Types of access methods allowed
Types of training provided	Types of security mechanisms
	Report-generating capability
	Retrieval capability
	Data definition capability

Suitability of the Data Base Approach

A practical explanation for the seeming reluctance of many organizations to embrace the data base concept and its concomitant potential gains are the rather significant costs that must be incurred: hardware purchases (main memory, a large processor, additional disk units), acquisition of a DBMS, upgrading of the technical staff, training of programmers and end-users, conversion of data files and application programs, disruptions of organizational activities during changeover, disruptions in organizational communication flows, and loss of individual control over data. The decision to move toward the data base concept cannot be taken lightly, but must follow a careful and thorough analysis. While this decision depends on many factors, CBIS environments with the following attributes generally benefit from adoption of the data base approach:

- Extensive sharing of data files,
- Concurrent access to data files,
- Complex file structures,
- Concern for security and backup of data files,
- On-line update and retrieval of data files,
- Ad hoc retrieval from data files,
- Diversity in data file users and usages, and
- Frequent modifications of application software.

DISTRIBUTED DATA PROCESSING

For the first two decades computers existed, economics favored centralizing information resources. *Centralization* here refers to the existence of a single organizational computer center providing information services through a large computer system and supporting staff and facilities. As shown in Figure 6.2, this in no way precludes accessing the single computer system from remote end-user locations. All processing and data storage, however, are centrally handled. Table 6.3 lists the major advantages of centralized computing.

While the economics favored centralization, this strategy was not without its disadvantages (listed in more detail in Table 6.3): end-users, being isolated from the CBIS staff and CBIS policymakers, often had little input in decisions on the best way to use computer resources; as all applications contended for a single computing system, response times were often long and conflicts over priority usage were common; with only one processor, there was no in-house backup in case of system failure; and there was little flexibility in expanding the computer system.

FIGURE 6.2
Centralized Computing Environment

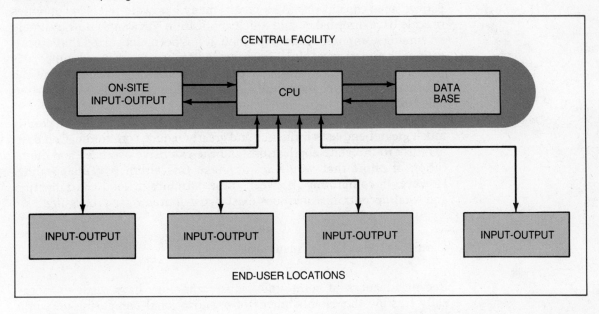

CENTRAL FACILITY

ON-SITE INPUT-OUTPUT ⟷ CPU ⟷ DATA BASE

INPUT-OUTPUT   INPUT-OUTPUT   INPUT-OUTPUT   INPUT-OUTPUT

END-USER LOCATIONS

TABLE 6.3
Characteristics of Centralized Computing

Advantages	Disadvantages
Economies of scale	*Diseconomies of scale*
More computing power for same financial investment	Large investment in one computer configuration
Less overhead for facilities, administration, and technical staff	Inability to react quickly to technological changes
Staff specialization	More overhead for hardware and operating system for many applications
Operations	*Operations*
More sophisticated, versatile applications	Isolation of end-users from computer services
Easier integration of applications	Computer personnel's lack of familiarity with end-user needs
Control over hardware, software, processing, expenses, standards, priorities, etc.	Response delays in servicing end-users
Hardware–software compatibility	No in-house backup

Three developments over the last decade have significant implications for the economics of computing. First, technological advances have drastically reduced the cost of computer systems while increasing their performance capabilities. As a result, many hardware-related economies of scale have diminished and much application software is now available on smaller computer systems. Second, it has been recognized that organizational performance often improves when computer-based support is provided where organizational activity occurs. Third, the portion of the information resource budget allocated to communications cost has risen substantially with centralized computing.

While *total decentralization* of information resources would permit much greater end-user influence and greatly reduce communication cost, inability to integrate applications and the extensive overhead and duplication of effort that would result make this alternative unappealing. However, a compromise between these extremes of total centralization and total decentralization does exist—*distributed data processing.*

Distributed Processing Advantages

Recent advances in communications technology have made economically feasible the establishment of organizational computing networks that provide the benefits of both centralization and decentralization. Such a network is pictured in Figure 6.3.

Distributed data processing entails the physical distribution of information resources (such as CPUs, storage devices, and input–output devices) and of information processing operations (such as data entry and file maintenance), throughout the organization. By servicing many information processing tasks locally but providing more powerful or specialized processing capabilities at central facilities, the system can meet the following interrelated goals:

- Improve end-user service by processing applications directly at the local site,
- Enable organization-wide applications to be processed at a central facility,
- Integrate applications by enabling computer systems, and hence applications, to communicate with one another, and
- Provide for a critical mass of personnel skills by maintaining a central staff of specialists.

As the most appropriate design for distributed networks depends on organization-specific attributes (e.g., size, geography, corporate structure, industry, and computer-based applications), it is impossible to prescribe an ideal, or even typical, configuration. It is fairly safe to surmise, nonethe-

FIGURE 6.3
Distributed Computing Environment

FIGURE 6.3 Distributed Computing Environment

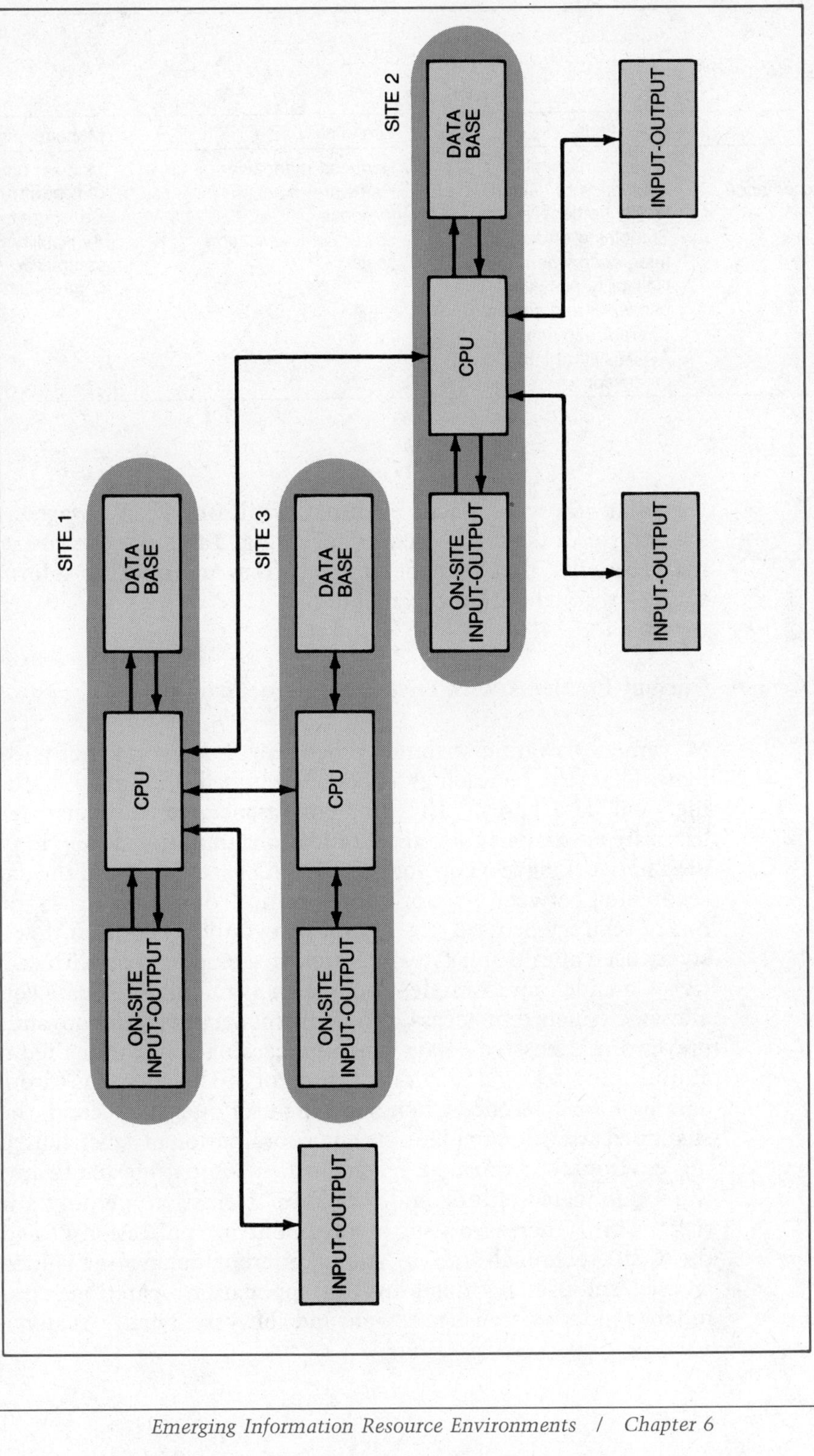

TABLE 6.4
Advantages of Distributed Data Processing

End-User	Operations	Economic	Management
User control	"Failsoft" capability	Reduced manpower needs	Modular upgrading
Enhanced user acceptance	Avoidance of central	Hardware matched	of hardware
Less paperwork	facility bottleneck	to needs	Configuration flexibility
Improved user access	Smoothing of demand	Lower communication	Availability of
Fast response	Integration when needed	costs	centralized planning,
	Reliability (simpler		control, and coordination
	hardware and software)		
	Shared resources		
	Availability of large		
	processor when needed		

less, that *all* organizations eventually will find it advantageous to adopt some form of distributed data processing. Table 6.4 categorizes the primary benefits that may be realized from distributing information resources throughout an organization.

Current Problems with Distributed Processing

Movement toward distributed processing, however, is not without problems. First, the technology *is* being stretched in terms of both networking[5] and data bases.[6] The problems associated with distributing data bases are particularly severe. Should each computer system in the distributed network have a copy of the full data base, or should the data base be segmented between network nodes so no redundancy exists, or should a mixed strategy be used (e.g., duplicating only sets of data that are extensively used at multiple sites)? Difficulties tend to arise with each alternative. Consider, for example, issues such as maintaining data consistency; allowing concurrent access; providing for security, backup, and recovery; preventing excessive delays when processing applications requiring data at multiple sites; and providing a directory to locate items throughout the data base for reference when handling user queries. Second, the need for sustained attention to planning and coordination of a distributed computing environment must be recognized. Incompatible hardware and software, duplicated efforts, and overcomputerization are only a few of the risks. Third, increased user involvement in application design requires the CBIS technical staff to adopt different behavioral values, and increased end-user responsibility for application operation requires more reliable and easy-to-use hardware and software. Finally, many costs associated with distributed processing are hidden[7] (e.g., increased involvement of users, program conversion, supplies, facilities, utilities, insurance, and physical security). Overall computer expenses may well increase with distributed data processing.

Suitability of Distributed Processing

As with the data base concept, distributed data processing is more appropriate in some organizational environments than others. Organizations characterized by functionally independent, geographically dispersed, relatively unsophisticated applications requiring fast response times are good candidates for an extensive distribution of information resources. Likely "locally handled" applications include order or client processing, shop floor control, and inventory control.

This discussion of distributed data processing has been couched in terms of a single organization, i.e., intraorganizational networking. Communications technologies can also be applied to interorganizational and international networking. An example of the three forms of computer networking should illustrate the variety of capabilities possible.

By installing and connecting terminals in over a hundred offices, Purolator Courier Corporation (a package-express firm) is using *intraorganizational networking* to quickly and economically transmit interoffice messages, alert offices to shipments, and track misrouted shipments.[8] In the future, it expects to support order handling through these same terminals. An *interorganizational networking* relationship between Sears and one of its suppliers, DeSota, Inc., has benefited both.[9] Sears' computer transmits purchase orders directly to DeSota's computer. As a result, Sears has greatly reduced its inventories by shortening delivery time, and DeSota has improved its manufacturing planning ability and cash flow. Finally, 3M Europe is employing *international networking* to link the computer systems of its fifteen independently operated subsidiaries.[10] The firm expects to enhance corporate control in finance, accounting, sales, shipping, marketing, distribution, and manufacturing by overcoming problems with high information processing costs and duplicate efforts, poor intercompany information flow, and overloaded computer centers with little backup capabilities. When information networking expands to the international domain, additional concerns must be faced. The political, economic, and ethical issues associated with international data flows are just beginning to surface and to be addressed by multinational corporations and governments. Considerable effort will probably be required over the next decade if these issues are to be resolved.

COMPUTER SECURITY AND EDP AUDITING

As discussed in earlier chapters, CBIS provide innumerable opportunities to improve an organization's internal functioning and to enhance its products or services. That CBIS also expose organizations to significant risks as they become increasingly dependent on information resources must be recognized as well. Most typically experienced through interrupted operations or a loss of assets, these dangers arise for the following reasons:

- Large, complex CBIS tend to be fragile, difficult to back up, and difficult to understand.
- Large, sophisticated corporate data bases can be accessed by knowledgeable criminals or naive end-users.
- On-line environments permit access to operating applications (which often involve one-step, invisible actions) and do not automatically provide for an audit trail.
- With data files replacing accounting ledgers, CBIS specialists, typically not as sensitive as accountants to the need for internal controls, become responsible for the integrity of organizational financial reporting.

Increasing the potential for disaster are the rapid rates of technological change being experienced with information resources and the current shortage of CBIS specialists.

Threats to CBIS security fall into four broad categories. First, many forms of *disasters* can destroy equipment, facilities, and program or data files. These include natural disasters, fires, power failures, and acts of sabotage (bombing, application of a magnetic field, programmer or operator actions), among others. Not only may such disasters disrupt normal operations, but the cost and time required to recreate program and data files can be exorbitant. Most disaster losses are associated with fires. Computer facilities are typically cramped and full of combustible material, and even small fires are accompanied by elements that can cause significant damage to electrical components, such as toxic fumes, smoke, heat, water, and high humidity.

Second, the potential for *errors*—be they associated with data entry, computer operations, programmer mistakes, or hardware—must constantly be faced. Even minor errors may have massive repercussions. For example, an operator error that causes a bank to miss a Federal Reserve collection deadline could prevent the use of hundreds of millions of dollars for a day! Figure 6.4 shows twelve control points that must be checked to detect information processing errors.

Third, the last decade has seen large increases in reported *computer crimes*. Computer crimes generally fall into two categories: fraud (the

FIGURE 6.4
CBIS Control Points

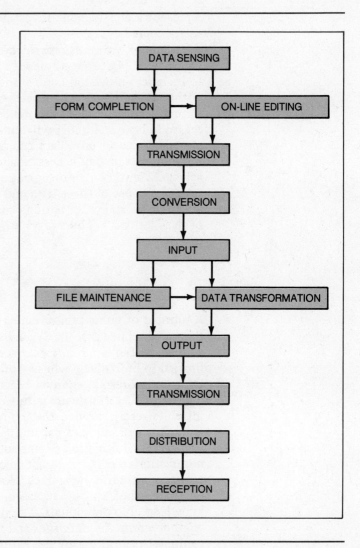

diversion of financial assets through the manipulation of programs, data files, or input data) and theft (the unauthorized appropriation or use of computer resources, programs, and data files). While all organizations are susceptible to computer crimes, financial institutions have been most vulnerable. The most likely targets in the future, however, are insurance companies, pension funds, investment houses, government agencies, and the many small firms from all industries that are making their initial acquisitions of information resources.[11] Theft of software has proven particularly perplexing, as most "business" software, which can represent a considerable investment, cannot be copyrighted but can be easily copied.

Finally, *information privacy* has been recognized as a basic right of a U.S. citizen.[12] Congress amended the Freedom of Information Act in 1974 to include a provision controlling access to personal information stored within CBIS by federal agencies and their contractors. The act provides for civil remedies and criminal penalties when discrepancies arise with regard to how and under what authority data are collected, how data are stored and used, how data can be disclosed to a third party, and how individuals can gain access to and request corrections in data on themselves. Essentially, an organization collecting data about citizens is borrowing the use of those data and must protect them from misuse. With many states and other nations enacting their own legislation, the threat of class action suits over privacy issues is affecting more and more organizations.

Security Measures

A number of protection or detection mechanisms are available to meet these and related threats. Seven basic categories of security measures are defined in Table 6.5. *Physical* access to information resources must be limited to individuals whose work requires direct contact. Additionally, information resources must be protected from natural as well as man-made disasters. *Hardware* failures can be prevented (or their effects minimized) directly through the hardware devices themselves or through a redundancy or fall-back capability built into a configuration. By inserting *software* modules into systems software (operating systems, DBMS, communications packages, etc.), one can monitor and selectively control access to information resources. However, since software mechanisms *are* programs, they can be accessed, analyzed, and then circumvented by knowledgeable individuals. The need to keep a tight physical inventory of all *program and data files* and to back up such files should be clear. If computer *operations* are not scrutinized for security gaps, they can provide innumerable opportunities for security violations. Attention to security gaps (e.g., passwords or account numbers on printouts placed in trash receptacles or left on unattended CRT screens), along with other mechanisms, can prevent many violations. *Software development*, if properly controlled, can prevent acts of omission and thwart acts of commission. Finally, *administrative procedures* provide the first line of defense against security threats. Many major violations have occurred solely because of inadequate attention to the assignment and supervision of tasks.

While most organizations recognize the need for security mecha-

TABLE 6.5
Security Mechanisms

Physical	Hardware	Software	Program and Data Files
Access to facilities	Multiple sites	Monitors	Multiple copies
Badges	Backup components	"Logon"	Off-site storage
Voice and fingerprints	Duplicate circuitry	File access and use	Inventories
Alarms	Read-only memory	Abnormal transactions	Dummy entries for entrapment
Site location and construction	Self-diagnostic circuitry	Shrinkage	
Fire protection	Preventive maintenance	Errors	
Air conditioning	Encryption circuitry	Volumes	
Uninterruptible power supply		Amounts	
Insurance		Access schemes	
		Encryption schemes	

Operations	Software Development	Administrative
Input–output controls	Standards	Authorization schemes
Processing controls	Documentation	Security classifications
Recovery procedures	Change control	Separation of duties
Console interaction		Supervision of operations
Logs		Rotation of personnel
Limited		Background checks
Changing access means		Removal of disgruntled employees
Keys		
Passwords		
Phone numbers		
Paper shredders		
Memory and screen blanking		

nisms, organizational responsibility for computer security is often fragmented among information resource, staff, and line management. However, the need to view security as a unified problem is increasingly recognized. Consequently, some organizations have established an independent *internal auditing* function that judges the adequacy of security and recommends improvements. For such an auditing group to maintain its objectivity, implementation and maintenance of security mechanisms should remain the responsibility of those organizational units that have authority over the resources involved.

The Role of the External Auditor

A related concern involves the role of the external auditor in computer security. Many CPAs feel that external auditors are not responsible for assessing computer security, that their sole obligation is to ensure generally accepted accounting practices are being followed in reporting financial statements. A series of court cases throughout the 1970s, however, resulted in decisions significantly extending the CPA's liabilities in computer security and drastically limiting the extent to which "due diligence" and adherence to generally accepted accounting principles may serve as a legal defense.[13,14] Currently, the external auditor's liability extends to computer security issues if the threat might materially affect the financial capacity, and hence financial reporting, of the firm.

Traditionally, the external auditor has assessed the integrity of computer-based financial reporting by auditing "around the computer." These techniques involve examining the inputs (transactions) and outputs (entries) for correctness, and thereby inferring the accuracy of the internal processing. While this is a low-cost approach requiring little technical sophistication, the inferences regarding processing integrity have little validity. A much preferred approach involves auditing "through the computer." By examining inputs and internal processing, one *can* make valid inferences about outputs. Examples of this approach include integrated test facilities using test data and dummy files to evaluate processing programs, special audit programs that look for and report on unusual conditions in corporate data files, and special audit programs that run parallel to the processing programs.[15] The best but most difficult and time-consuming technique, however, involves verifying the program code. Even here problems may arise, as the audited programs may not be the ones actually used. A developing trend finds the external auditor deeply involved with software development. This may eventually result in one or more of the following scenarios becoming commonplace:

- Inclusion of an external auditor on the CBIS development team to assess a design's integrity,
- Specification of software standards that ensure system integrity,
- Inclusion of audit procedures within DBMS, and
- Development of systems with embedded auditing mechanisms, such as collections of audit data bases and interactive audit software.

CONCLUSION

Continued advances in information technologies—particularly those related to information networking, microcomputer software, device intelligence, and natural language query interfaces—should hasten the adoption by organizations of information resource environments emphasizing data base structures and distributed processing. The initial impact of such capabilities will most likely center on TPS. The major benefits of such environments, however, will arise through the provisioning of higher-level support of organizational activity by IRS and DSS that are readily accessible and convenient to use.

Such environments, however, can inflict severe damage on an organization if proper controls are not established. Accessibility and convenience are two-edged swords, particularly in a CBIS that is extensively integrated and performs crucial organizational functions. While data bases and distributed processing disperse information resources throughout an organization, their effective use demands considerable organization-wide planning and control. This is perhaps most clearly seen in the need to develop organization-wide security policies.

Computer security can be enhanced in a number of ways. However, it is not economical to provide a totally secure computer system. In fact, it is impossible—disasters will occur that have not been prepared for previously and determined intruders, if they are technically capable, will be able to bypass many of the administrative and software security mechanisms that have been installed. Most computer crimes, for example, are detected by accident or chance. The best most organizations can do is to assess all security risks, install security mechanisms where risk and expected loss are highest, and ensure that all the low-cost mechanisms possible have been installed.

KEY ISSUES

The data base approach can overcome the following problems associated with the handling of data: redundant storage of data items, inconsistencies among various versions of the same data item, high direct storage costs, and high software development and maintenance costs.

By means of a data base management system, data can be managed so each data item is ideally stored only once and data and program structures are independent.

Many software vendors offer data base management systems.

To fully adopt the data base approach, data must be managed similarly to other critical organizational resources. Often a data administration function is established to handle these responsibilities.

Large financial and human investments are required to adopt the data base approach. Many organizations, however, can make effective use of the information resource without adopting the data base approach to data management.

Prior to the early 1970s, the economics of computing favored the centralization of computer resources.

With the cost reductions and performance gains observed with computer systems over the last ten years, the economics of computing have changed so that distributed processing (the shared use of processors and storage devices dispersed throughout an organization) is a viable alternative for many organizations.

Distributed technologies are being stretched, particularly with regard to networking and distributed data bases.

To be successfully adopted, distributed processing demands extensive planning and coordination.

Many hidden expenses can exist with distributed processing.

Significant organizational risks in terms of interrupted operations and asset losses arise whenever information technologies are employed to perform or support organizational activities.

The four major types of computer security threats are disasters, errors, computer crimes, and insensitivity to information privacy.

Numerous measures exist to overcome these security threats. Some are simple and inexpensive, while others are sophisticated and expensive. To determine which measures can be economically justified, comprehensive risk analysis programs should be conducted.

Responsibility for assessing security risks is increasingly being given to an independent internal audit function.

External auditors are being held more accountable for assessing the security of a firm's computer systems, along with maintaining the integrity of the firm's financial position.

DISCUSSION QUESTIONS

1. Explain why software development and maintenance costs might be expected to be higher with a file management approach, as opposed to a data base approach to data management.
2. Describe a situation in which two or more versions of a data item stored on a firm's files might be inconsistent.
3. What is a "data dictionary"? Using the example of the collection of data used by a bank to maintain customer checking and savings accounts, identify some data items likely to be stored. Then provide a comprehensive description of each data item.
4. What is the difference between a "query language" and a "report writer"?
5. Where in an organization's hierarchy should the data administration function be located?
6. Illustrate the concurrent access of data. How is this aided by adopting the data base approach to data management?
7. What are some disadvantages of centralized computing for applications run from remote locations?
8. Discuss the political implications of moving from centralized computing to distributed processing.
9. Derive a decision framework for deciding how best to distribute and then manage a data base.
10. Why are transborder data flows a sensitive geopolitical concern?
11. Why are so few computer crimes prosecuted? What are the implications of the low prosecution rate?
12. List those organizations that have information about you on their computer systems. Could any of this information be damaging if it were misused or otherwise allowed to get into the "wrong hands"?
13. Why might auditing firms resist enlarging their responsibilities for assessing the integrity of an organization's information systems?
14. Discuss various ways external auditors might become involved in the software development process. Which do you feel are most likely to occur?

BRIEF CASES

1. *Southside Auto Parts*
   Sam Hellick had just closed the biggest deal of his life. The owner of the city's largest auto parts company (eight branches spread out over a sixty-mile radius that included the entire metropolitan area) had decided to retire and sell out, and Sam was able to come up with the financial backing to purchase the operation. Instead of running one retail store, Sam now found himself with nine retail locations. In addition, his customer base had radically changed. Previously, Southside Auto Parts had primarily dealt with a walk-in trade. However, over 60 percent of the volume of the acquired company had been with small auto repair shops. Not only was this a highly

competitive market, but two new competitors had recently opened (one locally owned, the other a national franchise).

Sam felt this was the right time to finally computerize his business. With nine locations, he clearly had the volume to purchase his own system. Visits from a number of vendors, however, had left him perplexed. Everyone agreed that he needed to automate the basic transaction processing applications (accounting, accounts receivable, accounts payable, inventory, sales analysis, and payroll), but after this agreement ended. One vendor said he needed a separate computer at each location. Two others said he needed only one computer. Another agreed he needed one computer, but recommended he buy one or two terminals for each location. Finally, two vendors brought up the idea of a "distributed system." It was clear Sam could not make this decision on his own, but would have to find a consultant to advise him.

What computer system alternatives are available for a situation such as the one Sam Hellick faces? What are their relative advantages and disadvantages? What should he do?

2. *Bennison Construction Company*

Susan Allen, the recently appointed manager of Bennison's information system department, was putting the finishing touches on the expanded application portfolio she was preparing to present to the executive committee. Besides the project costing, scheduling, and control applications ordained by the executive committee, Susan believed anticipated benefits would more that justify three additional information systems: a cost forecasting system, an employee skills location system, and an equipment maintenance system. While all these information systems would not be implemented overnight, the entire portfolio, along with the already established accounting systems, represented an attractive information systems plan.

One major issue remained to be settled before the package was presented to the executive committee: Was this the time to implement a data base system? While additional expenses would be involved, it made sense to move this way now, rather than in five or ten years. If the data base approach was adopted now, no massive conversion effort (except for accounting applications) would be required. The critical concern, however, was whether a firm such as Bennison, with all its computing done at a central location, could justify adopting the data base approach to managing data.

Should Susan Allen's plan be devised along the lines of a data base approach to managing data?

3. *Mountain Community Bank*

Mountain Community Bank was a rapidly growing bank in one of the Rocky Mountain states. As with most successful banks, MCB recognized quite early that a critical factor in banking success is an efficient computer operation: the computer is a bank's production operation. Since MCB was based primarily in the state's three largest cities (separated by considerable distances), it had established three major computer centers. Each center handled all the computing needs of the branches in its region.

Many computing needs of the bank were met through remote terminals. With the bank's growth, the volume of traffic through each computer center was high. Occasionally response time was poor. Recently, however, Thomas McClinton, MCB's vice president for operations, felt that poor response time was becoming the norm. Tom was also well aware that it was commonly felt throughout the bank that "those computer jocks at the service center" had lost touch with (or had never understood) the needs of the bank's customers.

Tom was also familiar with the experiences of some major East and West Coast banks in distributed processing. While local processing might improve local services, certain efficiencies are lost. Also, effective deployment of distributed processing requires intensive planning and coordination not only by the computer group, but by all managers throughout a bank. The management team at MCB was not what Tom would consider "computer literate."

Looking to the future, Tom wondered what impact banking deregulation would have on the state's banking industry. Would the nature of competition change? What would be the effect of out-of-state banks' setting up branches? Would a distributed computing environment help MCB meet this new competition? One thing was clear. If MCB was going to distribute its computing, now was the time to do it. Market share was increasing and the bank was currently experiencing no major problems.

Is Tom really looking at a "night and day" situation? What are some of MCB's alternatives with regard to computing?

4. *Mercy Hospital*
The pace of work in the information systems department at Mercy Hospital had not seemed to lessen at all since Hank Thralpin had been appointed director six years ago. Hank had been brought in to straighten out the mess his predecessor had left on early retirement, and it was generally agreed that he had been successful. A series of major medical and administrative systems had been installed, a major hardware changeover had been carried out without any difficulty, and a hospital computer steering committee had been put in place. Hank was particularly proud of the hospital computer steering committee. When users were allowed to chart the future of computing at Mercy along with Hank and his key staff assistants, the entire procedure by which new systems were introduced had markedly improved.

Hank had just met with a senior member of the hospital's new audit firm. For the most part, the meeting went as Hank had anticipated it would. The auditor was overwhelmed by the progress Hank had made over the last six years. Well, almost overwhelmed. Things began to get a little tense when the auditor raised some questions about security. While Hank felt security might be an important concern for a bank or large manufacturing firm, he did not see it as a major concern for a hospital. His concern was with providing medical systems to save lives and with maintaining administrative systems to keep things running smoothly. It was not to play policeman. The auditor, however, did not see things in the same light. On leaving, she informed Hank that a complete report on the hospital's security program should be sent to her assistant.

What types of computer security risks exist within a hospital environment? Consider all four major types of risks: disasters, errors, computer crime, and insensitivity to information privacy.

NOTES

1. R. C. Sprowls, *Management Data Bases* (Santa Barbara, Calif.: Wiley/Hamilton, 1976).

2. G. M. Scott, "A Data Base for Your Company," *California Management Review* 19(1976):68–78.

3. R. M. Curtice, *Planning for Data Base Systems* (Wellesley, Mass.: QED Information Sciences, 1978).

4. I. B. McCririck and R. C. Goldstein, "What Do Data Administrators Really Do?" *Datamation* 26(1980):131–34.

5. J. C. Emery, "Managerial and Economic Issues in Distributed Computing," paper presented at IFIPS Congress '77, Toronto, 1977.

6. G. L. Powers, "Developing Your Distributed Data Base," *ComputerWorld* 15(1981):ID33–ID38.

7. K. M. Sullivan, "Does Distributed Processing Pay Off?" *Datamation* 26(1980):192–96.

8. *Information Systems News*, March 24, 1980.

9. *Information Systems News*, January 14, 1980.

10. *Information Systems News*, January 14, 1980.

11. M. G. Simkin, "Computer Crime: Lessons from the 1970s, Directions for the 1980s," *Proceedings of the 14th Hawaii International Conference on Systems Science* (Western Periodicals Co., 1981), pp. 709–16.

12. P. W. Howerton, "Privacy, Security and Auditing of Automated Systems," in W. W. Cotterman, J. D. Cougar, N. L. Enger, and F. Harold (eds.), *Systems Analysis and Design: A Foundation for the 1980s* (New York: Elsevier North-Holland, 1981).

13. Simkin (1981).

14. J. O. Mason, Jr., and J. J. Davies, "Legal Implications of EDP Deficiencies," *CPA Journal* 47(1977):21–24.

15. J. I. Cash, Jr., A. D. Bailey, Jr., and A. B. Whinston, "A Survey of Techniques for Auditing EDP-Based Accounting Information Systems," *Accounting Review* 52(1977):813–32.

Information Reporting Systems 7

ORGANIZATIONS WERE described in Chapter 3 as purposeful social systems striving to accomplish certain aims. However, numerous forces inhibit the realization of those intentions:

- Environmental changes as well as unexpected problems continually arise.
- Organizational subsystems often acquire vested interests far removed from organization-wide interests.
- The degree of coordination required to tie together interdependent but differentiated subsystems may be excessive.
- Errors always arise in communicating and executing organizational "purpose".

Consequently, organizational *direction* and *redirection* must be constantly attended to if organizational aims are to be achieved.

A simple illustration of how direction can be provided for any system is shown in Figure 7.1. Directives are prescribed for the system's processors by a *planning* function indicating how and when inputs are to be transformed into outputs. Concurrently, a *control* function can monitor system behavior (statuses and flow rates), providing feedback on how well these directives are being met. The arrows in Figure 7.1 going to and from the planning and control functions represent planning and control *information*. Essentially, the planning function plots a future direction for the system, while the control function assesses whether that direction is being maintained, whether the direction remains appropriate, and which corrective actions are needed when redirection is required.

Consider, for example, an interstate trucking firm. Considerable direction must be provided about truck, driver, and cargo availabilities and subsequent routing assignments. Without suitable direction (and redirection), organizational aims will probably not be met. Many things can dis-

FIGURE 7.1
Means for Providing System Direction

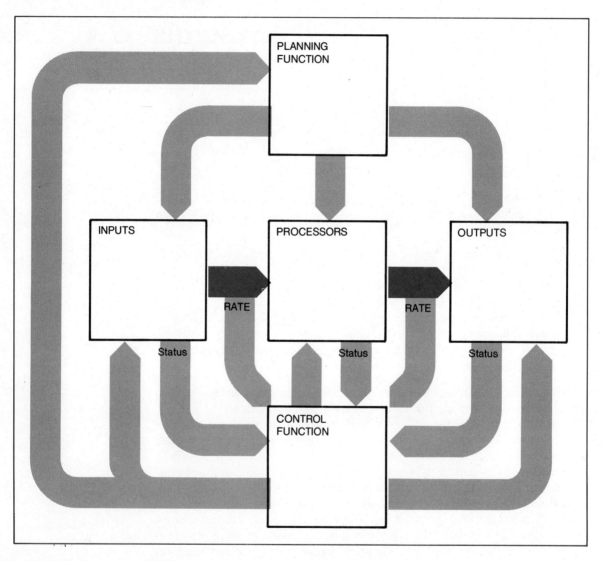

rupt what might otherwise have been an effective operation, including breakdowns, bad weather, and delays in preparing clients' cargoes for shipment. Through a constant monitoring of drivers, trucks, and clients, however, problems can be recognized and responded to (and opportunities exploited) without serious disruptions in operations.

The CBIS support systems known as *information reporting systems* (IRS) are used to provide such direction in organizations. An IRS cannot support the situation-specific activities of organizational members; rather, it induces desired behaviors by providing cues, by directing attention, by reviewing past performance, and by raising questions.[1,2] While such systems perform best in environments that are simple, static, and routine, IRS can also support activities of complex, dynamic organizational environments. For example, certain activities in all organizations tend to be well defined and repetitious, and variation in many organizational activities, while unpredictable, can be bounded. All organizational activities can be forecast, though poorly in many instances.

A key IRS characteristic prohibiting its use in situational support is that input data, procedures, and decision rules incorporated within processing programs, as well as output information, are *predefined*. The IRS users must specify their precise needs in advance. These needs are then reflected in the software that is developed or acquired, and any changes in the needs require that the software be modified or replaced (a step often requiring considerable delay and expense). Since the technology required to develop IRS is well understood and readily available and most organizational needs can be met at least partially by IRS, even with this limitation IRS currently account for most of the CBIS used in organizations for managerial and staff support.

Three basic reporting environments are observed with IRS. *Periodic* reporting involves the distribution of reports to individuals or groups of individuals at regular intervals. Examples include quarterly financial reports, monthly sales analyses, weekly expense reports, and monthly analyses of profit contributions of specific products or services. *Exception* reporting involves distributing reports to individuals or groups of individuals only when reports are triggered by a decision rule embedded in the processing program. Examples include listings of late shipments for the previous month (no report is sent if no shipments were late), notifications that inventory levels are dangerously low, and reports issued when maintenance expenses exceed a given amount. *Demand* reporting involves distributing reports only when they have been specifically requested. Examples include sales forecasts for particular product lines, analyses of wages and salaries for a personnel director, and detailed breakdowns of operating costs.

Each of these reporting environments provides a unique information context. Periodic reports tell organizational members which issues demand constant attention and serve as a ready information source for these issues. On the other hand, as the information being produced may not always be needed when the report is received, such reports may be viewed by some as not very useful. The costs of periodic reporting (processing, paper distribution, disruption, etc.) can become high relative to the benefits gained by organizational members unless the relevance of these reports is regularly assessed. Exception reports, which can meet 80–90% of an organization's IRS needs,[3] are not expected, and hence can very effectively trigger organizational actions. While the operating costs of exception reports are less than those of periodic reports, considerable effort must be devoted to assessing the meaningfulness of the decision rules that trigger reports. Even with well-designed exception reporting systems, much beneficial information is often not produced because of the decision rules being applied. Demand reports, while having extremely low operation costs, may never be demanded! If used effectively, however, demand reports can provide extremely useful information to organizational members facing complex but routine decision tasks.

In this chapter the purpose and potential of IRS will be examined. The chapter begins with an introduction to basic planning and control notions and continues with suggestions for how CBIS can best support these organizational functions. It concludes with an examination of the concept of management information and its presentation within IRS.

ORGANIZATIONAL PLANNING

Planning involves deciding on organizational objectives, strategies (directions, actions, resource allocations, etc.) to achieve the objectives, and goals that meaningfully represent the objectives. Basically, the aim is to develop and maintain an understanding of an organization and its environment so opportunities can be identified and exploited and problems can be foreseen and resolved.

For any organization facing a complex and uncertain environment to be successful, planning must be handled well. However, planning may be the most difficult task performed in organizations. Not only does it require skills, such as creativity and synthesis, that many individuals have not fully developed, but it is often preempted by current operating problems because of the tendency of many organizational reward systems to emphasize short-term performance. The gains that may be achieved by supporting planning efforts through CBIS are consequently significant.

Objectives and Goals

Objectives are statements of purpose an organization articulates to secure the support of those constituents (stockholders, clients, customers, regulatory bodies, employees, etc.) on which it critically depends for current functioning and survival.[4,5] Because of the diversity of expectations likely represented by an organization's key constituents, objectives tend to be stated vaguely and applied to an indefinite time horizon. Thus, objectives cannot be used to direct organizational activities in the immediate future.

Organizational *goals*, which may be put into operation as either desired ends or imposed constraints,[6] represent the intentions actually sought by an organization. While goals may emphasize some objectives more than others, they are necessarily bounded by the intentionally broad domain represented by stated objectives. As many planning goals are often stated in qualitative terms, goal statements are typically refined into planning *targets*—future conditions for which agreed-upon means exist that permit performance evaluation.

In assessing organizational performance, one should consider both effectiveness and efficiency. *Effectiveness* is the extend to which stated goals are attained. *Efficiency* is how well organizational resources are used in pursuing these goals. Effectiveness and efficiency targets give organizational members a fairly complete view of what to expect from organizational activity. The examples in Table 7.1, using the two organizational contexts developed in Chapter 3, illustrate differences between planning objectives, goals, and targets.

However, clear distinctions between effectiveness and efficiency do not always exist.[7] When resources are scarce, for example, efficiency may become the organization's primary goal. When resources are abundant or there is a crisis, however, efficiency may enter only minimally into assessments of organizational performance.

TABLE 7.1
Objectives, Goals, and Targets in Two Contexts

Context	Objective	Goals	Targets
Hospital emergency room	Provide good emergency care	Prevent loss of life (effectiveness)	Death rate Waiting time Accurate diagnoses
		Minimize resource usage (efficiency)	Cost per patient Idle time of staff
Materials management	Ensure that organizational activities are not interrupted by material shortages	Provide materials when needed (effectiveness)	Rejection rate Back orders Stockouts Worker idle time because of material shortage
		Minimize procurement and storage costs (efficiency)	Ordering cost per item Storage cost per item

The Planning Process

Three related issues affect the process by which planning occurs within organizations: the ordered sequence of activities that typically transpire, the multiple time horizons that must be addressed, and the need to hierarchically link the planning efforts of organizational units. Each will be briefly examined.

Certain generic activities occur, regardless of the focus of the planning effort. These include developing planning premises, deciding on planning goals, devising appropriate strategies, selecting a strategy, implementing the plan, and monitoring the plan.[8-11] *Planning premises* are those facts, trends, and assumptions that provide a context for planning. While it is impossible to define the issues to be addressed, aspects of each of the following will probably be included: the internal situation (strengths, weaknesses, competencies, and problems) of the organizational unit; projections associated with current activities (products, services, cash flow, and resources) of the unit; past, present, and future actions of key entities (other work units, competitors, stakeholders, suppliers, and regulatory bodies) in the unit's specific environment; and general trends regarding relevant components (social values, technology, economy, and demographics) of the unit's general environment. *Planning goals* evolve from a consideration of hierarchically communicated organizational objectives in light of the work unit's current planning premises. *Planning strategies* might reflect current actions, previously implemented actions, borrowed actions, or completely new actions. *Strategy selection* is the formal appraisal (applying agreed-on criteria) of the expected outcomes of each strategy, resulting in the selection of a plan. *Plan implementation* involves the allocation of necessary resources, delegation of the necessary authority, and communication of the plan to organizational members. *Plan monitoring* includes periodic assessments of whether the plan is being carried out as designed, whether progress has been made toward the planning goals, and whether the plan remains appropriate, given a continuously changing organizational context.

While the disciplined approach described above may seem highly rational, it is seldom observed in practice.[12] Planning often reacts dynamically to events as they occur and transpires over extended periods of time. Numerous actors are involved, each seeking particular objectives, and strategies emerge from varied sources, each of which attacks one aspect of the planning problem and then blends incrementally and opportunistically with the contributions of others.

Additionally, planning efforts oriented toward distinct planning horizons must be pursued and synchronized to permit a smooth, coherent passage from the present to the future. Table 7.2 suggests the variety of planning activities addressed within organizations.[13,14] An *operating*

TABLE 7.2
Planning Levels

Planning Effort	Planning Focus	Planning Horizon	Planning Purpose
Policy	Objectives	Infinite	Define organizational purpose Provide guidelines for strategic planning
Strategic	Goals	Operating cycle plus redeployment time	Develop a strategy set that moves toward organizational objectives
Financial	Budget	One year	Link action plans to the financial budgeting process
Operational	Actions	Operating cycle	Define specific actions to take in implementing strategies

TABLE 7.3
Differences in Planning by Organizational Level

Level	Focus	Degree of Uncertainty	Time Horizon	Relation to Actual Operations	Planner Discretion
High	Wide	More	Longer	Abstract	More
Low	Narrow	Less	Shorter	Concrete	Less

cycle refers to the time needed to develop capabilities and to begin to produce a product or provide a service. This might be more or less than a year, depending on the industry or function involved. Note also the distinction between "action" planning and "budget" planning. Both forms are necessary, as they serve distinct but complementary aims.

Finally, for effective planning to occur, the planning activities of work units throughout the organization must be tightly coordinated. Plans established at higher levels establish many of the planning premises of lower-level units, and the plans of horizontally related work units must be considered whenever a high degree of work unit interaction exists.

Accepting the fact that planning efforts occur throughout organizations means recognizing the diverse planning contexts in each organization. As one moves from higher organizational levels to lower, changes are invariably observed (see Table 7.3) in planning focus, amount of uncertainty to be faced, length of appropriate time horizons, proximity of planning actions to actual operations, and amount of discretion planners have in specifying objectives, premises, criteria, alternatives, etc. Likewise, planners in different functional areas normally focus on different issues. Coordinating such diffuse activities (and supporting these activities through CBIS) is no easy task.

Consideration of planning as a multilevel, multiphase activity leads directly to a major problem—goal displacement. Putting broad, abstract, and qualitative goals into operation often results in goal statements that may not completely or accurately reflect the higher-level planner's intentions. Restating a goal relating to sales contributions in terms of sales revenues, for example, may result in inappropriate actions by lower-level units. Related difficulties associated with goal displacement are misinterpretation, reluctance to drop prior goals (because of their established legitimacy or existing commitments), and the emergence of local, possibly conflicting goals attributed to the immediate needs of lower-level units.

Planning Support Needs

In supporting the information needs of planners, both data and their refinement must be considered. Data requirements cover financial (revenues, costs, investment needs, economic indicators and trends, etc.), quantitative nonfinancial (market share, market potential, productivity, etc.), and nonquantitative (technological trends, labor relations, community standing, political or social movements, etc.) measures. These data elements emanate from diverse sources: internally maintained data files, only some of which are likely computer based; the knowledge and insights of organizational members, particularly those who have developed relationships with critical environmental entities; and public sources (such as information services, reports, periodicals, and books).

Data analyses normally produce one of two types of planning intelligence: orientation reports and specific information.[15] Common orientation aids provided planners to fill in their knowledge bases include topical updates, speculations about future events, and relevant background materials. Such information support emphasizes information *scanning*, e.g., the surveillance of particular internal and external domains of interest. This involves monitoring both specific activities (closely tracing the occurrence and impact of particularly relevant events) and general movements (identifying and deriving the significance of broad social trends).[16] The need for such orientation reports increases as more dynamic environments are faced, concern focuses on marketing or technological issues, and the planning activity occurs at higher organizational levels.[17,18] Providing specific intelligence on request (capacity or demand forecasts, probabilities that certain events will occur, expected consequences of actions, reviews of past performance) requires *searching out* and quantitatively *analyzing* relevant data elements. Attention is thus directed at locating required data, capturing it in a form that facilitates analyses, and applying appropriate statistical and mathematical models.

An Illustration

The interstate trucking firm introduced earlier can be used to illustrate the variety of planning contexts that arise within organizations. Consider, for example, plausible planning targets—all evolving from an organization-wide objective to achieve a specific long-term return on investment—for three functional areas:

Operations	Route profit contribution (high level) Number of late shipments (low level)
Maintenance	Repair costs per route mile (high level) Number of overtime hours (low level)
Marketing	Market share (high level) Number of new customer contacts (low level)

The planning processes involved in addressing these issues would differ in relevant time horizons and the backgrounds of planners and would require widely varying support information (quantitative versus qualitative, internal versus external, financial versus forecast, scanning versus analysis, etc.). Furthermore, the plan produced by one group of planners (e.g., an action to reduce late shipments) may affect those of other planners (e.g., actions to increase a route's profit contribution or to reduce overtime by maintenance workers).

ORGANIZATIONAL CONTROL

The notion of control centers on organizational efforts to ensure that planned performance targets are achieved. Basically, the control function identifies and corrects deviations from the plan. Control is thus of benefit when it results in actions being taken that result in performance improvements.

The Control Process

The basic control cycle, which is adapted directly from engineering and general systems theory, involves the cybernetic notion that any system can be maintained on course by measuring current performance, comparing the measurement with what should have occurred had the system achieved its goal, and adjusting system behavior accordingly whenever actual performance differs from expected performance. Prior to implementing such a control cycle, however, one must specify control parameters and actions; this initial design is the crucial activity in implementing an effective control process. Essentially, then, control system design requires the following:

- Selection of control targets—the elements by which performance will be monitored,
- Derivation of control indicators—the actual measures used to represent control targets,
- Establishment of control standards—performance levels, stated in terms of the control indicators, that are appropriate for goal attainment and acceptable to organizational members, and
- Specification of corrective actions—adjustments required in behavior that return performance to a path consistent with that planned.

Control Targets. Control targets can focus on behavior itself or on behavioral outcomes.[19] While behavioral targets permit the fastest feedback (outcomes do not have to be reported), to use behavioral targets the relationship between behavior and outcome must be well understood. When that understanding is incomplete, outcome targets must be relied on.

The objective in selecting control targets is to arrive at a combination of indices that will provide sensitive, timely, and economic feedback. The best control systems are often very simple: they provide information on a few select strategic control points (factors found closely linked to the success of the activity involved), but permit more in-depth analysis when necessary.[20] Too many control points simply obfuscate an already complex world. Two key criteria to consider in arriving at control targets is that the control targets should adequately portray planned performance in terms of stated organizational goals and the behaviors or outcomes involved should be totally within the domain of the work unit being controlled.

Control Indicators. Control indicators are the collected measurements of organizational activity or performance that reflect the current status of control targets. A one-to-one relationship between targets and indicators is generally difficult to achieve; this difficulty increases as targets become qualitative, are ill defined, or relate to events or statuses external to the organization. In such instances, one must rely on target surrogates, each of which provides evidence about some facet of a control target.

Certain attributes of an ideal indicator have been suggested:

Useful	The indicator indicates when organizational behaviors require change,
Economical	The costs of measurement and reporting are less than the benefits of resolving the out-of-control situation,
Measurable	It is possible to collect the required data,
Unequivocal	There is a low probability that the message will be misinterpreted by its receiver,
Reliable	The measurement procedure would describe duplicate behavior similarly if data were collected at different times,
Accurate	The indicator accurately captures the behavioral characteristic involved,
Timely	The indicator provides evidence of inappropriate activities soon enough for corrective actions to be effective.[21,22]

The difficulty is that trade-offs must invariably be made regarding these attributes: utility versus measurability, timeliness and accuracy versus economy, unequivocalness versus measurability, and so forth. The danger always exists that poor indicators might give the appearance of control when little control actually exists.

Control Standards. Control standards are used to trigger the reporting components of control systems. As long as activities are within standards, no messages are transmitted. When standards are violated, notice is communicated so organizational behaviors can be adjusted. Most control standards tend to be defined in a negative sense—until problems arise, nothing happens. Greater efforts need to be directed at providing positive feedback to organizational members, as such feedback is growth promoting. Careful consideration must be also directed toward successfully integrating control systems within an organization's reward systems.

In setting standards for people, it is important to consider motivational effects.[23] Standards set too high or too low may prove dysfunctional. Standards easily achieved provide little motivation, while those impossible to achieve discourage individuals from striving toward the target. Standards should be tough but attainable, and should be accepted by those controlled as relevant to their organizational roles. Concern must also be directed toward what has been termed the "crawling peg" phenomenon within control systems.[24] The tendency exists for targets and standards to be determined by past performances. Overachievement becomes the standard for the future. The better one does, the more slack is removed and the more difficult it becomes to maintain a high level of performance. It is not surprising that individuals in such situations often aim to meet minimal requirements. Problems can also arise with overachievement. The sales plans of some manufacturing organizations are so finely orchestrated that too many sales can severely disrupt manufacturing operations or result in a loss of goodwill (eventually affecting market share) because of delivery delays.

A difficult decision regarding standards is whether to use a tight or loose control system. Tight control involves sensitive standards, multiple targets, detailed indicators, and more frequent measurement and reporting. Loose control involves the setting of a few critical, results-oriented targets and little if any monitoring of progress.[25] The obvious advantage of tight control is that the organization need not bear the costs of an out-of-control situation for any significant period. Potential disadvantages that might arise from too tight controls, however, include the following:

- Cost of data collection, processing, and reporting,
- Frequent disruption of activity,
- Organizational rigidity,
- Little opportunity for organizational members to exercise judgment, initiation, or imagination, and
- Negative reactions by organizational members.

Some general prescriptions to follow in arriving at a tight–loose balance are to employ tighter controls when organizational activities are more interdependent or when significant penalties arise from deviant behavior and to employ looser controls when organizational activities are independent or when the organizational context is dynamic.

Corrective Actions.   While it is impossible and undesirable to establish a corrective action for every possible observed deviation, considerable gains can be achieved by investigating the causes of problems and evolving strategies likely to resolve these problems. If the responsible individual is informed of a problem, its cause, and possible actions to take, reaction time and the likelihood that the individual will take a dysfunctional action are both reduced. Care should still be taken to prevent the control system from driving rather than supporting organizational behavior.

Additional Control Concepts

The desirability of designing a control system that anticipates, rather than reacts to, problems so steps can be taken to prevent out-of-control situations should be obvious. By developing an understanding of the conditions by which a particular problem arises, one can monitor organizational activity and use appropriate techniques (such as trend analysis and pattern matching) to predict the probable occurrence of a problem. Additional costs likely to be incurred with such a control system include the analysis needed to devise the algorithm, any additional data collection and processing expenses, and the dysfunctional aspects of forecasting a problem that would not otherwise have arisen.

While many control systems use the exception principle (i.e., control reports are issued only when the responsible individual needs to react to an evolving situation), exception reporting is one of the most underutilized mechanisms for supporting organizational activity. Two forms of exception systems exist. *Event-triggered* systems issue control information as soon as a deviation is detected, while *time-triggered* systems issue information on deviations only at periodic intervals and then only if at least one deviation has occurred. Event-triggered systems permit tighter control but are more expensive to implement. However, reducing the intervals between time-triggered reports makes it possible to approximate the advantages of an event-triggered system at far less cost.

As with planning systems, wide variances can be observed in the operating characteristics of control systems directed at different organizational functions or work units located at different levels in an organization's hierarchy. Typical differences likely to arise in vertically differentiated work units are shown in Table 7.4.

An Illustration

A critical concern of the trucking firm described earlier would be the customer service implications of late shipments. At first glance it might appear that a control system to detect repetitive late shipments would be fairly easy to implement. Deeper analysis, however, reveals the complexities that arise in designing effective control systems.

An obvious control target would relate to the percentage of late shipments. However, what is meant by the term "late"? Is it five min-

TABLE 7.4
Differences in Control by Organizational Level

Level	Focus	Subject	Frequency	Detail	Standards
High	Wide	Human	Less	Less	Loose
Low	Narrow	Activity	More	More	Tight

utes, fifteen minutes, one hour, or what? Does it differ from situation to situation? If so, how? Should the recognition of late arrivals occur at company freight stations or only at client locations? Exactly where does management's concern lie? Is it company-wide lateness, or is concern focused on drivers, routes, equipment, clients, etc.? Does the cause of lateness need to be identified and reported? Likely causes might include the driver, equipment, maintenance, client, weather, traffic, and accidents. Which are relevant? How is the appropriate cause identified? All these issues relate to selecting control indicators that facilitate recognizing, diagnosing, and resolving problems that arise.

Once appropriate indicators have been identified, questions related to collecting, processing, and reporting this control information arise. How are the data to be captured and who should collect them? Should the drivers be responsible? If so, should they keep a log book or phone the information in? Should clients and station masters be responsible? If so, should the data be placed on existing forms such as invoices or shipping logs? When should these be collected? How should they be collected? Who should evaluate the integrity of the collected data? How? How often should data files be updated? Should exception reporting be employed? If so, in what form? Who should receive control reports? How many types of reports should be generated? How often? Are all control indicators handled similarly, or should differences be maintained in control standards, frequency of processing and reporting, type of exception reporting, or depth of analysis?

COMPUTER-BASED SUPPORT OF PLANNING AND CONTROL

As illustrated in Figure 7.2, planning and control must be viewed as inseparable in practice. An organization's plans are the base on which controls are built, and controls indicate when a plan is inappropriate, given current organizational realities. Subsequent adjustments in a plan must be followed by adjustments in controls. To fully appreciate the high degree of interaction between planning and control, one could consider the set of linkages required to coordinate responsibility centers located horizontally and vertically throughout an organization, then add the need to allow for complementary planning and control activities covering short-term, intermediate-term, and long-term time horizons when the length of an appropriate time horizon may vary with each responsibility center. Often, however, organizational implementations of planning and control systems do not have a reciprocal relationship, so performance suffers. A practical explanation for such situations lies in the very different infor-

FIGURE 7.2
Integration of Planning and Control

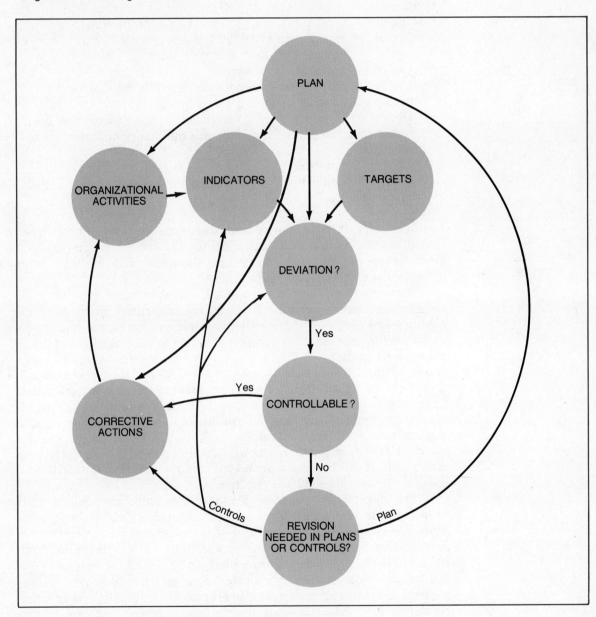

mation requirements of planning and control and, consequently, in the extent to which each tends to be supported by CBIS in organizations.

Most IRS are control-oriented applications. It is simply far easier to provide computer-based support for the control function than for the planning function. The following characteristics of the control function, for example, greatly simplify the CBIS design process.

- Control is a repetitious activity,
- Control specifications are implicitly provided by the planning function,
- Data needs for control primarily relate to the organization itself rather than environmental elements, and hence are more easily collected,
- Concern in control tends to focus on current activities, reducing the need to implement sophisticated information search and forecasting procedures.

As might be expected, a control facet absent from many computer-based control systems is that most different from the above characteristics—a means of recognizing when adjustments should be made in the planning or control activities currently in force.

Planning is a dynamic, unbounded, and nonroutine activity. It becomes economically feasible to design and implement fully integrated planning and control systems only in simple environments; in complex environments, the planning components tend to become obsolete before they can be exploited.[26] This is not to say that planning cannot be supported by an IRS, only that the roles of the CBIS and the human planner must be carefully delineated. An IRS can provide access to historical data bases, external as well as internal, and to analytic models that permit analyzing trends, forecasting, determining optimal strategies in allocating resources, evaluating alternative actions, and identifying significant variables as well as relations among variables, among other applications. As a result, it can become a productive component of an organizational planning system if employed effectively.

The objective in supporting planning and control through an IRS is to identify those organizational activities characterized by the features most amenable to IRS support, a need to quickly access large available data bases and a need to apply complex statistical or mathematical models, when both needs can be prespecified. An IRS should not drive organizational activities. Rather, it indicates when action may be desirable, it suggests directions for movement, and it provides information that, when combined with the experience, insight, and knowledge of an organizational member, enables actions to be taken that are likely to be consistent with organizational objectives.

REPORT DESIGN

The objective in report design is to provide the least information (to reduce the information processing burdens on both the CBIS and the human receiver) that meets the complete needs of the individual receiving the report. As the specified needs of organizational members are situation based and as an IRS by definition is prespecified, it becomes impossible to achieve this objective. Successful analysis of an individual's information requirements should, however, enable some of these needs to be met. When the organizational role played by an individual is routine and predictable, a sizable portion of the individual's information needs may be met by a carefully designed set of IRS reports.

Report design invariably requires that trade-offs be made among such issues as a report's currentness, completeness, relevancy, readability, cost, and accuracy. Consider, for example, the common trade-offs between accuracy, currentness, and cost. A need for extremely current information affects accuracy as less time is available for control procedures to be applied, and currentness or accuracy is improved only by additional investments in information resources. Organizational members for whom reports are being designed must understand these trade-offs and recognize that, while report accuracy and currentness are always desirable, neither need be *fully* achieved to obtain information support for most organizational activities. Inaccurate information is useful as long as the receiver is aware of the extent of inaccuracy that very likely exists, and a report remains useful if it is received prior to a decision or action deadline.

Management Information

All facts and figures (and their relationships) in a report should be recognized as abstract measures of reality. When these data are assimilated by a human mind, however, meaningful connections often enhance the individual's understanding of reality, reducing some of the uncertainty that previously existed regarding reality (for the moment at least). When this occurs, the facts and figures possess *information value*.

A comparison of the information potential of a report and the potential energy of a water reservoir can illustrate this concept.[27] Water stored in a reservoir on a hill can do work. Until the water is released, however, no work is performed. Data contained in a report likewise can reduce uncertainty; however, unless this information is meaningfully assimilated by an individual, the information value of the report is zero. The greater the meaning of a report to an individual (i.e., the more the report

TABLE 7.5
Information Differences by Functional Area

Information Characteristic	Marketing	Personnel	Production	Finance
External	Most	Less	More	Least
Historical	More	Least	Less	Most
Accurate	Least	Less	More	Most
Detailed	Less	More	Most	Least
Current	Least	Most	More	Less

changes the individual's current view in some way), the more uncertainty is reduced and the greater is the information value of the report.

The potential information value of a report can vary significantly, depending on the form in which information is presented and the individual who receives the report. Reports describing similar issues, for example, can vary in a number of information attributes, including scope (wide or narrow), source (internal or external), accuracy (more or less), currentness (more or less), time horizon (past, present, or future), and aggregation level (detailed or summary).[28] Such information attributes vary with the organizational level[29] and functional responsibilities[30] of the individual receiving the report. Tables 7.3 and 7.4 illustrate certain information requirement differences arising from an individual's level in the organizational hierarchy, and Table 7.5 suggests likely functional area differences. What might not be so clear is that information requirements may also vary with personal differences among organizational members.

The ease with which an IRS report is assimilated depends on each individual's human information processing system (HIPS).[31,32] As discussed in Chapter 3, individuals' varying experiential and educational backgrounds lead to differences in their ability to exploit fully the information potential of a report. These differences arise from a number of interrelated factors: failure to perceive the relevance of the information, cognitive discomfort in assimilating the information, or simply inability to make the required connections. While behavioral reactions to a report are impossible to anticipate fully because of situational factors (i.e., an individual faced with a pressing problem is likely to make effective use of a relevant report, even though it does not mesh well with his or her HIPS), certain general observations can be made:

- People with more technical backgrounds (engineers, accountants) tend to prefer quantitative information, while people with less technical backgrounds (advertising, personnel) prefer qualitative, visual information,

- People who are introverted tend to depend more on information provided in reports than do extroverts,
- People who dislike ambiguity tend to require more information,
- People with experience in the situation being faced tend to require less information.

While the individual receiving the report should be considered, it is normally uneconomical to design separate reports for each individual in an organization. Possible approaches to meeting individuals' needs are to categorize groups (financial analysts, salespeople, industrial engineers) within the organization by reporting preferences[33] and then design reports for each group, and to design reports in a very modular fashion (e.g., predefined sets of information varying in scope, form, detail, etc., are made available, permitting some flexibility in the information each user receives).

Displaying Information

Many ways can be used to increase the likelihood that the full information potential of a report will be extracted. Information can be presented in a variety of means through the creative use of tables, charts, and graphs. If accurate readings of reported information are crucial, tables must be relied on to a certain extent. However, as concern moves from extracting facts toward developing an understanding of an existing or evolving situation, the use of charts and graphs to "turn numbers into meaningful pictures" becomes more beneficial.

Trend analysis (actual versus forecast, rates of change), variance analysis (actual versus forecast), and direct comparison (amounts, rates) are greatly facilitated by the use of line graphs, bar charts, histograms, pie charts, area graphs, and maps. Such graphics can be applied with a single variable, multiple variables, time series data, and cross-sectional data. Deciding which type of graphics support to employ can only be done after the intended user has indicated what aspects of the issue are to be examined.

Many other ploys can be used to increase the *surprise* value of a report. Color can increase the "dimensionality" of a report, or it may be used for psychological motives (red indicating a "hot" item, blue indicating a "cool", etc.). Key items on a report can be highlighted by having the information blink on and off on a CRT screen, by encircling or isolating the information, or by using a different color. Other report design strategies (e.g., the use of relative rather than absolute numbers, the order information is presented, repetition of information) are limited only by the creativity of the report designer.

FIGURE 7.3
Total Revenue Trends

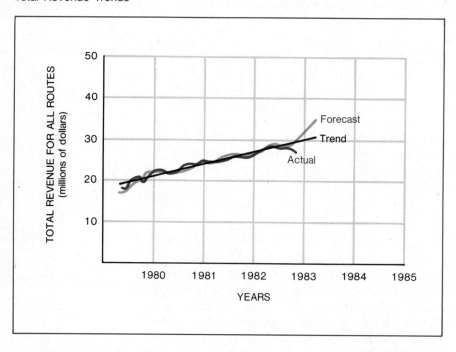

FIGURE 7.4
Deviation from Forecast, All Routes

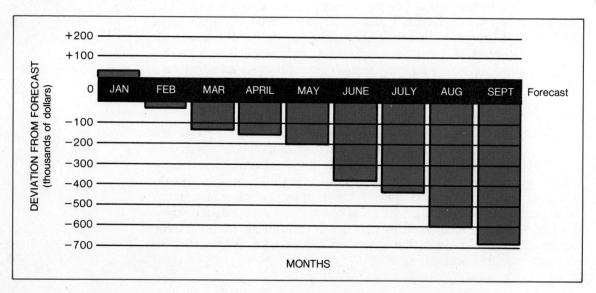

Part 2 / Choices

The accessibility of a report is as important as the quality of the information presented. Careful consideration must consequently be given to the ways reports are physically received by their intended users. Should the medium of exchange be technical (a terminal, microfiche) or human (voice output, a staff intermediary)? Should the user be provided a means to immediately initiate (through a terminal, for example) a response, request, or inquiry? If terminals are to be employed, how accessible and available should they be made? Should each user have an individual terminal or can group work stations be used?

An Illustration

The benefits of employing nontabular report designs to communicate information about problems and opportunities can be seen by referring back to our hypothetical interstate trucking firm. Assume the firm serves four major routes—A, B, C, and D. The firm's management might well receive a monthly report indicating actual and forecast revenues, along with a trend line, as shown in Figure 7.3. It can be seen that actual and forecast revenues generally follow the trend, but recent revenues seem to be falling below the forecast and trend lines.

If a bar chart illustrating the most recent deviations between forecast and actual revenues were also made available, the existence of a problem could be verified. An example of such a chart is given in Figure 7.4. Additionally, by using some recent time periods to contrast the revenue performances of the four major routes, one could detect an isolated problem (i.e., only one or two routes are affected). The pie charts in Figure 7.5 perform this function. Finally, by requesting a more detailed report on the revenue performance (deviation from forecast) of route A, one could confirm this diagnosis (Figure 7.6).

CONCLUSION

The objective of an IRS is twofold:

- To provide information (goals, targets, constraints, progress reports, data on problems, predictions of opportunities or problems, forecasts of likely results, etc.) that guides the behavior of organizational members, and
- To coordinate interdependent organizational activities through resource allocation and activity timing.

The aim is to provide each member of the organization with a particular action schema. The more routine and better understood are organizational purposes and processes, the more able an IRS is to help individuals

FIGURE 7.5
Proportional Revenue from Each Route

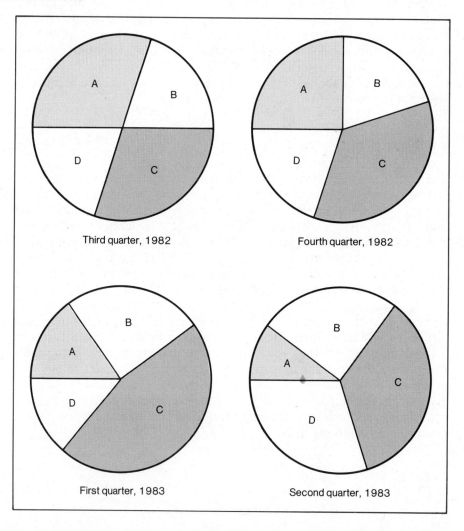

Third quarter, 1982

Fourth quarter, 1982

First quarter, 1983

Second quarter, 1983

work effectively and efficiently and align their individual goals with organization objectives.

If the inputs, outputs, and processing rules for an IRS application can be validly specified, development and operating costs can often be quickly recovered through accrued benefits. As organizational purpose and process become complex, dynamic, and nonroutine, it becomes increasingly difficult to validly specify IRS applications. What are often

FIGURE 7.6
Deviation from Forecast, Route A

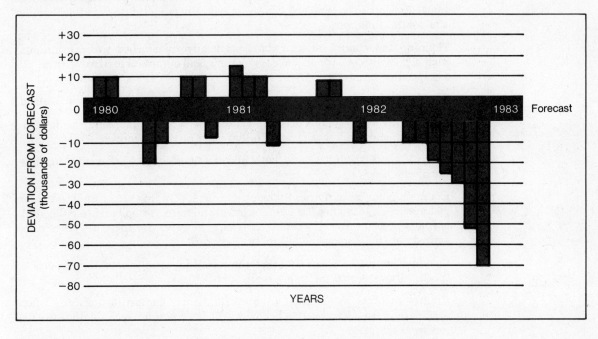

observed are irrelevant data in reports and irrelevant reports, inability to capture needed data, constant (expensive and time-consuming) modification of reports, and inability to modify reports. In such circumstances, computer-related costs rise, organizational members lose the incentive to access and use available information, and—worst of all—members may react to a report that does not represent organizational realities.

When correctly applied, IRS are of immense benefit to organizations and their members: they provide a very economical means of communicating behavioral guides to organizational members so the activities of relatively independent work units (and the individuals in these units) can be coordinated. However, if IRS are poorly designed or used inappropriately, the effects may prove quite harmful.

KEY ISSUES

Organizational direction and redirection must be regularly provided if organizational aims are to be achieved. These are typically provided through the planning and control functions.

Planning and control information is generally transmitted to organizational members by IRS. All inputs, processing rules, and outputs associated with an IRS are specified in advance of its use.

The three basic IRS reporting environments are periodic, exception, and demand.

Planning involves deciding on organizational objectives, strategies to achieve the objectives, and goals that meaningfully represent the objectives.

Plan elements should address both organizational effectiveness and organizational efficiency.

Common planning activities include developing planning premises, deciding on planning goals, devising strategies, selecting a strategy, implementing the strategy, and monitoring performance. It is rare, however, for these activities to be carried out in a sequential, disciplined fashion.

Planning intelligence usually takes the form of general orientation reports or specifically requested information elements.

Control involves measuring current performance, comparing these measures against the plan, and adjusting behavior whenever performance significantly differs from the plan.

Control system design requires selection of control targets, derivation of control indicators, establishment of control standards, and specification of corrective actions.

Anticipatory control systems are preferred to reactive control systems.

Exception reporting systems can be event triggered or time triggered.

Planning and control systems must be established for each of an organization's responsibility centers and must be specified across multiple time horizons. Successfully integrating such information systems can be difficult.

Most IRS are control oriented because it is far easier to implement control systems than to implement planning systems.

The objective in report design is to provide the least information that satisfies the information needs of the individual receiving the report. Such an objective invariably results in trade-offs in terms of a report's currentness, completeness, accuracy, and cost.

A report possesses information value when its reception reduces the uncertainty felt by an organizational member. A report's information value varies with the form in which information is presented and the personal attributes of the individual receiving the report.

DISCUSSION QUESTIONS

1. Generally, IRS support organizational activities in four ways: providing cues, directing attention, reviewing past performance, and raising questions. Illustrate examples of information being used for each of these support means for a purchasing manager evaluating vendor performance.

2. What are the positive and negative implications of the "predefined" nature of an IRS?

3. Compare the advantages and disadvantages of periodic, exception, and demand reporting.

4. Distinguish among organizational objectives, goals, and targets. Why might all three be incorporated within an organization's plans?

5. Provide examples of both effectiveness and efficiency measures for an advertising department in a consumer product manufacturing firm, for a fire department, and for the warehouse of an industrial supply wholesaler.

6. What is meant by the term "planning premises"? Give examples using the context of a mayor developing an annual budget for a large urban city.

7. Provide an example from your own experiences of goal displacement. How could this have been overcome?

8. Distinguish among control targets, indicators, and standards. Why must all three be formally specified when one is designing an effective control system?

9. Provide an example from your own experiences of a control target's not being totally within the domain of the individual or group being controlled. How could this have been overcome?

10. Describe a situation in which loose controls would be more appropriate than tight controls; then describe a situation in which tight controls would be more appropriate than loose controls.

11. Distinguish between time-triggered and event-triggered exception reporting. Which is generally more appropriate for most situations?

12. Illustrate the trade-off between report currentness, accuracy, and cost using the context of a report designed to help the manager of a word processing unit monitor the unit's performance.

13. Using experiences from your past, illustrate how different people can perceive the same information in different ways.

14. How can graphics improve the information potential of certain reports? What types of reports are most susceptible to graphics enhancement? Does color have the same impact?

BRIEF CASES

1. *Morningside Cereals*
   Morningside Naturals, Toni Sellek's family of natural food products, exceeded its sales target for 1982. While the initial success of these products resulted from the efforts of a large number of individuals, Toni knew the information system she had helped design provided an early warning of

market and distribution problem areas. Looking toward the future, she saw that continued success of the product line would depend largely on her ability to plan successful market expansion. Could information systems be as useful in supporting planning as they were in supporting control?

In examining the planning environment for Morningside Naturals, Toni recognized that a variety of planning activities were involved: strategic planning for the entire company, long-range planning for the Morningside Naturals line, annual budget and profit planning, project planning for each of the many current projects (advertising programs, merchandising programs, salesperson incentive programs, etc.), and replanning efforts associated with each of these. Toni was concerned about duplication of effort in setting up information systems to support these activities. Was there any overlap in the planning information needs of these planning activities? Should a single planning information system be designed, should separate systems be established for each planning activity, or should a mixed strategy be adopted?

Give examples of planning information elements that would be of general use. Outline a strategy for designing a planning information system for the Morningside Naturals product line.

2. *Greco Components*

Randy Fitzin, the systems development manager at Greco, knew he had a tough task ahead of him. Rose Leary, the sales manager, did not see much benefit from investing her time and resources in the development of an information system. Randy, however, understood quite well that the information systems division had been given a mandate to improve the way the sales group was managing its activities. In looking for an application that could immediately provide benefits to Rose, he felt a sales control system seemed a likely choice.

In planning his next vist to Rose, Randy realized the difficulty would be convincing her that the numbers being reported had real meaning. In their initial meeting, she had indicated that it was difficult to keep up with the progress of the sales staff in meeting their individual quotas and in "opening up" their sales regions. It was clear two types of control reports were needed, one going to Rose that reported on the activities of the sales staff, and one going to the sales staff to motivate them. What kind of information should be presented in each report? What data would be needed to produce these reports? Would any problems be encountered in capturing these data?

Randy wanted to go into his meeting with at least a sketch of the type of control system that could be implemented. What information would be needed about each report? Would this information overcome Rose's belief that computers cannot provide the "people" information needed to manage a sales force?

3. *The State Motor Pool*

One purpose of the vehicle information system was to monitor the operating and maintenance cost of each vehicle in order to signal when vehicles should be replaced. With the rising costs of replacement parts and labor, the breakeven point for replacing vehicles was occurring sooner and sooner.

Given the variety of vehicles the state owned, however, no single decision rule could be applied. Consequently, it was decided to regularly monitor vehicle operating and maintenance costs, compare these against the expected performance of new models, and then replace vehicles when the projected three-year costs of keeping a vehicle exceeded the projected three-year costs of buying and maintaining a new vehicle. While the design seemed simple, vehicles do not "gracefully" deteriorate. Often they fell apart overnight (or so it seemed).

The vehicle replacement control system is a good example of an exception reporting system. The objective of the system was to identify to responsible managers those vehicles that should be replaced. While failure to promptly replace one vehicle did not have drastic consequences, the state's weekly losses due to operating and maintaining inadequate vehicles approached $50,000. This loss included the direct costs of operation and maintenance, as well as indirect costs associated with inability to perform state business because of vehicle failures.

What type of design (event-triggered or time-triggered) would better suit the vehicle replacement control system? Why? Would you classify this control system as anticipatory or reactive? Explain.

4. *Bennison Construction Company*
Susan Allen, Bennison's information systems manager, was convinced that color graphics reporting could significantly improve management's ability to use the information systems that had recently been installed: the project costing, scheduling, and control systems; the cost forecasting system; the employee skills location system; and an equipment maintenance system. Moving in this direction, however, was not without its costs. Color graphics production would require equipment and software purchases, and perhaps the addition of a staff artist (such an individual could be used for duties other than those associated with information systems).

Susan was about to present her color graphics expansion program to the firm's executive committee. She wanted to identify an application that would benefit from color graphics, produce prototype graphics to aid management decision making, and then contrast color graphic reporting with the firm's current tabular reports.

Which of the listed applications should Susan select? With this application, where might color graphics be of benefit? Suggest some useful graphic features.

NOTES

1. C. T. Horngren, "Changing Accounting Packages for Reporting to Management," *National Association of Accountants Bulletin* 44(1962):3–16.

2. C. G. Schoderbek, P. P. Schoderbek, and A. G. Kefalas, *Management Systems: Conceptual Considerations* (Dallas: Business Publications, 1980).

3. J. P. C. Kleijnen, *Computers and Profits: Quantifying Financial Benefits of Information* (Reading, Mass.: Addison-Wesley, 1980).

4. R. M. Steers, *Organizational Effectiveness: A Behavioral View* (Glenview, Ill.: Scott, Foresman, 1977).

5. R. H. Miles, *Macro Organizational Behavior* (Glenview, Ill.: Scott, Foresman, 1977).

6. H. A. Simon, "On the Concept of Organizational Goal," *Administrative Science Quarterly* 9(1964):1–22.

7. Steers (1977).

8. D. R. Daniels, "Management Information Crisis," *Harvard Business Review* 39(1961):111–21.

9. R. J. Mockler, *The Management Control Process* (New York: Appleton-Century-Crofts, 1972).

10. W. H. Newman, *Constructive Control* (Englewood Cliffs, N.J.: Prentice-Hall, 1975).

11. A. S. Huff, "Strategic Intelligence Systems," *Information and Management* 2(1979):187–96.

12. J. B. Quinn, "Strategic Change: Logical Incrementalism," *Sloan Management Review* 20(1978):17–21.

13. D. I. Cleland and W. R. King, *Systems Analysis and Project Management* (New York: McGraw-Hill, 1975).

14. J. C. Camillus and J. H. Grant, "Operational Planning: The Integration of Programming and Budgeting," *Academy of Management Review* 3(1980):369–79.

15. Huff (1979).

16. J. E. Post and M. J. Epstein, "Information Systems for Social Reporting," *Academy of Management Review* 2(1977):81–87.

17. Schoderbek *et al.* (1980).

18. Horngren (1962).

19. Miles (1980).

20. Newman (1975).

21. E. E. Lawler III and J. G. Rhode, *Information and Control in Organizations* (Glenview, Ill.: Scott, Foresman, 1976).

22. E. G. Hurst, Jr., "Choosing Performance Measures," working paper 77–11–01, Wharton School, University of Pennsylvania, 1977.

23. Newman (1975).

24. S. Eilon, *Management Control* (London: MacMillan, 1971).

25. G. Hofstede, "The Poverty of Management Control Philosophy," *Academy of Management Review* 3(1978):450–61.

26. J. C. Henderson and P. C. Nutt, "On the Design of Planning Information Systems," *Academy of Management Review* 3(1978):774–85.

27. E. Hoffman, "Defining Information: An Analysis of the Information Content of Documents," *Information Processing and Management* 16(1980):291–304.

28. R. W. Zmud, "An Empirical Investigation of the Concept of Information," *Decision Sciences* 9(1978):187–96.

29. G. A. Gorry and M. S. Scott Morton, "A Framework for Management Information Systems," *Sloan Management Review* 13(1971):55–70.

30. G. B. Davis, *Management Information Systems: Conceptual Foundations, Structure and Development* (New York: McGraw-Hill, 1974).

31. I. Benbasat and R. N. Taylor, "The Impact of Cognitive Style on Information System Design," *MIS Quarterly* 2(1978):43–54.

32. R. W. Zmud, "Individual Differences and MIS Success: A Review of the Empirical Literature," *Management Science* 25(1979):966–79.

33. M. L. Bariff and E. J. Lusk, "Cognitive and Personality Tests for the Design of Management Information Systems," *Management Science* 23(1977):820–29.

Decision Support Systems and Programmed Decision Systems

8

REGARDLESS OF the effort spent designing effective planning and control systems, organizational success ultimately depends on the capabilities of organizational members—particularly those responsible for critical organizational functions—to competently carry out day-to-day tasks. While IRS reports may provide invaluable guidance to organizational members handling day-to-day situations, many of these situations do not involve clearly defined, well-structured, preanalyzed issues; today's world simply feels no compulsion to mold itself to the current design of an organization's existing CBIS.[1]

Organizational members, particularly those filling staff and managerial roles, spend much of their time on short-term, operating decisions: resolving a problem that unexpectedly arises, assessing a suggested alternative to a standard procedure, determining whether a potential opportunity should be explored in depth, and so on. These activities are largely unanticipated and rarely recur in exactly the same form. Additionally, they must generally be handled within a relatively short time, sometimes within one hour.[2] If resolved, they may lead to similar decision situations. Information support of such activities that fails to meet time constraints becomes irrelevant—the organizational member must employ whatever support is available and resolve the situation.

Task characteristics such as those described above apply as well to a number of other key organizational roles. Planners, high-level executives, and boundary-spanners (among others) often find themselves in nonroutine, semistructured situations in which the ability to access or analyze particular information elements can greatly contribute to a rapid, effective resolution of a problem.

The reporting capabilities of IRS lack the scope, timeliness, and flexibility to meet many information needs of these organizational members. What is *not* needed is simply more information—that could be provided by an IRS. To support ad hoc information needs, computer-based systems must provide convenient, easy, and quick access to data bases and analysis tools so decision-makers can "rummage around" to extract and manipulate data base fragments in ways that mesh well with the individuals' normal ways of viewing and resolving decision situations.

Recent technological advances—data base management systems, storage and retrieval of nonnumeric data, telecommunications, microprocessors, experience in producing user-friendly interactive facilities, etc.—provide a means to support these ad hoc decision situations by CBIS. Since a common impetus to the development of such CBIS is the need to find a means to resolve specific decision situations, these forms of organizational support are generally referred to as *decision support systems* (DSS).

In this chapter the properties and potential of DSS are introduced. The chapter begins with a review of some basic notions regarding the decision-making process and how CBIS might support this process. The DSS concept is then explored in depth, after which existing DSS and emerging DSS trends are discussed. Finally, another category of CBIS, *programmed decision systems* (PDS), is discussed briefly.

DECISION MAKING

Decision making consumes much of the time and efforts of organizational members. The need to choose between two or more action alternatives continuously arises: whether or not to move in a new direction, whom to assign a given task, how best to use a scarce resource, which complaint to address first, how to bypass an operational bottleneck, how best to mollify disagreeing subordinates, whether to begin a task now or delay it two months, etc. While individuals attack decision making in a wide variety of ways, a general understanding of what comprises a decision situation and how individuals resolve such situations is emerging.

A decision situation arises whenever an individual is unsure which of two or more options should be followed. Each option is associated with certain outcomes, and certain contingencies affect which outcomes are to be expected if particular events take place. One's understanding of options, outcomes, and contingencies may be fairly complete (i.e., a structured decision) or fairly incomplete (i.e., a semistructured or poorly structured decision). The less complete one's understanding is, the more situational uncertainty exists and the greater is the likelihood that a less appropriate action will be taken.

A number of researchers have undertaken to develop an understanding of the decision process.[3-6] The model of the decision-making process in Figure 8.1 reflects the findings of these researchers.

FIGURE 8.1
Steps in the Decision-Making Process

RECOGNIZING THE DECISION SITUATION
- Compare current realities with those expected.
- Diagnose the situation.
- Assess the situation's urgency and importance.
- Define the situation.

STRUCTURING THE DECISION SITUATION
- Arrive at appropriate criteria, objectives, variables, constraints, parameters, relationships, etc.
- Identify viable alternatives.

RESOLVING THE DECISION SITUATION
- Assign appropriate values to probabilities and outcomes associated with each alternative.
- Evaluate alternatives.
- Choose an alternative.

IMPLEMENTING THE DECISION ACTION
- Prepare (explain, persuade, etc.) to take action.
- Take action.
- Monitor action taken.

The first stage in decision making involves recognizing the need to make a decision. This activity is often bypassed as a superior, subordinate, peer, customer, or client explicitly presents a decision situation or as a formal organizational information system signals the existence of the situation. Nonetheless, the ability to recognize and diagnose decision situations is a valuable skill—possibly the most critical managerial skill an individual can acquire.[7]

Detection of a problem or opportunity leading toward a decision situation requires that a model of the "real world" be maintained and that real world activities be monitored so deviations from the model are recognized. Usually recognition arises by means of pattern matching—if a certain series of events occur, situation x exists. Situation recognition thus requires either a continuous monitoring of an activity or the ability to monitor the activity at discrete intervals. Key design issues related to such supports involve selecting appropriate models (historical trends, future plans, actions of competitors, desires of customers, etc.) and identifying relevant variables or critical events to monitor.

The second stage in decision making concerns the decision-maker's "framing"[8] of the decision situation and the generation of alternatives for resolving the situation. A decision frame represents the decision-maker's conceptualization of the objectives, criteria, constraints, and relationships that "model" the situation; alternatives are the actions that can be taken, along with associated outcomes and contingencies. Clearly, the frame adopted in response to an emerging situation will influence the actions, outcomes, and contingencies that seem most relevant.

Decision frames and sets of likely alternatives may already exist when a decision situation arises—especially if the decision circumstance, or a similar circumstance, has previously been observed. Searching and screening must then occur either in the decision-maker's mind or through support mechanisms, if the accumulated knowledge and experience about a situation are to be exploited. When a decision situation is unique or the individual involved is ignorant of existent frames or alternatives, the decision-maker must create an appropriate structure for the situation. Support mechanisms facilitating this design activity can be very helpful.

The third stage of decision making, situation resolution, involves evaluating alternatives and selecting the most appropriate. While some of the analysis accompanying these efforts is rational and quantitative, much of it requires decision-makers to exercise their judgment and intuition, as well as to negotiate among one another. Both types of analysis— the rational and quantitative and the subjective and political—can benefit from computer-based support mechanisms.

The final phase in the decision-making process is associated with efforts taken to implement a chosen alternative: preparing the organization for action (explanation, education, persuasion, etc.), taking action or directing others to take action, and monitoring organizational outcomes of taking action. Support mechanisms oriented toward communicating to others why actions are being taken and toward monitoring organizational outcomes are invaluable in facilitating these activities.

A number of caveats to this view of decision making are necessary. First, the stages of decision making should not be conceived of solely as a sequence of orderly activities. These activities are interdependent, and hence involve iteration and feedback. Second, when two or more individuals conspire to resolve a decision situation, they will probably work together on certain issues but independently on other issues. While this might lessen the time required to resolve the decision situation, the fact that these individuals possess unique human information processing systems, affecting the way each structures the decision and presenting communication difficulties, can add considerable complexity to the process of decision making. Finally, this view of decision making should be recognized as a very simplified model of what actually transpires.

By way of an illustration, consider the decision situation faced daily by an investment analyst who is responsible for managing a number of clients' accounts.[9] Each account consists of a portfolio of securities, and each client has stated certain risk and return objectives for his or her portfolio. The investment analyst's tasks revolve around interacting with clients, reviewing and revising portfolios, and analyzing the securities market.

A very common decision situation handled by the investment analyst is to assess whether or not any portfolios should be changed. All four decision-making stages are gone through if a change is made:

Recognition	Realizing that a certain portfolio is not meeting its planned objectives or that there is an opportunity regarding a particular security that is consistent with a portfolio's planned objectives
Structuring	Constructing a model of portfolio performance; identifying potential securities to add or delete; configuring alternative changes to be made
Resolution	Forecasting performance of alternative versions of the portfolio; contrasting performances with client's objectives; deciding on change to enact
Implementation	Initiating market transactions; explaining changes to client; monitoring performance of revised portfolio

Considerable uncertainty arises in each decision stage. However, by accessing and manipulating data describing the historical, current, and expected performance of a client's portfolio and of market securities, the analyst should be able to identify and take action that helps meet the client's objectives.

CBIS SUPPORT OF DECISION MAKING

The activities that make up decision-making behavior are highly varied. Nonetheless, it is possible to categorize these activities into a relatively limited number of decision tasks:

Search	Scanning or browsing through facts, figures, reports, previous results, etc.; may be directed or free-form
Computation	Applying mathematical, statistical, or qualitative analysis tools
Specification	Structuring a decision situation
Inference	Deriving conclusions from data

Assimilation	Pulling together fragments of a situation to arrive at an understanding of what is involved
Explanation	Justifying choices made in decision making to members of the decision group, superiors, implementers, etc.[10,11]

Each decision activity could well occur repeatedly, in varied forms, throughout the decision-making process.

The issue at hand is to assess how CBIS capabilities can best support such activities. Clearly the powerful computational capabilities of computers can directly support computation and enhance both inference and assimilation, and the facility to quickly access large numeric and textual data bases directly supports search and enhances specification. Some opportunities that may not be so clear are the use of computer graphics to aid in specification, inference, and assimilation and the benefit of imposing a consistent decision framework to overcome the communication difficulties that tend to arise in group decision making or negotiation.[12] Table 8.1 summarizes these decision activities and suggests how each might be directly supported through a CBIS.

It is through *combining* CBIS strengths, however, that the most significant benefits of computer-based support of decision making emerge. By searching through historical and current data bases, a CBIS might detect decision situations, suggest a diagnosis, provide a starting structure

TABLE 8.1
CBIS Support of Decision Making

Decision Task	Examples	CBIS Support
Search	Inquiring, browsing, briefing	Fast, convenient access to data and textual information sources
Computation	Evaluating, predicting, estimating, analyzing, simulating, optimizing	Fast, convenient access to computational models and results
Specification	Constructing, designing, forming hypotheses	Retrieval of previously used decision structures and alternatives, modeling tools, cues that facilitate modeling in particular context
Inference	Reaching conclusions, generalizing	Computational tools, visual aids for pattern recognition, retrieval of information about similar situations
Assimilation	Making sense of facts, pattern matching, determining relationships	Computational tools, visual aids for pattern recognition and relating elements, retrieval of information regarding similar situations
Explanation	Justifying choices made	All of the above to provide consistent, common, and objective decision framework

or an initial list of alternatives, or suggest analytic tools to use or decision facets that would benefit from examination. Such artificial intelligence enables a decision-maker to greatly improve his or her understanding of the decision context.[13]

Through effective CBIS support it is thus possible to *expand* the decision-maker's ability to resolve decision situations. However, CBIS support of decision making is limited by the characteristics of any computer-based system: all CBIS are directed by prespecified software, can access only data already stored on a computer-readable medium, are oriented toward quantitative analyses, and possess no natural creativity, insight, or reasoning capability. When supporting decision making through computer-based technologies, one should aim to create a human–machine decision-making team that exploits the capabilities of both the computer and the human decision-maker.

Such a view does not mean that the decision-maker must directly interact with a DSS—only that these computer-based capabilities are realizable.[14] Direct interaction with the DSS for its own sake is not the issue. What is of concern is providing an appropriate combination of people, data, interaction modes, hardware, and software to resolve a decision situation in a convenient, timely, and cost-effective manner. Exactly what combination is best depends on many factors: the decision situation, the personal characteristics of the decision-maker, the organizational climate, and the availability of computer-based resources.

Finally, decision-makers will not use CBIS support simply because it exists; they must see such utilization as in their best interests.[15] If the perceived costs of learning to use and then actually using a DSS exceed the perceived benefits, little use will occur. Successful decision-makers have arrived at personal strategies of decision making independent of computer-based support. Convincing such individuals to embrace computer technology is not easy, but it is precisely these *already* successful decision-makers who have the experience, insight, and knowledge about specific decision areas, as well as about the art of making decisions, who can best exploit DSS capabilities.

DECISION SUPPORT SYSTEMS

A Working Definition

These DSS capabilities represent a new role for computers in supporting organizational activities.[16,17] As their primary purpose is to provide fast, flexible, ad hoc decision support fully under decision-maker control, DSS make computers useful to organizational members who previously had not found CBIS to be *personally* useful, but who acknowledged their gen-

FIGURE 8.2
Visualizations of IRS and DSS

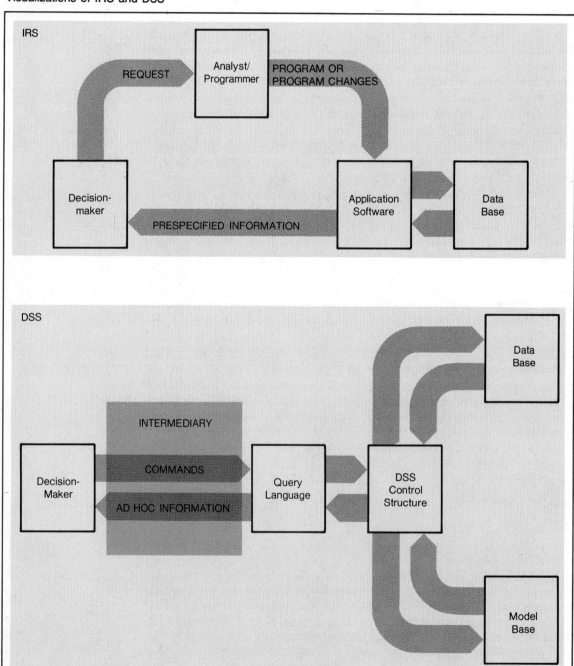

eral benefit to the organization. With DSS, CBIS support of nonroutine, short-term, day-to-day activities can become a reality.

Just how a DSS can provide such support can be seen in the following example.[18] To evaluate a proposed joint venture, Houston Oil and Mineral Corporation built a Monte Carlo risk-analysis model in only a few days. While the initial results of the analysis seemed favorable, an executive vice-president suggested that additional risk analysis was needed. In twenty minutes the additional modeling was completed and indicated considerable downside risk. The project was consequently dismissed. The key point is that a fast, economic response was made to a request based solely on a vague uneasiness felt by a decision-maker.

A DSS accomplishes its objectives by enabling decision-makers to converse with a computer-based system (in a language natural to the decision situation) so both data and models to operate on these data are conveniently accessed and manipulated. One means of describing a DSS is to compare it with an IRS. As shown in Figure 8.2, an IRS enables a decision-maker to receive prespecified reports produced by an application program specially written for that purpose by a computer specialist. A DSS, however, enables a decision-maker to initiate a sequence of commands to make use of a data base and a collection of models—a model base—in ways that need not have been precisely envisioned. As also shown in Figure 8.2, the decision-maker might interact directly with the DSS or through an intermediary. Table 8.2 presents characteristics of both IRS and DSS that more completely convey these distinctions.

What is being presented as a DSS is actually an ideal. Any CBIS directed toward the support of organizational decision making lies along

TABLE 8.2
Characteristics of IRS and DSS

IRS	DSS
Is a product	Is a service
Is a separate system	Is part of a decision-making system
Provides information as an input to the decision-making process	Provides direct support for decision making through the entire decision-making process
Has a time frame of days, weeks, and months	Has a time frame of minutes, hours, and days
Works within decision-maker's existing range and capabilities	Extends decision-maker's range and capabilities
Provides inflexible access to selected data by selected models	Provides flexible access to both data and models
Is controlled by software	Is controlled by decision-maker

a continuum anchored at one end by a pure IRS and at the other by a pure DSS. While many pure IRS exist, there are few if any pure DSS. Certain CBIS developed recently, however, lie near the pure DSS end of the continuum. Figure 8.3 describes the increase in data and model capabilities gained as one moves along the continuum.

DSS COMPONENTS

The basic building blocks of a DSS are listed in Table 8.3. A DSS is a *total* decision-making system; thus, the hardware, software, and human components should be viewed as an integrated whole.

The most crucial hardware element is an interactive graphics terminal that provides for responsive, natural, and rich communication between the human and software DSS elements. While microcomputers are becoming more powerful and can function as a limited DSS, to attain sophisticated DSS capabilities a terminal (or microcomputer in terminal mode) linked by telecommunications to a more powerful processor would likely be required. Telecommunication capabilities might as well provide access to external information services. Since a microprocessor is being used, local data storage devices can support a local data base capability, providing fast access to data and model elements.

FIGURE 8.3
IRS–DSS Continuum

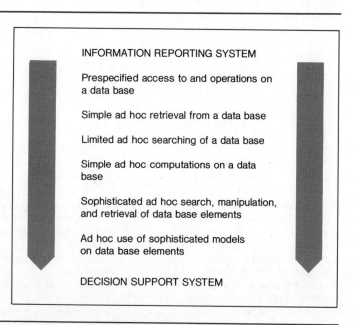

INFORMATION REPORTING SYSTEM

Prespecified access to and operations on a data base

Simple ad hoc retrieval from a data base

Limited ad hoc searching of a data base

Simple ad hoc computations on a data base

Sophisticated ad hoc search, manipulation, and retrieval of data base elements

Ad hoc use of sophisticated models on data base elements

DECISION SUPPORT SYSTEM

TABLE 8.3
DSS Components

Hardware	Software	Human
Interactive, graphics terminal	Data base management system	Decision-maker
Access via telecommunications to a powerful processor	Model management system	Intermediary (possibly)
Microprocessor at local site (possibly)	Query language that permits communication between decision-maker and DSS executive	
Secondary storage devices at local site (possibly)	Executive software that controls DSS processing	

At least four software components are required: a query language through which decision-maker commands are interpreted and DSS responses are presented, a data base management system, a model management system, and a DSS control structure that links these three. The query language should provide a set of commands—*graph, list, select, describe, get,* etc.—that relate to concepts in the decision-maker's mind.[19] Commands that tell what is desired rather than how it is produced are preferred.[20] The functions of data base management systems have been described elsewhere (Chapter 6). Model management systems are similar in function in that they provide a capability to generate, maintain, and use a collection of models.[21,22] Models, like data, are valuable organizational resources. An effective model management system supports the construction, testing, and maintenance of models in resolving a decision situation.

The human elements include the decision-maker and possibly an intermediary who interacts with the DSS in place of the decision-maker. There are, in fact, three human roles to be filled—model-builder, model-user, and decision-maker. The advantage of the decision-maker's filling all three roles is that the symbiotic benefits of *direct* decision support are greatest. The benefit of employing specialists for each role is that through specialization any dysfunctional aspects associated with learning and task interruption may be lessened.

DSS Types

While the emergence of DSS capabilities is a relatively recent event, a number of CBIS have been developed with characteristics approaching those listed for a pure DSS. This discussion of DSS examples is intended primarily to illustrate differences between DSS types and to indicate the

TABLE 8.4
Examples of Institutional DSS

Name	Description
AAIMS	Planning, financial, marketing, and operations analysis in airline industry
BRANDAID	Marketing analysis manipulating prices, advertising, promotion, and sales force
CIS	Analysis of production plan changes as they affect manufacturing operations for truck manufacturer
IMS	Evaluation of advertising strategies by accessing and manipulating consumer data base
IRIS	Personnel management and labor negotiation support by accessing employee data base
ISSPA	Policy analysis in state government
MAPP	Budget and cost analysis in bank
MYCIN	Medical diagnosis of infections by accessing data on patient symptoms and test results
NEEMIS	Energy-related policy analysis for New England states
PMS	Analysis of account and security data by investment managers in bank's trust department

variety of DSS currently available. More detailed descriptions of these and other DSS can be found elsewhere.[23-27]

Two basic types of DSS can be defined: institutional and general. *Institutional DSS* address a family of tightly defined, closely related decisions. Because the support provided is intertwined with a particular decision context, flexibility and range of use are reduced. The query languages used with an institutional DSS, however, can exploit this familiarity with a specific decision context and provide a collection of commands that parallel the terminology normally used by decision-makers. Table 8.4 lists a number of institutional DSS.

A *general DSS*, on the other hand, provides a generalized modeling language for building and executing a DSS. While its development requires considerable technical expertise, a general DSS enables DSS capabilities to be quickly, easily, and inexpensively provided throughout an organization. Often decision-makers themselves, rather than computer specialists, can develop these institutional DSS. As has occurred with data base management systems, the software industry—realizing that a market for DSS is emerging—has begun to market such software systems. For the most part, these systems are best described as *financial planning languages.*

A Sample Institutional DSS.   The Portfolio Management System (PMS), one of the early DSS development efforts, supports the activities associated with managing client investment portfolios.[28,29] The success of PMS is demonstrated by its adoption by a number of banks and by the fact that similar CBIS are currently used by many banks and investment houses.

With PMS, an account manager can access and manipulate three data bases: information on each client's portfolio (holdings, performance, objectives), information on market securities (historical as well as predicted performance), and up-to-the-minute market prices and activities. The investment analyst accesses these data bases with the PMS commands in Table 8.5.

An interesting illustration of how a DSS can be molded by users to support decision activities is provided by one incident in the PMS development history. In the prototype version of PMS, a CREATE command was made available that enabled an analyst to design a hypothetical portfolio and project its performance. This command, which required significant cognitive effort by the decision-maker, was not used during the test period, and it was not subsequently included in the initial operational version of PMS. Shortly after PMS was introduced, however, account managers requested that such a capability be added. Use of PMS increased substantially with the addition of this new command.

Financial Planning Languages. Financial planning languages (FPL) have evolved over the last decade to the point where they now provide CBIS support approaching that characterized earlier as pure DSS. The development of FPL from relatively unsophisticated, IRS-like systems to their current sophisticated forms is depicted in Figure 8.4. The earliest FPL

TABLE 8.5
Basic PMS Commands

Command	Function
DIRECTORY	Provide an overview of all accounts managed by analyst
GRAPH	Portray account, security, and market trends graphically
GROUP	Produce histogram of distribution of holdings for account by prespecified classification of securities
HISTO	Produce histogram of any available data item for account
ISSUE	Provide prespecified report on any security
SCAN	View holdings of any security (or group of securities) across all accounts managed by analyst
SCATTER	Examine relationship between two data items associated with securities held by account
SUMMARY	Provide prespecified report on account
TABLE	Provide capability to design ad hoc report assessing account

FIGURE 8.4
Development of Financial Planning Languages

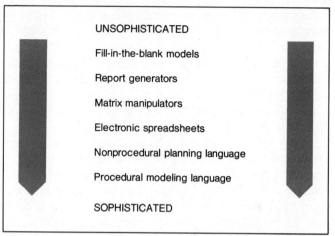

UNSOPHISTICATED

Fill-in-the-blank models

Report generators

Matrix manipulators

Electronic spreadsheets

Nonprocedural planning language

Procedural modeling language

SOPHISTICATED

were essentially parameterized IRS that allowed a decision-maker to select (by completing special input forms) a prespecified analysis to be performed. The technology advanced from ad hoc report generation (the decision-maker could obtain any report desired from a pool of data items) through matrix manipulators (the decision-maker could fill a matrix from a pool of data items and then manipulate this matrix in an ad hoc fashion) to today's more sophisticated FPL forms:

Electronic spreadsheets A matrix manipulator and report generator with financial functions,

Nonprocedural planning A modeling capability using predefined functions put into operation through commands,

Procedural modeling language A modeling capability using essentially any type of functions put into operation through both commands and more primitive operators.

The FPL packages offered by software vendors today represent these three forms.

While the analysis functions provided by FPL are oriented toward financial decision activities, a variety of analyses can be performed: mathematical, statistical, and forecasting procedures; sensitivity (i.e., a "what if" capability) analysis; goal-seeking and optimization procedures; risk analysis; financial functions such as depreciation, discounting, and return-on-investment; hierarchical consolidations; report generation;

TABLE 8.6
Application Areas for Financial Planning Languages

Accounting	Finance	Personnel
Budgeting	Capital budgeting	Recruiting needs
Pro forma statements	Feasibility studies	Wage and salary negotiations
	Investment analyses	
	Decisions to lease or buy	
	Cash flow	

Manufacturing	Marketing	Corporate Planning
Capacity planning	Product mix	Goal setting
Plant location	Distribution policy	Profit planning
Labor negotiation	Sales and pricing analysis	Mergers and acquisitions
Facilities planning	Advertising policy	New venture analysis
Production scheduling	Market planning	

FIGURE 8.5
Sample Questions for FPL Decision Activities

- What if raw materials prices go up 10 percent? 15 percent? 30 percent?
- How sensitive is net income to selling price? Material cost? Labor cost? Interest rates?
- Should we expand an existing plant or build a new plant? Where? When?
- Should we buy or lease capital equipment? Shall we plan on a three-year or five-year life?
- What impact will a 20 percent increase in fuel cost have on our operating ratio? 10 percent? 25 percent?
- What if the new labor contract calls for a 10 percent wage increase?
- What would happen if, because of a downturn in the national economy, our projected revenues fell by 20 percent?
- What would be the effect of a shorter accounts receivable cycle? A longer accounts payable cycle? A reduction in work-in-process inventory?

and graphic display generation. This financial orientation, however, does not preclude their use in other functional areas. Table 8.6 lists a number of applications across a variety of functional areas, and Figure 8.5 suggests the types of decision tasks normally handled. Not all FPL provide all these capabilities. Significant differences exist, which tend to be reflected in the costs of each package.

TABLE 8.7

Financial Planning Languages Available on Large Computer Systems

Company	Product	Delivery Method	Price	Required Hardware/ System Software
Management Decision Systems Inc.	Express	Timesharing, package	Variable $250,000–$330,000	IBM under VM/CMS Prime
Applied Data Research Inc.	Empire	Package	$48,000–$70,000	DEC 10, 20 And VAX IBM—TSO, VM/CMS, Roscoe
Boeing Computer Service	EIS	Primarily timesharing, also package	N/A	IBM—VM/CMS
Execucom Systems Corp.	IFPS	Timesharing, package	Variable $56,000	Most major mainframes and superminicomputers
Simplan Systems Inc.	Simplan	Timesharing, package, turnkey system	Variable $38,000–$61,000 $100,000	IBM—TSO And VM/CMS Prime (250 and up)
EPS Inc.	FCS	Package	$43,000–$60,000	Most major mainframes and minicomputers
Interactive Data Corp.	XSIM	Primarily timesharing, package	Variable $300,000	IBM—VM
Cuffs Planning & Modeling Ltd.	Cuffs	Timesharing, package	Variable $50,000	DEC 10, 20 IBM—VM/CMS
Decision Products Inc.	Reveal DSS	Package	$65,000–$88,000	Prime DEC—VAX IBM—VM/CMS, TSO
MDCR Inc.	Impact	Timesharing, package	Variable $52,000	IBM/370—OS/VS1, VM, MVS/TSO
Lloyd Bush & Associates	Model	Timesharing, package	Variable $16,000–$85,000	Prime DEC—VMS IBM—TSO, VM/CMS, VSPC Hewlett Packard Univac
Capex Corp.	Autotab II	Timesharing, package	$22,000+ $26,000–$30,000	IBM—OS, OS/VS, VM/CMS
	Autotab 300 Autotab 3000	Turnkey system Package	$75,000+ Due For Release 2nd Quarter 1982	HP 300 HP 3000
United Telecommunications Inc.	Foresight	Timesharing, package	Variable $45,000	Most major mainframes and minicomputers

Source: *Information Systems News*, Sept. 7, 1981, p. 23. Copyright © 1981 by CMP Publications, Inc.

Initially FPL were available only for large computer systems. Table 8.7 lists a number of these FPL, along with their prices and configuration requirements. These software packages can be acquired and placed on an organization's computer system or accessed through a time-sharing service. Acquiring a package to be placed on an organization's own large computer system requires not only that the software be purchased, but that a large computer system be available. Accessing a package through a time-sharing service reduces this massive up-front investment, but heavy utilization can easily lead to monthly expenses (terminal rental, line costs, time-sharing service charges) of $5,000–$10,000 or more. Clearly many organizations and individuals cannot use FPL because of such costs.

With the arrival of powerful microcomputers, the situation has changed markedly. Table 8.8 lists some FPL available today on microcomputers. Many others exist, and new packages are announced almost weekly. For a relatively small expense ($3,000–$6,000 for a microcomputer and $100–$1,500 for the FPL package), FPL capabilities are made available. The first of these micro-based FPL, VISICALC, has sold more than 100,000 copies since 1979. (It is the most popular piece of software ever written.)

The arrival of low-cost micro-based FPL has not spelt doom for the FPL that are executed on large computer systems. If an organization has a large computer system, it can acquire one package and make it available to hundreds of decision-makers through interactive terminals. With micro-based FPL, each user must acquire both a microcomputer and a copy of the FPL package. Moreover, FPL that run on large computer systems are more sophisticated and more capable. However, this performance differential will probably diminish in the near future; at least two large system vendors (the developers of IFPS and Cuffs) are planning versions of their products that will run on 32-bit microcomputers.[30]

DSS Experiences

Although the DSS concept is a relatively recent phenomenon, case studies have been conducted of decision-maker DSS behaviors.[31-35] Table 8.9 summarizes the major findings of these studies. These observations, as well as others on human–machine interaction,[36,37] suggest that, if organizational members are to become active and eager DSS users, a DSS should do the following:

- Capture and reflect the way decision-makers (hence managers) think.
- Support multiple decision processes and multiple decision styles.
- Be easy and convenient to use and not require extensive training.

TABLE 8.8

Financial Planning Languages Available on Microcomputers

Company	Name/Cost	Configuration
Advanced Mgmt. Strategies Inc.	TARGET $195	48K Apple II Plus; SoftCard; Language System: *CP/M 2.2; two drives.* Or 64K TRS-80 Model II; Lifeboat CP/M 2.2
Apple Computer	Decision Evaluator System $400	48K Apple II Plus, one disk drive
	Plan 80 $185	64K Apple II, Pascal, one drive
	Info. Analyst $250	Apple III; AppleSOS, two drives
Carolina Bus. Comp., Inc.	REPORT WRITER $149	Any 48K CP/M System; Microsoft BASIC
C4P, Inc./Lifeboat Assoc.	FPL $99	48K CP/M system; 120K-byte drive, compiled version
Digital Marketing	Plan 80 $295	CP/M 1.4 and higher, one drive 56K or 64K TRS-80 Model II
Ferox Microsystems (also—Addison-Wesley Pub.)	RCS $1,500	64K Apple II Plus; three disk drives; Pascal language card; TI 810 printer
Financial Planning Assoc. (sold by WESTICO, Inc.)	MINIMODEL $495	48K CP/M; CBASIC 2
Hayden Publishing	FINPLAN $69.95/cassette $74.95/disk	TRS-80 16K; cassette or disk based
Lifeboat Associates	T-MAKER $150	48K CP/M systems; two disk drives
Ohio Scientific	PLANNER PLUS $200	OSI C4P or C8P; two disk drives
Personal Software	VISICALC $99 to $299	Apple II 48K; 48K Atari 800; CBM 32K; HP-85; TRS-80 Model II and III
	DESKTOP/PLAN II $195	Apple II 48K
Spectrum Software	Universal Computing Machine $99	32K Apple II with Applesoft in ROM; DOS version 3.2, 32K TRS-80 Model 1; TRSDOS version 2.3
Vector Graphic	EXECUPLAN $150	Vector Graphic VIP, System B or 3000; two drives

Source: *Personal Computing*, 5(June 1981):70. Reprinted with permission. Copyright © 1981 Hayden Publishing Company.

TABLE 8.9
Characteristics of DSS Use

Characteristic	Explanation
Little on-line decision-making	Few decision situations are resolved during DSS interaction. Rather, DSS use brings about learning, communication, and explanation that supports off-line individual, group, and organizational decision processes.
Unintended uses	DSS use frequently deviates widely from that expected by DSS designers. Users personalize the inherent capabilities of the DSS and evolve others over time as experience is gained.
Variety of uses	Unintended use along with considerable individual differences in use result in a wide spectrum of DSS uses.
Little decision-maker use	Managerial work habits and styles often do not mesh well with terminal use. Much DSS use occurs through intermediaries.
Decision-maker design	While decision-makers might not personally interact with a DSS for decision resolution, they often personally develop the decision models embedded in the DSS.
Limited DSS working set	DSS users typically work with a limited set of DSS capabilities (data and models) during terminal sessions. This working set may vary considerably over a sequence of terminal sessions aimed at resolving a particular decision situation.
Decision-maker problems	Many DSS users have difficulty defining decision situations, identifying relevant data elements and models, and otherwise initiating the decision-making process.

- Allow a decision-maker to adapt it as experience is gained in DSS capabilities.
- Provide aid to decision-makers in structuring decision situations and in the initial stages of resolution (most current DSS contribute little to these decision process stages).
- Be "user-friendly" (prompt, meaningful, and "pleasant" responses, under user control, minimal user-memory requirements, error-tolerant, comfortable physical environment, natural physical interaction).

Probably no DSS today possesses all these characteristics. (The president of Execucom, the developers of IFPS, concurs with this assessment.[38]) However, the time when such DSS will be available is not that distant.

EMERGING DSS TRENDS

Manager's Work Station

An idea attracting considerable attention is that of the manager's or executive's work station.[39] By combining DSS technologies with those associated with office automation (Chapter 5), one can provide a readily accessible and convenient cluster of computer-based support mechanisms to handle those information processing tasks that dominate the workload of management and staff personnel. Equipment at such a work station could include an interactive terminal or a microcomputer with local storage devices, and might also include a hard-copy printer, a copier, and microform reader and files. Through this work station, an individual would also have access to a more powerful processor, the organization's entire data base, and external information services.

While the technology exists to produce such work stations, the costs are still prohibitive for most organizations. However, there is a natural evolution toward this goal—organizational members are acquiring terminals, personal computers, and word processors, which are being interconnected and linked to other organizational CBIS through telecommunications.

As an aid to envisioning what might be possible with a full-scale manager's work station, consider the following description of what the White House terms the "information-efficient" Presidential aide.[40] On arriving at work, the aide sits at a terminal and reads any messages that arrived during the night; checks the day's schedule, reviews documents of relevance, and obtains background information on issues to be addressed and people to be met; checks the status of ongoing projects; and browses through articles from the morning's newspapers selected by "key word" searches. Prior to going to any meeting, the aide again sits at the terminal and accesses data or document files stored in a personal or White House data file, accesses external data or document files (other agencies, news services, *Congressional Record*, etc.), uses computational and modeling capabilities, and writes or revises reports (text, graphics, data analysis and presentation, etc.).

Group Decision Support

The idea of a corporate "war room" or "chart room" is not new. By bringing together individuals with specialized knowledge and different perspectives and by presenting background and operating information through charts and slides, one can obtain *group* resolution of a decision situation. A major source of discontent regarding corporate war rooms is the static nature of presented materials. By exploiting DSS technologies, this limitation can be overcome.

One strategy for supporting group decision making with DSS is through a concept known as the "planning laboratory."[41] In such a room each participant has an interactive graphics terminal with DSS capabilities. This terminal can be used in three ways—as a source of *individual support* for each participant (e.g., offering access to data or documents, acting as a computational tool); as a *group slave* (e.g., enabling the group to jointly build, modify, and use models, to view background or current operating data); or as a *message system* (e.g., notifying a staff assistant to produce needed materials, receiving notification of critical events). A valuable quality of such support is the anonymity allowed participants making sensitive judgments, as in voting, estimating, forecasting, rating, or brainstorming.

DSS Support of Intuition

Research on the human brain demonstrates that the two hemispheres undertake quite distinct information processing activities: the left cerebral hemisphere is characterized by rational, sequential, and analytic processes, while the right is characterized by intuitive, simultaneous, and holistic processes.[42] While everyone at various times uses both sides, most people, because of their educational background and unique experiences, tend to emphasize one or the other. Interestingly, many successful managers and executives seem to favor intuitive processing.[43]

Organizational decision making can be successfully accomplished with either form of processing. A thought-provoking question arises, however, over how best to provide decision support with a DSS. Should a DSS be designed to match a decision-maker's dominant style of decision making, or should it complement this dominant style by supporting those processes that are underdeveloped?[44] The ideal approach, clearly, would be to do both.

Because of the inherent characteristics of computer systems and the tendency for analysts and programmers to prefer analytic decision styles, CBIS have historically emphasized analytic approaches when supporting organizational decision making. One of the most exciting aspects of DSS technologies is their potential for supporting *intuitive* processes in decision making. Verbal and visual information presentation modes, which are becoming increasingly available, have vast potential in this area. Exactly how they can realize it, however, is just beginning to be explored.

PROGRAMMED DECISION SYSTEMS

When a decision situation becomes so structured that explicit decision rules can be specified that handle the situation effectively most of the time, a program can be written to incorporate these decision rules within a CBIS. Such CBIS are referred to as *programmed decision systems* (PDS). By employing a PDS, one can transfer the *act* of decision making from a human to the CBIS. A PDS behaves much the same way as a transaction processing system (TPS), with the major distinction being that a decision can be identified that was previously made by a human.

Some common PDS applications involve loan or credit approval, inventory reordering, college acceptance, and Internal Revenue decisions about whom to audit. As might be expected with such applications, areas often arise in which the rigid application of decision rules may not be appropriate. In such instances a likely PDS action is "no action," with the act of decision making being returned to human decision-makers who, through experience or insight, should be able to resolve the situation.

While the act of decision making can be delegated to a PDS, *responsibility* for the decision remains with human decision-makers. A decision rule—no matter how well thought out—can never cover all aspects of a situation. And as decision rules must evolve in response to changes in the organization or its environment, the fragility of such rules should be clear. Thus, PDS decision rules must periodically be assessed and revised to maintain their correctness. Often, however, an assessment occurs only after a problem has arisen because of an invalid PDS action.

Currently implemented PDS can be described as *rule following*—that is, actions are chosen according to programmed rules. Any changes in these rules require human intervention. Research is underway, however, to use techniques borrowed from studies of *artificial intelligence* to provide PDS with a self-adjustment capability. If the results of the actions taken by a PDS are monitored, captured, and stored in a local data base, generalized analysis rules can also be programmed that enable the PDS not only to detect when its operating rules are becoming less effective, but to also modify these rules. Given such capabilities, a PDS should be able to react to environmental changes without direct human intervention. Providing such capabilities even minimally, however, requires considerable technical expertise plus an extensive understanding of the decision context involved.

CONCLUSION

A DSS provides a computer-based capability to support organizational activities for which CBIS support was previously deficient—those day-to-day or nonroutine situations that cannot be prespecified. As such organizational activities represent many tasks engaged in by management and staff personnel in organizations, the potential impact of DSS technology on organizations is large.

Situations particularly suited for DSS applications are characterized by at least a partial decision structure so relevant information elements and appropriate operations on these elements can be identified. While the objective of DSS support does *not* include provision of a solution, a general framework to facilitate decision conceptualization, resolution, and implementation must exist. If such conditions are met, both recurring and one-time decision situations can be aided.

Suitable DSS technologies exist today; most seemingly technical problems are associated with the costs of configuring appropriate hardware and developing needed software. With hardware price decreases expected to continue and with the availability of general DSS through proprietary software packages, these cost barriers will be reduced to a level where all organizations can benefit from DSS capabilities. Difficulties most likely to persist with DSS implementations for some time involve attaining sufficient *organizational* understanding of a decision situation so a framework for resolution can be prescribed, capturing and making available through the DSS the information elements crucial for decision resolution, and successfully addressing the human factor issues associated with meeting the information processing needs of a wide variety of organizational members, many of whose work habits are far removed from those traditionally associated with computer usage.

A PDS can be implemented whenever decision actions, information elements, and explicit rules resulting in the effective resolution of a decision situation can be incorporated within a computer program. In such cases, the organizational activity involved can be handled more accurately and consistently and less expensively by PDS than by human decision-makers. Applications are most successful when applied to simple, repetitious, and stable decision situations.

When implementing a PDS, one must recognize that responsibility for decision resolution remains with the organization's members, and that the continued validity of the decision rules must be closely monitored. Additionally, the danger of alienating customers, clients, vendors, or employees always arises when organizational activities are delegated to automated processes. Consequently, organizational and behavioral procedures—or the lack thereof—that accompany PDS services are crucial to their eventual success.

KEY ISSUES

Much organizational activity involves unanticipated, nonroutine, and poorly structured situations. Supporting such activities by CBIS requires convenient, easy, and quick access to data bases and analysis tools. A DSS provides such capabilities.

Decision making involves choosing among alternatives under conditions of uncertainty.

Four major steps comprise the decision-making process: recognizing the decision situation, structuring the decision situation, resolving the decision situation, and implementing the decision action.

Typically, CBIS support of decision making involves aiding the following decision tasks: search, computation, specification, inference, assimilation, and explanation.

A DSS enables a decision-maker to converse with a computer-based system to access and manipulate both data and models to operate on these data in ways that need not have been precisely specified. The decision-maker may converse directly with the DSS or indirectly through a human intermediary.

Two basic types of DSS can be defined: institutional DSS, which address families of tightly defined decisions, and general DSS, which provide a modeling capability for building and then using a DSS.

The most readily available general DSS are financial planning languages. These software packages have been produced for most computer systems. Their cost and sophistication vary widely.

It is unlikely that a decision-maker will use a DSS if the personal costs involved in learning about and then using the DSS are believed to be greater than the benefits.

An intriguing area of DSS support for decision making involves the aiding of intuitive as well as analytical decision styles.

A PDS can be an effective means of decision support whenever explicit decision rules can be incorporated into computer software. In such situations, the act of decision making is transferred from a human to a CBIS. Responsibility for the decision, however, remains with the human.

By applying artificial intelligence principles to PDS, one can construct PDS that are self-adjustable.

DISCUSSION QUESTIONS

1. Why are IRS unable to meet many day-to-day situations organizational members face? Why isn't it possible to design reports complete enough to handle all situations?

2. Identify a decision you face on a periodic basis. Specify the alternatives that exist, their associated outcomes, and any known contingencies that suggest a particular outcome is desired.

3. Do people really go through the decision process specified in Figure 8.1? Provide examples from your own experiences in which all four major steps were executed, in which some steps were bypassed, and in which some steps were repeated.

4. How are decision structures built? Do general structures exist that can be used for a variety of decision situations? Provide some illustrations of such general structures.

5. Consider the corporate decision to build a new manufacturing facility. Provide illustrations of decision activities involving each of the following decision tasks: search, computation, specification, inference, assimilation, and explanation.

6. Exactly what does it mean to "create a human–machine decision-making team"?

7. What is a "model base"? Using the decision context of production planning, provide examples of what might be included in a model base.

8. Can the DSS concept as introduced ever be more than an ideal? Why or why not?

9. Three human DSS roles were defined: model-builder, model-user, and decision-maker. Discuss the advantages and disadvantages of employing a human intermediary in each role.

10. Why do decision-makers favor DSS commands that identify what is to be done, rather than how it is to be done? Do you see any disadvantages with such commands?

11. It is still quite expensive to configure systems such as a manager's work station and group decision support facilities. In which managerial contexts might such decision support be most easily cost justified? Why?

12. Propose some computer-based means of supporting intuition. Illustrate your proposal using any decision situation you choose.

13. What advantages does a PDS offer over a human decision-maker? Are there any disadvantages?

BRIEF CASES

1. *Mountain Community Bank*

    Major decisions facing the rapidly expanding Mountain Community Bank were determining where to locate new branches and which banking services to offer at each new branch. Sharon Tinker had been given the assignment of designing a DSS to support these critical decisions.

    The branch location decision was a very complex one involving urban growth patterns, size of the client base, location of competitors, location of other MCB branches, real estate costs, and so on. Deciding which services to emphasize at each bank was less complex, as it depended largely on the makeup of the client base.

One of Sharon's key design decisions revolved around which of the decision steps to support with the DSS. Could all four steps (recognition, structuring, resolution, and implementation) be supported? If not, which steps could be adequately supported?

Which decision process steps should be emphasized in the design of this DSS? Propose some specific support mechanisms.

2. *Southside Auto Parts*

One of the biggest headaches Sam Hellick faced with his auto parts company involved deciding when to drop items from his inventory. The need to stock over six thousand parts tied up a large amount of cash that could otherwise be used to finance further expansion of the firm.

The owner of a local software house had approached Sam at the monthly meeting of the community service club they both belonged to with an intriguing proposal. The owner believed there was a huge market for an "inventory maintenance" DSS to be marketed to businesses like Southside Auto Parts. He proposed that, if Sam would work with the house in the design effort and let his company serve as an initial test site for the software, the resultant DSS, along with any other of the house software products, would be made available to Southside at no cost. Sam agreed.

It was recognized early on that most likely purchasers of the DSS product would have little knowledge of or experience with computer-based systems. Accordingly, the DSS command language would be a key feature of the product. If the DSS commands were not easily understood by prospective purchasers, it would be difficult to convince them to buy the DSS. Sam's first task was to categorize the types of analysis that were regularly pursued when a parts inventory was examined to uncover items to drop.

What decision tasks would be involved in such an analysis? Identify likely tasks and associate each with a DSS command phrase. Assume that this "inventory maintenance" DSS would include an inventory tracking and control system.

3. *Hickory Manufacturing Company*

The corporate planning group's initial success in supporting planning activities through computer-based means resulted in the establishment of a task force to assess the desirability of acquiring a financial planning language to further computerization of the planning function. The mandate given this task force, however, was wider than simply selecting a financial planning language for the corporate planning group. All decisions were to be made from a corporate perspective, in that (1) any package selected would have to satisfy all potential corporate users and (2) the economic evaluation of any decision would have to consider this large group of end-users.

The task force's initial efforts were spent identifying the size of the potential user base for a planning aid. This study determined that there were eighteen sites with a total of eighty-eight users who could make immediate use of a financial planning capability. Thirteen of the sites were connected to the firm's mainframe computer. While this mainframe computer could easily handle a sophisticated DSS, the existing time-sharing configuration was reaching its full capacity.

What alternatives are there for acquiring a financial planning language? Which alternative would best fit the needs of Hickory Manufacturing?

4. *Greco Components*

Randy Fitzin was deeply concerned with the progress of his project to develop a sales control system. Putting it as politely as possible, Rose Leary was not overly impressed with the initial design. Her first comment to Randy was, "Just as I expected! Numbers! Numbers! Numbers!"

Randy now realized that the last thing Rose wanted was a weekly one-inch stack of computer printouts. An alternative approach that might prove successful would take on the quality of a DSS. That is, Randy could provide Rose with a capability to interactively examine an on-line data base that contained relevant data on sales force activities. The key question was how to do this so it would seem natural to a "people person" such as Rose.

Describe some ways to support Rose with DSS capabilities. At this point be as creative as possible. Worry about costs later.

NOTES

1. V. A. Vyssotsky, "The Use of Computers for Business Functions," in M. C. Dertouszos and J. Moses (eds.), *The Computer Age: A Twenty-Year View* (Cambridge, Mass.: MIT Press, 1979), pp. 129–145.

2. P. Berger and F. Edelman, "IRIS: A Transactions-Based DSS for Human Resources Management," *Data Base* 8(1977):22–29.

3. H. A. Simon and A. Newell, *Human Problem Solving* (Englewood Cliffs, N.J.: Prentice-Hall, 1972).

4. W. F. Pounds, "The Process of Problem Finding," *Industrial Management Review* 11(1969):1–19.

5. L. P. Schrenk, "Aiding the Decision Maker—A Decision Process Model," *Ergonomics* 12(1969):543–57.

6. H. Mintzberg, D. Raisingham, and A. Theoret, "The Structure of 'Unstructured' Decision Processes," *Administrative Science Quarterly* 21(1976):246–75.

7. Pounds (1969).

8. A. Tversky and D. Kahneman, "The Framing of Decisions and the Psychology of Choice," *Science* 211(1981):453–58.

9. P. G. W. Keen and M. S. Scott Morton, *Decision Support Systems: An Organizational Perspective* (Reading, Mass.: Addison-Wesley, 1978).

10. R. B. Miller, "Archetypes in Man–Computer Problem Solving," *Ergonomics* 12(1969):559–81.

11. P. G. W. Keen, "Decision Support Systems and the Marginal Economics of Effort," CISR working paper no. 48, Sloan School of Management, MIT, 1979.

12. S. A. Alter, *Decision Support Systems: Current Practice and Continuing Challenges* (Reading, Mass.: Addison-Wesley, 1980).

13. J. J. Elam and J. C. Henderson, "Knowledge Engineering Concepts for Decision Support System Design and Implementation," *Proceedings of the 14th Hawaii International Conference on System Science* (Western Periodicals Co., 1981), pp. 639–43.

14. Alter (1980).

15. Keen (1979).

16. Keen and Scott Morton (1978).

17. P. G. W. Keen, "Value Analysis: Justifying Decision Support Systems," *MIS Quarterly* 5(1981):1–15.

18. D. J. Simpson, "Making Business Models Easy to Use," panel presentation at 1979 National Computer Conference, New York, 1979.

19. P. G. W. Keen, "Adaptive Design for Decision Support Systems," *Data Base* 12(1980):15–25.

20. R. H. Bonczek, C. W. Holsapple, and A. B. Whinston, "Future Directions for Developing Decision Support Systems," *Decision Sciences* 11(1980):616–31.

21. H. J. Will, "Model Management Systems," in E. Grochla and N. Syzperski (eds.), *Information Systems and Organizational Structures* (Berlin: DeGruyter, 1975), pp. 467–82.

22. J. J. Elam, J. C. Henderson, and L. W. Miller, "Model Management Systems: An Approach to Decision Support in Complex Organizations," working paper 80-08-04, Wharton School, University of Pennsylvania, 1980.

23. E. D. Carleson (ed.), "Proceedings of a Conference on Decision Support Systems," *Data Base* 8(1977).

24. Keen and Scott Morton (1978).

25. Bonczek *et al.* (1980).

26. Alter (1980).

27. R. H. Sprague, Jr., "Decision Support Systems: Implications for the System Analyst," in W. W. Cotterman, J. D. Cougar, N. L. Enger, and F. Harold (eds.), *Systems Analysis and Design: A Foundation for the 1980s* (New York: Elsevier North-Holland, 1981).

28. Keen and Scott Morton (1978).

29. Alter (1980).

30. R. L. Perry, "Crystal-Balling on Micros," *Computer Decisions* 13(1981):58–72, 161–74.

31. E. D. Carlson, B. F. Grace, and J. A. Sutton, "Case Studies of End User Requirements for Interactive Problem Solving Systems," *MIS Quarterly* 1(1977):51–63.

32. P. G. W. Keen and G. Wagner, "DSS: An Executive Mind-Support System," *Datamation* 25(1979):117–22.

33. Keen (1980).

34. Alter (1980).

35. Keen (1981).

36. B. Shneiderman, *Software Psychology* (Cambridge, Mass.: Winthrop, 1980).

37. L. Martin, "Ergonomics: A Growing Concern in CRT Design," *Mini-MicroSystems* 13(1980):119–21.

38. G. Wagner, "DSS in the Office of the Future," paper presented at the TIMS College on Information Systems seminar on Information Systems in the Office of the Future, Colorado Springs, Colo., November 9, 1980.

39. R. R. Panko, "Integration in Office Automation," *Proceedings of the 14th Hawaii International Conference on System Science* (Western Periodicals Co., 1981), pp. 685–89.

40. *MIS Week*, Sept. 24, 1980.

41. Wagner (1980).

42. W. Taggert and D. Robey, "Human Information Processing in Information and Decision Support Systems," *MIS Quarterly* 6(1982):61–73.

43. T. S. Issack, "Intuition: An Ignored Dimension of Management," *Academy of Management Review* 3(1978):917–22.

44. M. DeWaele, "Management Style and the Design of Decision Aids," *OMEGA* 6(1978):5–13.

MIS STRATEGIES

The five MIS Strategies that follow illustrate both the variety of computer-based information systems to be found in organizations today and the problems that can arise if attention to careful planning and analysis does not precede the use of information resources.

As is clearly seen with Hewlett-Packard, American Airlines, and Mellon Bank, the key to effective use of computer resources lies first in implementing information systems that "drive" an organization's mainstream operations and then in exploiting the resulting store of data to provide information that supports higher-level managers. The trends toward integrating an organization's information systems and using very high level languages to enable ad hoc end-user processing are represented. Arguments for adopting both the data base approach and distributed processing can be found, as well as a convincing case against distributed processing (illustrating that technical decisions must be made in the light of organizational objectives and concerns).

Accompanying these gains from using computer technologies, however, are numerous risks. The danger of becoming overly dependent on information resources and the necessity for considering all contingencies and for controlling input errors are strongly brought out in the story on Paine Webber. The need to continually reassess decision rules incorporated within information systems is pointed out through the Dallas Cowboys scouting report. The disadvantages of being a "technological pioneer" are suggested by Mellon Bank.

Opportunities for exploiting the information resource exist in virtually all organizations. Each organization, however, presents a unique context within which these technologies are implemented. If success is to be achieved, decisions leading toward organizational computerization must reflect a high degree of both technological and organizational understanding. These MIS Strategies illustrate just such a mix.

American Air Unifies DP Systems

For American Airlines, comprehensive relational data base tools cannot come soon enough to help ease the task of serving the host of users inside the country's second largest domestic airline.

In the meantime, however, the airline's data processing operation is hardly standing still. American is busy consolidating the various systems that have developed over the years to provide faster decision making for management.

Recent events such as the deregulation of the industry and the air traffic controller's strike have underscored the need for timely data and decision making for the nation's air carriers.

"The industry is not very healthy," notes Stephen G. Emery, senior director of marketing information systems.

Therefore, the three major thrusts of the airline's MIS strategy—passenger services, flight operations, and commercial data processing—have been integrated so that information from one can feed another and improve productivity for the company as a whole.

However, the data bases that serve these information systems have not proved as amenable to consolidation, and that has kept Max Hopper, vice-president of data processing and communications services, a very busy man.

"The relational data base tools that, hopefully, will come down the road in a few years will enable us to utilize common data bases in ways we cannot now," he says. "We would like to build as common a data base as we can to eliminate redundancy when these tools become available."

Hopper explains that many of American Airline's various DP systems were developed before the advent of data base technology. In addition, the complexity of running an airline has increased in recent years, especially from an economic standpoint.

Since the company wants to put as much computer power as possible into the hands of the user, the structuring of data in a format that can be accessed by users armed with nonprocedural inquiry tools has become a high priority.

Toward this end, American Airlines is attempting to consolidate its 50 most often used data bases into one, which will reduce the total number of data elements over 50 percent. However, this represents an enormous task that can be counted in many man-years of effort.

Hopper hopes that when the expected relational technologies appear, they will save the company much time and effort that can be more profitably applied to other areas. "We need a tool that will allow users to extract data and, in effect, create a new relational data base for them to inquire against," says Hopper. "There is no real tool for this type of processing available at this time."

An example of the firm's current approach is found in the Marketing Information Reporting System (MIRS)—a data base that has been created out of many separate applications systems. Its development, which took approximately 10 man-years of effort, according to Hopper, gives the marketing department direct access to data it needs for fast, accurate decisions.

Such decisions were never more important than in the recent air traffic controllers strike, when airlines were forced to curtail their schedules. American used a system that drew upon the giant MIRS data base to help it through this difficult period.

This system, the Segment Profitability Analysis Network (Span), is administered out of the marketing information department. Span actually creates a separate profit and loss statement for each leg of the thousand flights the firm operates each day. This capability is especially important because American does a large part of its business in connecting flights.

During the strike, the marketing department used Span to determine the effect that eliminating a route would have on overall profitability, and what flights to either add to or delete from the schedule.

"The primary purpose is to identify the principal revenue flows," says Emery. "It is very difficult to match revenues to a particular passenger and the leg of a flight without such a facility," he says. "If we can add one more passenger per flight, the system can pay for itself many times over.

"It is a tool I suspect no other airline has, and it provides us with an intelligent response where there was only an educated guess before."

The Span system uses the Mark IV information management system from Informatics Inc., Canoga Park, Calif., which not only provides them with the ability to create a catalogue of commonly requested reports, but allows a nontechnical user to develop an ad hoc request when necessary.

"The vast majority of the reports generated from the Span system were set up by users," reports Hopper. He explains that in the restructured data base, the data organization appears very flat, as it would in a relational system. The Mark IV system can access this type of data base very well, he adds, which puts control of the information in the hands of the user.

"We want it [control] to be the user's system, not our system," he says. "We try to encourage the users to be as proficient as possible in defining the requirements of the system and how it is to be implemented. But it all comes down to getting answers quicker." In the future, Hopper hopes to have an alternative to the time-consuming practice of reorganizing a data base for different users.

"If we had had the relational tools then, we could have built the MIRS data base out of existing data bases with a minimum of effort, without the need to develop an entirely new system," he says.

Otherwise, American Airlines will maintain its three-part DP operation, whose whole thrust is "to provide services to aid in the distribution of our product."

Chief among American's three DP facilities is the Semi-Automatic Business Research Environment system (Sabre), which handles the airline's reservations and passenger services. Developed by American from 1958 to 1964 in conjunction with IBM, the system has been upgraded numerous times since then.

"When it was first completed it handled from 12 to 15 messages per second, but now it is up to 600," says Hopper.

In addition to reservations, Sabre tracks baggage, meals, check-in, and prearranged seating for American Airlines passengers. The over 5,000 commercial travel services that work with American provide input to the system, as do American's own reservation personnel.

A second major system, for flight operations, is a "resource tracking system that allows us to monitor operating efficiencies," says Hopper. It helps formulate flight plans, tracks planned routes compared to actual routes, maintains fuel requirements, and handles many key administrative functions, including the payroll of flight personnel.

In addition, the system tracks spare-part inventories and the status of the airline's over 220 airplanes, and schedules maintenance personnel.

"It has gone a long way toward making us an efficient operator," says Hopper, "and it gives us the kind of tools we need."

The firm's third major system is commercial, and most clearly fulfills American's need for timely decision making. It handles financial matters and performs simulation.

"There is a tremendous amount of time-sharing in which we model the best possible routes for aircraft," says Hopper. "The systems are very highly related, and data from each are fed back to the others."

The aim of all this can be traced to four essential principals, says Hopper—distribute the product, provide a quality product to customers, increase internal productivity, and provide decision support to American Airline's management.

By William P. Martorelli. From *Information Systems News*, November 30, 1981. Copyright © 1981 by CMP Publications, Inc. Reprinted by permission.

HP System Manages to Give Detail

The art of translating a manufacturing firm's product into profit demands that management learn to speak the language of blue-collar information. Yet management information systems designed to provide white-collar workers with that nuts-and-bolts vocabulary often seem to speak in incomplete sentences.

"I don't think anyone's done a good job in summarizing operational information to the detail necessary to be useful to the management decision-making process," says Cort Van Rensselaer, manager of corporate information systems at Hewlett-Packard Co.

But he and the information systems organization of the Palo Alto, Calif.-based computer manufacturer seem to have overcome a large part of the linguistic distance between the production line and the bottom line, particularly at divisional MIS levels. And good reviews plus strong demand for their work within the HP organization make Van Rensselaer hopeful that corporate management will soon benefit as well.

Since 1974, HP's information services organization has been developing the facility management system (FMS). Substantially completed in 1978, FMS consists of several modular applications, including general accounting, cost accounting, production planning, materials management, and purchasing. The decentralized system runs on an HP 3000 minicomputer. Most of HP's 45 manufacturing divisions now use some modules of FMS, and a few use the entire system.

"What's been missing," Van Rensselaer observes, "is a way to create on-line, active decision-making systems for upper-level management." The master scheduling module, now under development, is what he hopes will provide that facility. (HP's General Systems Division sells a master scheduling package that the information systems group is considering.)

"Part of the problem—in fact one of the greatest problems we have had—is finding people who understand the business functions that the systems are designed to support," he comments, but adds that is being overcome by training and user education.

"We've done well at the operational level, and have increased productivity and job effectiveness there," he notes. IS hopes to duplicate those successes at top management levels.

One operational systems success Van Rensselaer points to is the ability of lower-level personnel to become more involved in the management decision-making process, "thus freeing the manager to become more effective in his role."

"For some time we've been putting the access to data bases at the fingertips of clerical people, such as stock clerks," he says. "Now, when unplanned issues of stock are ordered, a clerk can check inventories through a CRT terminal before the stock issue is made and check for possible stock outages.

"If one occurs, the clerk can then call the manager in the area for which the stock was ordered and advise him of the situation. Likewise, an early warning system for stock outs has been created for the purchasing function. It allocates stock against future orders.

"Yet forecasting, cost accounting, the identification of bottlenecks, purchasing, and other functions are equally important at the corporate level," Van Rensselaer explains. The problem, as he sees it, is that "most manufacturing support systems are a little more narrow gauge than what we've planned."

Part of the problem is in presentation, which he says is and will be solved by colorgraphics terminals. "A manager needs information coordinated for him, and the graphics terminals, particularly colorgraphics terminals, present it to him in an easily identifiable manner."

But the consolidation of the material itself is where the greatest difficulties lie. "Data interpretation is extremely dependent on how data are collected. Unless the parameters of what is needed are understood exactly the same way by all the parties you need to get information from, there are going to be problems," Van Rensselaer says.

Master scheduling with an evaluation of constraints—capacity limitations, people, space, the matching of inventory with demand and availability, purchasing information—is the challenge, according to the HP IS manager. And to schedule quickly is the real trick, he adds.

"A materials requirements planning 'explosion'—simulating possible changes in a manufacturing operation to measure the impact of that change (for example, to handle a large order for a product)—is very detailed and takes a long time to run," Van Rensselaer observes, "often five to 10 hours.

"If we could do that in five minutes," he says, "then a manager could run simulation after simulation, and make his choice." This kind of "abbreviated master scheduling" is what the IS organization is after. Expectations are that the system will be in place by the end of the year.

Defining what is needed is the first problem, even at the divisional level— discovering what elements are crucial in the manufacturing process, for example, that will be used to give a reliable answer.

At the corporate or multidivisional level, the problems are obviously multiplied. But they can be overcome, explains Van Rensselaer. He points to the HP Computer Systems Group, which has developed a master scheduling module of its own.

That module, using computer graphics, can figure and quickly display the printed-circuit board needs of the nine different divisions within that group, plus the several divisions of the HP Instrument Group. Basing its projections on those divisions' own master schedules, it can graphically compare those needs against the anticipated output of HP-owned printed-circuit-board plants.

Since only one fabrication plant is now operating, the projection with this system makes it easier to design long-term contracts with outside printed-circuit-board vendors on a more precise basis.

"What we're really talking about here is an ability to greatly increase productivity, the effectiveness of top management, and the effectiveness of the entire organization," Van Rensselaer says.

From *Information Systems News,* August 25, 1980. Copyright © 1980 by CMP Publications, Inc. Reprinted by permission.

How Paine Webber Tackled "Paper Blizzard"

While the "paperless society" remains largely a futurist's fantasy, Paine Webber Inc. had to bring much of that dream into reality for its securities processing operations over the past several months—and fast!

For the $500 million–revenue Wall Street brokerage found itself at the turn of the decade in the middle of a paper-induced nightmare. The company teetered on the brink of disaster as automated systems failed to keep up with an unprecedented trading-volume increase.

The headaches began to subside by June, after arduous nonstop efforts by the entire organization, particularly the computer and communications department, headed by Donald Brown, a senior staff vice president. He is quick to point out that the cure for the immediate problem is not the final remedy.

"Much work still needs to be done," he notes.

Dougald Fletcher, who took over as executive vice president of operations (Brown reports to him) last May 5, echoes Brown's comment: "We're in the stage of thinking through what we've learned. It's easy to just say we're applying it, but it's all part of a larger issue involving the impact of technology on the company and the industry as a whole. We're trying to get it down in real terms."

"After the *Titanic*," quips Brown, a 14-year Paine Webber executive, "everything we've done to our systems has included long-term thinking toward higher capacities and keeping our options open."

His sense of humor belies the heavy pressure he and his 388-person staff have been under. (The staff has grown from its 300-plus level at the beginning of the year. Most of the personnel increase came in the systems programming area, which has added almost 70 people since April.)

That intense stress is mirrored by some of the effects the fiasco had on the corporation itself: The company's second quarter, ended March 31, showed a loss of $10.2 million; top management changes were effected; more than a quarter of its 950 salesmen left; and the New York Stock Exchange and the Securities and Exchange Commission each launched investigations into Paine Webber's problems.

On the surface, those difficulties appeared to arise from an untimely combination of events: a huge increase in trading of all types of securities hit the market in December 1979, just as Paine Webber was putting the final touches on a major acquisition.

The firm completed a $45-million deal with INA Corp. for Blyth, Eastman, Dillon & Co., another brokerage, in January. From that point until midyear, Paine Webber started falling behind.

Its computer systems could not keep pace with the massive demand of increased trading volumes. It appeared to many that systems planning had failed to anticipate correctly the impact that the merger and the heavy trading—both known about in advance—would have on computer and systems capacity.

Yet that was not the full systems story. In fact, the conversion of Blyth's Honeywell Inc. 6060 mainframe-based systems to Paine Webber's IBM-based environment running under TCS/SOM (Telecommunications Control System/Securities Order Match) software was accomplished by November 1979, prior to the merger's consummation.

And systems planning had created a good track record, anticipating business needs and innovating where necessary. Back in 1973, for example, the company was the site of the first major installation of IBM's TCS/SOM, which controls an integrated on-line system that handles trade processing, settlement-day processing, and on-line entry and retrieval for listed stocks (securities traded on major exchanges).

In 1976 a CRT-based interactive on-line network for its branch offices (which now total 233) was implemented, replacing the traditional Teletype network.

And even before the proposed merger was known within the company, the computer and communications department ran a "Snap/Shot" simulation in April 1979 at IBM's Raleigh, N.C., facilities. That test emulated a 100-million-share day with Paine Webber's existing systems. As a result, a 3032 was brought in during March 1979 to join the 370/158 AP already in place.

Another "Snap/Shot" simulation was run in October 1979 following announcement of the merger. "We want to make sure we had enough capacity to handle the additional Blyth load plus any increase in business," Brown says. On the strength of that test, a 3033 was ordered for August 1980, and a major conversion to IBM's TCS/ACF (Advanced Communications Function) was also begun.

It appears that systems planning was again meeting perceived needs. "The on-line systems performed beautifully in the tests," Brown says. "But that turned out to be part of the problem.

"What wasn't anticipated was the growth of trade products that weren't fully automated, like over-the-counter stocks and municipal bonds that were manually prepared and had to be handled by Entrex keypunch systems."

During December 1979 and January 1980, municipal bonds soared to over five times above previous volume levels, over-the-counter stock trades quadrupled, while other semi-automated systems such as options and institutional investments doubled in volume.

"We had the equivalent of sustained 80-million-share days here throughout December and January," Brown notes. "What happened was that 'Snap/Shot' only gave us a true picture of the total on-line processing capacity of existing fully automated on-line trading systems. Meanwhile, each of the off-line production systems [such as 'munis' and 'OTCS'] had some form of automation, but we couldn't foresee with the test what increases in volume in those would do to the systems' capacity overall.

"What we found out," Brown observes, "is that each off-line system didn't have enough automation." So, while the computers in place were technically capable of handling high volumes, the manual preparation that preceded the automated processing of the varied products made the task impossible.

Processing on the hand-tended systems by keypunch normally began between 5 and 6 P.M. daily. The increased volume pushed that time back to midnight and beyond. Meanwhile, inexperienced help hired in droves to post the trade figures before they got to keypunch greatly increased the error rate. The problem snowballed, eventually affecting the automated systems. Paine Webber was thrown into chaos.

The computer and communications department began reacting immediately to the problem, creating ad hoc reporting mechanisms to keep management apprised of the situation on a daily basis and to speed up the process of resolving problems. It began laying out a recovery plan in January that included three "waves" of action:

• Wave One—A series of 26 short-term systems improvements were instituted to regain management control of the situation. The 3033 on order from IBM, due in

August, was brought in during March and was up and running in one week's time, according to Brown. An IBM liaison man is quoted as saying that during the crisis, Paine Webber personnel "did five years' work in five months' time."

• Wave Two—The 26 projects were expanded to 33 and scheduled for completion by the second quarter of 1981. This second phase was designed to capitalize on the improvements gained in Wave One, and maintain the control realized.

"We're putting as much in the user's hands as possible," Brown says, "with up-front editing and extensive order trails to track transactions, in an effort to get manual handling down to an absolute minimum."

So far, he sees the projects as successful, with all being completed "on or ahead of schedule." And the proof of their effectiveness is characterized in the area of data collection. "In September, during the heaviest trading since the crisis period," Brown relates, "only 3,000 trades a day were handled manually—out of about 20,000—in the systems that had been giving us trouble."

He also says that all production, which was several weeks behind during the earlier part of the year, is now "all completed prior to 8:30 A.M. the following day." Error rates, running well over 1,000 a day not too long ago, are now below 400. "Our goal is to get them down as low as possible, and longer-range improvements in the systems will take care of that."

• Wave Three—Long-term improvements scheduled for completion over the next two to three years will make sure Paine Webber "never loses control again, no matter what." Communications plans are important to this portion of the plan, Brown says, but will not elaborate except to say that satellites may be involved.

The current picture at Paine Webber has improved tremendously, but the company is not out of the woods yet. "I don't want to leave the impression that we're finished, by any means. But we've gotten on top of most of the problems, and so far, everything has worked just about perfectly," Brown says.

The turnaround at Paine Webber could be classified under the heading of "minor miracles," judging from a report that Brown prepared for top management on the status of the various projects. Of the 26 projects begun in June as part of Waves One and Two:

• Fifteen have been completely implemented.
• Two are completed and scheduled.
• Three are in parallel operation with existing systems.
• One is undergoing required testing.
• Three are being developed as subsequent phases to projects already implemented.
• Two have been deferred by users and higher priority projects have been substituted.
• Since June, nine related projects have been identified; three of these are completed and six are in various stages of development.
• In general, the bulk of the projects were in place by September.

Cowboy DP Scouting Avoids Personnel Fumbles

Fifteen consecutive winning seasons, two Super Bowl championships, and 17 straight opening-day victories have been highlights of the Dallas Cowboys' history in the National Football League, making it the most successful franchise in the history of the NFL.

One reason for this consistent success is the use of computerized scouting to evaluate and rank collegiate talent in preparation for the annual draft, which the Cowboys were the first to use, and which they use more extensively than any other team.

As a result, the Cowboys have gained a reputation as a cold and impersonal organization that somehow uses computers to judge talent above and beyond what is possible with manual methods—a reputation reinforced by the cool, imperturbable presence of coach Tom Landry on the sidelines at every game, the very picture of precision and dispassionate competence.

Yet, as any data processing manager can tell you, computers cannot do more than they are told, and their value is subject to the quality of input their masters provide.

"The biggest fallacy in the minds of the fan on the street is that the computer can do something magical. But the old 'garbage in, garbage out' theory still applies," says Texas E. "Tex" Schramm, president and general manager of the Cowboys.

What the computer can and does do, however, is provide a useful tool to save enormous amounts of time and provide protection against the possibly misleading tendencies of the human mind. The Cowboys use their computerized Player Evaluation and Selection System to gain an added measure of accuracy in predicting which players will prove adequate.

"Of course, the final decision for selecting a player will always remain with the club management, namely Tom Landry and Gil Brandt [vice-president and director of player development], but the computer has been a tremendous asset," says A. Salam Qureishi, developer of the system and now president and chairman of Sysorex International Inc., a Santa Clara systems development company.

It was the pooling of Qureishi's skill with Schramm's and Brandt's vision that led to the creation of the system, the only one of its type in organized sports.

"In my opinion, the Cowboys have been a consistent winner because they had the foresight to use advanced mathematical techniques and large-scale computers in their player selection," says Qureishi.

Schramm's interest in computers began during his tenure with the Los Angeles Rams in the late 1940s and '50s, when the league and its scouting methods were growing out of infancy.

At first, teams would rely on word-of-mouth recommendations from friends on college campuses or coaches who would work for the league on a part-time basis. With football rapidly rising in popularity, the need for talented prospects increased, and teams soon began hiring regional scouts to find players.

With this expanded scouting, however, came an increasing amount of information, and the more there was to assimilate, the more difficult the task became. In addition to the problem of simply going through this vast amount of data, it became more difficult to grade players consistently on the same basis.

"We found that people's personal preferences had a tendency to color their perception and their grading of players," says Schramm. For instance, he says, speed was his personal fetish; if any player had speed, he would tend to attribute other good qualities to him as well, and ignore possible negatives. Although the Rams had developed a grading system to protect against their tendency, it still presented a problem to general managers, scouts, and coaches.

After Schramm left the Rams, he served with Columbia Broadcasting System Inc. in New York. One of his jobs was to produce the telecast of the 1960 Winter Olympics in Squaw Valley. IBM was involved in the official scorekeeping and timekeeping of the games, and the telecast originated from an IBM building in New York.

Knowing that he would eventually get back into football, Schramm began talking to IBM and started investigating the possibility of using computers to eliminate both the enormous time required to rank prospects and the subjectivity involved.

"We wanted to put the criteria by which we judge players into the computer without the personal bias," he says.

In 1960 when the Cowboys were formed, Schramm approached a friend within IBM who put him in touch with the Service Bureau Company, which at that time was a subsidiary of IBM. He eventually hooked up with Qureishi, who was then an employee of SBC and an expert in this type of analysis.

A long and difficult project ensued, in which the primary task was to define those qualities that made a good football player, and to develop a language that could describe these qualities.

"We had to start from scratch, because coaches used different terms that meant different things," when they were describing players, Schramm says.

For instance, the term "character" had meanings that ranged from "someone who would knock your head off," to "a real leader." It took four years of research and the viewing of countless films to let the coaches decide exactly what such terms meant and how they could be used consistently.

"We didn't get a printout with any kind of reliability until 1965," says Schramm, "and it was still pretty rough for a few years." The Cowboys kept refining the system, as time provided feedback.

"To check our model, we started feeding back the results of what happened to the player once in the league and started getting predictability as to what particular factors led to success in particular positions.

"The program basically stays the same, but the ingredients within it are continually changing," says Schramm.

Since the requirements for quarterback and defensive lineman differ, the Cowboys use a different set of criteria to judge each. Adjustment of those factors and what they contribute to success is a continuing effort for Schramm and his staff, who re-examine them every year.

In addition, scouts differ in the way they rate players, says Schramm, and differences in their methods have been taken into account. For instance, the input of each scout is weighted differently, and each scout's accuracy is measured by reviewing his past predictions. If a scout has been wrong about several players in the past, his relative weight will be lowered within the system.

However, use of the Player Evaluation and Selection System is only a part of the Cowboys' method of selecting draft picks, and the team still collects scouting reports in loose-leaf binders to be read individually. That provides a check for errors made by the computer, by scouts, or by coaches.

"All of the computer's data and evaluations are matched against what we do manually and physically," says Schramm. "That provides us with a computer ranking from which to start, and a very good guide to measure out manual methods against.

If there is a wide discrepancy between the two, we will take a very close look to find out why."

After a few years of working with the system, the Cowboys decided to find a more cost-efficient alternative to SBC's service. Because of the high cost, the Cowboys said, "To hell with SBC, let's form our own company," Schramm reports.

Thus, Optimum Systems Inc. was born. It served the Cowboys and a shifting complement of other NFL teams until portions of the firm were sold in 1980 because the company was growing so rapidly. The Dallas Cowboys are now the sole user of the system, which was originally a joint venture between the Cowboys, the Los Angeles Rams, and the San Francisco 49ers.

Optimum Systems is still half owned by Cowboys' owner Clint Murchison. He felt that from a business standpoint, the scouting service was merely "an appendage" to the company as a whole.

The Cowboys are now served by On-Line Business Systems Inc., Santa Clara, which purchased the Player Evaluation and Selection System from OSI. "We pay them a monthly fee, and while we may be paying them more than we paid to SBC, it feels like less," Schramm says.

The system itself runs on an IBM 360 under MVS and is still written in its original FORTRAN IV, according to Richard Rust, and OSI employee for over 10 years who is now with National Semiconductor Inc. Most of the programs that comprise the system are now over 10 years old.

"We had a harder time than many other computer users because there wasn't much around to go on," he says. "There are thousands of banking systems out there that allow people to see mistakes that are made and what would happen if they were to start over again. We did not have that ability, and had to go through it ourselves by trial and error."

Now, even though manual methods are still employed, the system is considered to be indispensable. "The people on the field have more time to be innovative," says Schramm. "Before, we spent all of our time gathering the data, rather than putting it to use."

However, he emphasizes that computerization, while useful in football, can never supplant the human element.

"In football there is concern with the end result, as with any business. But it is also important how you get there," he says. "Otherwise we could put all the data into the computer and have it determine who wins the game. That is not what the people want, however, and the computer serves us primarily as an aid to human judgment."

Schramm suggests that the use of the Player Evaluation and Selection System may even be more humane to potential NFL players, by helping to gauge their chances of playing in the league.

"It is very humiliating for a player to be picked high in the draft and then not make a team," he says. "The players who are truly the best should be picked early, and it is better for those who may not make the grade to know early. We are trying to use every means possible to evaluate a human being, and in the long run it is in the best interest of the individual."

Yet the motivation for computerizing the selection process was not born out of a desire for technology for its own sake, but from a keen sense that a competitive advantage might exist there, an advantage best utilized before anyone else.

"You get to feel uncomfortable with all the advances in computers today. There's a feeling there is more out there than you can keep an eye on, and that someone else might find it first," says Cowboys president Schramm. "Before it felt like you were on top of the pile and directing the computer, but now the computer sometimes seems to be directing you.

"Football, like any other business, must keep up with the times. But everything was a lot more fun before everything got so technical and sophisticated."

On the other hand, Gil Brandt, who is the primary user of the system, is more enthusiastic about what computerization has meant to the team.

"Today I am very excited about the system, and how we now can get the percentage a player has of playing in the league, what percentage he has of starting, and what are the most and least important qualities that make up a successful football player," he says. "When we started, we had a four-room house of gray vanilla—and it ended up being a mansion."

"We have an advantage because we've been doing it the longest," says Schramm. "Other teams take a simplistic approach and don't specifically rank players the way we do. They may use the computer more in terms of simply listing what players are available in which positions, and their size."

Although it is difficult to document, the system seems to be a success. At least, the Cowboys have come up with a steady stream of talented players, and after a somewhat shaky start this year, seem to be gathering steam in their bid for yet another Super Bowl trophy. "Life is percentages," says Brandt. "If we can arrive at a 52 percent probability rather than 50 percent we will be that much better off."

By William P. Martorelli. From *Information Systems News,* November 16, 1981. Copyright © 1981 by CMP Publications, Inc. Reprinted by permission.

Mellon Bank Holds Down Costs with "Big Iron"

Everything about Mellon Bank is big, especially its computers.

The bank, headquartered in Pittsburgh, is the fifteenth largest financial institution in the United States, with assets of over $16 billion, and the biggest bank outside the money centers of New York, Chicago, and Los Angeles.

The bank's computers are large, partly because of the views held by George P. DiNardo, senior vice-president and director of the bank's Information Management and Research Department.

"We believe entirely in the economies of scale, and therefore I am a devotee of the big iron," DiNardo says, adding that he has long resisted the widespread trend to implement minicomputers and other methods to distribute processing.

"I stood alone for 10 years while the rest of the world went into distributed data processing. But now they're coming back into my camp," he says. "We eschewed the medium-sized hardware when it came out. And the bigger the machine, the better we like it."

Mellon Bank currently has one IBM 3081 processor—with plans to add two more—along with two 3033s and two 370/168s.

But it is more than simply a preference with DiNardo. The "big iron" he wholeheartedly embraces is there for a purpose: to support the more than 160 highly integrated systems that drive Mellon's array of banking services. To Mellon, integration means the ability of one system to feed data to the next, without human intervention.

"If you are offering integrated systems, you'll need a big piece of machinery to drive them," DiNardo says. "Our goal is to reduce the cost of computing per unit of work by 10 percent per year, a goal we have achieved for the last five years. Big computers help us do it."

DiNardo's Information Management and Research Department serves all of Mellon Bank, which has 120 branches in contiguous counties in Pennsylvania, and services the other subsidiaries of Mellon National Corp., Mellon Bank's holding company, as well.

It is also responsible for servicing almost 300 correspondent banks in 12 states. That makes Mellon Bank "perhaps the largest bank-owned DP service bureau in the U.S."

"We are also, we believe, the most automated financial institution in the country," DiNardo says.

"We have proven to the management of this bank that the trade-off of capital equipment versus labor is an attractive one," says David Moore, vice-president of the Software and Telecommunications Division. Moore is responsible for both communications and operating software, as well as capacity planning.

However, providing integrated systems is no easy task, regardless of the size of machine on which it is performed.

"There is a very complex stream of jobs to perform to integrate systems properly, but we looked at distributing our DP and found it a very difficult problem that approached the unmanageable," Moore says.

"We have continually studied the applicability of minicomputers and distributed data processing to our problems, but they have always come up short in terms of integration," Moore says. "New innovative services are possible through the marriage of processors and I/O systems."

According to Moore, managing the services Mellon Bank provides to its own customers, other banks, and corporate customers is greatly eased through systems integration. Managing the data communication between all of these sites is also a challenge, one that is primarily Moore's responsibility.

Providing integrated systems that support customer services has called for more than a little innovation on Mellon Bank's part. That is why the bank has been at the forefront of more than one technological advance.

However, "the problem with being a pioneer is that the fourth guy in line finds it much easier than the first," Moore observes.

He says Mellon Bank was a leader in the development of large customer-information files, where bank customers' records can be kept with a minimum of redundancy.

"We began in the late 1960s when there were no products available," Moore says. "Back then everybody was a number, but we wanted to look at a customer as a person."

The effort to create the file took "an amazing amount of programming," especially in the creation of an alphabetic key to enable a search for a customer when his full name was unknown.

Another area where Mellon Bank has been a leader is in automation of the teller function. It was the first in the United States to install automated teller terminals, Moore says. The bank currently uses Docutel ATMs and over 7,000 CRT terminals for data entry and inquiry.

Mellon Bank also did "a lot of development work with Job Entry Subsystem 2 (JES2)," Moore says, to allow the entry of a job as well as its output from any processor. "We put a pretty sizable investment into that software," which is now distributed as an official modification from Share, the user group for large IBM users. This software allows much greater flexibility in working with multiple processors, Moore says.

"As a shop gets into its second big processor, they have a whole new set of problems to deal with, and this is one of them."

Mellon Bank also claims it is the first company to get IBM's MVS/SP operating system into production, out of the 13 firms that comprised IBM's Early Support Program.

"We are also very heavily involved with standards, to help us avoid duplication of effort and to help develop utility programs that can be used across applications." Also, Moore says, the strict enforcement of standards avoids the problem of a confusing array of different procedures at the teller terminal, because "the teller doesn't want 60 ways to input data."

Mellon Bank has developed its automated banking systems so that every system feeds the next "without human intervention," in DiNardo's words. Customers at both Mellon branch locations and correspondent banks can access a full array of banking, cash management, and other services without having to visit another location.

Banking documents also remain at the branch location, since there is no need to clear them through Mellon's corporate headquarters.

"When a customer comes in to one of our branches, that is where they stay," he says, "and although insurance companies have this capability, I don't know of any banks that do."

DiNardo is in charge of a staff of 296 application programmers, but makes no distinction between development and maintenance work.

"Our group is functionally oriented, and my goal is to make the systems staff work as directly for the user as possible." However, he says he likes to retain ultimate control over his staff in order to protect both his interests and theirs.

"I am afraid that if the programmer did indeed work for the user, we would lose the synergy, the emphasis on career development, and the programmers themselves might lose interest."

DiNardo calls Pittsburgh a "good old ethnic town," where mobility is less than that found in larger cities. Mellon Bank has registered a turnover rate of only 7 percent annually over the last two years. Since the city is heavily populated by company headquarters, however, there is no shortage of opportunity.

DiNardo admits that Mellon has experienced some problems with big iron, and says there were times when he and his staff were "sweating bullets." However, on the whole, he says, large centralized processors are increasingly attractive as the state of the art improves.

"Each iteration of big hardware has higher levels of reliability and price performance," DiNardo believes.

"For example, IBM has really outdone itself with the 3081, and we are very, very pleased with it," he says. "The point is—with competition, you're getting a better product no matter whom you get it from, and these improvements have done away with most of the reasons why people were afraid of going big iron."

Sticking to his guns in regard to large processors has paid off in another dimension, DiNardo says. "We got a head start in integrated systems, as well as in tying the big iron together," while others were concerned with spreading it out.

By William P. Martorelli. From *Information Systems News*, June 16, 1982. Copyright © 1982 by CMP Publications, Inc. Reprinted by permission.

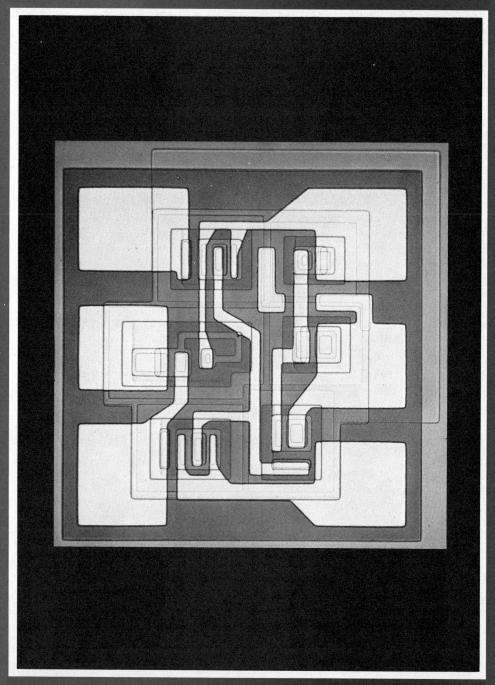

1964.
*Radio frequency amplifier/multiplier. The first consumer-
oriented linear integrated circuit in the world, still on the
market today.*

Implementation **3**

CBIS
Implementation 9

A SERIES OF activities must normally be undertaken to provide CBIS products for organizational use. Three groups of problems are addressed:

Product fitting	Arriving at CBIS product requirements that meet both immediate and longer-term needs of the initiating work unit(s) and are compatible with organization-wide concerns,
Technical development	Fabricating an appropriate hardware–software configuration,
Organizational deployment	Inserting the CBIS product into the organization so intended benefits are attained.[1]

While all basic activities associated with CBIS implementation will be introduced in this chapter, particular attention will be paid to tasks that profit most from active user participation.

The phrase *CBIS implementation* is often understood to denote only the third problem area above. It is becoming increasingly evident, however, that these three areas are not independent, and in many situations they are tightly interrelated. In recognition of that fact, "CBIS implementation" refers here to an overall process that complements all the creating, designing, and changing activities involved in developing and using a CBIS.[2]

This view of CBIS implementation recognizes the importance of software in making possible the harmonious cooperation of people and machines characteristic of any successful CBIS product. All software products, however, are human creations. They begin as an idea, take shape in their designers' minds, become progressively more visible as development proceeds, and eventually are physically experienced through their inputs, outputs, and supporting documentation. The quality of any software product thus ultimately depends on the quality of its initial design and the ways the design is expressed (and communicated) during its elaboration and development. The importance of design—and in a more general sense planning—will be stressed throughout these discussions.

The chapter begins with discussions of problems commonly experienced in software development and ways these problems are being resolved through the application of modern software practices. The activities that comprise CBIS implementation are then examined. Two perspectives are presented: the traditional view of the implementation life cycle, and alternative life-cycle representations that reflect the interrelatedness of CBIS implementation activities. The role of non-computer specialists—users and managers—in CBIS implementation is then examined. The chapter concludes with brief introductions to the remaining four chapters of Part 3.

SOFTWARE DEVELOPMENT PROBLEMS

One obvious characteristic of software is its *cost*. In an era marked by dramatic decreases in hardware costs, the portion of organizational budgets allocated to the information function continues to rise, and more and more of this budget allocation is associated with software.[3]

Many factors have contributed to this rise in software costs. Some are uncontrollable. Today's CBIS applications are more sophisticated and complex than those of a decade ago. Furthermore, a shortage of computer specialists has resulted in high salaries and the need to assign less experienced and possibly less capable analysts or programmers to software development tasks. Others, however, are controllable.

Prior to a discussion of how modern software practices provide a means of addressing the high cost of software, a brief discussion of three major problems with software development—that it is labor-intensive, very changeable, and difficult to manage—is provided.

The *labor-intensive* nature of software development raises three critical issues. First, software expenses rise along with the salaries of computer specialists; thus, the cost of software directly reflects inflation, an extremely tight labor market, and the skill requirements of an application. Second, the personal nature of design and programming activities results in project control and quality assessment difficulties and a tendency for analysts and programmers to identify with the product of their efforts (and hence be unwilling to listen to criticism). Third, the innate capabilities of individuals must be relied on. Productivity improvement thus must be directed not only at providing tools, but also at improving the thought processes of those individuals assigned implementation tasks.

Because of evolving organizational needs, a continuing emergence of new information technologies, and the inevitability of errors, all CBIS undergo *periodic restructuring*. As the need for restructuring differs with the nature of each CBIS product, it is difficult to specify an ideal change frequency. A general characterization, however, has been suggested: TPS might require changes every three to five years, IRS and PDS every one to two years, and DSS every one to two weeks.[4]

Efforts to change CBIS products after their introduction fall into the category of software maintenance. While the importance of maintenance has only recently been recognized, it normally accounts for 50–90 percent of the expense associated with software products.[5] Figure 9.1 illustrates how maintenance expenses might mount with a typical CBIS product. Immediately after its introduction, errors in design or coding appear and must be corrected. Gradually these disappear. Throughout the life of the CBIS, efforts to perfect the product take place as organizational members realize how they can exploit CBIS capabilities to accomplish organi-

FIGURE 9.1
Software Maintenance Expenses

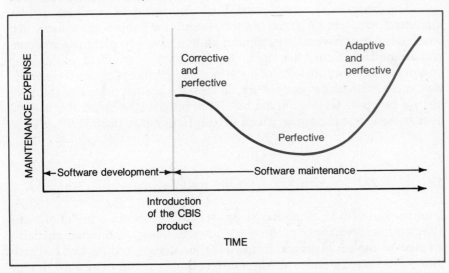

zational activities. Sooner or later the organizational context within which the CBIS has been placed changes. Then the software product must be adapted to its evolving context. These adaptive forces tend to intensify with time.

Software maintenance is much more expensive than initial development for many reasons. Often the programmer who initially developed a product is not available to insert the required changes. The new programmer assigned this task must thus first figure out how the program works. To make matters worse, the product's documentation may be outdated or the program and its documentation may have been poor to begin with. Maintenance tasks are often assigned to junior staff members who lack the skill or experience to make the change quickly and effectively. Software maintenance involves considerable testing. Not only must the inserted code be tested, but care must be taken that the new code does not produce errors in other portions of the CBIS product. Finally, and most important, as changes are inserted into software, its design integrity tends to degenerate, making future changes more difficult and expensive. When a CBIS product's design integrity is destroyed, it is more costly to modify the existing CBIS than to design and develop a new CBIS.

Long-lived software is characterized by other costs as well. Organizational members may continue to follow old work habits that are inappropriate, given current organizational realities; these individuals may also be required to interact with a CBIS in inefficient ways. Furthermore, obsolete hardware may be retained and a highly skilled staff tied up in maintenance tasks, either of which might well prevent potentially valuable, innovative applications from being undertaken.

The complexity, size, invisibility, and newness (analysts or programmers are seldom given projects similar to those they have just worked on) of software development all contribute to planning and control difficulties.[6] Schedules and budgets are poorly estimated, monitoring of progress and coordination of the efforts of a project team are formidable tasks, and balancing a need to "freeze" designs against the inevitability of change becomes almost impossible. What results is software that is late, over budget, and (from the user's perspective) unsatisfactory.

MODERN SOFTWARE PRACTICES

Over the last decade, computer scientists have evolved a number of techniques to resolve these problems. Although these techniques initially focused on the act of programming (program design, coding, and testing), they have been extended to the more complex realm of system design (configuring a collection of programs to accomplish wider functions than those typically associated with a single program). The intent in introducing these techniques is to identify and illustrate key concepts to be applied to the even more complex CBIS implementation context.

The objective in software development is to produce software products that are *relevant* (complete, correct, reliable, and usable), *maintainable* (configured to be easily adapted to environmental changes), and *portable* (configured to be easily adapted to internal changes). Not surprisingly, these objectives are best accomplished if a software product (code plus supporting documentation) has a simple, clear structure. The human mind can grasp any amount of complexity as long as it is presented in easy-to-grasp chunks that together comprise a whole. By breaking a complex object, such as the intended functions of a software product, into a collection of simpler parts, one can produce program and system designs that are easily understood, communicated, and, hence, changed.

These modern software practices, commonly referred to as *structured* approaches, are based on three interrelated concepts: abstraction, stepwise refinement, and modularity. While each will be introduced separately, they are best viewed as a unit if the expected benefits of structure are to be realized.

A primary means of achieving simplicity in design is to make effective use of *abstraction*. A design should initially reflect only the essence of an entity or function. Trivialities must be left out and details suppressed until their knowledge becomes necessary. The idea is not to exhaustively model reality (which is impossible), but to create a reduced representation that makes sense, given the problem addressed. Guidelines to follow in abstraction include an analysis of what, not how, and employment of terms and concepts natural to the problem.

A technique contributing to both simplicity and adaptability is the use of *modularity*. Understanding is enhanced by dividing a design into small, well-defined, relatively self-contained modules. Each module should perform one logical task and possess as few linkages as possible with other modules. This facilitates adaptability, as future changes can be limited to a few modules.

Abstraction and modularity are put into operation through the process of *stepwise refinement*. Designs should be produced in layers, with the top layer being very abstract (and close to human thought in form) and the bottom layer very explicit (closely representing the targeted real-world context, in this case a particular programming language). Each layer should reveal how the prior layer accomplished its purpose, but as little as possible should be revealed with each step. By too rapidly detailing a certain design aspect, one may impose constraints on other design elements. Also, each layer should be complete in itself so the completeness and correctness of the evolving design can be examined at any point.

FIGURE 9.2
A Systems Model of the Dish Washing Process

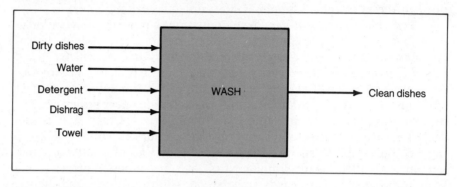

The everyday process of washing dishes clearly illustrates these ideas.[7] Figure 9.2 offers an overview of this process and Figure 9.3 a structured representation. This example illustrates a *top-down* design, a design approach that will reappear throughout this discussion of CBIS implementation. With a top-down design, one begins with a high-level statement of purpose and then refines it by disclosing detailed activities (or other requirements). The strength of a top-down design is that the entire effort is focused on the high-level target. Its weakness lies in the fact that critical constraints may not be realized until after a considerable investment in design effort has been made. For example, with the dish washing example, the capacity of the drying rack is likely to require a multicycle washing process.

An alternative design approach is *bottom-up* design. In this case one starts with the basic details associated with some purpose and then combines these to facilitate coordination. The strength of bottom-up design is that all basic entities or activities are explicitly addressed. With the dish washing example, a bottom-up design would first identify required activities (gather materials, fill basin, scrub dish, dry dish, stack dish, etc.) and any associated problems. Hence, the drying rack size constraint should be recognized early. The weakness of this approach lies in the danger that current means may dictate future ends.

Good designers often use both top-down and bottom-up approaches to produce effective designs.

In the remainder of this section, specific modern software practices are presented and their overall qualities discussed. The techniques selected possess general applicability and are easily understood.

FIGURE 9.3
A Structured Description of the Dish Washing Process

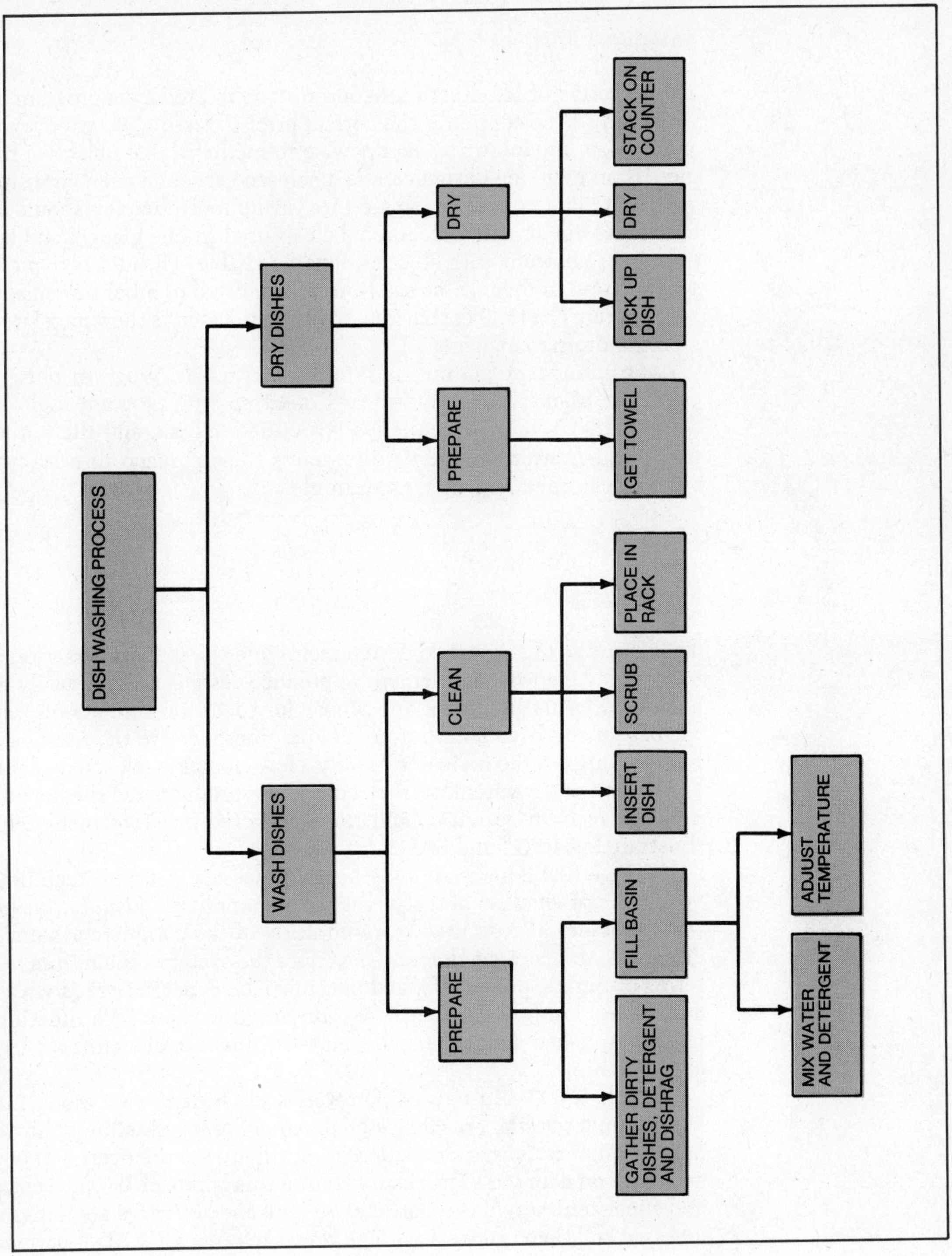

Structured Programming

The objective of structured programming is to produce a program that is very likely to be complete and correct prior to testing. By effective use of abstraction, modularity, and stepwise refinement, this objective may be met, as an evolving design can be disclosed early and then continuously validated. The conceptual logic of a structured program should reveal how tasks are actually executed, be captured in one glance, and be read from top to bottom with all control paths visible. The idea is to produce a program design that can be easily communicated to other humans, not to a computer. The final design (i.e., the bottom layer) is then translated into a programming language.

Structured programming is often written in *program design language*, or *pseudocode*. This means of expressing program logic uses a combination of pidgin English, a structured syntax, and the purposeful use of indentation. Figure 9.4 illustrates this approach to programming with a customer credit check example.

Structured Design

The objective of structured design techniques is to use abstraction, modularity, and stepwise refinement to produce designs that are easily understood and easily modified, and whose key decisions are visible early in the design activity. Common to all such methods are the use of graphic representations, the inclusion of only a few elements in each diagram, the production of documentation as a design by-product, and the portrayal in a design of both activities and the data acted on. Two techniques are illustrated—HIPO[8] and SADT.[9,10]

The HIPO (Hierarchy plus Input, Processor, Output) technique involves the production of three types of documents. A *visual table of contents* provides a structured representation of the complete system being designed. An *overview diagram* describes the system's major functions in terms of inputs, processors, and outputs. The concern here is with what and where, not how. A *detail diagram* describes how each function will be accomplished. Figures 9.5, 9.6, and 9.7 illustrate diagrams for an order entry example.

With SADT (Structured Analysis and Design), two models of the system under design are constructed. An *actigram* illustrates the flow of data through activities, and a *datagram* illustrates the operation of these activities on data sets. The theory behind this approach is that a complete and consistent design is most likely if data and activities are individually assessed and then interrelated. The central element of SADT is the SADT box, shown in Figure 9.8. By developing a hierarchical representation in

FIGURE 9.4
Program Design Language for Credit Check

LEVEL   PROGRAM DESIGN

1.   Perform credit check

2.   If credit conditions favorable
                  then
                          approve order
                  else
                          reject order

3.   If order criteria favorable
                  then
                          approve order
                  else
                        if past payment history favorable
                                then
                                    approve order
                              else
                                    if past payment history unfavorable
                                          then
                                              reject order
                                        else
                                                  print exception report

4.   If order amount + current balance ≤ credit limit
                  then
                          approve order
                  else
                        set flag to approve
                        while there are past orders to examine
                              if payment past due over 90 days
                                  then
                                    set flag to reject
                                else
                                    if payment past due over 30 days
                                        then
                                          set flag to question
                      if flag set to approve
                          then
                              approve order
                        else
                              if flag set to reject
                                then
                                  reject order
                              else
                                  print exception report

FIGURE 9.5
HIPO Visual Table of Contents

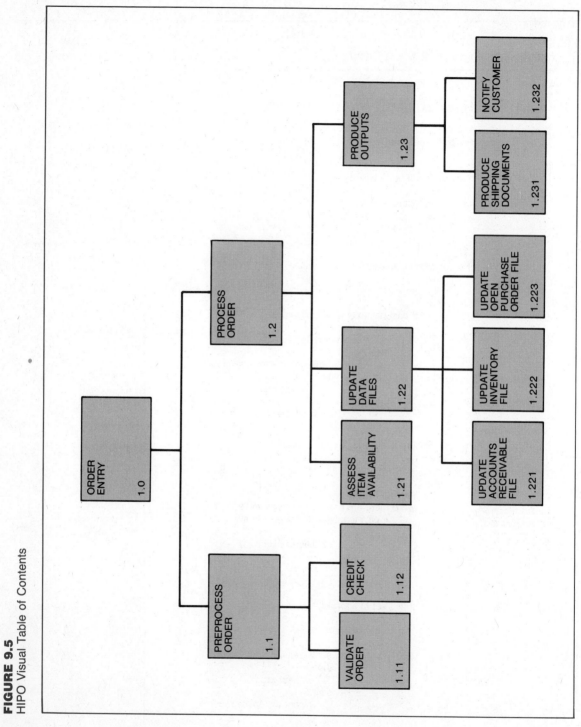

FIGURE 9.6
HIPO Overview Diagram

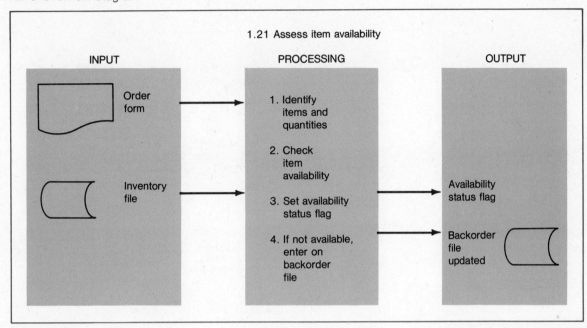

1.21 Assess item availability

INPUT	PROCESSING	OUTPUT
Order form	1. Identify items and quantities	
	2. Check item availability	
Inventory file	3. Set availability status flag	Availability status flag
	4. If not available, enter on backorder file	Backorder file updated

FIGURE 9.7
HIPO Detail Diagram

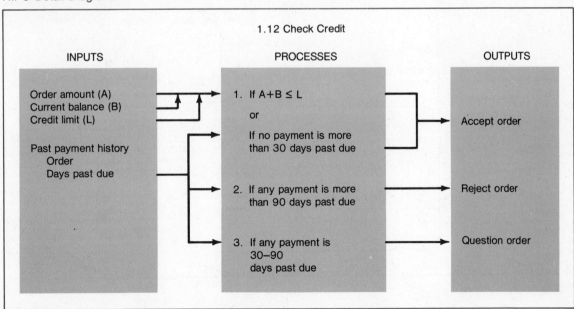

1.12 Check Credit

INPUTS	PROCESSES	OUTPUTS
Order amount (A) Current balance (B) Credit limit (L)	1. If A+B ≤ L or If no payment is more than 30 days past due	Accept order
Past payment history Order Days past due	2. If any payment is more than 90 days past due	Reject order
	3. If any payment is 30–90 days past due	Question order

FIGURE 9.8
SADT Box

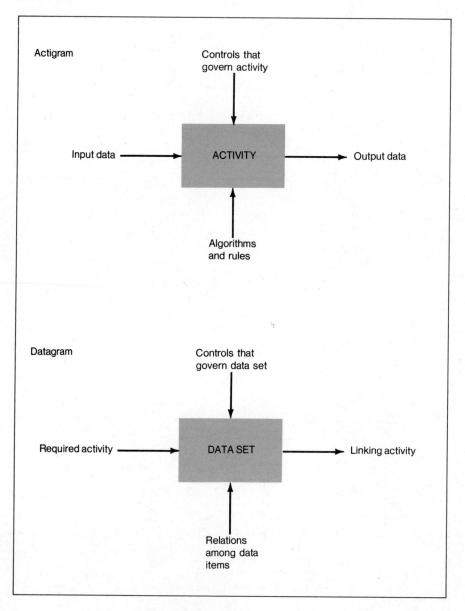

which such boxes are the design modules, one can readily grasp the crucial functions and data sets that underlie a design. Figures 9.9 and 9.10 illustrate, respectively, partial SADT actigram and datagram structures for an order entry example.

Other Modern Software Practices

A successful means of uncovering errors (design, code, test, etc.) early in the development process is that of *structured review*, which involves formal, early, and continuous team critiques of development products. The team climate is crucial, as the product and not the author must be the subject of the review. The best-known methods of performing structured reviews are the walkthrough (in which an analyst or programmer traces the development of a product with a group of peers) and the inspection (in which a team of inspectors critically examine a product and recommend corrections).

Top-down development incorporates structured methods directly in program development.[11] Development proceeds layer by layer (design-code-test) so each layer can be verified for correctness. Attention is first directed at developing control modules, with "stubs" being used to represent as-yet-undeveloped functional modules.

Implications of Modern Software Practices for CBIS Implementation

Most modern software practices share a number of attributes:

Conceptual integrity	Simple and unambiguous designs,
Discipline	Early formal exposure of designs and solutions,
Continuity of thought	Visibility of an evolving product through standard documentation procedures,
Continual validity	Early and continuous critiques of designs and solutions by groups with different perspectives,
Receptivity to change	Willingness to anticipate, plan for, and control change.

In general, *comprehension* and *planning* are emphasized. The aim is to have all critical decisions expressed early in an understandable form so

FIGURE 9.9
Sample SADT Actigram

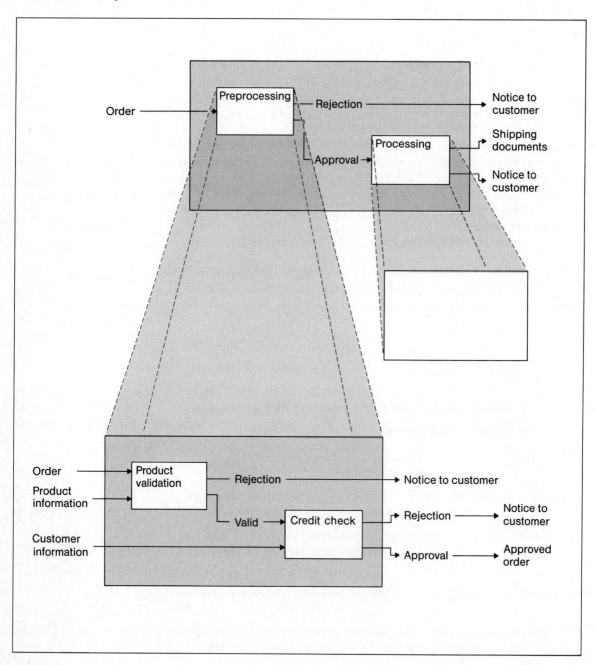

FIGURE 9.10
Sample SADT Datagram

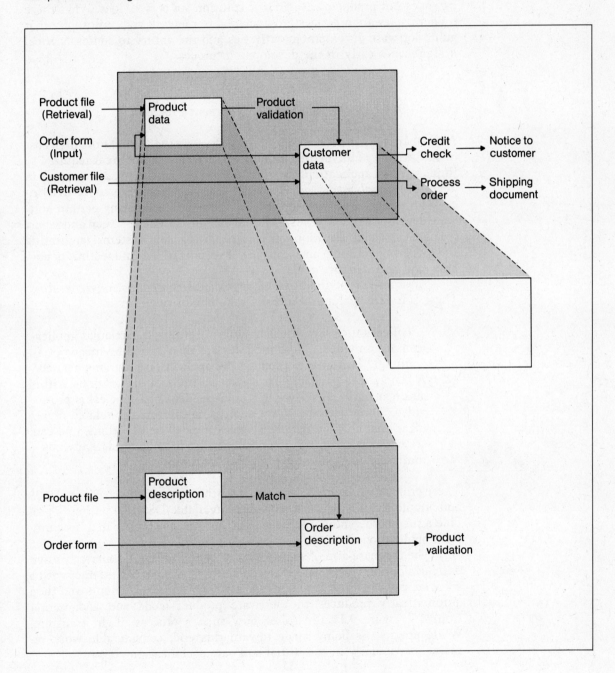

others may point out potential problems and verify correctness and completeness before expensive commitments are made.

These techniques are not strict recipes to be followed. A methodology does not produce a design or a solution—a person does. What these modern software practices provide are a framework and philosophy that guide software development activities and the ability to address critical design issues early in the development process.

Other Approaches to Software Development Problems

A number of other developments are under way that address the high cost of software by reducing the amount of software development required to implement an application. Considerable recent progress has been made in developing *application development software* (software tools that increase analyst or programmer productivity by automating certain software development activities).[12] Prime examples include screen and report formatters, documentation generators, interactive systems facilitating the gathering, refining, and verifying of specifications, and testing, debugging, and maintenance tools.

Another recent trend is the appearance of *application generators*. These software packages generally take one of two forms:

1. A collection of functional modules useful in a particular application are provided. These modules are then joined by means of a command language to produce the application programs desired.
2. A generalized package that handles a number of functions within an organizational setting (e.g., independent pharmacies) is provided, along with questions addressing information-related organizational characteristics. By answering these questions, one can set parameters within the package that provide a relatively customized collection of application programs.

These program generators are limited for the most part to traditional TPS and simple IRS applications. However, available DSS-like packages provide a means to generate CBIS support for more sophisticated, less uniform applications.

The ultimate aim of such efforts is to provide an *automated design and development* capability whereby a user or analyst can interact with a software package that first helps specify software requirements and then automatically produces the software product (code and documentation).[13,14] Figure 9.11 illustrates how such a process might transpire. While progress is being made toward this end, considerable work remains, particularly in the initial software specification stage.

FIGURE 9.11
Automated Design and Development

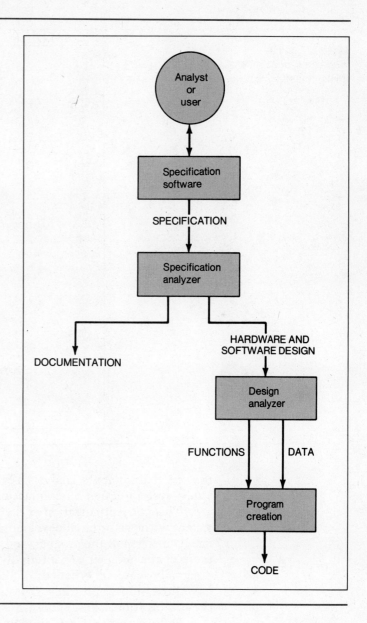

A TRADITIONAL VIEW OF THE CBIS
IMPLEMENTATION PROCESS

The sequence of activities traditionally followed in implementing a CBIS
is illustrated in Figure 9.12 and defined in Table 9.1. These activities—
aside from training and documentation—generally occur *sequentially*;

FIGURE 9.12
Traditional Sequence of CBIS
Implementation Activities

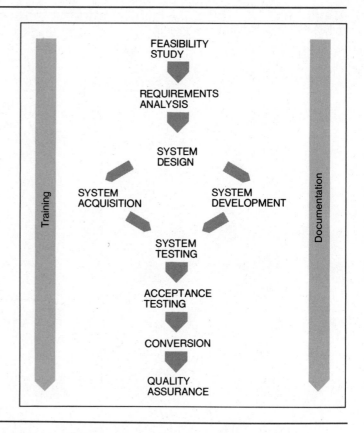

that is, requirements analysis begins on completion of the feasibility study, system design on completion of requirements analysis, etc.

This conceptualization of the CBIS implementation process is consistent with the internal development of a CBIS product, with the external acquisition of the product, and with situations in which certain portions of the product are internally developed while the remainder are externally acquired. Where the CBIS product is actually fabricated should have little impact on the activities undertaken from the perspective of the organizational unit sponsoring the project.

Following the CBIS implementation implications derived from modern software practices and the text's orientation toward the CBIS user, rather than the technical specialist, emphasis is placed on implementation activities that are directed at "planning" or "purpose" issues and that stand to benefit most from extensive user involvement. These activities include the feasibility study, requirements analysis, acceptance testing, and quality assurance. These topics will be covered in depth in

TABLE 9.1

Descriptions of CBIS Implementation Activities

Implementation Activity	Description
Feasibility study	Analysis to generate information to determine whether or not to commit organization resources and implement the CBIS product
Requirements analysis	Determination of the input, processing, and output attributes of the CBIS product so it meets organizational needs
System design	Configuration of hardware, software, and human components that enable a set of CBIS requirements to be achieved
System acquisition	Effort to develop proposals and solicit and evaluate bids when hardware or software must be acquired from vendors
System development	Internal programming effort to provide a software product
System testing	Assurance of the correctness of an internally developed software product
Acceptance testing	Evaluation of a CBIS product, acquired externally or developed internally, by the product's sponsors (users) prior to accepting "ownership" of the product
Conversion	Introduction of the CBIS product into the sponsoring organization
Quality assurance	Continual evaluation of the organizational "fit" of the CBIS product (and subsequent maintenance) after its introduction
Training	Provision of necessary skills, knowledge, and understanding to facilitate the implementation effort
Documentation	Description of the evolving CBIS product and creation of a history of the implementation effort.

the remaining chapters of Part 3. So the relationships between these user-dependent activities and the remaining implementation activities may be understood (particularly from the standpoint of the user's role throughout the implementation process), brief descriptions of these remaining activities are provided here.

System Design

System design is the predominantly technical task of configuring hardware, software, and human (procedural and human–machine interaction) components to meet stated requirements, given economic, technical, and behavioral realities. Primary concern should be directed toward establishing appropriate linkages among the CBIS product's components and between these components and those of other applications, of systems software, and of other organizations that interface with the CBIS product. All information processing tasks associated with the CBIS product must be addressed: data capture, entry, processing, storage, and dissemination.

Once a system design has been completed and software acquisition or development commences, the costs of significant CBIS product changes substantially increase. It is thus desirable for users to review and evaluate a system design on its completion. Users need to visualize whether or not requirements will be met by the design and assess requirements—costs trade-offs.

System Acquisition

System acquisition refers to efforts to prepare proposals, solicit and evaluate bids, and negotiate contracts with hardware and software vendors. Given effective requirements analysis and system design tasks, proposal preparation should be relatively straightforward. The remaining acquisition tasks, which tend to be quite specialized, were discussed in Chapter 2.

The user role is again that of reviewing and critiquing. Users must ensure that proposals represent organizational needs, that criteria used to evaluate bids are consistent with organizational objectives, and that contracts include adequate organizational protection.

System Development

Most efforts to improve the CBIS implementation process have involved *system development* tasks—software design (structuring a software product as a collection of programs), program design (structuring a program as a collection of modules), module coding, and program testing. These efforts and the problems they address were covered in the preceding two sections of this chapter.

Software development tasks are by far the most technical tasks associated with CBIS implementation. In few instances is intensive user involvement beneficial. Interestingly, much of the current activity associated with "application development" software is aimed at bypassing these purely technical tasks through automated design or development.

System Testing

System testing refers to efforts by system developers to increase the likelihood that a CBIS product will perform as specified when introduced into the organization. The intent is to exercise the entire requirements domain of a CBIS product: the complete range of inputs and outputs, every possible condition or situation that might arise, peak processing loads, all manual procedures, linkages with other systems, etc. Such an objective, however, is unreasonable, given the enormous number of circumstances to be tested with most CBIS.

The key to effective system testing, thus, is to compile a relatively small set of test data that accounts for much of the CBIS product's domain. Test data are an important organizational resource, a resource worthy of considerable investment in design and preparation. Generally included in such collections of test data are the most common values expected, common errors, and boundary values. Some test data are "artificial"—that is, created solely for test purposes. Progress is being achieved in developing software that automatically generates artificial test data after analyzing a piece of software.[15] The remainder of the test data would be "live"—that is, extracted from an organization's data and transaction files. It is here that an important user role emerges—working with system developers to compile the test data.

The act of testing itself often requires considerable effort and time. Testing often uses up half or more of the time devoted to software development. Compiling a quality set of test data thus results in a number of benefits: development time should be shortened, fewer errors should appear when the CBIS product is introduced, and maintenance expenses should be reduced.

Testing shows only the presence of errors, not their absence. Only through *design* can efforts be directed toward producing error-free CBIS products.

Conversion

If a CBIS fails to perform as expected on its organizational introduction, a number of harmful consequences are likely to arise. For example,

- Inability to perform specific organizational functions with the introduced CBIS may prevent those functions from being performed at all;
- Even if partial operation is realized, organizational disruptions may be severe;
- Failure is usually accompanied by negative psychological impacts that may impede future CBIS activities;
- Additional development costs will be incurred as CBIS staff members work to resolve the situation.

The probability that some failure will occur with any CBIS implementation is fairly high. Not only is it unlikely that all errors will be caught through system testing, but the original requirements specification may have been faulty and the time lag between when these specifications were derived and when the CBIS product was introduced might be long enough for naturally occurring organizational changes to invalidate certain requirements. The larger, more sophisticated, or more innovative the CBIS product is, the higher is the probability of failure. The aim in selecting a conversion strategy is to reduce the risk of a *disastrous* failure occurring but to do so at an acceptable cost.

A number of conversion strategies have been suggested, with the four most common pictured in Figure 9.13. The *parallel* strategy has the greatest potential for reducing the risk of failure. Both the CBIS being replaced ("old") and that being introduced ("new") run simultaneously for a time. In addition to having the old CBIS performing the function in case the new fails, one can compare the outputs of the old and new CBIS. (With many implementations no old CBIS exists and this strategy cannot be used.) The expense and the organizational confusion of operating parallel systems, however, can be great. The least costly strategy is to perform a *direct* conversion—i.e., at a certain point the old CBIS is replaced by the new. The risk inherent in such a strategy, however, should be clear. Two other strategies represent compromises between the parallel

FIGURE 9.13
Common Conversion Strategies

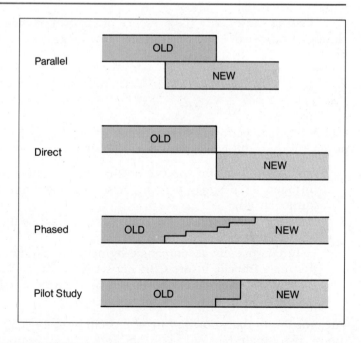

and direct conversion extremes. With a *phased* strategy, the new CBIS is incrementally introduced by dividing it (by subfunctions, complexity layers, organizational subunits into which it is introduced, etc.) and introducing each segment only after experience is gained with its predecessor. With a *pilot study* strategy, one segment of the new system is introduced and experienced, after which the remainder of the system is introduced. The objective with both the phased and pilot study strategies is to uncover problems early in the conversion effort so later introductions have lower risks of failure.

The following characteristics of CBIS products are typically assessed in selecting a conversion approach: their urgency, importance, and extent of organizational dependence, organizational impact, and required human interaction (input and output). Assessing such factors and planning a conversion effort clearly require user involvement. When the CBIS product being introduced is large or complex, it is common to find mixed conversion strategies in which particular segments of the system are introduced according to their unique attributes. The final CBIS product may often appear quite different from the original design as a result of two change processes: organizational members' being exposed to the CBIS product, and the CBIS product's "experiencing" the organizational context in which it has been inserted.

Training

Implementation efforts usually require that a variety of organizational members (top management, managers of the operating units sponsoring the CBIS product, users of the CBIS product, CBIS management, system analysts, and programmers) perform a wide range of tasks. For these tasks to be carried out effectively, participants must have certain knowledge, skills, and background information.[16] Table 9.2 summarizes representative requirements. A training effort must consequently be carried out that provides implementation participants with the knowledge and skills each requires. This training should not be a one-time event; rather, an organization-wide CBIS training program should exist on an ongoing basis that is supplemented as needed for any CBIS implementation project.

Documentation

Documentation is an integral element of a CBIS product, as it provides users with both product visibility and product understanding. Additionally, documentation can become the medium by which implementation

TABLE 9.2
Implementation Knowledge Requirements

General Areas of Required Knowledge	Specific Areas
Organizational overview	Objectives, purpose, opportunities, constraints, internal and external functioning
General CBIS	Hardware and software concepts, CBIS potential, organizational CBIS policies and plans, existing CBIS applications
Technical skills	Methods and techniques required to perform implementation tasks
Organizational skills	Interpersonal behavior, group dynamics, project management
Target organizational unit	Objectives, purpose, functions, resources, links with other internal and external units, problems
CBIS product	Purpose, design, required procedures, impacts on individuals

participants obtain a common view of the CBIS product and through which individual contributions are conveyed.

Historically, CBIS implementation efforts have been deficient in documentation. Documentation has generally been viewed as a secondary work obligation to be undertaken on completion of software development (often by a junior staff member, not the actual developer). That such a situation exists is not surprising, given the existence of reward systems focused on delivery of a software product by a given date. Software development activities not directly associated with program design, coding, or testing are naturally seen as unproductive.

When reward systems begin to stress the provision of easily maintained software products, this perception of documentation should change. The growing concern with documentation can be seen in the fact that many modern software practices provide documentation as a by-product.

At least three documentation packages should be provided: a user's manual, operator's manual, and project manual.

The user's manual tells how to use a CBIS product and informs potential users about the capabilities of the product. It consequently must contain general information (a narrative description of purpose, environment, basic structure, benefits, limitations, individuals to contact for more information, etc.), specific information (on hardware, basic system flow, inputs, outputs, processing mechanisms and conditions, data files, etc.), and detailed operating procedures (manual procedures, input formats, output layouts, error conditions, recovery procedures, etc.). The importance of producing a clear, correct, and complete user's manual cannot be overemphasized, as it is through this document that

CBIS use occurs. It has been recommended that preparation and approval of the user's manual be the first "product" of an implementation effort.[17]

The operator's manual gives computer operators all the information they need to schedule, prepare, and execute a run and to distribute output from the CBIS product. Thus, it should describe the system flow, inputs, outputs, data files, processes, errors, recovery procedures, hardware, setup, data entry procedures, output distribution, normal run cycle, etc. The importance of a comprehensive operator's guide increases as the organization's CBIS portfolio grows and operators can no longer maintain a complete understanding of each CBIS product in their minds.

The project manual provides, at any point in the life of a CBIS product, a description of what has transpired, what the product's current state is, and what is expected to occur in the future. It should reflect not only all key decisions (objectives, plans, designs, evaluations, etc.), but also the reasons behind these decisions. A project manual provides a guide for the product's developers, evaluators, or maintainers, and also reduces the vulnerability of a project to personnel turnover. Essentially, the project manual should provide summary and detailed descriptions of the efforts, decisions, and outcomes associated with each implementation activity.

CHARACTERIZATION OF THE TRADITIONAL APPROACH TO CBIS IMPLEMENTATION

The traditional view of the CBIS implementation process just presented describes the basic activities necessary to implement a CBIS and represents the sequence of activities most commonly observed. What it does not disclose are the distribution of responsibilities among implementation participants and the major criteria that drive implementation efforts.

This traditional approach can be characterized as follows:

Technological emphasis   Concern is focused on the efficient use of information resources,

Change minimization   Attention is directed toward "freezing" designs early so the technical staff can concentrate on devising the best technical solution,

System analyst control   Users are only passively involved, as the system analyst first interviews users to ascertain their needs, then examines the existing means for handling the targeted organizational function(s), and finally prescribes the new CBIS.[18]

The universal appropriateness of this approach is currently being challenged. The following story[19] may help explain why.

One manufacturing firm decided to develop an inventory control system within three years. The inventory control staff members who best understood the situation were too busy to commit themselves to the project, so surrogate experts with time on their hands were assigned to the project. After considerable effort, a requirements specification was produced. It was incomplete and inconsistent, as it was based on amateur opinions about inventory control and the existing situation. This specification was then frozen to shield the programmers. After three years of development, the inventory control system was introduced into the organization.

The inventory control staff quickly grew skeptical about the CBIS (operating procedures were cumbersome, needed information was not provided, and strange results were produced now and then), but the CBIS eventually was accepted and incorporated into the day-to-day routine of the inventory control staff. (However, the suspicions of staff members about the limits of computer-based technologies were reinforced. Most damaging, few of the new ideas developed by staff members over the past three years were incorporated into the CBIS.) One year later, management could not understand why inventory problems persisted even with this investment in information resources.

ALTERNATE VIEWS OF THE CBIS IMPLEMENTATION PROCESS

Challenges to the traditional CBIS implementation approach center around the notion of *adaption*. As CBIS are often subject to constant and dynamic changes, the desirability of creating and managing implementation processes that facilitate change, improve communication flows, provide for quick feedback, and span implementation activities seems clear.

For example, even with the sequential approach to CBIS implementation, considerable *iteration* (backtracking to previously performed activities) is often encountered as early assumptions or design decisions prove inappropriate or infeasible. As implementation proceeds, organizational learning always transpires, resulting in a more accurate understanding of the opportunities, problems, constraints, benefits, and costs associated with the CBIS product. Thus, even when a traditional approach to CBIS implementation is adopted, mechanisms should exist (in the form of checkpoints allowing reviews, reevaluations, and replanning) that permit management of an iterative, rather than sequential, series of activities.

Two approaches to the CBIS implementation process, both of which involve a succession of iterations through partial CBIS products, are presented: evolutionary[20] and prototyping.[21,22] Each addresses a particular set of problems that may arise when a CBIS product is implemented. After each approach is discussed, an overall framework for selecting an implementation approach is suggested.

Evolutionary Development

Large, complex CBIS typically are characterized by a long interval between the specification of requirements and the conversion activity. During this development period, changes are likely to occur that invalidate some of the stated requirements. Furthermore, during these primarily technical tasks, users are frozen out of the implementation effort. With a lengthy development period, valuable feedback from those using a CBIS product is absent.

The evolutionary approach to CBIS implementation strives to address these difficulties. With this approach, the CBIS product is broken into predefined versions that are successively developed and introduced into the organization. If each version has a relatively short development period (a few months at most), a portion of the CBIS product will probably be introduced before significant organizational changes occur, and user feedback on these early versions can be incorporated into later versions. Typically the initial version is a skeleton of the full CBIS product, and succeeding versions add refinements until a complete product is configured. Figure 9.14 portrays such an approach.

Prototyping

When the organizational functions to be supported by a CBIS product are poorly understood, it is difficult to state a valid requirements specification. Such situations are most quickly recognized with DSS applications, as much of the anticipated use of the CBIS product remains to be shaped through user experiences. Difficulties in stating requirements arise with many IRS applications as well.

With the prototyping approach, a "quick and dirty" version of the CBIS product is developed in a very short time (a few weeks at most) and provided to users. After experience with this prototype, users are more likely to recognize how the CBIS can help them perform their organizational responsibilities. Feedback from users is then incorporated into successive versions of the CBIS product. The CBIS product is thus designed and developed through a process of continual user learning and product adaptation. Figure 9.15 illustrates this approach.

FIGURE 9.14
Evolutionary Approach to CBIS Implementation

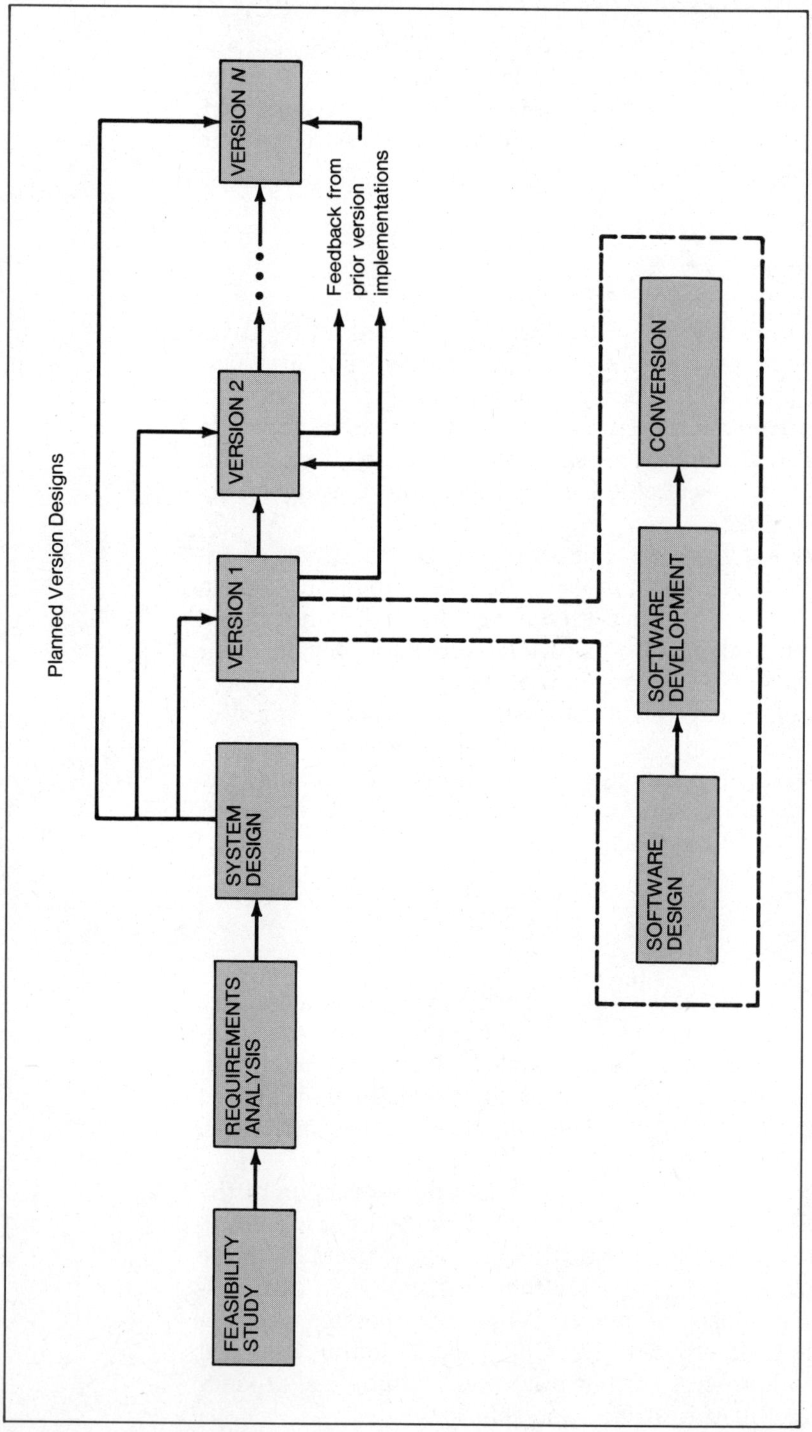

FIGURE 9.15
Prototype Approach to CBIS Implementation

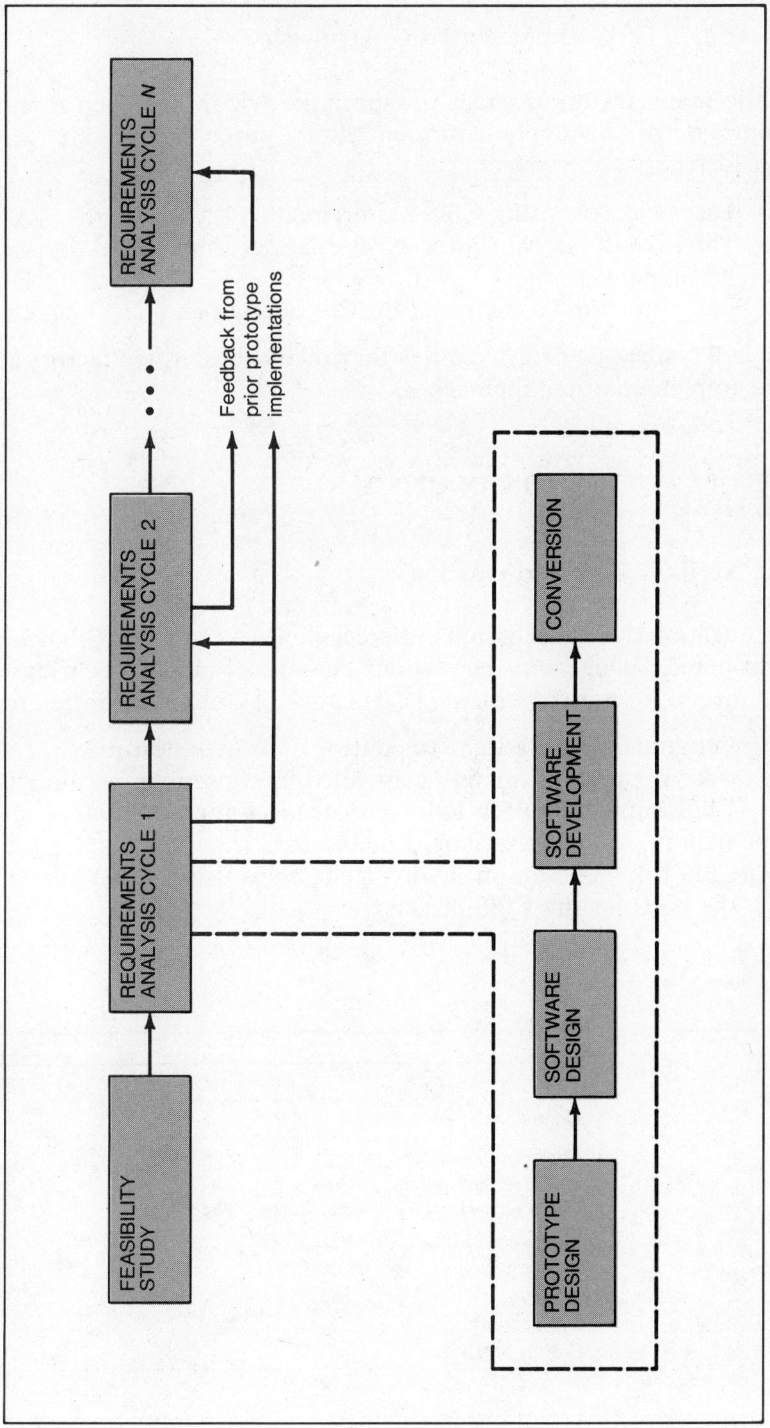

Selecting a CBIS Implementation Approach

While many factors interact to determine which approach is most appropriate for an implementation effort, three factors are generally considered:

- Ease of determining CBIS requirements,
- Presence of relevant prior experiences of implementation participants,
- Length of time anticipated for CBIS design and development.

Table 9.3 suggests decision rules that relate these three factors and the four implementation approaches.

USER PARTICIPATION IN CBIS IMPLEMENTATION

The Need for User Participation

Throughout these discussions, the desirability of user involvement has been noted. Aside from the obvious benefits of tapping user knowledge and insight, user involvement is advocated for a number of other reasons:

- Individuals have a right to control their own destinies.
- Activities are ultimately controlled by those who perform them.
- CBIS implementation involvement often increases users' understanding of organizational functioning.
- CBIS implementation involvement helps users better appreciate the need for the CBIS product.

TABLE 9.3
Framework for Selecting an
Implementation Approach

	Situations			
Conditions	1	2	3	4
Clear requirements	Yes	?	Yes	No
In-house experience	Yes	?	?	?
Large project	No	No	Yes	?
Actions				
Sequential	X			
Iterative		X		
Evolutionary			X	
Prototyping				X

- CBIS implementation involvement enhances users' understanding of and commitment to the CBIS product.[23–25]

Whether or not these benefits are actually achieved depends on the effort put forth by user participants.

For users to commit themselves to implementation activities, they must have the requisite knowledge and abilities, understand how they will personally benefit from the CBIS, and believe their contributions will be incorporated within the CBIS. The first two conditions are partly achieved through appropriate training and participant selection. All three conditions are most influenced, however, by the assignment of implementation roles to participants.

User Implementation Roles

Three generic roles can be defined for CBIS implementation participants. A *consultant* role finds an individual responding to questions asked by the person directing the implementation task. These responses are not necessarily incorporated into task outcomes. A person in an *influence* role also responds to questions posed by another, but the responses are incorporated (directly or indirectly) into task outcomes. In a *responsibility* role, an individual leads the implementation task and is responsible for its success or failure. If users are to be motivated to commit themselves to implementation tasks, they should at least be assigned influence roles.

The importance of user participation and the roles assigned users can be seen in the following example.[26] In 1972 an agreement was reached at an administrative level among Danish library organizations initiating a national effort to develop a CBIS for cataloguing and lending. The project followed the traditional approach to CBIS implementation. The project team consisted of library administrators and computer specialists. When the system design was completed in early 1975, the project team wanted to present the proposal to librarians across Denmark to obtain feedback for "fine tuning" the design. Consequently, a newsletter was established and a series of meetings were held. Unexpectedly, the librarians became very interested. After studying the proposal, a number of librarian groups began to question some objectives of the proposal. Believing significant changes were required, these groups attempted to influence the system design. As this was not the role assigned them by the project team (who viewed the librarians solely as a reservoir of knowledge to be tapped), the project stalled while a heated debate was carried out in the national press. After one third of all Danish librarians signed a petition to halt the project, it was terminated at the system design stage in the summer of 1977.

The Contingent Nature of Implementation
Role Assignments

Clearly the makeup and size of implementation teams and the roles assigned implementation participants vary with the implementation activity.[27] Certain stages, such as software development, are dominated by technical specialists, while others, such as the feasibility study, are dominated by users.

Furthermore, the nature of the CBIS application itself influences implementation role assignments. User involvement is not without costs: it is expensive and time consuming, and ineffective implementation processes may alienate users or give them unrealistic expectations. If the organizational functions involved are structured and stable and involve little human–machine interaction (such as an accounts receivable application), it might be best to minimize user participation. On the other hand, the need for extensive user participation (including assigning responsibility for certain implementation activities and for the entire project) increases when the organizational functions are poorly understood, innovative, and dynamic, have significant individual or organizational impacts and significant organizational dependence, and require large financial investment and substantial human–machine interaction.[28,29]

PLAN OF THIS PART

Implementation failures are often due to the implementers' inability to manage the uncertainty that pervades CBIS implementation. These uncertainties can be attributed to a number of sources:

- The dynamic nature of information technologies,
- The large number of technical, economic, and behavioral factors involved,
- The natural human tendency to overlook factors until they become problems,
- The political nature of CBIS,
- The diverse backgrounds and interests of implementation participants,
- Participants' lack of understanding of their own and others' implementation roles,
- Difficulties in determining requirements,
- Difficulties in predicting CBIS organizational impacts,
- Pressure for fast, successful, cost-effective implementations.[30–32]

CBIS implementation is an information-intensive activity that, if it is to succeed, must facilitate information discovery, information exchange, and the attainment of a consensus on CBIS purpose among participants and between CBIS specialists and users. One view of the CBIS implementation process addresses a series of information processing tasks believed necessary to resolve the uncertainties associated with CBIS implementation (Table 9.4).[33] This conceptualization emphasizes planning activities as well as activities requiring intensive user participation—precisely the activities covered in the remaining chapters of Part 3.

Chapter 10 centers on *planning* issues. While not directly concerned with the implementation of a specific CBIS, the first two topics—developing a master plan and selecting a project—are included in recognition of the need for each project to be viewed against the organization's entire CBIS portfolio. Next the objective of and processes involved in a feasibility study are discussed, with emphasis placed on assessing CBIS benefits and costs. The chapter concludes with an analysis of factors and strategies associated with devising an implementation plan, once the decision is made to develop a CBIS.

It is generally accepted that the most critical implementation activity with most CBIS involves arriving at a valid requirements specification. Chapter 11 provides a thorough coverage (from the user's perspective) of the objectives and methodologies of requirements analysis. The techniques emphasized reflect structured approaches to determining information requirements.

The need to regularly assess the results of CBIS implementation efforts is critical if the information resource is to be effectively exploited.

TABLE 9.4
A Radical Model of the CBIS Implementation Process

Activity	Goal
Scouting	Problem identification; analysis of appropriateness of a CBIS solution
Entry	Realization of a need for solution; commitment to CBIS project by users and CBIS specialists
Diagnosis	Achievement of problem understanding
Planning	Agreement on CBIS objectives, requirements, and evaluation criteria
Action	CBIS design and development; training; conversion
Evaluation	Insurance of a continued fit of CBIS product through evaluation and maintenance
Termination	Internalization of CBIS product within users' behaviors; departure of CBIS specialists from project

Chapter 12 discusses four CBIS evaluation activities—stating measurable CBIS product performance objectives, performing the quality assurance function for operational CBIS, performing an acceptance test, and judging the overall effectiveness of an implementation effort.

Chapter 13 concludes Part 3 by focusing on common causes of CBIS failure and on steps organizations can take to increase the likelihood that information resources will be used effectively.

KEY ISSUES

"Implementation of a CBIS" refers to the overall process of initiating, designing, developing, installing, using, and maintaining a CBIS product.

Software development difficulties are a major factor in both the high cost of CBIS products and the existence of CBIS products that do not meet the needs of organizational members. Many problems associated with software development are a direct result of its labor-intensity, its changeability, and management difficulties.

The objective in software development is to produce products that are relevant, maintainable, and portable. The structured approaches to software development reflected in modern software practices help achieve this objective by emphasizing design, comprehension, and communication throughout the development process.

A considerable effort is being made to automate software development activities.

The major software development activities include feasibility analysis, requirements analysis, system design, system acquisition, system development (program design, coding, and testing), system testing, conversion, quality assurance, training, and documentation.

The traditional approach to software development views these activities as occurring sequentially. Additionally, the traditional approach tends to be directed by systems analysts and tends to emphasize technical concerns.

Alternative approaches to software development explicitly recognize that CBIS are subject to constant and dynamic change. Hence, the CBIS implementation process is oriented to facilitating change by improving communication flows among participants and permitting rapid feedback from users to developers. Two alternatives are the evolutionary and prototype approaches.

User participation in CBIS implementation activities provides numerous benefits, but these are not without costs. There is great variety in the way users can participate in CBIS implementation. Deciding on the proper roles for both users and technical specialists requires consideration of the task requirements of each implementation activity and the nature of the CBIS being implemented.

Failures of CBIS implementation can usually be traced to the implementer's inability to manage the uncertainty that pervades CBIS implementation.

DISCUSSION QUESTIONS

1. Explain what is meant by the "invisible" nature of a software product at the beginning of a development project. What are some software development problems that directly result from this invisibility?
2. How do modern software practices improve the "thought processes" of the individuals responsible for designing, coding, and testing software products?

3. How do modern software practices enhance communication? How do they force key decisions to be brought out early in the design process?

4. Consider the relatively routine task of making change for a ten-dollar bill for a purchase of less than ten dollars. Using the notation of structured programming illustrated in Figure 9.4, design a program to handle this task.

5. A major problem facing organizations is that many of their current CBIS products are very old. As a result, these applications are costly to maintain, do not exploit current information technologies, and do not accurately reflect current organizational realities. Why do organizations tend to use CBIS products longer than their ideal useful lives?

6. Consider the relatively routine job of changing a flat tire. Using the concepts and techniques of structured design, document the activities involved in changing a flat tire.

7. What do you believe will be the impact of automated design and development tools on career opportunities for programmers and system analysts?

8. Devise some decision rules regarding when to apply a parallel conversion strategy. Do the same for a direct conversion strategy.

9. What are the main advantages of the evolutionary and prototype approaches to CBIS implementation over the traditional approach? Can you suggest situations in which the traditional approach might be the most appropriate approach to take? Explain.

10. Why is user participation in CBIS implementation absent in many organizations? Is this absence ever justified?

11. Often users on CBIS design teams have little real influence on the implementation process. Is this preferable to not involving these individuals at all?

BRIEF CASES

1. *Mercy Hospital*

   The final approval for the interactive pharmacy inventory control system had just reached Joe Engles' desk, along with a note from the director of the hospital's pharmacy department. Joe was being put in charge of the inventory project. His first task was to meet with Sara Lytle, the system analyst assigned to the project, and develop an implementation strategy. Joe was glad Sara had been assigned to the project. As a pharmacist, he had little experience with computers. Sara and he got along fine, however, and she was acknowledged to be one of the more technically skilled analysts employed by the hospital.

   The current pharmacy inventory control system was a batch processing system in which transactions were processed at six-hour intervals throughout the day. This system was essentially an inventory tracking system from which daily reports of drug levels were produced. Ordering was done manually by means of these reports (drugs with low stock levels were flagged on the reports). With an average of 2500 orders a day, the manual system was simply being overwhelmed. Orders were often received late, stock-outs of drugs were occurring (requiring expensive rush deliveries), and the error rate had gotten too high.

The new inventory system would involve a complete rewrite. Not only was the processing environment changing to an on-line data entry, immediate processing environment, but a number of additional functions were being added to the system. The major enhancements involved automatic reordering; checks on patient–drug interactions; checks against a patient's prior drug orders to identify overdoses, duplicate orders, or instances of two drugs being ordered that might produce harmful reactions; and a on-line inquiry capability for both pharmacists and doctors. As might be expected, an elaborate security system was also being designed to prevent unauthorized use of the inventory system.

In their previous meeting, Sara had given Joe a report produced by the information system department that described various approaches to managing an implementation effort. Sara told Joe to read through the report, as their first task would be to put together an implementation plan. Three approaches stuck in Joe's mind as he began to prepare for the meeting with Sara: a sequential approach, an evolutionary approach, and a prototype approach.

What implementation approach would you recommend for the interactive pharmacy inventory control system project? Why?

2. *Mountain Community Bank*
Helen Thompson had been directed to lead the implementation effort on the bank's loan approval and control system. This project involved a number of enhancements in the bank's existing loan approval system. The current system was a pure batch system. The major enhancements involved changing to an on-line loan application data entry process, enabling loan officers to interactively query the status of any loan application, collecting statistics on the payment performance of customers receiving loans, and producing reports on the effectiveness of the loan approval process. These reports were to be used to evaluate loan officer performance and to suggest revisions in current decision rules regarding loan approval.

Helen felt very strongly that user participation was necessary with most CBIS implementations. This application, however, seemed straightforward. Everyone was satisfied with the current loan approval system, and even though no interactive systems had been developed for loan applications, the bank was experienced in interactive applications. Aside from developing some training programs for the clerical staff in the loan department, there seemed little need for user participation.

Do you agree with Helen's views on the need for user participation in the loan approval and control system project? In discussing your answer, include references to each of the major activities associated with CBIS implementation. You can assume the feasibility study has already been performed.

3. *Woodstock Heaters*
The decision was made to purchase a software package to handle the manufacturing control application. A consultant was hired to work with the

firm's small information systems staff to determine requirements and select a package. Since many of the production employees had been with the firm for some time and hence had no experience with computer-based systems, as much weight in selecting a package was given to ease of operation (data entry, report production, etc.) as to manufacturing control capabilities. The basic functions performed by the software package were scheduling the manufacturing steps for an order, tracking the order through its manufacturing process, and providing a rescheduling capability in case rush orders or major production problems arose.

While the selected software package was already written, it had been tried out in only two locations. Neither of the two manufacturing firms that had purchased the software package had an internal environment similar to that of Woodstock Heaters. Subsequent enquiries revealed that no major installation problems had been encountered by either firm, both of which had considerable experience with computer-based manufacturing applications.

The manufacturing process at Woodstock Heaters involved three separate assembly lines, one for each of the solar heaters the firm sold. Each line was best viewed as a job shop, with fifteen to twenty discrete manufacturing steps required to produce a solar heater. As the heaters for the most part were produced on order, it was critical to maintain current information on manufacturing statuses. Customers were continually calling about delivery dates. Additionally, many components used in manufacturing a heater were quite expensive, and the firm could not afford to maintain a large components inventory. Efficient production required the capability to order components from suppliers so a heater's components arrived just before they were needed.

Each of three assembly lines was composed of five "shops," with related manufacturing functions performed in each shop. While a heater might keep moving between shops during the manufacturing process, each manufacturing step was relatively independent of the other steps.

Propose a conversion strategy to be used by Woodstock Heaters to implement the manufacturing control package.

NOTES

1. N. Szyperski and T. Tilemann, "Challenges and Consequences for Future Research on Implementation," in N. Szyperski and E. Grochla (eds.), *Design and Implementation of Computer-Based Information Systems* (Alphen an den Rijn, The Netherlands: Sijthoff & Noordhoff, 1979), pp. 353–64.

2. N. Szyperski, "State of the Art of Implementation Research on Computer-Based Information Systems," in Szyperski and Grochla (1979), pp. 5–28.

3. B. W. Boehm, "The High Cost of Software," *Proceedings of a Symposium on the High Cost of Software* (Palo Alto: Stanford Research Institute, 1973), pp. 3–14.

4. J. H. Moore and M. G. Chang, "Design of Decision Support Systems," *Data Base* 12(1980):8–14.

5.   L. A. Belady and M. M. Lehman, "The Characteristics of Large Systems," in P. Wegner (ed.), *Research Directions in Software Technology* (Cambridge, Mass.: MIT Press, 1979), pp. 106–38.

6.   F. P. Brooks, *The Mythical Man-Month* (Reading, Mass.: Addison-Wesley, 1974).

7.   H. W. Lawson, *Understanding Computer Systems* (Linkoping, Sweden: Lawson Publishing, 1979).

8.   M. Bohl, *Tools for Structured Design* (Chicago: SRA, 1978).

9.   D. T. Ross and J. W. Brackett, "An Approach to Structured Analysis," *Computer Decisions* 8(1976):40–44.

10.   D. T. Ross, "Structured Analysis: A Language for Communicating Ideas," *IEEE Transactions of Software Engineering*, SE-3(1977):16–34.

11.   H. D. Mills, "Top Down Programming in Large Systems," in R. Rustin (ed.), *Debugging Techniques in Large Systems* (Englewood Cliffs, N.J.: Prentice-Hall, 1971), pp. 41–56.

12.   J. Ewers and I. Vessey, "The Systems Development Dilemma—A Programming Perspective," *MIS Quarterly* 5(1981):33–45.

13.   D. Teichroew, W. J. Rataj, and E. A. Hershey, "An Introduction to Computer-Aided Documentation of User Requirements to Computer-Based Information Processing Systems," in E. Grochla and N. Szyperski (eds.), *Information Systems and Organizational Structure* (Berlin: DeGruyter, 1975), pp. 438–66.

14.   J. F. Nunamaker, Jr., B. R. Konsynski, Jr., T. Ho, and C. Singer, "Computer-Aided Analysis and Design of Information Systems," *Communications of the ACM* 19(1976):674–87.

15.   G. Myers, *The Art of Software Testing* (New York: Wiley, 1979).

16.   R. W. Zmud and J. F. Cox, "The Implementation Process: A Change Approach," *MIS Quarterly* 3(1979):35–44.

17.   W. S. Donelson, "Project Planning and Control," *Datamation* 22(1976):73–80.

18.   M. J. Ginzberg, "Participative System Design," in Szyperski and Grochla (1979), pp. 215–20.

19.   H. D. Mills, "Software Development," *IEEE Transactions of Software Engineering* SE-2(1976):265–73.

20.   R. W. Zmud, "Management of Large Software Development Efforts," *MIS Quarterly* 4(1980):45–55.

21.   J. Berrisford and J. Wetherbe, "Heuristic Development: A Redesign of Systems Design," *MIS Quarterly* 3(1979):11–19.

22.   P. G. W. Keen, "Adaptive Design for Decision Support Systems," *Data Base* 12(1980):15–25.

23.   H. C. Lucas, Jr., *Toward Creative System Design* (New York: Columbia University Press, 1974).

24.   R. J. Boland, Jr., "The Process and Product of System Design," *Management Science* 24(1978):887–98.

25.   E. Mumford, "Participative Systems Design: Structure and Method," *Systems, Objectives, Solutions* 1(1981):5–19.

26. H. Clausen, "Concepts and Experiences with Participative Design Approaches," in Szyperski and Grochla (1979), pp. 231–42.

27. Zmud and Cox (1979).

28. Zmud and Cox (1979).

29. R. J. Schonberger, "MIS Design: A Contingency Approach," *MIS Quarterly* 4(1980):13–20.

30. M. L. Markus, "Power, Politics and MIS Implementation," working paper, Sloan School of Management, MIT, 1980.

31. E. Mumford, "Implementing EDP Systems—A Sociological Perspective," *The Computer Bulletin* 13(1969):10–13.

32. E. Mumford and A. Pettigrew, *Implementing Strategic Decisions* (London: Longman, 1975).

33. M. J. Ginzberg, "A Study of the Implementation Process," *TIMS Studies in the Management Sciences* 13(1979):85–102.

CBIS 10
Planning

INCREASED ATTENTION to software *design* has enabled software groups to develop products that satisfy specified requirements and that are produced on schedule and within budget. These achievements have been realized through reaching an early consensus on a software product's requirements; emphasizing a software product's basic control structure so natural, simple linkages occur among the product's modules and between the product and other software products; and anticipating likely future modifications and enhancements so they are allowed for in a software product's basic control structure. Similar attention to CBIS *planning* activities (i.e., defining information resource strategies and policies, selecting CBIS applications to implement, developing an application portfolio, assessing the feasibility of an application, designing an implementation plan, etc.) must be applied to provide organization-wide schemas to drive all CBIS implementation efforts.

The goal of all CBIS-related activities is to effectively meet the organization's information needs while managing the uncertainty that tends to surround the information resource. The extent of this uncertainty (associated with resource scarcity, dynamic technological and organizational environments, intra- and interorganizational dependency, and functional complexity) increases with time, which intensifies the need for CBIS planning. In the absence of effective planning, CBIS efforts become reactive, resulting in the information resource's being confronted rather than exploited.

This chapter introduces four closely related CBIS planning activities. Two—developing a master plan and selecting a project—are directed toward reducing the uncertainty associated with charting an organization's entire CBIS effort. The other two—performing a feasibility study and designing an implementation plan—focus on identifying and resolving uncertainties associated with individual CBIS projects.

A CBIS MASTER PLAN

A common goal of many organizations in the 1960s was the development of a "total system," a global but fully integrated information system that encompassed all aspects of an organization and that could be implemented at one time. Attempts to implement such total systems invariably met with (at times spectacular) failure. Not only do organizations present "moving targets," but the effort involved was simply too large, complex, and demanding in terms of the required organizational resources.

The goal of developing a total system remains, but is viewed as an unachievable ideal. The current view conceives of an organization's CBIS efforts as resulting *over time* in a cluster of information systems that differ markedly in their interdependence but that can be integrated as required. Each CBIS is designed individually but with concern for current and future CBIS interfaces.

This evolving design that includes current and future CBIS applications is the CBIS *master plan*. Along with identifying applications, the master plan describes the data, hardware, systems software, personnel, and financial resources required and the sequence in which applications and resource commitments will arise. Objectives that underlie development of a master plan include the following:

- Ensuring that all CBIS efforts are consistent with, contribute toward, and eventually influence organizational strategies,
- Ensuring that CBIS applications address critical organizational information processing needs (opportunities and problems),
- Defining (and communicating throughout the organization) the role of the information function,
- Conveying to the organization the extent of current and future CBIS resource commitments,
- Enhancing communication between the information function, top management, and users,
- Ensuring that a solid CBIS foundation (TPS applications associated with mainstream functions) is built on which more sophisticated IRS and DSS applications can be based,
- Cultivating a core group of organizational proponents (users and top management),
- Controlling and directing the acquisition and deployment of information resources,
- Ensuring that the CBIS staff remains technologically current.[1,2]

The remainder of this section will define the components of a CBIS master plan and describe the processes associated with developing such a plan.

Master Plan Components

A CBIS master plan should contain the following four components: a definition of the charter of the information function, statements disclosing current CBIS strategies and constraints, a project inventory, and visual portrayals of the planned evolution in CBIS capabilities and resources.

A *charter* delineates the scope and organizational role of the information function. Statements relating to *scope* essentially define the information resource. Is it limited to traditional (EDP) information processing activities, or does it extend into word processing, records and forms management, interoffice and interorganizational communication, graphic arts, and library services? All information systems must be reflected in a master plan if integration is to be attained and redundancy eliminated. A CBIS can play various organizational *roles:* source of clerical, operations, or management support; competitive or strategic force; mechanism for facilitating organizational development or fomenting organizational change; and political tool. Since such roles vary in their importance across organizations (as well as over time) and in their impact on organizations, invoked roles should be clearly understood by planners.

A coherent *strategy* that directs CBIS implementation activities must be communicated to implementation participants, along with an explanation of all *constraints* on implementation efforts.[3] The strategies should tell organizational members the relative priorities of various CBIS efforts to focus attention, to induce commitment, and to facilitate resource allocation decisions throughout the organization. Also, desired CBIS design orientations (end-user concern, cost, technology, etc.) must be clarified so they can be incorporated where appropriate within CBIS products. Relevant constraints might be imposed by external entities (regulatory agencies, competitors, the industry, etc.) or by the organization itself (budget or personnel limitations, hardware and software capabilities, risk position, time frames, access to external information services, etc.), or they may reflect environmental influences. Again, the intent is to focus the behaviors of organizational members whenever organization-wide concerns must be addressed.

A *project inventory* identifies and describes existing CBIS applications, those under development, and those planned for future development. Included with all project descriptions are project name, functional description, hardware and software architecture, primary outputs, data requirements, mode of operation, relations with other applications, and status (existing, being developed, planned for future). Additional information regarding future applications might include ways to implement (acquire or develop), expected time schedule and costs, and priority. A secondary aim of the inventory is to quickly inform organizational members of existing and future CBIS applications.

Time-phased diagrams illustrating the sequence in which CBIS capabilities are to be acquired should also be produced. Such diagrams disclose organizational intentions over time on a number of issues, such as CBIS applications, data resources, hardware and software environment, CBIS staffing needs, and financial outlays. A single diagram usually illustrates the planned evolution within each issue; taken together, these diagrams allow one to visualize the entire master plan. Figure 10.1 suggests an applications sequence for a hypothetical wholesale firm.

Master Plan Development

An organization's initial efforts to develop a master plan might require considerable human resources and time. Thereafter, however, master plan redesign should not require a major commitment of resources. The appropriateness of the current master plan should be reassessed at least once a year (to coincide with annual budget preparation). Reassessments should also occur whenever major changes occur in the organization (a new CEO, a merger, or a reorganization), in the organization's environment (a constituency change or a strategic action by a competitor), or with information technologies.

A major decision in devising a master plan is adopting a specific planning horizon. Behaviors should be forecast as far ahead as possible, but little is gained when predictions are unlikely to come about. A planning horizon should only extend into a future that will probably transpire. In stipulating a time horizon, one must examine a number of environmental "stabilities": product or service markets; resource availabilities; regulatory influences; economic, cultural, and political forces; and information technologies. In the past, the dynamic nature of information technologies mandated fairly short time horizons (e.g., three to five years).[4] Now, however, because of market pressure, vendors' new products are generally compatible with their existing products; consequently, an organization can adopt a CBIS master plan time horizon more consistent with that of its strategic plan.

The dynamic nature of information technologies, however, will continually result in striking discontinuities over time. Regardless of how well an organization has planned, evolving technological realities will eventually make prior plans (and resource commitments) obsolete. Today, for example, many organizations that earlier (and appropriately, given existing technologies and organizational realities) invested substantially in establishing centralized information facilities now find themselves facing user demands for microcomputers, minicom-

FIGURE 10.1
Applications Sequence Diagram

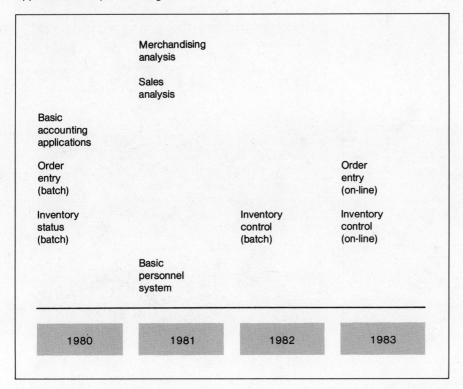

puters, distributed networks, local processing, etc. How well these demands are responded to and the manner in which subsequent changes are effected will substantially affect managerial attitudes throughout such organizations.

Clearly, it is advantageous for organizations to establish a formal or informal capability to monitor and assess evolving information technologies, as well as their potential organizational impacts. The more dependent the organization is on information services, the more critical is this need.

Figure 10.2 summarizes the process of developing a CBIS master plan. The first task is to understand the organization's current and future contexts: its external environment (market, competition, economy, legislation, resources), its internal environment (unique capabilities, culture, problems, finances, expected work volume changes, personnel changes,

FIGURE 10.2
Steps in Developing a CBIS Master Plan

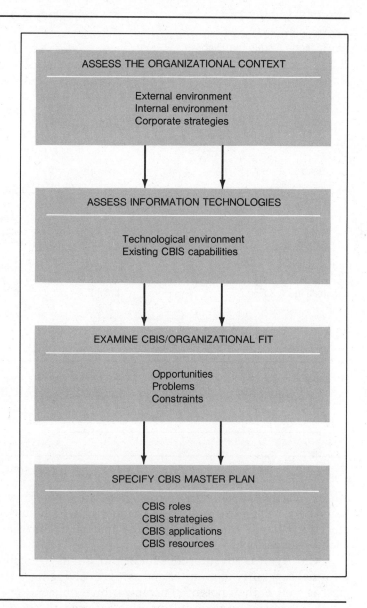

organization structure), and its policies and strategies (risk philosophy, growth philosophy, objectives, domain targeting, action plans, financial strategies). Then the CBIS technical environment must be appraised to identify capabilities and potentials. Existing CBIS applications and resources must be inventoried, the development of information technologies over the plan's time horizon must be assessed, and any organizational constraints on CBIS opportunities must be recognized. Next, the ways CBIS might resolve organizational problems and contribute to organizational opportunities must be examined. For example, a CBIS could perform clerical tasks, support operations, support managerial planning, control, and decision making, provide better products or services, and provide new products or services. Finally, all these factors should be interrelated so decisions can be made on CBIS roles, strategies, and applications.

CBIS Master Planning Methodologies

Because of the broad scope and unstructured nature of planning activities, it is difficult to devise mechanistic sequences of procedures to follow when deriving a CBIS master plan. Numerous frameworks, however, have been suggested. Two widely different methodologies, both developed by IBM, are Business Systems Planning (BSP) and Business Information Analysis and Integration Technique (BIAIT).[5]

The first, BSP, involves a two-phase process of developing first a broad understanding of an organization and then a CBIS master plan. The fundamental idea is to identify the information necessary for the organization to achieve its objectives. An overview of this process is shown in Figure 10.3. Phase one emplois a top-down modeling approach to identify the organization's mission, strategies, and functions. This is followed by an analysis of how CBIS can best be used to support these functions, paying particular attention to assigning priorities to CBIS applications. In phase two, current CBIS capabilities are assessed, major CBIS deficiencies identified, and organization functions (or users) located that share data to highlight CBIS integration requirements. Finally, a master plan consistent with organizational objectives and sequenced over time is produced. To be done well, BSP requires many organizational members to make considerable investments of time and effort. A common sentiment among the many organizations that have used BSP is that they were glad they did it but would never do it again!

A totally different approach to CBIS master planning is taken by BIAIT. After considerable research, IBM researchers identified seven questions the answers to which suggest which of several standard CBIS master plans to use:

1. Do you bill customers or accept cash?
2. Do you deliver products immediately?
3. Do you create and maintain records of customer buying habits?
4. Do you negotiate price?
5. Do you rent or sell your product?
6. Do you perform product recalls or updates?
7. Do you make to order or produce for stock?

FIGURE 10.3
Overview of the BSP Methodology

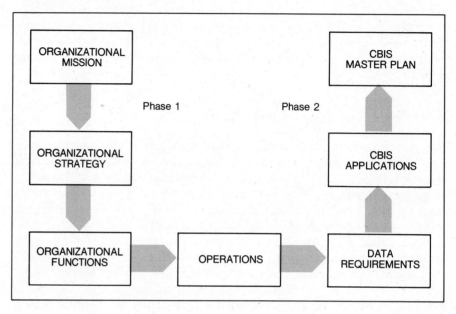

This plan is then customized to fit the unique characteristics of the target organization. Consequently, BIAIT adopts a bottom-up approach requiring far less commitment of time and effort by organizational members than BSP. The danger involves the relevance of the generic model to the target organization. For small organizations involved with a small number of functions, such an approach might be appropriate, but larger, more complex organizations might require a BSP-like methodology.

Links Between CBIS Master Planning and Organizational Strategic Planning

The need for organizations to link CBIS master planning and organizational strategic planning is increasing because of three major forces. First, an enlarging symbiosis between information technologies and organizational strategic activities is becoming evident: new information technologies increasingly provide strategic opportunities, and major shifts in an organization's products or markets are invariably followed by requested changes in CBIS services. Second, the growing amount of funds committed to providing information services requires that top management provide considerable direction to and control of the information function. Poor management of the information function is quickly reflected in an organization's bottom line. Third, the peculiar nature of information technologies (extended time lags for implementation, the need to acquire and develop specialized personnel skills, difficulty in reversing prior decisions regarding hardware or software architectures, etc.) requires that they be explicitly considered when alternative organizational strategies are being evaluated.

Furthermore, the extent of linkage between CBIS master planning and organizational strategic planning varies with the strategic and operational importance of information services to an organization's success. In certain organizations (such as a bank), it is quite reasonable to expect CBIS planners to play a lead role in setting organizational strategies. In other organizations (such as a process manufacturer in a stable market), an appropriate role for CBIS planners regarding organizational strategic planning might be that of a passive source of knowledge. In any case, CBIS master planning and organizational strategic planning integration should ensure that information resources, when applied, directly contribute to the attainment of organizational objectives, and that information resources, when appropriate, are seen as strategic tools.[6]

PROJECT SELECTION

Ordinarily, organizational demands to undertake CBIS projects exceed organizational resources (financial, personnel, and hardware and software). As a result, *project selection* mechanisms to discriminate between alternative requests must be used. This might be done in an ad hoc fashion or formally by means of prescribed rules and procedures. To ensure compatibility and consistency, the adoption of formal mechanisms is advocated. Methods to apply with such a procedure are given in Appendix A.

Project selection should not involve a detailed analysis of benefits and costs—such in-depth analyses are performed elsewhere (in feasibility studies, requirements analyses, etc.). Rather, project selection should be directed toward *screening out* inappropriate projects (those that misuse organizational or information resources), determining *priorities* for accepted projects (identifying projects addressing critical organizational needs), and obtaining a *balanced* CBIS portfolio. Balance here includes the trade-off between payoff and risk, the range of CBIS applications (TPS, IRS, DSS, PDS), organizational functions supported, and organizational units supported. These objectives suggest the close relationship between master planning and project selection: master planning activities activate project selection mechanisms, and project selection activities undertaken independent of master planning efforts should use the master plan as the central focus in project selection procedures. Particularly important are the time-sequencing aspects of the master plan—while a specific application might not in itself address a critical organizational need, it might have to be implemented so a crucial application can be implemented in the future.

Not all CBIS projects need to go through a formal screening mechanism. Projects requiring only limited organizational resources and affecting single organizational units might be acted on independent of other CBIS investment alternatives and, hence, are best decided by local decision-makers, rather than higher-level project selection committees. Determining the criteria that allow formal selection mechanisms to be bypassed is a critical policy decision.

Clearly, CBIS projects have diverse origins, are proposed for many reasons, and are evaluated by a variety of criteria. Potential sources of CBIS project ideas include top management, users, CBIS specialists, consultants, vendors, literature, professional groups, peers of organizational members, and educational programs (external as well as internal). The need to invest personal effort and organizational resources in cultivating such sources cannot be overstated. The CBIS projects might arise as modifications, extensions, or total redesigns of existing applications, or they

---

TABLE 10.1
Reasons for Initiating CBIS Projects

General Reason	Examples
Organizational needs	Growth
	Change in objectives
	New products, services, or markets
	Change in operations
	Reorganization
	Personnel changes
	Attainment of resource constraints
	Operational bottlenecks
	Need for better operational efficiency and effectiveness
	Need for better management information
Environmental needs	Regulatory, legislated, or industry mandates
	Competitors' actions
	Economic climate
Growth in technology	Hardware or software acquisitions
	Need to improve hardware or software efficiency
Growth in education or experience	Discovery of CBIS potentials by users
	Recognition of CBIS opportunities by CBIS specialists

TABLE 10.2
Representative Project Selection Criteria

Criteria	Issues Addressed
Economic benefit	Resolving a critical problem or opportunity Realizing a direct or indirect dollar outcome
Master plan compatibility	Fitting in with sequencing demands of the existing master plan
Project risk	Categorizing a project as difficult or innovative
	Recognizing that personnel are inexperienced, that major problems exist in the area to be automated, or that the area to be automated is not understood very well
	Recognizing that significant changes will be required in the manner in which organizational activities are to be performed
	Recognizing that the personnel in the area to be automated are likely to resist the changes to occur
Required resources	Assessing the adequacy of hardware, software, and personnel
Politics	Recognizing that the project has the support of the organization's "power elite" or that the project will serve an organizationwide education role

might represent new applications. Table 10.1 indicates the diverse forces that trigger CBIS project proposals. Because of this diversity, as well as the importance of organizational contextual or situational considerations, it is inappropriate to apply one set of selection criteria in all cases. Table 10.2 lists some representative selection criteria.

FEASIBILITY STUDY

Once a CBIS project proposal has gone through (or bypassed) the project selection mechanism, the desirability of beginning implementation is assessed in a feasibility study. Because of the "invisibility" of most CBIS projects at their inception, there is considerable uncertainty about costs and benefits. The purpose of the feasibility study is to resolve much of this uncertainty so an appropriate decision can be made about committing organizational resources to the implementation effort. Possible decision outcomes include implementing the full CBIS, implementing a portion of the CBIS now and postponing the remainder, postponing the entire project, deleting the project from current and future consideration, and asking for more analysis (i.e., no decision). The last outcome should be chosen with caution. Feasibility studies are expensive, primarily because of the salaries of participants and the costs of interrupting key organizational members. More analysis should be undertaken only if substantial gains are to be had (e.g., a critical factor emerges after the initial feasibility analyses are performed). The objective in a feasibility study is not to eliminate uncertainty, but to reduce it to a point where it can be realistically grappled with by the organizational members responsible for the implementation decision.

A difficult consideration in any feasibility study is determining depth of analysis. Clearly, this situational concern reflects such factors as the investment required, the organization's dependence on the implemented CBIS product, and the urgency of the implementation effort. Later implementation activities (particularly requirements analysis and system design) require very detailed study. Consequently, the feasibility study should not be viewed as a one-time activity. Feasibility must be addressed periodically throughout the implementation effort, with the decision to stop a project at any time depending on the project's relative advantage *at that time.*

Another argument for iterative studies are decreasing marginal returns in uncertainty reduction. The rate of uncertainty reduction typically decreases during an analysis session. By performing a series of analyses (each following other implementation activities that facilitate organizational learning), one can reduce uncertainty much more at comparable costs (Figure 10.4).

The underlying motive of a feasibility study is to ensure that investments in information resources are treated similarly to other organizational investments. This has not always occurred, probably because of the unfamiliarity of nontechnical organizational members with information resources. There are two general guidelines in doing feasibility studies:

- CBIS investments should be made only when the expected return on investment compares favorably with alternative uses of the investment funds, and
- Only incremental (i.e., out-of-pocket) costs and benefits should be considered.

One exception to the adoption of such an investment perspective is the implementation of individual DSS.[7] Two characteristics of DSS applications—an inability to predict all uses and their evolvability—make it difficult to state costs and benefits. A number of alternative approaches to justifying DSS are possible:

- One can compare DSS alternatives to existing practices,
- One can treat the DSS investment like management training and development investments, and
- One can build a low-cost, low-risk prototype.

As the last approach permits *visualization* of DSS benefits and costs and can be applied iteratively in evolving the DSS, it is strongly advocated.

Prior to a description of some major considerations in a feasibility

FIGURE 10.4
Uncertainty Reduction and Costs in
One-time Studies and Iterative Studies

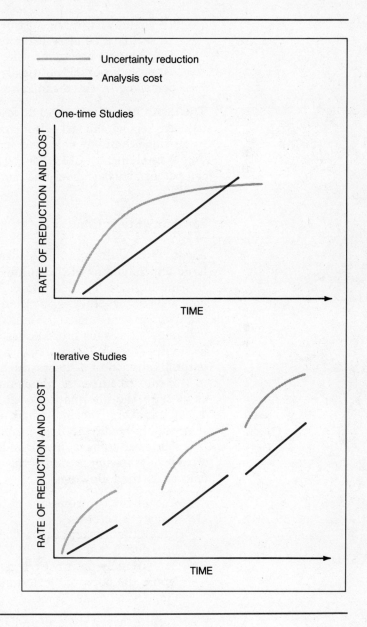

study, two related issues must be addressed. First, many CBIS products are *mandated* (i.e., they must be implemented because of corporate policies, management edicts, industry pressures, or regulatory or legislative requirements). Even so, a feasibility study should be performed for several reasons:

- To ensure that a low-cost design is employed,
- To realize secondary benefits of the product,
- To provide a basis for future evaluation, and
- To protect oneself politically (a mandated product may later be perceived by the organization as a mistake).

The depth of analysis in such cases, however, would be expected to be reduced. Second, the real reason many feasibility studies are undertaken is to provide seemingly objective support for a politically influenced decision to implement a CBIS. For the same reasons given above, a thorough, competent analysis should be performed.

Feasibility Study Context

A variety of skills and knowledge is required for a feasibility study. A basic understanding of the following is typically desired: CBIS capabilities and limitations, the existing CBIS portfolio, the organizational purpose and strategy, the organizational function, organizational and human behavior, and the financial condition of the organization. As few individuals understand such broad issues, teams are typically formed to perform feasibility studies. The more perspectives there are on a team, the greater is the likelihood of a successful study.

Figure 10.5 lists the actors normally involved in feasibility studies, along with the information each primarily provides. The "responsible decision-maker," the individual who makes the implementation decision, should be directly responsible for the investment.

The need to have diverse individuals interact in a feasibility study often results in *suppression* of the uncertainty in a situation. Participants tend to do the following:

- Accept the contributions of others as certain when they are anything but certain,
- Ignore the impact of user "learning" once a CBIS product is introduced,
- Be extremely optimistic regarding their own contributions,
- Ignore the potential for errors by others, and
- Emphasize "easy" issues.

What results invariably is an underestimation of costs and an overestimation of benefits.

For these reasons an environment must be created that promotes criticism and cross-education among participants. If participants understand each other's perspectives, capabilities, limitations, and biases, the likelihood that all uncertainties will be recognized and accounted for is greatly increased.

FIGURE 10.5
Feasibility Study Actors

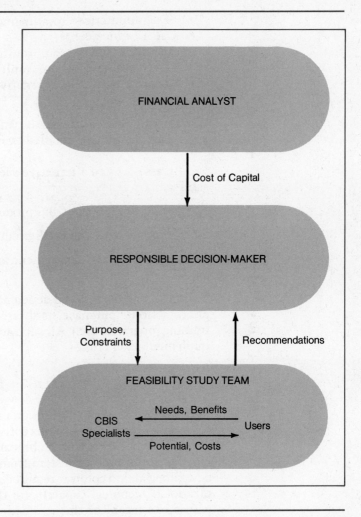

Feasibility Considerations

The major concern in a feasibility study is to identify all likely CBIS solutions, evaluate the feasibility of each, and present these findings to the responsible decision-maker. A common failing of many studies is that too few alternatives are considered. Depending on the situation, a wide range of alternatives should be readily identifiable (with other alternatives arising as the analysis proceeds). The following represents the range of suitable alternatives:

• Retain present system (should always be included),
• Enhance present system (multiple designs possible),

- "Decomputerize" to a manual system,
- Use a service center,
- Acquire a new system (multiple choices possible),
- Develop a new system (multiple choices possible),
- Consider non-CBIS alternatives (workflow or job redesign, reorganization, etc.).

Certain alternatives, of course, can be easily screened from consideration and never go through detailed evaluation.

In assessing an alternative's feasibility, three sets of criteria must be assessed:

Technical   Can the CBIS product be provided?

Operational   Will the CBIS product be used?

Economic   Is the investment an appropriate use of organizational resources?

Technical and operational deficiencies can be overcome by taking appropriate actions (purchase hardware, hire CBIS specialists, develop user training programs, etc.). All such activities, however, add to the cost of an implementation effort.

Technical Feasibility.   There are two major considerations involved in assessing the technical feasibility of a CBIS product. The first concerns the organizational capabilities and availabilities of technical information resources—hardware, systems software, and personnel. It is important to distinguish between true technical problems and technical constraints; most apparent problems stem from unwillingness (which certainly may be appropriate) to commit required resources.[8] The second concerns organizational technical capabilities: the existence of documented rules or procedures regarding the application area and the availability of needed data. The existence of such rules and data is a mark of organizational *maturity*.

Operational Feasibility.   The ability of organizations to develop CBIS products far outweighs their ability to induce people to use them.[9] If organizational members are to exploit the full potential of a product, they must believe that they can do so, that it is to their advantage to do so, and that such behavior is advocated by their superiors. Critical issues to resolve thus revolve around user readiness to use a CBIS, user expectations regarding the relevance and impact of a CBIS, and user perceptions of superiors' attitudes toward a CBIS.

Resistance to CBIS implementation efforts does arise.[10,11] This might take the form of overt actions to block the implementation or to misuse the CBIS product, or it involves covert actions, such as failure to make a commitment to implementation tasks or underutilization of the CBIS product.

Such resistance is most often rational when the CBIS is viewed from the user's perspective. Some CBIS products can be real threats to an individual's security, power, or status. The work context is often changed (organization boundaries may be redrawn, social work groups upset, communication, authority, and influence patterns revised) and the work itself may be affected (increased complexity, unfamiliarity, pressure, or rigidity, less autonomy, fewer interesting or challenging duties).

If dysfunctional consequences seem apparent after the CBIS is viewed from the user's perspective, the question should be raised, Is this form of the CBIS product necessary? If the answer is "yes", appropriate steps must be taken to overcome user resistance. Such actions will be suggested in the next section of this chapter. If the answer is "no", the feasibility study team in conjunction with user representatives should compose a more compatible form of the CBIS product and then assess its feasibility.

Economic Feasibility. The purpose of appraising the economic viability of a CBIS project is to enumerate *all* costs and benefits over the life of a CBIS product and to determine whether or not the investment is worthwhile, given alternative uses of scarce organizational resources. This analysis may be extremely difficult, particularly when an unstructured, complex, or broad application is involved. As a result, decisions about a project's feasibility are often made in the absence of an economic analysis, and poor analyses are invariably regarded as good.

Cost–Benefit Analysis

Because of the importance of performing a meaningful cost–benefit analysis, key considerations regarding CBIS costs and benefits are presented. Methods to apply in such analyses are suggested in the Appendix.

Typical costs and benefits associated with CBIS implementations are summarized in Tables 10.3 and 10.4, respectively. The costs fall into two categories:

One-time   The expense occurs only once, usually with efforts to procure, develop, and introduce the CBIS.

Recurring   Expenses accrue regularly as the CBIS is used and maintained.

TABLE 10.3
CBIS Costs

Category	Examples
One-time	Salaries and other direct expenses associated with an implementation up to and including conversion activities Site preparation Freight Organizational disruption
Recurring	Processing costs (supplies, data entry, data storage, CPU charges, etc.) Dedicated hardware and system software expenses (rental, maintenance, insurance, taxes, etc.) Application software maintenance expenses

TABLE 10.4
CBIS Benefits

Category	Examples
Cost-reducing and cost-avoiding	Reduction in CBIS hardware, software, and personnel needs Improvement in operational capacity and efficiency Better utilization of organizational facilities, cash, equipment, personnel, materials, etc.
Value-enhancing	Improvement in product or service effectiveness New products or services Better management decision making through improved information or organizational learning (improved planning and control, improved coordination, more flexibility, quicker reaction to opportunities and problems, product or service mix improvements, etc.)

Benefits can be placed in three categories:

Cost-reducing Upon introduction of a CBIS, an immediate and continuing cost-related benefit is realized.

Cost-avoiding The presence of the CBIS negates future organizational resource commitments.

Value-enhancing The CBIS provides an organizational capability that otherwise would not be realized.

As mentioned earlier, all costs and benefits associated with a CBIS implementation effort must be identified. This usually is easier with costs than benefits, as the secondary benefits of a CBIS may be at least as important as its primary benefits. Consider, for example, CBIS implementation directed at improving inventory control. Possible primary benefits might include reduction in information resources, reduced investment in inventory (capital, cost of capital, taxes, and insurance), less spoilage, obsolesence, and theft, and lower purchasing and transportation costs. However, by incurring fewer stock-outs, one should improve customer satisfaction (finished goods inventory) and encounter fewer manufacturing bottlenecks (raw material, procured components, and work-in-process inventories). Identifying all secondary benefits is difficult, but the potential organizational gains in increased sales and manufacturing productivity improvements may far outweigh the direct inventory benefits.

Another issue associated with enumerating CBIS costs and benefits is *tangibility*. A cost or benefit is tangible if it can easily be assigned a dollar value. Monthly payments to a vendor and the elimination of a clerical position are very tangible. Other costs (organizational disruption) and benefits (improved information) are quite intangible. What makes tangibility a complex issue in CBIS cost–benefit analysis is that costs are usually tangible, while benefits, particularly those with the greatest potential organizational impact, are often intangible.

When tangible costs and intangible benefits arise, a common reaction is to refrain from pursuing a strict analysis of economic feasibility. Often such ad hoc decisions turn out poorly—a CBIS is implemented whose costs outweigh the benefits (tangible plus intangible). Additionally, future CBIS product evaluations focus on the tangible (mostly cost-related) outcomes, suggesting little was gained from the earlier investment.

Such ad hoc decision making should never take place, for CBIS products always have meaningful organizational impacts and any perceived effect can be estimated. The expectation of organizational benefits, though perhaps ill-defined, does exist. If the impact is truly unmeasurable, the application is so poorly understood that it should not be undertaken at this time.

Such a perspective does not imply that arriving at tangible expressions of value is easy. The task is often very difficult, and the resulting measures are characterized by substantial uncertainty. However, this uncertainty can be dealt with by using statistical methods or by discounting highly uncertain estimates.

A number of techniques have been suggested for determining the value of intangible benefits. (Similar techniques could obviously be used with intangible costs.) The most simple, and least reliable, is to ask the sponsors of the CBIS product how much they would be willing to pay for the product—i.e., to establish a *market price*. An approach requiring more effort is to have sponsors provide *bounded estimates* (most optimistic, most likely, most pessimistic) of the product's value and then use each estimate to perform an analysis.

A technique requiring even more sponsor effort involves determining the value of the *least expensive* tangible alternative to the CBIS product. Two ways of obtaining the same "service quality" improvement from an inventory control system are to increase the level of items stored in the inventory and to build another warehouse. Each could readily be stated in terms of expected costs, and the lower could represent the value of the inventory control system. (Such an approach is valid only if one alternative actually would be undertaken if the CBIS product were not implemented.)

The final technique for estimating benefits is best, even though it requires the most intense sponsor analysis of CBIS impacts. By stating benefits in their intangible form and then tracing them through to their *tangible consequences,* analysts can best uncover all CBIS organizational impacts. Figure 10.6 shows in a simplified manner how such a procedure might work.

An interesting alternative to deriving the value of intangibles is the approach taken by one major corporation, which it terms the *"prudent manager" axiom.*[13] This corporation believes its managers regularly make decisions under conditions at least as uncertain as those associated with the CBIS feasibility decision. Consequently, if a manager is told the expected cost of a CBIS product and still desires it, the CBIS is provided. The manager's budget, however, is charged for the cost of the CBIS plus the prevailing cost of capital.

This last example makes clear an important fact of each valuation technique: the estimates that result are only as good as the effort put forth by the individuals providing them. To produce valid estimates, individuals must thoroughly understand the projected impacts and costs of a CBIS product and must directly feel the consequences of poor estimates. A suitable organizational climate cannot be established overnight. However, it can be established over a number of years by gradually increasing both the penalties associated with poor estimates and the rewards associated with good estimates.

THE IMPLEMENTATION PLAN

There are three key factors in the eventual success of any CBIS implementation.[14] First, the organization's climate (resources, reward systems, access to information sources, extent of individual discretion allowed, etc.) must support the implementation effort. Such influences, however, do not ensure success—they simply permit it. Second, implementation participants must become committed to their tasks, and a favorable predisposition toward the CBIS must be instilled in its intended users. Third, implementation planning must be comprehensive, timely, and complete.

FIGURE 10.6
Tracing Intangible Benefits to Tangible Consequences

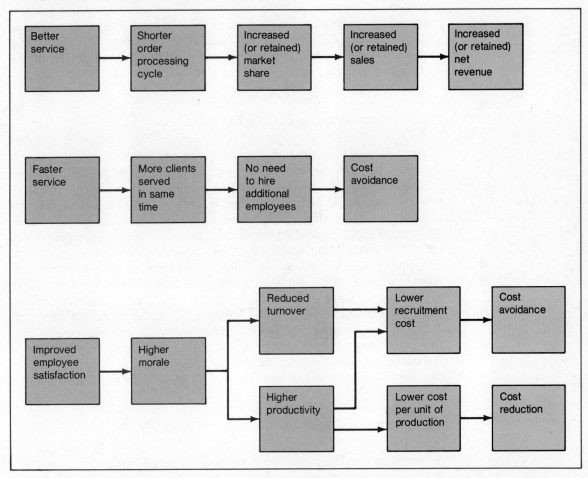

Much uncertainty associated with an implementation effort and many potential deficiences of the first two factors can be dissolved by designing an implementation plan that matches the implementation context.

A CBIS implementation is a highly situation-dependent activity that must be managed so key issues and likely impediments are recognized and addressed *early*.[15-17] Minimally, this entails establishing implementation objectives, diagnosing the implementation context, devising an implementation plan, and monitoring the plan as implementation proceeds.

Implementation Objectives

Implementation objectives for the most part represent constraints imposed on the implementation effort that divert effort from the primary objective, providing the best possible CBIS product. Objectives might include (but are not limited to) minimizing implementation cost, implementation time, organizational disruption, and risk of failure, and maximizing implementer credibility.

Diagnosing the Implementation Context

Three potential sources of implementation impediments should be investigated, organizational barriers, implementation risk factors, and personnel assessments.[18-22] Organizational barriers are organizational deficiences that should be overcome (or at least lessened) prior to initiating an implementation. If these deficiences (some of which are listed in Table 10.5) prove significant, the potential for failure looms large, regardless of individual efforts. Implementation risk factors are deficiencies (the more common of which are listed in Table 10.6) specific to various implementation contexts. While some factors may be unresolvable over the life of the project, others may be fully or partially resolved as implementation proceeds. Personnel assessments are analyses of the traits, abilities, and stakes in the project of both participants and users. Some questions that should be answered are shown in Table 10.7. While the composition of the user group must usually be treated as a constraint, there is normally considerable discretion in the selection of implementation participants.

Ingredients of the Plan

An implementation plan should consist of the following:

Project description	Statements on the purpose, objectives, and functioning of and evaluation criteria for the CBIS,
Project tasks	Time-phased ordering of all implementation activities that indicates the schedule and budget for each activity, as well as associated milestones,
Participant assignments	Assignments of organizational members to implementation activities with their roles clearly indicated.

TABLE 10.5
Organizational Barriers

Barrier	Examples
Culture	Norms, beliefs, or values antagonistic to CBIS usage
Social relations	Internal conflict, little acceptance of outsiders
Top management support	"Power elite" that is not pro-CBIS
Receptivity to change	Aversion to risk or satisfaction with status quo
History	Little organizational experience with CBIS-related change

TABLE 10.6
Implementation Risk Factors

Factor	Explanation
Technology	Lack of needed hardware, software, or skills by CBIS staff or application area specialists
Motivation	Lack of felt need by users for CBIS
Resources	Insufficient personnel, finance, facilities, time, etc.
Application area	Organizational immaturity Uncertainty regarding needs or CBIS impacts Severe organizational problems unrelated to CBIS
Participants	Lack of experience Lack of consensus regarding CBIS need, purpose, use, etc.

TABLE 10.7
Personnel Assessment Questions

Target Group	Major Questions
Users	Who are they? What stakes do they have in the CBIS project? How will they be affected by the CBIS product? How do they perceive the CBIS product? How will they behave?
Participants	Who are they? What stakes do they have in the implementation effort? What do they perceive their role to be? Do they understand and trust each other? How will they behave?

Additionally, strategies for resolving identified barriers, risk factors, or personnel deficiences must be decided on and incorporated into the implementation plan. Strategies that have proved successful in actual CBIS implementation efforts include the following:

- Make a prototype of the CBIS product.
- Slowly evolve the CBIS product.
- Break the CBIS product into modules.
- Emphasize simplicity in user interactions with the CBIS product.
- Provide appropriate education, training, and assistance.
- "Sell" the CBIS product.
- Build up the implementer's credibility.
- Informally refine the CBIS product through ad hoc review groups prior to initiating a full-scale, formal implementation effort.
- Anticipate resistance and prepare countermoves.
- Appeal to a higher authority.
- Isolate the CBIS implementation effort and then introduce the product throughout the organization through coopted users.[23-26]

Monitoring the Plan

Finally, mechanisms should be developed that provide for evaluations of conformity to the plan (Is it on schedule? If not, why not?) and the quality of the plan (Should the plan be revised because of environmental events, organizational learning, or any outcomes of enacted strategies?). Strategic control points must consequently be identified and regularly assessed.

Developing the Plan

While an implementation plan is finalized and set into operation only after a project's feasibility has been established, most of the analysis associated with developing the plan should occur during the feasibility study. As implementation activities account for a significant portion of the cost of most CBIS, the implementation plan (and its expected cost) must be determined in the feasibility study. Otherwise, a realistic representation of the project's costs will not likely be produced.

CONCLUSION

An organizational model particularly relevant to CBIS implementation is that suggested by Leavitt, who asserts that organizations consist of a homeostatic web of relations among technologies, tasks, people, and structures, and a change in any one tends to be resisted and to cause associated changes in the others.[27] As most CBIS implementations affect all four elements, it may be useful to view CBIS implementations as a particular type of organizational change effort.

If one adopts such an "organizational change" perspective, one should undertake the following tasks to effect CBIS-related change:

- Fostering a felt organizational need for the CBIS product,
- Establishing an organizational consensus about the goals, purpose, and functioning of the CBIS,
- Putting into operation CBIS goals and purpose so the CBIS product becomes visible to organizational members,
- Instilling commitments to the implementation effort and the CBIS product in organizational members,
- Helping organizational members understand each other's interests, capabilities, and biases.[28,29]

The CBIS planning topics covered in this chapter, if effectively handled, are a necessary first step to the realization of such outcomes.

Finally, a number of guidelines have been suggested for achieving planning success.[30] These general rules apply to the four planning issues covered in the chapter. Sufficient resources (time, personnel, facilities) must be allocated for planning activities and for management review and follow-up. Management throughout an organization must support and become involved in planning efforts. As a consequence, all plans must be expressed in generally understood terms and membership on planning groups should be rotated. Planning procedures and directives must be formally defined and followed. If planning occurs in an ad hoc fashion, performance quality can vary widely and planning tasks may well be viewed as unimportant. Above all, specified plans must be carried out. If this fails to occur, organizational members will probably not be committed to their assigned planning tasks.

KEY ISSUES

A CBIS master plan is an evolving design for all current and future CBIS applications, along with the major hardware, software, and personnel actions required to implement these applications.

There are four components in a CBIS master plan: a charter defining the scope of the information function; a strategy statement that discloses the specific roles being played by information resources in accomplishing organizational objectives, as well as the organizational constraints that limit the application of information resources; a project inventory that describes existing applications, those under development, and those planned for the future; and visual portrayals of the sequential nature of the master plan.

All organizations should develop an internal capability to monitor the external environment in order to recognize the emergence of new information technologies that can be used to enhance organizational performance.

It is not always desirable for CBIS planning to exert a main role in the development of an organization's strategic plans. Often the proper role of CBIS planners is that of serving as a passive source of knowledge. Determining the extent to which CBIS planning should drive an organization's strategies is an important policy decision.

Formal project selection mechanisms should be established and followed. The purpose of these mechanisms should be to screen out clearly inappropriate applications, to set priorities for appropriate applications, and to ensure that a balanced CBIS portfolio is obtained.

Not all CBIS project proposals need go through formal project selection. Determining the criteria for allowing a project to bypass this formal procedure is an important policy decision.

It is the responsibility of all organizational members to initiate CBIS project proposals.

The objective of the feasibility study is to remove much of the uncertainty that surrounds a CBIS implementation effort so an appropriate decision can be made regarding the desirability of committing organizational resources to the implementation effort. The objective is not to eliminate all uncertainty.

Feasibility studies should not be viewed as one-time events. Rather, feasibility assessments should occur at regular intervals throughout the implementation effort.

Because of the varied knowledge needed to assess the feasibility of most CBIS applications, teams are usually established to perform feasibility studies. To uncover all the uncertainty associated with a project, team interaction should take place within an environment that promotes criticism and cross-education.

Three types of feasibility must be examined: technical, operational, and economic.

All feasibility decisions should ultimately be based on an objective consideration of the project's costs and benefits. If the benefits of an application are truly intangible, the project is probably ill defined and should not be undertaken. Assessments of the feasibility of a DSS application are the major exception to this general rule.

Four key factors affect the eventual success of most CBIS implementation efforts: a supportive organizational climate should exist, implementation participants should be committed to their assigned tasks, the intended CBIS users should be favorably predisposed toward the CBIS product being implemented, and comprehensive, timely, and complete implementation planning should occur.

In diagnosing an implementation context, one should examine the following sources of implementation barriers: organizational climate deficiencies, project risk factors, and the personal characteristics of key participants and users.

Implementation of CBIS must be viewed as an organizational change effort.

DISCUSSION QUESTIONS

1. What notions inherent in the modern software practices discussed in Chapter 9 suggest the importance of planning to CBIS success?
2. What was the original concept of a "total information system"? How does the current view of this concept differ from the early view?
3. One CBIS master plan objective is to ensure that a solid CBIS foundation is built. What does this mean? Explain your answer in the context of a chain of large retail department stores.
4. Discuss how the role of the information resource might likely differ for organizations in the following organizations: a bank, furniture manufacturer, industrial wholesaler, and state agriculture department.
5. What issues are stressed with the BSP planning methodology? What issues are stressed with the BIAIT planning methodology?
6. Describe some situations in which a proposed CBIS project should not have to go through a formal project selection procedure. Propose some guidelines for establishing policies about which applications can bypass this formal mechanism.
7. What should be done when a project is proposed that is not within the CBIS master plan?
8. Provide an example of when it might be appropriate to ask for additional analysis at the conclusion of a feasibility study.
9. Why do you think many organizations have treated decisions to invest in the information resource differently from other investment decisions?
10. How can "user learning" after a CBIS product has been introduced affect a feasibility study?
11. Using the implementation context of office automation, suggest situations in which organizational members might rationally resist the introduction of the new technology.

12. Using the implementation context of a comprehensive personnel information system, illustrate each of the following benefit categories: cost-reducing, cost-avoiding, and value-enhancing. Do the same for an information system intended to help advertising managers assess the effectiveness of their advertising programs.

13. Using the implementation context of an on-line order entry system being introduced within a mail-order firm, provide an example of an intangible cost and trace this cost to its tangible outcomes.

14. Why is it important that implementation participants become committed to their assigned tasks? Can't one rely on the existing organizational control systems to ensure that these tasks are performed effectively?

15. List crucial questions to investigate in assessing the risk associated with a CBIS implementation effort. Each question should have a "yes" or "no" answer.

16. A number of strategies were suggested for overcoming potential implementation problems. Select any three and describe a situation in which each might be effectively applied.

BRIEF CASES

1. *Big Apple Promotions*

   Bill Butler, president of this growing New York advertising firm, was not very satisfied with how the company was making use of computers. The push eight years ago to automate the firm seemed to stall after the basic accounting and billing systems were installed. While the manager of the firm's information systems group was technically proficient, she was still not comfortable with the advertising world after being with the firm for three years. Also, the firm's employees were not overly enthusiastic about computers. It wasn't that they resisted automation, but rather that they had difficulty suggesting ways computer technology could be exploited. This was not too surprising, considering their backgrounds.

   What started Bill thinking about the firm's lack of progress was the meeting he had attended yesterday afternoon. One of the major hardware vendors had offered a seminar on computer applications in the advertising industry. While the meeting was clearly a sales pitch, many of the speakers' comments deserved consideration. The topic that had impressed Bill the most was the role of the chief executive in developing a successful information systems program. Bill had never seen himself as having any such role. The speaker had emphasized that a firm's chief executive had to vocally support the information system program and clearly identify the organizational roles information systems were to play in the firm. If this was not done, there would be little direction or incentive for others to become actively involved with information system activities.

   Consequently, Bill decided to prepare a memorandum setting forth his views of how information systems should be applied within Big Apple Promotions, stressing his strong endorsement of efforts to develop information systems, and encouraging others to respond with their own ideas. Bill was going to end his memorandum with the statement that this was the first step toward developing an information system strategic plan for the firm.

What types of roles can information systems play in an advertising firm? Can information systems be a strategic tool?

2. *Southside Auto Parts*

Southside's current information systems portfolio consisted of a batch-oriented accounting package and the sophisticated inventory planning and control system that Southside had developed with a software vendor. Sam Hellick recognized that the firm could not afford to haphazardly introduce applications whenever chance provided an opportunity to do so. With Southside's multiple retail locations and plans for expansion out of its current market region, the dangers associated with duplication and incompatibility were significant.

In discussing these concerns with the president of the software vendor with whom he had developed the inventory system, Sam came up with the idea of developing a master plan. It was finally agreed that one of the software vendor's senior analysts would be assigned to help Sam develop the master plan. The only "charge" was the understanding that the software vendor's products would be seriously considered if Sam decided to implement a particular information system.

Propose a CBIS master plan for an auto parts retailer such as Southside. Your plan should include the following elements: a sequential ordering of applications to be developed, a view of the firm's data resources (file inventory) over time, and an indication of the hardware acquisitions that would likely be required to implement this plan. The firm's current information systems portfolio is as described above. Its current hardware consists of a state-of-the-art minicomputer, one terminal at each retail location, and required communications equipment.

3. *The State Motor Pool*

The latest information systems project to emerge involved the implementation of a statewide purchasing system to coordinate the purchase of repair parts, supplies, and tools needed to maintain the thousands of vehicles owned by the state. The proposal for the maintenance purchasing system had to be approved by the state's Informations Systems Policy Committee. Given the budgetary problems faced by the state, it was evident that the "economics had to be there" if the proposal was to be approved. As a result, it was extremely important that all the benefits expected from the information system be explicitly identified and tied to dollar amounts.

List the likely benefits to arise from a purchasing information system as has been described. Then clearly describe how you would arrive at dollar values for each benefit. Be sure to include both primary and secondary benefits.

4. *Greco Components*

Randy Fitzin was pleased with the progress that had been made with the sales control system. His initial rough design had struck a positive chord in Rose Leary, the sales manager, and their joint proposal had been accepted by the firm's top management. Now the real work was to begin.

It was clear to Randy that the sales staff was going to play a key role in the success of the system. The contributions to the final design were going to be important, particularly with regard to the reports the salespersons themselves were to receive. Even more important, much of the required input data would have to come from the sales staff. While Rose was now enthusiastically behind the project, she warned Randy that her sales force might not be so receptive. Remembering that it had taken almost a year to convince Rose to accept the idea of computer-based support, Randy took this warning to heart.

Randy's next step was to develop an implementation plan. Not only did he have to lay out the tasks to be accomplished, but he had to select who was going to work on the project, assign each of these individuals their tasks, identify likely problem areas, and then devise strategies to overcome each identified problem. It was going to be a long week!

What activities would require the participation of Rose Leary? What activities would require the participation of representatives from the sales force? Would these individuals be willing to work on the project? Do you see any difficulties in getting cooperation from the sales force with regard to data capture? How about their use of the reports being sent back to them? Do you have any ideas how identified implementation barriers might be overcome?

NOTES

1. E. McLean and J. V. Soden, *Strategic Planning for MIS* (New York: Wiley, 1977).

2. R. V. Head, *Strategic Planning for Information Systems* (Wellesley, Mass.: QED Information Sciences, 1979).

3. W. R. King, "Strategic Planning for Management Information Systems," *MIS Quarterly* 3(1978):27–37.

4. Head (1979).

5. B. Bowman, G. Davis, and J. Wetherbe, "Modeling for MIS," *Datamation* 27(1981):155–62.

6. W. R. King and R. W. Zmud, "Managing Information Systems: Policy Planning, Strategic Planning and Operational Planning," *Proceedings of the Second International Conference on Information Systems* (Boston: Second International Conference on Information Systems, 1981), pp. 229–308.

7. P. G. W. Keen, "Value Analysis: Justifying Decision Support Systems," *MIS Quarterly* 5(1981):1–15.

8. S. A. Alter, *Decision Support Systems: Current Practice and Continuing Challenge* (Reading, Mass.: Addison-Wesley, 1980).

9. M. J. Ginzberg, "A Prescriptive Model for System Implementation," *Systems, Objectives, Solutions* 1(1981):33–46.

10. G. W. Dickson and J. K. Simmons, "The Behavioral Side of MIS," *Business Horizons* 13(1970):59–71.

11. M. L. Markus, "Power, Politics and MIS Implementation," working paper, Sloan School of Management, MIT, 1980.

12. P. G. W. Keen, "Information Systems and Organizational Change," *Communications of the ACM* 24(1981):24–33.

13. G. Matlin, "What Is the Value of Investment in Information Systems?" *MIS Quarterly* 3(1979):5–34.

14. R. W. Zmud, "System Implementation Success—Behavioral/Organizational Influences and Strategies for Effecting Change," paper prepared for the Nonfuels Minerals Demand Workshop, National Research Council, Arlie, Va., 1981.

15. S. Alter and M. Ginzberg, "Managing Uncertainty in MIS Implementation," *Sloan Management Review* 20(1978):23–31.

16. J. Anderson and R. Narasimham, "Assessing Project Implementation Risk: A Methodological Approach," *Management Science* 25(1979):512–21.

17. J. S. Hammond III, "A Practitioner-Oriented Framework for Implementation," *TIMS Studies in the Management Sciences* 13(1979):35–61.

18. G. Zaltman and R. Duncan, *Strategies for Planned Change* (New York: Wiley, 1977).

19. Alter and Ginzberg (1978).

20. Anderson and Narasimham (1979).

21. Hammond (1979).

22. M. Radnor, "The Context of OR/MS Implementation," *TIMS Studies in the Management Sciences* 13(1979):17–34.

23. Alter and Ginzberg (1978).

24. J. R. Galbraith, "A Change Process for the Introduction of Management Information Systems: A Successful Case," *TIMS Studies in the Management Sciences* 13(1979):219–33.

25. J. H. Manley, "Implementing Change in Very Large Organizations," *TIMS Studies in the Management Sciences* 13(1979):189–203.

26. Keen (1981).

27. H. J. Leavitt, "Applied Organizational Change in Industry: Structural, Technological and Humanistic Approaches," in J. G. March (ed.), *Handbook of Organizations* (Chicago: Rand McNally, 1965), pp. 1144–70.

28. M. J. Ginzberg, "A Study of the Implementation Process," *TIMS Studies in the Management Sciences* 13(1979):85–102.

29. Keen (1981).

30. Head (1979).

Requirements Analysis 11

IT SHOULD BE increasingly evident that the key to CBIS success lies in planning and design. Accordingly, establishing a valid set of requirements to guide product design is the most critical activity undertaken in CBIS implementation.[1] If the requirements statement is inconsistent, ambiguous, incomplete, or otherwise incorrect, the following outcomes are likely:

- Costly design errors are made,
- Testing becomes difficult,
- Modern software practices cannot be used,
- It becomes difficult to manage the CBIS development process,
- User–CBIS staff communication problems abound,
- Users have little real influence,
- Maintenance costs increase,
- User dissatisfaction rises.

Table 11.1 suggests the impact such outcomes have on the overall cost of a CBIS project.[2] If errors are recognized early, the project cost increases negligibly, but if product changes must be introduced later in the product's life cycle (when the code has been written, testing has been completed, or the system has become operational), costs can increase substantially.

Requirements, however, are often very difficult to derive and, as pressure to produce a CBIS product increases, tempting to delay or avoid doing thoroughly. This difficulty may arise for many reasons. The organizational functions may be complex or ambiguous. The CBIS specialists may not fully grasp what is involved in the functions. The users may not realize what they need (e.g., they may not know what is possible through CBIS support, or they may not have formally analyzed their tasks). Even

TABLE 11.1
Relative Impacts of Requirements Changes

Stage When Change Is Initiated	Relative Cost of Implementing Change
Requirements analysis	1
Coding	1
Program (module) testing	2
System testing	10
Acceptance testing	15
Field deployment	450

when a valid set of requirements has been stated, an organization's natural evolution may eventually make the specification outdated.

This last point requires some elaboration. Requirements should be stated in terms of the forecast life of the CBIS product. Requirements must initially be specified in terms of the organizational realities expected to exist when the CBIS is introduced into the organization (not the realities that existed when the project began), and the basic design should allow for all changes expected to arise throughout the product's useful life. If these changes are not allowed for in the product's initial control structure, future changes are likely to be very expensive (and perhaps impossible).

In this chapter a number of issues regarding requirements analysis will be discussed. First the form of a requirements specification and a suggested process to follow in deriving a requirements specification will be presented. Next, the information sources and techniques commonly used in performing a requirements analysis will be examined. Finally, a selection of requirements analysis approaches will be introduced and illustrated.

THE FORM OF A REQUIREMENTS STATEMENT

The objective of an effective requirements specification is to provide a comprehensive, formal depiction of a CBIS product from the *user's perspective*. At the least, an overview, detailed description of outputs and of inputs required to produce the outputs, description of the processing environment, and forecasts of future changes in the CBIS product should be included (Table 11.2).

The *overview* should clearly describe why the CBIS product is being introduced and what it is to accomplish. To convey such an understanding of CBIS purpose, narrative or visual descriptions of the organizational

TABLE 11.2
Form of a Requirements Specification

Component	Contents

Overview	Descriptions
	  Reasons CBIS is being implemented
	  Goals of CBIS

Outputs	For each document, report, or inquiry
	  Basic properties
	  Organizational influences
	  Samples

Inputs	For each processed data item
	  Basic properties
	  Relationship to outputs
	  Samples

Processing environment	Particular needs
	  Hardware and software components
	  Mode of operation
	  Security

Future changes	Forecasts
	  Modifications
	  Enhancements
	  Extensions

functions involved, the way the CBIS product will perform or support these functions, and current organizational problems and opportunities are prepared. The overview should conclude with a formal statement of project objectives (i.e., what specifically should be gained from the CBIS implementation), and an informal appraisal of expected organizational impacts, both positive and negative.

Outputs of CBIS are the documents, reports, and inquiry capabilities that directly support organizational functioning. Each output should be identified and described in terms of its basic properties and organizational influence. By *basic properties* is meant such attributes as medium, layout and format, accuracy and currentness levels, contents (along with value types and ranges, measurement scale, codes, etc.), transformation rules or algorithms, and input data required for transformations. *Organizational influences* of each output refer to issues such as who will receive the output, how, when, and how often they will receive it, and how it will be used. These types of concerns are included in a requirements statement because they tie each output to the overview, and they initiate valuable dialogues among implementation participants (often resulting in an improved set of requirements).

Inputs are data items that trigger processing or are directly used in the processing activity. Each input item should be identified by name and by its relationship(s) with CBIS outputs. Also included should be data item attributes such as source (data file or entry), currentness and accuracy, value types and ranges, measurement scale, codes, layout or format, medium, and retention policy.

To further increase the visibility of the CBIS product being described, samples of inputs and outputs should be provided whenever possible. Such samples might include illustrations of formatted screens, report layouts, punched card layouts, tape or disk layouts, source documents, or human–machine dialogues.

The *processing* environment includes the hardware and software environment, the mode of operation, and security concerns. All hardware (input–output devices, storage devices, processors) and software (data base management system, other CBIS applications) directly linked with the CBIS product should be identified. Visual representations (a systems flowchart, for example) provide a very concise and informative means of identifying these hardware and software elements and illustrating the relation of each with the CBIS product. The mode of operation reflects the actual processing context with which organizational functioning is supported:

- Batch, on-line, or real-time processing,
- Resulting response times, throughputs, and turnaround times,
- Input, output, and storage volumes,
- Assigned priority in scheduling or execution.

Security covers access or use restrictions, backup (redundancy), fallback (no redundancy), recovery, privacy, and input–output controls.

Finally, *forecasts* of product modifications, enhancements, or expansions over the life of the CBIS should be indicated. Such changes could affect any facet of the requirements statement; thus, the full anticipated impact of each change on the complete set of requirements must be described.

THE REQUIREMENTS ANALYSIS PROCESS

Poor CBIS products are frequently due to the adoption by requirements analysis participants of overly narrow perspectives. Too often participants take as givens for their analysis the initial situational diagnosis, existing organizational structures, and current organizational procedures. What often results is the provision of an inflexible CBIS product, a product that resolves only the easy (visible) problems, or a product that totally ignores underlying organizational deficiencies.

For example, rising concern about problems such as declining productivity, excess inventories, missed shipments, customer complaints, and material shortages has encouraged many manufacturers to develop CBIS to help manage their materials and their production operations. These CBIS, however, have not experienced overwhelming success, with 40–50 percent of the manufacturing organizations reporting dissatisfaction with them.[3] The basic cause of these failures lies not with faulty CBIS designs, but with basic manufacturing system design flaws (i.e., manufacturing systems that are not consistent with the strategic and organizational requirements of the organization).[4] Effective manufacturing CBIS cannot be implemented when existing manufacturing systems are ineffective.

It might prove beneficial to view the requirements analysis activity as an opportunity to redesign the organization. Initially, little should be taken as fixed, and any strategy for improving organizational functioning should be examined. The *ideal* result of a requirements analysis effort might be a relatively simple organizational redesign requiring little, if any, organizational investment in information resources.

The requirements analysis process to be presented adopts a perspective that can overcome the overly restrictive approach representative of many requirements efforts. (Nonetheless, this process is rarely observed in practice.) The overall sequence of activities is shown in Figure 11.1. Essentially, a conceptual model of the target organizational context is developed and then iteratively refined so multiple interests, constraints, and alternatives are consolidated in an integrated, holistic fashion.

FIGURE 11.1
The Requirements Analysis Process

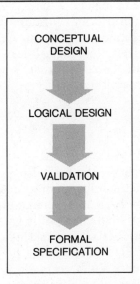

CONCEPTUAL
DESIGN

LOGICAL DESIGN

VALIDATION

FORMAL
SPECIFICATION

Conceptual Design

The objective in conceptual design is to construct a normative model of the organizational context in which the CBIS product is to be introduced and an ideal means of CBIS support. The normative model should reflect the critical factors affecting the organization (environmental forces, organization-wide goals and policies, current and anticipated problems and opportunities, etc.) and the basic resource, product, and service flows that represent organizational functioning. This initial CBIS solution should not be bound by organizational realities, as to do so might impose undue constraints on what could be achieved. Most important, these designs must be documented in a way that is readily grasped by *all* organizational members.

There are three major purposes behind the conceptual design activity. First, it provides for a common view among users, managers, and CBIS specialists that should facilitate communication when their interaction is required. Second, it serves as a base of knowledge for all implementation participants that should permit the cross-education necessary for implementation success. Third, it acts as a frame of reference to guide the gradual evolution of the requirements statement from an abstract notion to a formal set of detailed specifications.

Logical Design

The purpose of logical design is to appraise the conceptual design, given relevant organizational (resources, maturity, attitudes, politics, priorities) and technological (existing CBIS capabilities, data availabilities, personnel) realities. The logical design should provide a CBIS product that can be implemented and that is consistent with the basic structures in the conceptual design.

Validation

Prior to preparing the formal requirements specification (which is then used to drive the implementation effort), it is advantageous to subject the logical design to an analysis that provides some assurance that if the CBIS product were implemented, it would provide the anticipated outcomes. The impossibility of this task is clear—the CBIS product does not yet exist. However, these steps can help determine whether or not a valid set of requirements has been produced.

First, users other than those participating in the requirements analysis effort must examine and critique the requirements. Reviewers should include users involved with all aspects of the CBIS product—data entry, output utilization, evaluation, etc.—and should examine both conceptual and logical design.

Reviewing written specifications, however, can be a tedious, difficult, and time-consuming task, particularly for nontechnical organizational members. A second means of validation involves "hands-on" experience through providing users with report or screen mock-ups.[5] Such a strategy is especially useful when organizational members are expected to have difficulty understanding how CBIS capabilities might enhance their task environments.

As will be shown later in this chapter, there are many ways one can determine CBIS requirements. The approaches emphasize different organizational factors and require different organizational perspectives. If multiple requirements approaches result in essentially the same set of requirements, one might assume a valid set of requirements exists. Even if the requirements differ, a final specification that integrates the key features of each should be more valid than the individual specification. This, then, becomes a third means of validation.

Finally, if a considerable investment must be made in CBIS implementation or if CBIS failure would prove disastrous, it may be advisable to have two teams independently determine the requirements specification. The advantages include those given above for employing multiple approaches, *plus* the benefits of having requirements specifications that probably represent different sets of assumptions and individual perspectives. While using multiple teams is expensive, it may prove worthwhile when the costs of an invalid set of requirements are considered.

Formal Specification

The final task is to prepare a document that clearly and completely communicates the results of the requirements analysis. Organizational standards should define *what* is to be included in a requirements specification and *how* it is to be described. Otherwise, requirements specifications tend to be presented in an ad hoc fashion that causes misunderstanding.

Requirements Analysis Strategies

As with CBIS implementation in general, the sequence in which a requirements analysis takes place may vary considerably, depending on factors associated with the ability of participants to cope with the uncertainty faced. A number of strategies are possible:

- No requirements analysis activity is needed, as a requirements specification already exists (e.g., an existing manual system is to be automated as is).
- Participants sequentially move through conceptual design, logical design, validation, and formal specification.
- Substantial iteration between these stages is observed.
- Prototyping is employed.[6]

The more unstructured the organizational situation, the more naive are participants about their requirements analysis roles, and the more innovative the application, the more desirable are strategies that allow for information discovery and exchange.

INFORMATION SOURCES AND REQUIREMENTS TOOLS

While determining a valid set of requirements is difficult, there is much one can do to facilitate the process. The major focus is on capturing, analyzing, and describing information. Tools for each activity will be covered briefly after a discussion of information sources to tap when one performs a requirements analysis.

Information Sources

The most obvious information sources are those directly associated with the target organization functions:

- Managers of the functions,
- Organizational members whose organizational roles touch on the functions,
- Customers, clients, vendors, and other outsiders associated with the functions,
- Existing procedures (manual and computer-based) employed in performing and supporting the functions,
- Existing forms, data files, reports, and documents associated with the functions,
- Performance appraisals, letters, and memos associated with the functions.

Certain formal organizational documents should be examined as well, as they provide a sense both of history and of future direction regarding the functions: organization charts, job descriptions, product or service flow documents, procedures manuals, and plan and budget statements.

Numerous sources of information outside the organization should also be explored. Trips can be made to organizations performing similar functions, particularly those using information resources in innovative ways. Hardware and software vendors can be invited to demonstrate how their products can be applied. Since many of these vendors are likely to have considerable experience with the functions under consideration, their insights—when viewed as *information* and not necessarily as *solutions*—can be invaluable. Most professional groups (accounting, purchasing, personnel, materials management, marketing, sales, etc.) have national societies that fund studies of ways information technologies can enhance their members' organizational effectiveness. Finally, much information about the application of information technologies can be found in trade magazines, professional journals, books, and computer industry information services (such as the Datapro and Auerbach reports).

In fact, there may be *too much* information available when one considers all the alternatives. It would require a great effort to search through all these sources at one time. Consequently, self-education about information resources should be a continuing activity of all organizational members.

Information Collection Tools

Most of the commonly employed collection tools—observation, interviews, and questionnaires—need little explanation. Becoming adept at employing such methods, however, is another matter. These methods should be used so one complements the other. For example, examining procedures manuals for visible wear and tear may validate statements by organizational members about critical work flows or recurring problems. Many organizations have recognized this fact and initiated training programs to improve their members' abilities, particularly in observation and listening.

Certain other tools are useful in special circumstances. *Monitors* can be placed on equipment (including computer terminals) to measure physical behaviors (rates, statuses, and types). Organizational members can be asked to record what they do, whom they interact with, what information they use, etc. To develop an appreciation of how a seemingly ad hoc task is handled, *protocol analysis* may be employed in which individuals performing the task explain their step-by-step actions. If such explanations are tape recorded for a variety of situations and individuals, they can be analyzed for patterns so an understanding of the task may emerge. Finally, when data become voluminous or the time allowed to meet requirements is short, *statistical sampling* techniques are often necessary. By employing appropriate sampling strategies, one can gather large collections of data at low costs.

Requirements Analysis Tools

Again, most commonly employed analysis techniques—statistical methods, simulation studies, optimization methods—require little explanation, but effective use of such techniques requires considerable skill.

Two methods of particular relevance to requirements analysis are utility analysis and "ABC analysis." *Utility analysis* includes a variety of methods that enable one to measure and use one's own or another's opinions. Such a capability is useful in many CBIS situations, as it is often difficult to quantify someone's appraisal of a problem, solution, design, CBIS product attribute, etc. A very simple example of utility analysis is included in Appendix A (the weighting-scoring model). *ABC analysis* is one of the oldest and simplest analysis tools. A commonly observed phenomenon of organizational activity is that a relatively few events or entities monopolize a large portion of organizational resources. For example,

- Twenty percent of inventory items account for 80 percent of all inventory movements.
- Twenty percent of a product line accounts for 80 percent of sales.
- Twenty percent of clients account for 80 percent of the service load.
- Twenty percent of employees account for 80 percent of absenteeism.

In other words, there is a relatively well defined group (of items, products, clients, employees) that, *if managed well*, can greatly increase organizational effectiveness or efficiency. The underlying philosophy of ABC analysis is that one should focus one's initial attention on identifying and handling this A group.

Information Description Tools

Regardless of the effort devoted to searching for, capturing, and analyzing information, unless results are expressed so the understanding attained is readily communicated to others, the effort is for the most part squandered. Presentation tools, consequently, are crucial to a requirements analysis.

While statistical profiles and narratives can provide meaningful descriptions, they are usually not sufficient when the intent is to demonstrate relationships. Three tools particularly suited for illustrating CBIS-related relationships are decision tables, matrices, and data flow diagrams.

Decision tables are an easily understood way of expressing well-structured decision situations. The general structure of a decision table and an example are shown in Figure 11.2. Rule 1 indicates that a definite decision to buy from a vendor requires that the vendor offer the lowest price *and* have previously demonstrated satisfactory performance in both delivery time and product quality. This example employs only "yes" and "no" conditions, but other relationships (satisfactory or unsatisfactory, favorable or unfavorable, obtained or not obtained, etc.) could be used.

FIGURE 11.2
Decision Tables

GENERAL STRUCTURE		Rules	
	Condition stubs	Condition entries	
	Action stubs	Action entries	

VENDOR SELECTION

	1	2	3	4	5	6	7	8
Lowest price	Y	Y	Y	Y	N	N	N	N
Past delivery time acceptable	Y	N	Y	N	Y	Y	N	N
Past quantity acceptable	Y	Y	N	N	Y	N	Y	N
Buy	X							
Consider buying		X	X		X		X	
Do not buy				X		X		X

One nice attribute of decision tables is that programs known as "decision table processors" can translate a decision table specification into a programming language, such as COBOL.

While *matrices* can be used to indicate relationships in many ways, they differ primarily in the type of relationships identified. Figure 11.3a, for example, illustrates the simplest use—denoting the existence of a single relationship (that a report uses data from a given data file) between two entities. In Figure 11.3b, three relations (who executes the function, who can be consulted, and who must be notified) are used in linking shipping employees to shipping functions. The variety of relations that can be so represented is limited solely by the imagination of the describer.

Data flow diagrams are similar to the systems models introduced in Chapter 3. Their purpose is to depict the flow of data, materials, or clients through an organization so changes in the flow or condition of data, materials, or clients are easily observed. Major additions to the systems model are data file representations. As can be seen in Figure 11.4, these identify where particular sets of data are accessed and manipulated during organizational functioning.

REQUIREMENTS ANALYSIS APPROACHES

A variety of approaches for performing a requirements analysis have appeared over the last two decades. While they often seem similar, close examination reveals that each adopts different perspectives and emphasizes different organizational issues. Approaches included in this chapter were selected on the basis of two major considerations:

- Structured analysis should be emphasized.
- The set of selected approaches should cover most key concerns to be explored when CBIS requirements are determined.

Structured requirement analysis follows the structured design concepts (introduced in Chapter 9) of abstraction, modularity, and stepwise refinement. Briefly, the advantages of such design concepts are as follows:

- Both an overall design (the abstract, top level) and a concrete design (the bottom level) are provided,
- One aspect of a problem at a time is analyzed while a current view of the whole problem is maintained,
- Iteration can be employed in moving horizontally or vertically through an evolving design,
- the completeness and correctness of the evolving design can continually be assessed.

FIGURE 11.3
Matrices

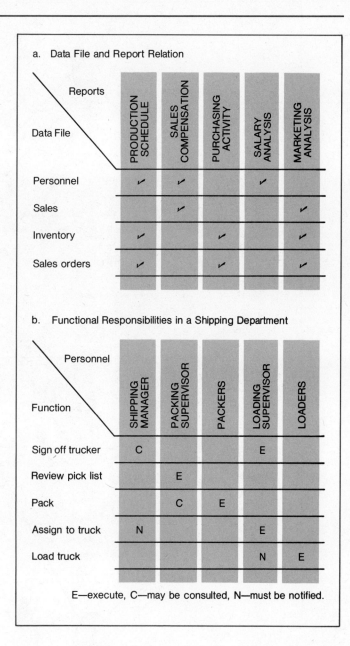

a. Data File and Report Relation

Data File \ Reports	PRODUCTION SCHEDULE	SALES COMPENSATION	PURCHASING ACTIVITY	SALARY ANALYSIS	MARKETING ANALYSIS
Personnel	✔	✔		✔	
Sales		✔			✔
Inventory	✔		✔		✔
Sales orders	✔		✔		✔

b. Functional Responsibilities in a Shipping Department

Function \ Personnel	SHIPPING MANAGER	PACKING SUPERVISOR	PACKERS	LOADING SUPERVISOR	LOADERS
Sign off trucker	C			E	
Review pick list		E			
Pack		C	E		
Assign to truck	N			E	
Load truck				N	E

E—execute, C—may be consulted, N—must be notified.

FIGURE 11.4
Service Flow in a Professional Job Placement Agency

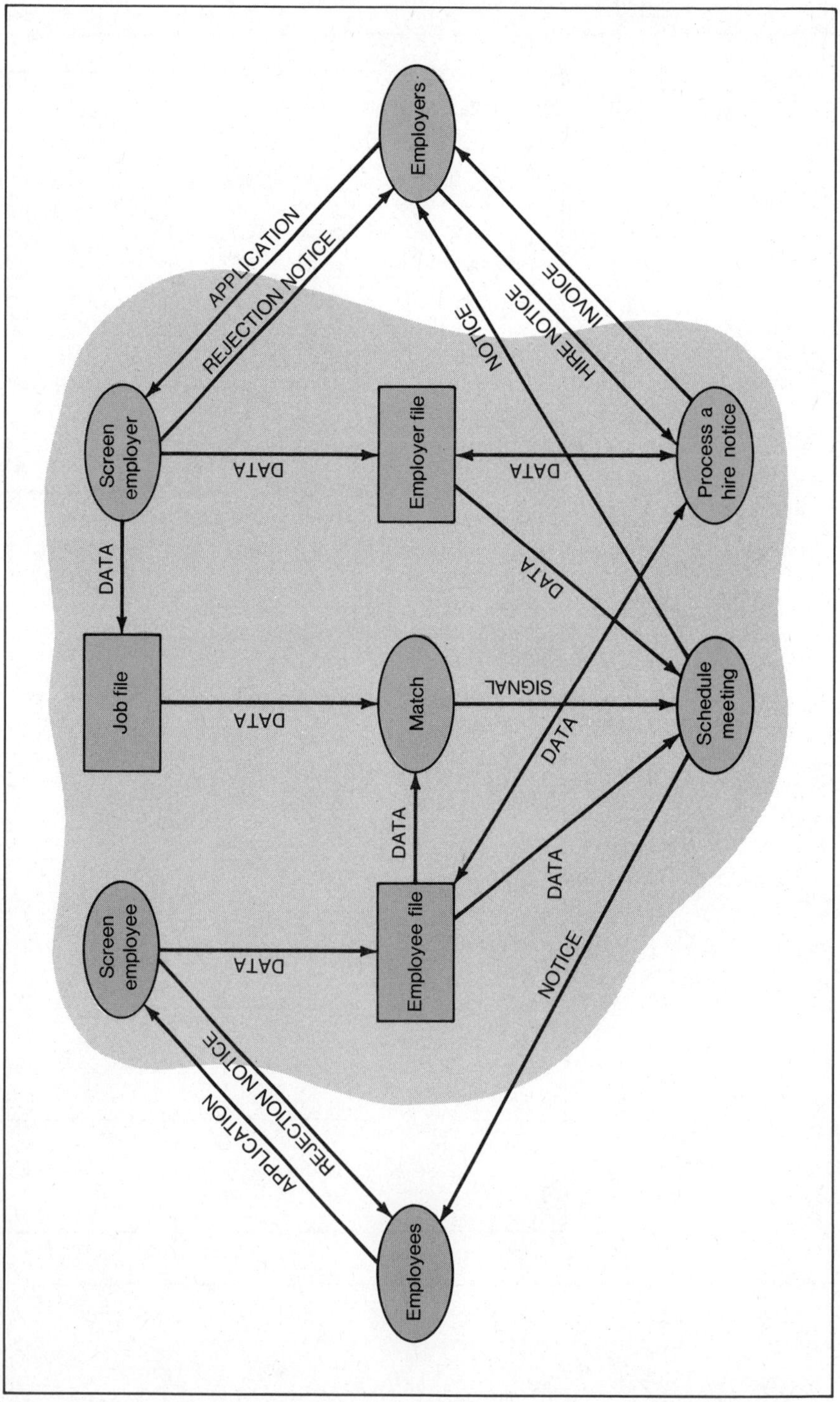

Thus, through the use of structured analysis one obtains both a frame of reference to guide design and a precision and clarity of expression that facilitate communication of the design.

Two approaches covered, operational modeling and information analysis, are structured methods. They consequently provide frameworks to guide the requirements analysis effort. The remaining three approaches—variance analysis, critical success factors, and future analysis—touch on issues that embellish the evolving design.

Decision-Oriented Versus Data-Oriented Analysis[7]

With decision-oriented analysis, as shown in Figure 11.5a, one begins by identifying organizational objectives, traces these to key management decisions, and then derives information needs to support these decision situations. By focusing on objectives and critical functions, one increases

---

FIGURE 11.5
Decision-Oriented and
Data-Oriented Analysis

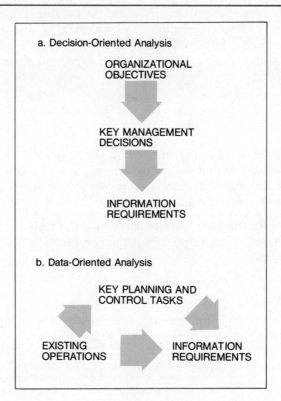

a. Decision-Oriented Analysis

ORGANIZATIONAL
OBJECTIVES

KEY MANAGEMENT
DECISIONS

INFORMATION
REQUIREMENTS

b. Data-Oriented Analysis

KEY PLANNING AND
CONTROL TASKS

EXISTING
OPERATIONS

INFORMATION
REQUIREMENTS

---

the likelihood that the requirements specified will include those issues most relevant to the long-run aims of the organization. Additionally, decision-oriented analysis tends to stress normative solutions to organizational problems, and thus is less subject to organizational bias and narrowness.

With data-oriented analysis, on the other hand, one focuses on current operations and the existing means (manual or computer-based) of information processing. Initially, current problems or short-run aims are identified and examined. Then decisions associated with issues such as allocating resources, evaluating operations, and ensuring that materials to be used are available are defined and analyzed relative to required information support. Data-oriented analysis tends to more completely describe the range of current activities than does decision-oriented analysis. Figure 11.5b provides a schematic view of data-oriented analysis.

Decision-oriented analysis is generally more expensive than data-oriented analysis because it is best directed by managers or users, rather than CBIS specialists, it requires more participants and higher participant opportunity costs, and it tends to take longer. However, it often results in a better set of requirements when the organizational functions involved are less structured, emphasize planning tasks, or are tightly linked to the future. Table 11.3 provides a decision rule to apply in deciding which form of analysis to adopt in a given situation. If possible, both should be employed.

Operational Modeling[8]

Operational modeling employs a data-oriented analysis approach that first obtains an understanding of how the organization functions and then derives information requirements. A two-cycle process is thus employed. The first cycle includes three steps:

1. State the key operations (gross units of work specialization) that must be accomplished if the organization's mission is to be attained.

TABLE 11.3 Situation Criteria for Choosing Analysis Form	Decision-Oriented Analysis	Data-Oriented Analysis
	Unstructured	Structured
	Planning-control oriented	Operations-control oriented
	Future oriented	Present oriented

2. Build a systems flow model that interrelates these jobs, tasks, or functions.
3. Define the suboperations of each key operation.

These steps are repeated until an appropriate level of concrete reality is reached. This should occur when the model reflects the level of task aggregation used in operational planning, procedure descriptions, job descriptions, and so on. Once this level has been reached, the remaining steps are taken:

4. State the significant managerial planning and control actions (selecting courses of action, adjusting expenditures, allocating resources, etc.) required to successfully pursue and coordinate these operations.
5. Specify the outcomes of each action and the producing relationships.
6. Define the information required for each action.

Thus, on completion of the operational model, one should have a systems model of organizational functioning (with required inputs and resulting outputs) and an understanding of the managerial information required to plan and control organizational functioning.

Information Analysis[9,10]

Information analysis is a decision-oriented analysis approach that again—because of the refinement activity—involves a two-cycle process. The first cycle involves building a model that represents the information "determinants" of successful organizational functioning, while the second involves a detailed analysis of each component of this model. The first cycle includes four steps:

1. State an abstract "information kind"—goal, result, etc., that reflects organizational purpose.
2. Determine the horizontal "information precedents" (information sets, actions on information, actions on transactions or resources) required to produce the "information kind"; some of these may be external to the focal organization, while others might be intermediate.
3. Check the current model for completeness and consistency.
4. Break each identified "information element" into subelements (a deeper level of abstraction).

These steps are repeated until an appropriate level of concrete reality is reached. Throughout this analysis, *processing* is not considered—the intent is to simply represent the information structure of the organization. Once the appropriate level of concreteness is reached, the second stage of analysis commences:

5. Define the specific components of each information element.
6. Derive all controls necessary to provide each information element.
7. Specify the transformations that operate on each information element.

At the conclusion of this process, a complete specification of information requirements—inputs, outputs, and processing environment (controls and transformations)—should exist.

Variance Analysis[11-13]

Variance analysis is one methodology embodied in a philosophy of work design known as *sociotechnical system* (STS) design. (More on this design philosophy will be presented in the following chapter.) Basically, variance analysis is a data-oriented analysis approach whose main objective is to expose the weak points of the existing mode of organizational functioning.

Four steps are followed in performing a variance analysis:

1. Identify the organization's "unit operations" (i.e., sets of integrated tasks separated from others by a change in the state of inputs).
2. Select some "ideal model" (historical performance, current plan, standards, client or customer views, etc.) that represents how the organizational work system should function.
3. Compare this ideal model against reality to identify key variances—those that significantly impair the ability of the work system to meet its objectives.
4. Analyze each key variance by examining the following:
   • Interactions between variances,
   • Where each variance originates,
   • Where each variance is observed,
   • Where each variance is corrected,
   • How each variance is corrected,
   • Who corrects each variance,
   • What information is needed for correction,
   • Where this information originates.

Variance analysis should lead to a definition of the information required to overcome the current problems of the work system.

Critical Success Factors[14]

An analysis method that has met with considerable management acceptance is that of focusing on an organization's (or manager's) *critical success factors*. Regardless of the scope involved, most organizational responsibilities can be characterized by a relatively limited number (three to six) of critical factors—tasks, objectives, or decisions that must go right if success is to result. These factors should receive continued, careful attention by organizational members. Critical success factors, which may be based on both industry and organizational characteristics, tend to reflect control issues, rather than planning issues.

The steps in employing the critical success factors method are deceptively simple:

1. Identify critical success factors.
2. Define measures representing each factor.
3. Design reports containing these measures.
4. Specify inputs, controls, and transformations required to produce these reports.

This approach requires intensive management participation to be effective.

Future Analysis[15,16]

None of the prior analysis approaches explicitly consider changes likely to occur over the life of the CBIS product. (The critical success factors method allows for building as well as monitoring factors, but these are directed toward the short term.) As future considerations are a fundamental component of a complete requirements specification, analyses specifically directed at discovering and evaluating future changes are beneficial.

Future analysis involves having a group of experts—organizational members most aware of the environments (organizational and information technology, economic, legal, etc.) involved—formally discuss what might occur. Many group processes have been suggested for facilitating such exchanges, such as the "interacting group," the "nominal group," and the "Delphi" methods (described in the appendix).

The following steps should occur in any effort at future analysis:

1. Predict those factors likely to change over the life of the CBIS product.
2. Assess the probability that each change will take place.
3. Assess the impact of the most likely factors on the organization and then on the CBIS product.

Such an analysis effort should produce the forecast life of the CBIS, a revised list of objectives, and statements of how (functions, volumes, performance conditions or characteristics, etc.) the requirements specification is likely to evolve over time.

Review of the Approaches

These analysis approaches serve three main purposes:

- They provide a framework on which to build an analysis.
- They ensure that certain issues will be addressed.
- They cause key issues to be raised early.

However, the approaches differ in the specific framework provided, factors emphasized, and issues examined. Table 11.4 summarizes the major attributes of the five approaches. Selection of an approach must be based on careful consideration of the situation being faced, including such factors as the purpose of the CBIS product, the characteristics of the organizational situation, and the urgency and importance of the project. Furthermore, the success of any requirements effort ultimately depends on the capabilities, knowledge, skills, and experience of participants. Analysis methodologies do not perform the analysis. Determining a valid set of requirements remains a largely human endeavor demanding creativity and insight, neither of which can be obtained from a design methodology.

TABLE 11.4
Comparison of the Requirements Analysis Approaches

Attribute	Operational Modeling	Information Analysis	Variance Analysis	Critical Success Factors	Future Analysis
Orientation	Data	Decision	Data	Decision	Decision
Focus	Current work flow	Organizational objectives	Current operational problems	Organizational success	Future events
Advantage	Handling of current activities complete	Strategic issues addressed	Current problem areas addressed	Issues critical to organization's ability to serve domain addressed	Likely changes incorporated into CBIS design structure
Disadvantage	Current activities might not be appropriate	May overlook low-level but necessary activities	Perspective limited to existing task domain	Limited to management control issues	Difficult to accurately forecast future

ILLUSTRATION OF THE APPROACHES

Since it is difficult to envision how these requirements analysis approaches are employed, an example of how they might be applied is provided. The aim is not to illustrate a detailed requirements analysis, but to convey the manner the approaches would be applied and, as a by-product, to illustrate the features of each approach.

The situation considered depicts initial steps involved in the development of a *conceptual design* for a regional airline reservation and information system. (This example is derived from one conceived by Yeh *et al.*[17]) As this application is very broad and cuts across many organizational levels, multiple requirements analysis approaches must be applied.

In the example, a small regional airline (serving ten cities and a thousand-mile flight range) is considering implementing a CBIS to support its functioning. It expects both clerical and managerial support: reservation clerks will use the CBIS to make, change, cancel, or confirm reservations, and managers will use it to add or delete flights and to request information to support other decisions. Two elements of the CBIS have already been determined:

- A flight file, holding data such as flight number, origin, destination, number of seats, available seats, passenger list, and departure and arrival times,
- A load factor report, listing percentages of filled seats for all scheduled flights, available by 8:00 A.M. each day.

The first analysis effort might be *operational modeling*. Figures 11.6 and 11.7 show the first two levels of abstraction in developing operational models of the reservation and operations management functions, respectively. Each model would be made more concrete, after which associated planning and control actions would be identified. Sample actions for the reservation function include maintaining customer service at a high level (short wait, fast response), staffing an appropriate number of clerks, minimizing reservation errors, and maintaining up-to-date booking data. Sample actions for the operations management function might include maintaining an appropriate number of available aircraft, ensuring profitable operations by adding and deleting flights when appropriate, and maintaining a high level of customer satisfaction. The idea in operational modeling, thus, is to understand how the target organizational unit functions and to ascertain both the operational information and managerial information necessary to ensure effective and efficient performance.

Once a functional model of the organization has been constructed, it might be appropriate to use a *variance analysis* to identify existing problem areas. Assume this has been done, and three key variances are observed: low loads at takeoff, too much food being catered, and failure to

FIGURE 11.6
Reservation Model

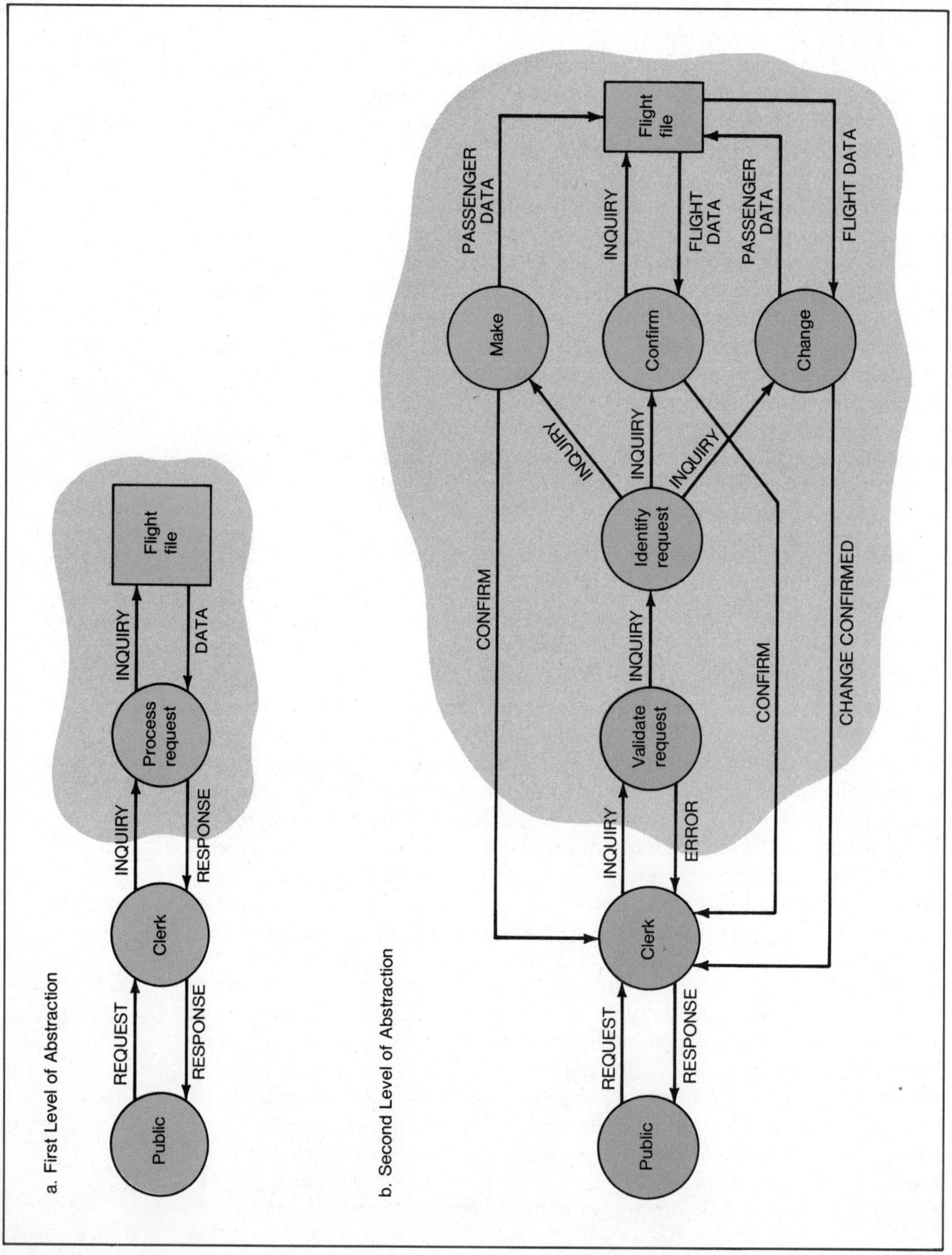

a. First Level of Abstraction

b. Second Level of Abstraction

FIGURE 11.7
Operations Management Model

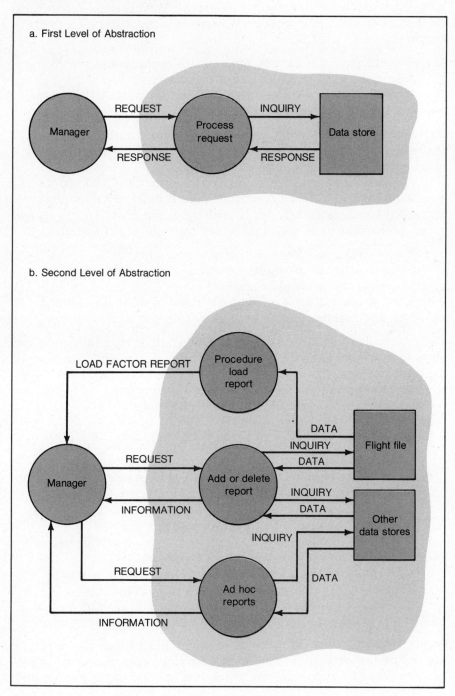

a. First Level of Abstraction

b. Second Level of Abstraction

add flights when demand exists because it is not known if an airplane is available. Another key variance is associated with the public: numerous complaints about lost luggage have surfaced. Tracing these variances to their sources and analyzing ways to correct them indicate three major requirements for the CBIS:

- Need to maintain current and accurate booking data,
- Need to institute a luggage tracking capability, and
- Need to maintain current data on aircraft availability (i.e., maintenance information).

By identifying critical problems, one can recognize desirable features of the abstract CBIS and visualize particular CBIS product attributes that are necessary in the evolving set of requirements.

At this point it might be useful to ensure that the CBIS product will contribute to organizational objectives by performing or supporting organizational activities directly linked with these objectives. First, a *critical success factors* analysis yields three key concerns of management:

- Need to react quickly to fluctuating ride patterns,
- Need to maintain customer satisfaction (good food, no luggage problems, few schedule changes),
- Need to control costs, particularly those associated with food, fuel, and maintenance.

These considerations, as well as those attained through operational modeling and variance analysis, enter into an *information analysis* effort to logically structure the information requirements. Figure 11.8 suggests the first two abstraction levels of such a design activity. This analysis reveals that the following information elements of the CBIS product are desirable:

- Maintenance of current booking data in a *flight file*, which is the same as originally specified plus a luggage component,
- Maintenance of an *aircraft file*, which holds maintenance activity and cost and usage data on each aircraft,
- Maintenance of a *historical flight file*, which records costs and revenues associated with all previous flights,
- Provision of a *add or delete flight report*, which reveals not only the load factor but the availability of aircraft,
- Provision of a *schedule appraisal report*, which evaluates the profitability of current routes and suggests alternatives,
- Transaction processing relating to *reservations, aircraft maintenance, food preparation, luggage handling,* and *fuel usage.*

Finally, to assess what external events might affect the airline, a *future analysis* is undertaken. The following developments are identified as likely to occur over the next five years: fuel scarcity, rapidly rising fuel

FIGURE 11.8
Information Analysis

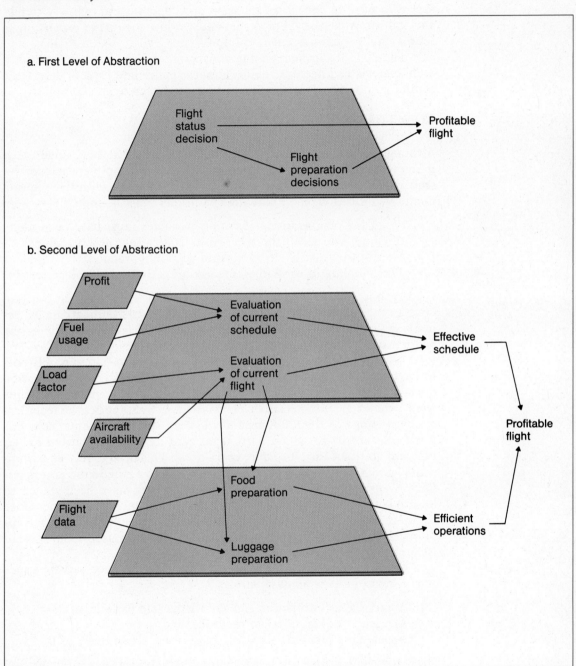

a. First Level of Abstraction

b. Second Level of Abstraction

costs, increased competition with other modes of transportation, and expansion of the airline's market. These projections underscore the already identified concern for fuel efficiency and customer satisfaction, suggest a need to collect information on economic and industry trends, and indicate that the CBIS design must allow for future expansion in routes, flights, and passenger volume.

Figure 11.9 summarizes the conceptual design that has evolved. If each analysis had been carried to a more appropriate level of detail, the resultant conceptual design would be more concrete and complete.

CONCLUSION

Although requirements analysis is the most critical activity undertaken in implementing a CBIS, it is impossible to derive a complete and correct requirements specification in most cases. To produce a definitive requirements specification, the following conditions must be met:

- All of the organizational system's variables must have been identified, as well as all the relationships affecting these variables,
- The future must be "frozen" into the CBIS product,
- The handling of each implementation activity must be perfect.[18]

Clearly, one cannot produce *definitive requirements*, but one can produce a successive iteration of partial requirements specifications by formally describing and validating each partial specification and by creating and managing structures that facilitate the inevitable changes.

Moreover, requirements analysis is, for the most part, a purely cognitive effort. The quality of resulting specifications is largely a function of participants' *intents* (what users want, think they want, or state they want; what the CBIS specialists perceive these wants to be; the technical predispositions of the CBIS specialists; etc.) and participants' *commitment* (the extent to which participants are motivated to use *all* their inherent abilities, insights, and experiences). This need to rely on participants' commitment reflects how difficult it is to evaluate the efforts put forth by participants. Certain processes, however, have been shown to lead to better requirements specifications. These include the emergence of "up-front" conflict, which is then productively resolved,[19] lack of communication barriers between participants,[20] and joint user–CBIS specialist problem solving so cross-education results.[21]

Given these observations, three conditions seem necessary for a successful requirements analysis effort:

- Appropriately motivated and knowledgeable participants,
- Application of appropriate methods, and
- Appropriate planning, control, and reward structures.

These three conditions can be met with effective management practices.

FIGURE 11.9
Conceptual Design of Organizational Information Needs

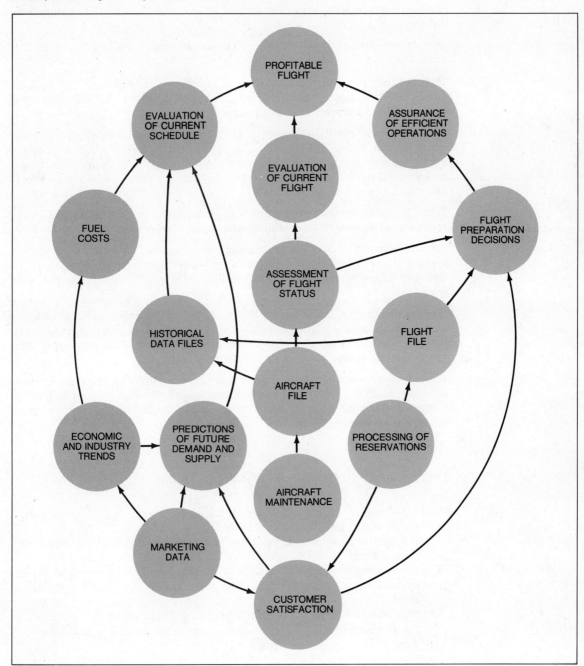

KEY ISSUES

Specifying a valid set of requirements, a formal depiction of a CBIS product from the user's perspective, is the most critical activity undertaken in CBIS implementation.

A requirements specification must consider the entire forecast life of a CBIS product.

Included in a requirements specification are an overview of the CBIS product, detailed descriptions of its outputs and inputs, descriptions of its processing environment, and forecasts of future changes.

The first step in specifying requirements is to build a conceptual design, an ideal configuration, of the CBIS product. This is followed by the construction of a logical design, a pragmatic version of the conceptual design. This design should then be subjected to a validation process. Finally, a formal depiction of the specification should be prepared.

When considerable uncertainty arises about requirements, iteration and prototypes are often used in the requirements analysis process.

The most important tools in performing a requirements analysis are those that are used to communicate an evolving design. Three description tools particularly useful in requirements analysis are decision tables, matrices, and data flow diagrams.

Five requirements analysis approaches were presented: operational modeling, information analysis, variance analysis, the critical success factors method, and future analysis. These approaches differ from each other in the framework provided to guide analysis and in the issues they emphasize.

While a requirements analysis can be aided by employing an appropriate analysis approach, success ultimately depends on the contributions of the human participants. Thus, the quality of the resulting specifications depends largely on participants' intents and commitment.

DISCUSSION QUESTIONS

1. Explain why errors caught late in the implementation process are more costly than those caught very early.
2. If definitive requirements can never be stated, why is requirements analysis so important?
3. How is the control structure of a software product destroyed if future changes are not allowed for in the initial design? Why is a control structure critical?
4. Why should one go through the conceptual design step when specifying a set of requirements? Which situations might not require a conceptual design?

5. A number of validation procedures were discussed. Which do you feel would provide the best assurance that a valid set of requirements had been determined? Explain.

6. Is there any danger in not looking outside the organization when determining requirements?

7. Construct decision tables that capture the decision processes you have gone or are going through in selecting a restaurant, a graduate school, and a summer job.

8. Construct a matrix that shows the relationships between the courses you are currently taking and major concepts, theories, and skills being emphasized. Is there much overlap between any of these courses?

9. Construct a data flow diagram that depicts the course registration process at your school.

10. Construct a data flow diagram that describes the functioning of the textbook department (orders and sales) of a student bookstore.

11. Using the context of financial management, identify a CBIS application whose requirements might best be captured by a decision-oriented analysis method. Then identify an application for which a data-oriented analysis method might be preferred.

12. Why do the structured analysis methods, operational modeling and information analysis, both employ a two-cycle process?

13. Would the critical success factors approach be appropriate for determining the requirements for a DSS? Why or why not?

14. Identify a CBIS project in which little cognitive effort might be required to determine a set of requirements.

15. Why might "up-front" conflict between participants improve the quality of a requirements specification?

BRIEF CASES

1. *Morningside Cereals*
   Toni Sellick wanted to receive a monthly report that would enable her to evaluate the sales performance of each product in the Morningside Naturals line. After talking with the systems analyst who had been given the assignment of developing this report, she realized he did not understand exactly what type of report she wanted. As they were not making much progress, the analyst suggested Toni prepare a detailed specification of the report requirements. Toni asked the analyst exactly what was needed. The analyst responded that the report should be sketched out and that each information element should be defined in terms of its required input data, calculation, and use. The analyst suggested that once this specification was prepared, the process of designing procedures to produce the report should go smoothly.

   Do you agree that the requirements analysis should go smoothly once this report specification has been produced?

2. *Greco Products*

One major component of the sales control system Randy Fitzin was design-ing involved a monthly report to be sent to each sales representative that accomplished two primary objectives: providing feedback to the representa-tive about the person's performance that month and year to date, and pro-viding marketing information (industry trends, economic indicators, inno-vative packaging ideas being proposed, etc.) to support the direct sales effort. The initial design of this report had been put together by a team composed of Randy, Rose Leary, and three key individuals from the sales force. The initial design seemed to meet the needs of the organization and the individ-ual sales representatives, but one thing bothered Randy. Would this specifi-cation be appropriate five years from now, or even two years? The sales control system already represented a sizable investment of both time and money. It consequently was unlikely that any major revisions would be approved in the near future.

Is Randy overly concerned? Can you identify future changes that might be required in a monthly report such as that being sent to the sales repre-sentatives? Could any of these changes have a significant impact on the basic design of the sales control information system? If so, what changes would those be?

3. *Mountain Community Bank*

The branch location DSS project that Sharon Tinker had been working on for the past two months was finally beginning to take shape. Most of the system's modules had been designed and approved by management. The last module of major consequence involved a set of reports that evaluated branch revenue performance and productivity.

In planning how best to manage the requirements determination step for this last module, Sharon was unsure what type of validation procedure to employ. She had an uneasy feeling that the different managers she would interview would have varied ideas about what was needed to evaluate a branch's performance. Unless agreement was reached on the validity of a set of requirements, the project might reach the snag Sharon had so far avoided.

Suggest a validation procedure for Sharon to use and explain why this procedure is appropriate.

4. *Mercy Hospital*

Susan Horowitz' latest idea for updating the management processes at Mercy Hospital involved the implementation of an interactive system to support the annual budget preparation task. Each department's manage-ment staff spent at least six weeks every year putting together their budget (or so they claimed). Most of this time was not what might be termed pro-ductive work—it consisted largely of handling the many revisions required whenever a department's budget did not fit the overall budget for the hospi-tal. It seemed to Susan that if the departmental budgets could be stored within a computer system, they could be retrieved and revised fairly quickly. Assuming that the financial modeling system that had been imple-mented earlier could be tied into this interactive budget system, Susan believed that most of the hospital's departments would be able to complete their budgets within a week.

Which requirements analysis approaches would be appropriate for determining requirements for this interactive budget preparation system? Why? Would you advise using more than one approach? If so, which ones and why?

NOTES

1. G. B. Davis, "Information Analysis for Information System Development," in W. W. Cotterman, J. D. Cougar, N. L. Enger, and F. Harold (eds.), *Systems Analysis and Design: A Foundation for the 1980s* (New York: Elsevier North-Holland, 1981).

2. M. G. Walker, *Managing Software Reliability* (New York: Elsevier North-Holland, 1981).

3. J. G. Miller, "Fit Production Systems to the Task," *Harvard Business Review* 57(1981):145–54.

4. Miller (1981).

5. J. Berrisford and J. Wetherbe, "Heuristic Development: A Redesign of System Design," *MIS Quarterly* 3(1979):11–19.

6. Davis (1981).

7. M. C. Munro and G. B. Davis, "Determining Management Information Needs: A Comparison of Methods," *MIS Quarterly* 1(1977):55–67.

8. J. C. Miller, "Conceptual Models for Determining Information Requirements," *Proceedings of the Spring Joint Computer Conference* (Arlington, Va.: American Federation of Information Processing Societies, 1964), pp. 609–20.

9. B. Langefors, "Analysis of User Needs," in G. Bracchi and P. C. Lockemann (eds.), *Information System Methodology* (Berlin: Springer-Verlag, 1978), pp. 1–38.

10. L. B. Methlie, *Information Systems Design* (Bergen, Norway: Universitetforlaget, 1978).

11. R. P. Bostrum and J. S. Heinen, "MIS Problems and Failures: A Socio-Technical Perspective—Part II: The Application of Socio-Technical Theory," *MIS Quarterly* 1(1977):1–28.

12. J. Hawgood, F. Land, and E. Mumford, "A Participative Approach to Forward Planning and System Change," in Bracchi and Lockemann (1978), pp. 39–61.

13. E. Mumford and D. Henshall, *A Participative Approach to Computer System Design* (New York: Wiley, 1979).

14. J. F. Rockart, "Chief Executives Define Their Own Data Needs," *Harvard Business Review* 57(1979):81–92.

15. Hawgood et al. (1978).

16. F. Land, "Adapting to Changing User Needs," in *Life-Cycle Management*, Vol. 2 (Maidenhead, Berkshire, England: Infotech International, 1980), pp. 135–62.

17. R. T. Yeh, A. Araya, R. Mittermeir, W. Mao, and P. Evans, "Software Requirements Engineering: A Perspective," in P. J. L. Wallis (ed.), *Structured Software Development*, Vol. 2 (Maidenhead, Berkshire, England: Infotech International, 1979), pp. 313–42.

18. Walker (1981).

19. D. Robey and D. Farrow, "User Involvement in Information System Development," *Management Science* 28(1982):73–85.

20. A. Edstrom, "User Influence and The Success of MIS Projects: A Contingency Approach," *Human Relations* 30(1977):589–607.

21. R. J. Boland, Jr., "The Process and Product of Systems Design," *Management Science* 24(1978):887–98.

CBIS Evaluation 12

COMPUTER-BASED INFORMATION SYSTEMS that significantly enhance an organization's performance serve meaningful organizational roles, are used, and remain relevant over their planned life. Two factors inhibiting such outcomes are the invisible nature of a CBIS at its inception and organizations' natural evolution over time. Product invisibility makes it extremely difficult for organizational members to foresee the potential roles of a CBIS, thereby resulting in "underdesigned" products and in users' lacking the motivation to learn about and use these products. The evolving nature of organizations requires that CBIS products change over time to maintain an appropriate fit with organizational needs.

In this chapter, two topics that directly aid organizational efforts to deal with product invisibility and organizational evolution are discussed. By stating CBIS product *performance objectives* and *assessment criteria* in measurable terms and by instituting a *quality assurance* program, one can help make CBIS products concrete for managers and users and one can recognize when and how products need to be modified. The sooner measurable performance objectives and their indicators are stated and quality assurance criteria and mechanisms are specified, the sooner can management, users, and implementation participants achieve a consensus on the CBIS product.

This chapter also covers two other CBIS evaluation topics: *acceptance testing* (an evaluation activity in which the user accepts ownership of the CBIS product) and *project review* (an evaluation of both the outcome and process of an implementation effort on its conclusion). All four activities require high levels of management and user participation to be successful.

MEASURABLE PERFORMANCE OBJECTIVES

Leavitt's model of an organization, shown in Figure 12.1, was described in Chapter 10.[1] Viewed in this framework of interrelated technologies, tasks, people, and structures, CBIS are directed toward inducing technological and task changes. These changes, however, invariably affect people and structures through changes in the work context (i.e., authority, influence, communication, political, social, etc., relationships) and through changes in the nature of work (i.e., its complexity, rigidity, interest, variety, autonomy, norms, familiarity, etc.). As a result, it is important to state performance objectives that touch on both technology and task issues (improving the effectiveness and efficiency of the work system) and people and structure issues (enhancing the fit between what different individuals or groups are seeking from the work system).[2,3]

The ultimate aim of CBIS implementations, thus, is to achieve a "technological bonding" in which the CBIS product enhances both organizational performance and the quality of work life.[4] With certain implementations, this is often difficult to achieve (e.g., when work relationships are revised or when information technologies replace humans). While it may not always be possible to improve everyone's work situation, as few people as possible should suffer.

The *targets* for performance objectives might be elements of the CBIS, the organization itself, or the organizational environment.[5,6] At times CBIS projects are undertaken solely to improve the efficiency of an existing computer-based system, to incorporate new hardware or software technologies that reduce the cost of an application or that increase operating performance (in terms of throughput, response time, number of terminals handled, etc.) at a minor cost increase. More typically, however, the major aim of a CBIS project is to improve organizational func-

FIGURE 12.1
Leavitt's Organizational Model

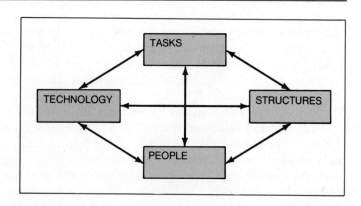

TABLE 12.1
Measurable Performance Indicators

Category	Example
Financial	Cost reduction or avoidance
	Sales or revenues
	Profit, ROI, or market share
Organizational functioning	Service time, productivity, or capacity
	Product or service quality
	Errors or complaints
	Customer or client satisfaction or turnover
Personnel	Employee satisfaction, morale, or turnover
	Employee job security, income, or advancement
	Task scope, variety, responsibility, or status
CBIS system	Capacity or volume
	Execution time, response time, or access time
	Security, flexibility, reliability, or accuracy

tioning so direct benefits are observed in the organization's internal or external environment. Internally, this might result in enhanced operations, improved planning or control capabilities, or improved employee attitudes, as seen in productivity gains, better use of resources and assets, product or service quality advances, and increased sales or service capacity. Externally, improved relationships with clients, customers, stakeholders, the community, vendors, or regulatory and legislative bodies often result from improvements in operational efficiency or organizational effectiveness.

All three targets are often affected by a single CBIS product. In fact, it is desirable that this occur: the more comprehensive the set of performance objectives, the more likely it is that the CBIS product has been analyzed from all relevant perspectives.

There are a variety of ways to make performance objectives measurable, the more common of which are listed in Table 12.1. Performance measures can be expressed in a number of ways: absolute gain or reduction, percentage gain or reduction, relative gain or reduction, etc. As the manner in which an indicator is stated can affect its interpretation, measurable performance criteria must be selected with great care.

QUALITY ASSURANCE CRITERIA

As stated earlier, organizations naturally evolve in response to changes in their internal and external environments. Even if a valid set of requirements is specified for a CBIS product, aspects of the product will eventually require modification or extension for the CBIS to enjoy a continued fit with its organizational context. *All* requirements specifications are deficient in at least a few respects. As these defects are not normally realized until the product is introduced into its operating environment, a way is needed to identify these deficiencies so they can be corrected.

Four classes of criteria can be used in a quality assurance program:

- Organizational performance objectives,
- Actual use of the CBIS product,
- Individual performance, and
- User satisfaction with the CBIS product.

While each class touches on particular aspects of the CBIS product, these criteria are interrelated (Figure 12.2). Each class has certain limitations, as well, so an effective quality assurance program should employ evaluation criteria from all four classes.

Organizational Performance Objectives

It is desirable to focus on the expected organizational impacts of the CBIS product, as these form the basis for the organization's decision to invest in the CBIS project. If performance objectives are attained (and continue to be attained), the CBIS product is likely performing as it should. If performance objectives are not being attained (or have slipped), product defi-

FIGURE 12.2
Relationships Among Quality Assurance Criteria Classes

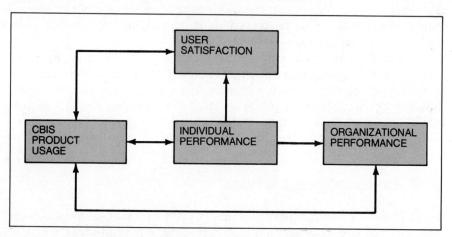

Part 3 / Implementation

ciencies probably exist. These performance objectives (as discussed in the preceding section) should be stated in measurable terms so they can be readily assessed.

There are a number of disadvantages with using performance objectives as the sole quality assurance mechanism. First, they are static: performance targets are set relative to a particular organizational context. Efforts made to revise these targets over time so they reflect organizational changes are subject to considerable bias. Second, these indicators primarily serve notice that an expected outcome is not being realized. They typically do not indicate where or how modifications or extensions should be undertaken. Third, many causes of observed organizational performance outcomes may be unrelated to the CBIS product. Controlling for such influences can be extremely difficult.

CBIS Product Utilization

If a CBIS product is used as intended, it is likely performing as expected. If it is not being used, it may have been found deficient in one or more respects by the users. However, these interpretations are not always accurate. Use might be mandated, or an inferior product might be used because there are no alternatives. Nonetheless, use is a viable mechanism for assessing the continued appropriateness of a CBIS.

If the CBIS product being evaluated is used through interactive terminals, it is fairly easy to monitor use (who uses what product capabilities) through the software itself. With batch environments similar measurements can be obtained, though not with the same degree of detail, through the operating system's job accounting routine. Other ways of assessing usage are to periodically have users "red-line" a report when they refer to it (put a mark by the information accessed) or to temporarily discontinue a report (or portion of a report) or temporarily deny access to a certain program or data file and then monitor complaints. While such techniques are disruptive, they can prove quite informative.

Individual Performance

With IRS and DSS, organizational performance is enhanced through improvements in the way individuals perform assigned responsibilities: better decision making occurs, tasks are completed sooner, more comprehensive solutions to problems result, etc. Additionally, while it may not be explicitly stated, an aim of most CBIS implementation efforts is to change the behaviors of organizational members.[7] This may occur even if the CBIS product is not introduced because of learning from implementation activities such as the feasibility study, requirements analysis, and implementation planning.

Changes can be tracked in both decision behaviors (information sought, methods used, etc.) and the decision-makers themselves (their perspectives, confidence, problem understanding, etc.). Doing so, however, often proves difficult, time consuming, and expensive, and it again becomes important to control for outside influences.

User Satisfaction

User satisfaction criteria measure users' perceptions of the usefulness and usableness of CBIS products.[8,9] By capturing user satisfaction when a CBIS product is introduced, one can determine the product's inherent deficiencies. By monitoring user satisfaction over time, one can identify deterioration in the fit between the CBIS and its organizational context.

Perhaps the greatest advantage of assessing user satisfaction is that virtually any facet of a CBIS product can be examined. It is often possible to identify exactly where product defects lie and how they can be cor-

---

TABLE 12.2
User Satisfaction Assessment Criteria.

Characteristic	Examples
Time	Frequency, turnaround time (batch system) Response time (interactive system) Currentness (reports, data base)
Controls	Errors, integrity (data entry, data storage) Security, privacy (data base, programs, operations)
Delivery system	Accessibility, availability, physical discomfort, reliability, query language, aids (user manual, CBIS staff)
Data entry	Convenience, disruption, relevance
Decision aids (models)	Relevance, currentness, completeness, understandability
Report content	Relevance Completeness (problem finding, context provision, problem structuring, problem solving, solution tracking) of support, scope of support Quantity, detail, accuracy, redundancy
Report form	Media (CRT, paper, microform, etc.) Format (tables, charts, graphs, narratives, etc.) Conciseness, clarity, readability, understandability

---

rected. Table 12.2 lists some CBIS product characteristics often assessed by user satisfaction mechanisms.[10-12]

User satisfaction can be assessed through interviews, questionnaires, and complaint tracking. Interviews (individual or group) generally provide the most meaningful information, as a dialogue is established. However, interviews are time consuming and may be subject to bias because of group pressures or reluctance to be critical in face-to-face encounters. Questionnaires can be a very economical way to elicit feedback from all users. Developing reliable and valid questionnaires, however, is not simple. Complaint tracking may be the easiest method to employ, but it is doubtful that all complaints will be voiced. Also, complaint tracking does not capture favorable user perceptions.

Product Efficiency

The quality assurance criteria discussed thus far have been directed toward ensuring product *effectiveness*. It is also important to periodically analyze the *efficiency* of each CBIS application—that is, to identify hardware, software, or procedural improvements that can reduce the cost of providing the CBIS product. While examinations of product effectiveness are primarily a responsibility of users, product efficiency realistically must be assessed by CBIS specialists.

If the actual costs of the information resources used in providing a CBIS product are compiled and if hardware or software monitors measure those resources during CBIS operation, transaction costs can be tracked over time and compared with those for similar CBIS. This information can then be used to evaluate the costs of possible CBIS modifications. Few organizations formally assign responsibility for such analyses to CBIS specialists, but formal assignment is recommended, as it is difficult to motivate CBIS specialists working on ongoing implementation efforts to review the efficiency of an already implemented CBIS.

ACCEPTANCE TESTING

Acceptance testing is best understood in the context of acquiring a CBIS product from a vendor. When an organization accepts a CBIS product from a vendor, the vendor's contractual obligations have essentially been met, the organization is obligated to pay for the product, and required product changes come under the category of maintenance and associated costs tend to be borne by the organization. It is consequently to the advantage of vendors to discourage the inclusion of acceptance criteria in contracts. Without such clauses, most contractual disputes are concluded in favor of the vendor; at best, the user may win a long, costly legal battle.

With comprehensive, detailed, and relevant acceptance criteria inserted in the contract, the user is protected against poor vendor performance. Payment does not begin until all acceptance criteria are met, and default or late penalties may be charged to the vendor. The inclusion of acceptance criteria in a contract thus becomes a major negotiation goal. If the acceptance criteria are too weak, the user is not protected; if they are too tough, the vendor will not accept the contract.

Acceptance criteria can likewise prove valuable when a CBIS product is being developed internally. A real or "psychological" contract specifying acceptance criteria aids both developers (the information function) and sponsors (the target organizational units). The product becomes "frozen", thus facilitating communication between developers and sponsors and guiding the design and development effort, and sponsors can assess very early the product being delivered. Essentially, sponsors commit themselves to particular product attributes and developers commit themselves to producing that product.

The major problem in developing an appropriate set of acceptance criteria is that they must not refer to CBIS product attributes that can be assessed only after the CBIS has been put into normal organizational use, for then the vendor could claim implied acceptance of the product. Consequently, many criteria put into a request for proposal are not appropriate for acceptance testing. Only criteria that can be examined through preconversion testing are recommended, such as measuring system performance (e.g., response time, throughput, turnaround time, volume limits, service time, number of terminals handled) and ensuring that the entire range of data types and values are handled, that file processing is handled as required, that all documents and reports generated are complete and accurate, that all prescribed security provisions are met, and that all prescribed documentation is provided.

PROJECT REVIEW

When a CBIS conversion has been completed and users have become familiar with their required CBIS behaviors (i.e., the CBIS product has become "institutionalized"), two questions need to be answered:

- Was the outcome successful?
- What findings during the implementation effort can be generalized to other CBIS efforts?[13]

By answering the first question, one can affix responsibility for the initial investment decision and for the implementation effort itself. Previous feasibility assessments and measurable performance objectives form the basis for these evaluations. By answering the second question, one can formalize and transfer to future CBIS projects the learning that occurred throughout implementation about organizational functioning, CBIS capabilities and limitations, implementation analysis, planning, and control techniques, participant roles, etc. This, however, can occur only if the implementation effort has been well documented. A repository containing information on all implementation activities and their associated costs, all project communications, and all key implementation decisions and outcomes should be maintained. If such information is not made available at the project review, many critical problems and valuable insights will be forgotten or diminish in significance.

CONCLUSION

The primary objective of engaging in CBIS evaluation activities is to ensure that an implemented CBIS product remains relevant throughout its life. However, CBIS product success requires more than making quality products available for use. Three additional factors that comprise a minimal set of success conditions are organizational awareness of a CBIS product, organizational capability to use a CBIS product, and organizational desire to use the CBIS product.[14–17] These three factors are highly interrelated and evolve from educational and motivational programs, from efforts of individuals (users, managers, and CBIS specialists), and from the information resource policies established by the organization's top management. Engaging in the implementation activities covered so far in Part 3 should lead to the establishment of an implementation context conducive to CBIS product success. Additional steps that can be taken by an organization are suggested in Chapter 13.

KEY ISSUES

Two key factors limiting the successfulness of CBIS products are their initial invisibility and the inevitability that user needs will change over the products' planned lives. Various CBIS evaluation procedures address both these issues.

Measurable project objectives should be specified for both organizational performance and quality of work life.

Project objectives may be targeted at CBIS functioning, organizational functioning, or an organization's environment.

All CBIS products are deficient in some respects. The purpose of a quality assurance program is to identify these deficiencies so they can be corrected.

The four classes of quality assurance criteria include measurable performance objectives, the actual use of a CBIS product, user performance, and user satisfaction.

Acceptance testing is performed prior to a user's acceptance of a software product. Until the acceptance tests are met, the software product remains the responsibility of the software developer.

All acceptance testing must be performed prior to an organization's decision to begin using the CBIS product in support of organizational activities.

After a CBIS product has been introduced into an organization, a comprehensive review should be made of the implementation effort.

DISCUSSION QUESTIONS

1. How might the invisible nature of a CBIS product dampen user motivation to participate in an implementation effort or to use a CBIS once it has been implemented?
2. Illustrate from your own experiences (including outside reading) how the introduction of a CBIS can change the work context and the nature of work itself.
3. How might the work context be affected if a corporate planning group implemented a CBIS whose major attribute was that the planners now had on-line access to both a corporate data base and external information services?
4. One prime benefit of many TPS is that personnel reductions are possible. How can one state "quality of work life" objectives in such situations?
5. Consider an application whose major objective is to reduce the time it takes to process a customer order. Propose performance objectives that relate to the CBIS itself, to improvements in organizational functioning, to improvements in the organization's quality of work life, and to the organization's environment.
6. While user satisfaction measures are very flexible quality assurance mechanisms, they are subject to considerable bias. What biases might result in distorted user attitudes?

7. Explain the difference between system testing and acceptance testing.
8. What is meant by the statement that a CBIS product has become institutionalized.
9. Which is the more important aspect of a project review, evaluating the CBIS product that had been implemented or evaluating the implementation process itself? Explain.

BRIEF CASES

1. *Bennison Construction Company*

   A major enhancement was being proposed for two of Bennison's most important information systems: the project scheduling system and the project control system. As both systems were currently batch processing systems, management was dissatisfied with the currentness of the information made available. An even greater source of dissatisfaction was that the two systems could not be integrated. As a result, many manual gyrations were required to arrive at schedule revisions when the control system identified a problem with an existing schedule.

   The project under consideration addressed both concerns. The new information system was to combine both the scheduling and control functions in an on-line environment. Files would be updated three times a day.

   Propose some measurable project objectives for the proposed information system. Be very explicit as to how you would calculate your measures.

2. *The State Motor Pool*

   Two information systems implemented by the State Motor Pool were the vehicle replacement control system (an exception reporting system that identified vehicles to be replaced) and the maintenance purchasing system (an extensive information system that supported and coordinated the purchase of maintenance parts, supplies, and tools across the entire state). While the quality assurance program would eventually be extended to all the CBIS implemented by the State Motor Pool, quality assurance mechanisms were initially to be developed for only these two applications.

   Would it make sense to develop a single collection of quality assurance measures and apply them to both information systems? What measures, if any, would apply to both? What measures, if any, might apply to one system but not the other?

3. *Power King Tools*

   Power King Tools had a work force of over eight thousand employees, over six thousand of whom were blue-collar workers. Maintaining personnel records on this work force was becoming a massive undertaking, particularly as many of the workers had specialized skills. Manufacturing problems had arisen in the past because of the firm's difficulties replacing skilled employees, only to subsequently find out that those same skills were underutilized elsewhere in the company. In the face of these difficulties, the decision was finally reached to purchase a sophisticated personnel information system.

   The chosen package performed a number of functions, including collecting daily work records, maintaining extensive personnel records, performing work-force productivity analyses, providing a skills location capability, and facilitating employee career planning. The system's processing environment provided on-line data entry and retrieval through standard screens and menus, as well as a fairly flexible ad hoc retrieval facility.

Assume you were given the responsibility for the acceptance testing of this software product. What conditions would you wish to insert into the contract? Be very explicit regarding the software attributes being assessed. Then explain exactly how you would manage the acceptance testing. When, where, and how would it be done?

NOTES

1. H. J. Leavitt, "Applied Organizational Change in Industry: Structural, Technological and Humanistic Approaches," in J. G. March (ed.), *Handbook of Organizations* (Chicago: Rand McNally, 1965), pp. 1144–70.

2. R. L. Schultz and D. P. Slevin, "A Program of Research on Implementation," in R. L. Schultz and D. P. Slevin (eds.), *Implementing Operations Research/Management Science* (New York: American Elsevier, 1975), pp. 31–51.

3. J. Hawgood, F. Land, and E. Mumford, "A Participative Approach to Forward Planning and System Change," in G. Bracchi and P. C. Lockemann (eds.), *Information Systems Methodology* (Berlin: Springer-Verlag, 1978), pp. 39–61.

4. E. Mumford, "Values, Technology and Work," in Bracchi and Lockemann (1978), pp. 142–59.

5. E. D. Carlson, "Evaluating the Impact of Information Systems," *Management Informatics* 3(1974):57–67.

6. D. Seibt, "User and Specialist Evaluations in Systems Development," in N. Szyperski and E. Grochla (eds.), *Design and Implementation of Computer-Based Information Systems* (Alphen an den Rijn, The Netherlands: Sijthoff & Noordhoff, 1979), pp. 285–300.

7. M. J. Ginzberg, "Finding an Adequate Measure of OR/MS Effectiveness," *Interfaces* 8(1978):59–62.

8. D. F. Larcker and V. P. Lessig, "Perceived Usefulness of Information: A Psychometric Examination," *Decision Sciences* 11(1980):121–34.

9. E. B. Swanson, "Measuring User Attitudes in MIS Research: A Review," working paper, Graduate School of Management, UCLA, 1980.

10. E. B. Swanson, "Management Information Systems: Appreciation and Involvement," *Management Science* 21(1974):178–88.

11. R. W. Zmud, "An Empirical Investigation of the Dimensionality of the Concept of Information," *Decision Sciences* 9(1978):187–95.

12. A. M. Jenkins and J. A. Ricketts, "Development of an Instrument to Measure User Satisfaction with Management Information Systems," working paper, School of Business, Indiana University, 1979.

13. G. I. Susman, "Planned Change: Prospects for the 1980s," *Management Science* 27(1981):139–54.

14. C. D. Schewe, J. L. Wick, and R. Dann, "Advanced Marketing Information Systems: An Empirical Investigation of System Usage Problems," *Proceedings of the AIDS National Meeting* (Atlanta: American Institute for Decision Sciences, 1974), pp. 356–59.

15. H. C. Lucas, Jr., *The Implementation of Computer-Based Models* (New York: National Association of Accountants, 1976).

16. D. Robey, "User Attitudes and Management Information System Use," *Academy of Management Journal* 22(1979):527–38.

17. H. C. Lucas, Jr., "The Implementation of an Operations Research Model in the Brokerage Industry," *TIMS Studies in the Management Sciences* 13(1979):139–54.

CBIS Failure and Success 13

ORGANIZATIONAL CBIS SUCCESS is not necessarily reflected in the size of an organization's CBIS budget, the absolute number of CBIS applications, or the sophistication of acquired hardware. Rather, success is attained in the following situations:

- Information resources are used to increase organizational *effectiveness* and *efficiency* in those areas where it should be used,
- Particular attention is paid to areas *crucial* to organizational success,
- The investment in information resources provides a return consistent with other uses of investment funds.

The following organizations might be considered to be experiencing CBIS failure, regardless of the other CBIS applications each has implemented:

- An insurance company that does not use the information resource to support sales, claims handling, or actuarial analyses,
- A police department that does not use the information resource to support emergency services or manpower deployment,
- A retail store that does not use the information resource for cash or inventory management.

How does an organization audit itself to determine how successful it is? One strategy would be to identify the organization's critical success factors, examine how these might ideally be supported through TPS, IRS, DSS, and PDS applications, and periodically assess its actual CBIS portfolio against this ideal portfolio. A second strategy would be to state measurable CBIS objectives and then regularly assess whether or not these objectives have been achieved. A final strategy—the most common and easiest but least informative—would be to compare an organization's

CBIS budget to industry averages. While this may enable an atypical situation to be recognized, it does not address CBIS success in terms of *organization success*.

Because CBIS success cannot be separated from organization success, actions leading to CBIS success are quite context dependent. Nevertheless, general observations and guidelines can be offered. Common indicators, causes, and consequences of CBIS failures exist, and steps to follow in striving for CBIS success can be identified that are suitable to most organizations.

CBIS FAILURE

As discussed above, "CBIS failure" refers to an organization's inability to fully exploit the information resource. As with CBIS success, there are innumerable ways CBIS failures occur. Failure rarely arises because of one large and clearly identifiable misdirection of effort. Rather, it tends to result from a series of misdirections, most often traceable to lack of managerial attention to CBIS-related issues that should be addressed on a continual basis.

It is often difficult to recognize that information resources are not being managed well, particularly in organizations lacking a strong tradition of CBIS activity. Table 13.1 lists a number of *indicators* that an

TABLE 13.1
Indicators of CBIS Failure

Issue	Indicators
Hardware	Overutilization, underutilization, incompatible components, frequent component failures, numerous configuration changes, inability to easily upgrade or expand configuration
Software	High maintenance costs, late or overbudget development efforts, incompatibility, inflexibility, difficulty in modifying or enhancing, inadequate documentation, excessive backlog of development projects, old software products
Operations	Excessive reruns, missed schedules, inadequate response time or turnaround time, excessive errors (data entry and processing), inadequate documentation, lack of availability of CBIS products
Data	Nonexistent data items, inaccuracy, inaccessibility, inconsistent data files, lack of currentness, improperly measured data items
CBIS staff	High turnover, invisibility, rapidly increasing budget, extensive or inadequate use of consultants
Users and managers	Disinterest, distrust, fear, dissatisfaction, anger
Organization	Crisis atmosphere

organization is mishandling the information resource. These general issues should be periodically examined for signs of the indicators.

These indicators do not *explain* why failure has occurred; they only suggest its presence. If a number of indicators are evident, an effort should be made to diagnose the situation. Common causes of CBIS failures include a machine orientation; inadequate planning, requirements analyses, resource acquisition processes, technical capabilities, and user participation; and user–CBIS specialist conflict. Often these causes interact to influence CBIS activities, thereby making it difficult to pinpoint the reason for a deteriorating situation. A suggested strategy is to assess each possible cause whenever failure seems evident.

Machine Orientation

Because of their background and personality, many CBIS specialists, when given the option, are inclined to employ innovative and sophisticated information technologies to meet information requirements. This is fine as long as the design arrived at has proved more effective than alternatives and the risk inherent in this approach is recognized. Other behaviors reflecting a machine orientation are managerial emphasis on hardware or systems software efficiency, rather than organizational effectiveness (with new information resource economics, application software should drive CBIS activities), and an organizational philosophy that the proper role of CBIS is to replace organizational members, rather than to extend their capabilities.

Inadequate CBIS Planning

As brought out in Chapter 10, the dynamic and interdependent environments surrounding an organization's CBIS use make CBIS planning of paramount importance. All major decisions—creation of a master plan, hardware and software acquisition, project selection, feasibility analysis, etc.—must be formally addressed from an organization-wide perspective characterized by concern for the future.

Inadequate Requirements Analysis

If one does not allocate enough time or limits organizational representation when deriving information requirements, one will probably not produce clear, correct, consistent and complete requirements specification. As pointed out in Chapter 11, poor requirements lead to CBIS implementation problems, as well as a poor fit between the implemented CBIS and its organizational context.

Inadequate Resource Acquisition Processes

Much dissatisfaction with acquired hardware and software products could be eliminated if organizations approached the acquisition of information resources with the same fervor and conservatism demonstrated in acquiring other resources. Too often only a single vendor is contacted, vendor claims are taken at face value, and vendor-prepared preprinted contracts are accepted. As indicated in Chapters 2 and 12, organizations can do much to protect themselves when negotiating with hardware and software vendors.

Inadequate Technical Capabilities

A great deal of specialized skill, knowledge, and experience is required to successfully exploit information technologies. When an organization's use of information resources involves standard applications, much of the needed expertise can be borrowed from vendors and consultants. However, as information resources begin to be applied to CBIS applications that reflect unique organizational characteristics, organizational understanding becomes at least as important as technological understanding and the need for in-house capabilities intensifies. Substantial investments in human resources are required to implement those CBIS applications that tend to produce the largest organizational benefits.

Inadequate User Participation

It is very tempting for both CBIS specialists and users to allow the users to abdicate responsibility for the information resource: many CBIS specialists do not enjoy interacting with users, as it distracts them from technical tasks, and users have other tasks to accomplish that seem more pressing. Related to this is a tendency for organizations to make poor decisions when selecting project participants. The individuals assigned to implementation activities should be those who best understand the technical and organizational issues involved. Invariably, however, it is believed that such individuals cannot be spared from their primary organizational responsibilities. As a result, CBIS products are implemented that may prove adequate but that do not enhance organizational functioning to the extent possible.

User–CBIS Specialist Conflict

Users and CBIS specialists tend to differ in backgrounds, interests, and general outlook, which can result in communication difficulties that inhibit the cross-education so beneficial to CBIS implementation success. These differences can be reflected in approaches to problem solving, attitudes toward CBIS purpose and toward change, vocabularies, organizational loyalties, views of each other (values, interests, abilities, etc.), and so on. While these differences can be attributed primarily to educational and experiential factors that cannot be prevented, they are also influenced by factors that can be modified, such as reward systems, salary and status distinctions, task boundaries, and CBIS-related role assignments. The more users and CBIS specialists interact in purposeful ways, the more they can learn about and from each other.

Implications of Failure

Failures of CBIS tend to build on one another because of the interrelated nature of CBIS applications and the damaging impact of a series of failures on an organization's CBIS climate. Obvious implications of CBIS failure are the high costs that result and the projected benefits that are not realized. A deteriorating CBIS climate, however, has other effects that may prove even more damaging in the long run. Among them are the following:

- Retention of existing systems,
- Misuse or underuse of existing systems,
- Personnel disinterest in the information resource,
- Organizational distrust of the information function.

The following section discusses steps to take to improve an organization's CBIS climate.

CBIS SUCCESS STEPS

While this text has emphasized individual contributions to CBIS success, individual behaviors occur within specific organizational contexts. A negative CBIS climate can easily impede individual contributions or prevent them from occurring; a positive CBIS climate permits and enhances individual contributions. Prior to an examination of steps all organizations can take to improve their CBIS climate, a number of factors that moderate an organization's CBIS climate are introduced.

Moderating Factors[1]

Organizational size, environmental complexity and change, organizational structure, organizational time frame, and the availability of extra-organizational resources can affect organizational CBIS behaviors. Two facts, however, limit the actions that can be taken to resolve unsatisfactory situations: the time required to affect change is well beyond most CBIS project time horizons, and the information function can do little by itself to rectify the situation. These facts still must be considered in organizational CBIS planning, as they constrain organizational options and indicate where special emphasis must be placed to achieve CBIS success.

Organizational Size. Generally, the larger the organization, the more likely it will be to achieve CBIS success. There are a number of reasons for this:

- With organizational slack, more investment funds are available and riskier projects can be undertaken.
- With personnel economies of scale in effect, CBIS staff specialization can be pursued.
- With organizational specialization and impersonality, a need to understand and document organizational functioning arises independent of the CBIS function.

Smaller organizations, in contrast, tend to have fewer communication barriers, and their members usually have developed working relations with one another and are better able to relate their individual tasks to organization-wide functioning.

Environmental Complexity and Change. More complex, dynamic organizational environments provide ample opportunities to employ information resources for strategic, tactical, and operational purposes. Implementing such CBIS products, however, is difficult. The need to make modules of software and hardware elements and to provide integrative control structures consequently requires particular attention in planning and design.

Organizational Structure. Centralized organizations provide natural mechanisms for ensuring control and coordination of the information resource. Decentralized organizations, on the other hand, facilitate the delegation of decision-making responsibility to local units, where knowledge of organizational functioning is greatest. Each structure, thus, has advantages for CBIS-related activities. With each alternative, however, concern must be emphasized for the strengths of its opposite: centralized organizations must develop effective means of instilling local responsibility, and decentralized organizations must provide for a centralized control and coordination mechanism.

Organizational Time Frame. "Organizational time frame" refers to three timing characteristics of organizational decision making:

- The speed with which organizational members can react to problems and opportunities,
- The length of time until decision outcomes can be appraised,
- The overall pace of organizational life.

Because of cultural, industry, and organizational differences, considerable variations in time frames can be observed across organizations. The organizational time frame influences CBIS activity by affecting the determination of appropriate time horizons for a master plan, implementation effort, hardware acquisition, etc.

Extraorganizational Resources. Geographic location can severely limit an organization's CBIS capabilities if access to vendors, services, consultants, professional groups, CBIS specialists, etc., is difficult. In such cases, information and expertise must be acquired at far greater costs. Most likely, much information will not even be known to exist.

Creating a Positive CBIS Climate

All organizations can take five major steps to increase their likelihood of achieving CBIS success:

- Improve organization maturity,
- Improve CBIS maturity,
- Enhance relationships between the information function and the rest of the organization,
- Enhance the internal structure of the information function,
- Improve the psychological climate for CBIS.

While responsibility for effecting such changes lies with top management, the purposes and implications of these actions must be appreciated by all organizational members. Many seemingly minor actions taken by individuals throughout an organization can greatly ease the transitions involved and amplify the attained benefits.

Organizational Maturity. An effective CBIS product cannot be implemented without first achieving (and documenting) an understanding of organizational functioning. This means the following must be analyzed and expressed (for both the entire organization and each operating unit) in a clear, easily accessible form:

- Organizational purpose and objectives,
- Organizational strengths and weaknesses,
- Organizational resource availabilities,
- Key environmental factors,
- Key activities, tasks, and decisions,
- Major product, service, and resource flows,
- Captured (or capturable) data elements.

Such an understanding must exist when one develops a CBIS master plan, performs a feasibility study or a requirements analysis, evaluates a CBIS product, etc. The CBIS activity will be accomplished more smoothly, quickly, and (probably) successfully if a *formal* understanding of organizational function exists prior to initiation of the activity.

Consequently, any organization contemplating CBIS-related activities should ensure that an adequate level of organizational maturity (i.e., understanding of itself) exists. Are formal planning and control systems in place? How are such tasks handled? Do policy and procedure manuals exist? Are they current? Have service flows, work flows, material flows, transportation flows, etc., been detailed? Is the supporting documentation easily understood? Do current job descriptions reflect the actual tasks assigned to organizational members? This type of self-analysis should ideally be done independent of any CBIS implementations.

CBIS Maturity.   The more formal and disciplined CBIS activities are, the greater is the likelihood that CBIS outcomes will be comprehensive, consistent, forward-looking, compatible with organizational purpose, and consistent with one another. These activities cannot be handled in an ad hoc fashion. Well-defined procedures must be followed for all major CBIS activities, including master planning, hardware and software acquisition, project selection, feasibility analysis, requirements specification, CBIS evaluation, project planning and control, security and internal control, and software development.

Organizational Position of the Information Function.   Most organizations initially placed the information function in an existing operational area. This typically was the office of the controller, as accounting tended to be the first user of the information resource. In two recent trends, the organizational position of the information function is being established independent of any single functional area, and it is being placed higher in the organizational hierarchy. A number of reasons exist for each movement.

The need to establish an independent information function reflects the ever-enlarging scope of CBIS applications. The information resource cannot be viewed as primarily serving a single functional arm of the organization—it should be seen as being appropriately applied wherever the opportunities for achieving organizational success are greatest. Placing the information function within a particular operating area often results in an unbalanced CBIS portfolio, as the responsible area quite rationally uses the information function to serve its own functional or political purposes, as well as organization-wide purposes.

Rising CBIS budgets, the convergence of data, information, and word processing, recognition of the strategic role of information resources, and greater concern for the impact of information resources on an organization's "bottom line" have tended to raise the information function in the organizational hierarchy. Exactly where in the hierarchy the CBIS director is located depends on the organizational role played by information resources.[2] When information resources are used as competitive tools and comprise the primary mechanism driving organizational operations (as in banking), the information function should be located at the highest organizational level. When information resources are employed in supportive roles, it makes little sense to elevate the information function to such a high level.

There is another reason why many organizations elevate the CBIS director. Since the demand for information resources usually exceeds organizational resources, a considerable amount of negotiating and bargaining is involved in allocating information resources and services. To effectively engage in such activities, the CBIS director must have power comparable to that held by individuals (often vice-presidents) maneuvering to gain larger shares of information resources.

Another means of contending with the political maneuverings of organizational units is through the establishment of a CBIS *steering committee*. This is a top management coordination group that serves as a policymaking body and negotiating table for deciding issues related to CBIS plans, budgets, resource allocations, etc. Selecting people to serve on the steering committee is itself a political decision. Often both permanent and rotating positions are defined to prevent the bias that could arise if certain organizational functions were never represented on the steering committee.

Internal Structure of the Information Function. The internal structure of the information function involves two related issues. First, the information function is comprised of quite different functional units that might benefit from varied organizational structures. Second, CBIS-related decisions must be made throughout an organization. Exactly where major decision responsibilities lie must be determined.

A useful way of viewing the information function is to divide it into operations, implementation, and planning. Operations (data entry and storage, application processing, hardware maintenance, etc.) tend to be relatively stable, narrow in scope, predictive, and control oriented, so they might benefit from more mechanistic management structures and styles. Planning, on the other hand, tends to be relatively dynamic, broad in scope, futuristic, and politically oriented. Organic management structures and styles thus might prove most advantageous. Implementation falls between these two extremes. In efforts to structure the CBIS implementation function, two somewhat opposing aims are desired: encouraging creativity, openness, and concern for likely organizational or technological changes, and establishing standards and methodologies to follow to achieve the necessary discipline. Devising an appropriate structure for CBIS implementation, thus, is not easy. One solution is to allow for structural arrangements that vary with the implementation activity being pursued.[3,4]

In selecting an appropriate locus of CBIS decision making, one must consider the relative advantages of centralization (all CBIS activities directed by a central group) and decentralization (local units making their own CBIS-related decisions).[5,6] Centralization facilitates CBIS planning, control, and integration, all of which are critical to CBIS success. It also encourages the adoption of global rather than local perspectives and provides for certain economies of scale (particularly with regard to staffing the information function). Decentralization tends to result in quicker, more flexible, and more appropriate responses to local needs, as local decision-makers direct CBIS activities. It also establishes a sense of local accountability for the effective and efficient use of the information resource. (Furthermore, the adopted "locus of CBIS decision making" should be consistent with organizational policies on the centralization–decentralization issue.)

Clearly, certain elements of both centralization and decentralization are desirable. The following trends are taking place in many organizations:

- Central planning and coordinating groups are being established to ensure consistency among CBIS decisions to facilitate orderly movements toward achieving both organization-wide and local purposes,
- Centralized organizational systems groups are being established that provide the expertise needed for handling hardware and software acquisition, CBIS training, and technical assessment and for developing standards, and that are responsible for implementing and maintaining systems software and organization-wide applications software,

- CBIS operation and implementation, whenever possible and appropriate, are being decentralized.

The intent is to arrange decision-making responsibility to allow for overall coordination, staff economies of scale, and local autonomy and responsibility.

The difficulty in arriving at an appropriate structure can be seen in the organizational location of systems analysts. When all analysts are assigned to a central pool, specialization is permitted and peer interaction should maintain a stimulating technical environment. When analysts are hired and housed in operating units of an organization, they should be more responsive to organizational needs, as they have closer working relations with organizational members and a better understanding of organizational functioning, and are evaluated by operating unit management rather than CBIS management. Again, a variety of arrangements are possible. For example, analysts may reside in a central pool but develop continuing relationships with individual operating areas. In addition, a member of the operating area can serve as a "CBIS boundary spanner" for the area and establishes a close relationship with the analysts assigned to work on CBIS projects for that area. A side benefit of this user-liaison position is the use of such a role as a managerial training or development aid. Individuals assigned to such positions not only learn about information technology, but attain a thorough exposure to their operating area and a working understanding of most other organizational functions.

Psychological CBIS Climate.   As has been repeatedly emphasized, CBIS success ultimately depends on the individual behaviors of organizational members—users, managers, CBIS managers, and CBIS specialists. Participants in CBIS planning, implementation, and evaluation must perform their assignments to the best of their abilities and in a manner that reflects organizational objectives. Users must fully exploit the CBIS products available.

As shown in Figure 13.1, CBIS behaviors might be considered to evolve from individuals' predispositions to engage in their assigned tasks. Individuals' *commitments* to assigned tasks tend to be strongest when they believe it to be personally rewarding to contribute their time and effort. These predispositions toward CBIS behaviors reflect individuals' understanding of the likely implications of CBIS implementation participation or of a CBIS product's impact on the individuals' organizational roles. This knowledge of CBIS purpose and impact is believed to be derived from a variety of factors:

- Formal education or organizational training programs that touch on CBIS issues,

FIGURE 13.1
Factors Influencing CBIS Behavior

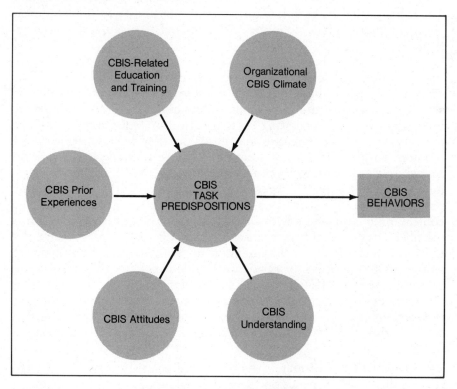

- Individual attitudes about CBIS purpose and CBIS-induced change,
- Prior CBIS implementation experience or CBIS product use.

All of these, however, are greatly influenced by the organization's CBIS climate:

- The clarity with which the CBIS purpose has been stated,
- The training provided on CBIS issues,
- The existence of reward systems that encourage CBIS participation and use,
- The provision of adequate resources to undertake CBIS activities,
- Visible expressions of top management support for CBIS behaviors,

- The establishment of structural arrangements that expose organizational members to the information function, that inform CBIS specialists about organizational purpose and functioning, and that encourage a sense of trust and mutual understanding among users and CBIS specialists,
- The existence of control mechanisms that encourage individual accountability for CBIS behaviors.

To illustrate how an organization's CBIS climate can be affected by management policies and actions related to these issues, the last will be discussed in some depth.

Most organizations have established internal budget and charging mechanisms to control information resources.[7,8] The objectives of such control mechanisms are three:

- To allocate the costs of providing CBIS products or services to organizational units,
- To allocate scarce information resources,
- To encourage more intelligent and responsible CBIS behavior.

While CBIS management tends to emphasize the first two objectives, the third makes by far the most valuable contribution.

Depending on how CBIS budgeting and information resource pricing are handled, a variety of behaviors can be produced:

- Users can be allocated CBIS-specific funds to encourage experimentation.
- Users can be forced to trade off using information resources against using other organizational resources, thus instilling an "investment alternatives" approach to CBIS decision making.
- Prices charged for particular information resources can be manipulated to encourage certain behaviors or to ration specific resources.

Charging systems can cover a variety of information resources—hardware, applications software, systems software, data sets, analyst or programmer time, etc. The point is that quite different behaviors can be triggered by different budget and charging systems.

CONCLUSION

Computer-based information systems success evolves from a series of interrelated decisions and actions by individuals and groups throughout an organization. All organizational members must contribute to this effort. Their behaviors will reflect global, local, and personal interests, hidden agendas, and organizational, personal, and environmental constraints. While a few guidelines can be offered that apply to most organizations, much CBIS behavior depends on the organizational and situational contexts. How well these contexts are diagnosed and responded to is determined by the abilities of organizational members to execute their own CBIS responsibilities, to be cognizant of the organization-wide implications of their behaviors, and to recognize the purposes of the CBIS-related actions of others throughout the organization.

KEY ISSUES

Organizational CBIS success reflects the extent to which information resources are used to promote organizational effectiveness and efficiency (particularly for those areas critical to organizational performance). Furthermore, investments in information resources should provide returns consistent with an organization's general investment policies.

Failure to achieve organizational CBIS success usually results from a series of misdirections, rather than one mistake.

The major causes of CBIS failures include the adoption of a machine orientation, inadequate planning, requirements analyses, resource acquisition processes, technical capabilities and user participation, and conflicts between users and CBIS specialists.

The importance of establishing an overall organizational climate conducive to CBIS success cannot be overemphasized.

The five major steps to take in establishing a favorable organizational climate include improving organizational maturity, improving CBIS maturity, enhancing relations between the information function and users, providing adequate organizational structures for handling CBIS responsibilities, and creating a psychological climate that encourages all organizational members to actively participate in CBIS activities.

An organizational climate favorable to CBIS success would be characterized by a clear understanding of CBIS purpose, adequate CBIS education programs, appropriate organizational structures, planning and control mechanisms and reward systems, and visible expressions of top management support.

DISCUSSION QUESTIONS

1. Suggest CBIS applications that would generally have to be implemented for each of the following organizations to experience CBIS success: an airline, a manufacturer of major appliances, a manufacturer of household cleaners, the tax office of a large county government, a large management consulting firm, and a savings and loan institution.
2. Would you expect highly professional CBIS specialists to exhibit a "machine orientation"? What are the organizational implications?
3. Suggest some actions an organization could take to reduce the potential for user–CBIS specialist conflict.
4. What are the long-term implications of an organization's decisions to retain existing systems, rather than engaging in periodic enhancements or redesigns of their CBIS?
5. What problems might a large organization face in CBIS implementation that would not be faced by a small organization? What problems might a smaller organization face that a large would not?

6. What CBIS implementation problems might be faced by organizations with fairly lengthy time frames? What about organizations with short time frames? In each case, provide an example of an organizational context that would apply.

7. Would you expect certain types of organizations, as a general rule, to be characterized by considerable immaturity? If so, give some examples.

8. Why is the accounting function usually the first to exploit the information resource?

9. Suggest some industries in which the information function might well be positioned at the vice-presidential level. Why?

10. There has been considerable dissatisfaction with executive CBIS steering committees because they often become involved with day-to-day decisions, rather than longer-term policy and strategic decisions. Why do you think this occurs?

11. Suggest some actions an organization's top management could take to demonstrate the importance it attaches to organizational efforts to make effective use of information resources.

12. How might an organization's reward systems discourage individuals (both CBIS specialists and users) from becoming actively involved in a variety of CBIS-related behaviors? Provide some specific illustrations.

BRIEF CASES

1. *Big Apple Promotions*
   In addition to formalizing the CBIS planning process, Bill Butler, president of Big Apple Promotions, believed it was necessary to establish some formal annual procedure by which the firm could assess its progress in using information resources. Exactly how this could be done was not obvious. The only data currently collected detailed the costs attributed to the provision of information services. Bill could compare this to industry averages published by the Association of Advertising Executives, but was unsure exactly what those statistics meant. If his costs were below the industry average for firms of a comparable size, it might mean he was being very efficient. However, it might just as well reflect that he was not making sufficient use of information resources.

   Propose a mechanism (or set of mechanisms) for Bill to use to implement an annual assessment of the success Big Apple Promotions was experiencing in using information resources. Be specific: identify the data to be collected and the information to be presented, and discuss what these information elements should indicate.

2. *Mountain Community Bank*
   The bank's vice-president of operations, Tom McClinton, was not satisfied with the way information systems were being implemented. On average, maintenance expenses were exceeding original development expenses within three years. The bank's inability to produce valid requirements specifications seemed to be the most likely explanation. What bothered Tom

most was that he had made a considerable effort to put together a comprehensive manual to follow in performing a requirements analysis. The procedures outlined in this manual incorporated most of the guidelines suggested by leading software development experts.

In thinking about this problem, Tom decided that perhaps the wrong users were being assigned to requirements analysis teams. A related notion was that even if the right individuals were assigned, they spent little real effort on their assigned tasks because of constant interruptions to handle problems back in their departments. Tom wondered what he could do to encourage departments to assign their best people to requirements analysis activities and to motivate these individuals to devote their considerable energies to the difficult task of specifying valid requirements.

Propose some actions that might induce the behaviors Tom is thinking about.

3. *Mercy Hospital*
The hospital's executive steering committee was involved in a very heated discussion. There was considerable dissatisfaction in some of the departments about the system analysis support they were receiving. (A full chargeback of system analyst support costs had recently been instituted.) The most common complaint was not that the analysts assigned to work on particular projects were incompetent, but that they spent a significant amount of time (which was charged against departmental operating budgets) learning about the functions to be automated and about the individuals who would be using the implemented CBIS. Currently, all the hospital's analysts worked out of a central pool. An effort was made to assign analysts with prior experience with a department to projects involving that department. However, this was often difficult, as required technical skills usually dictated analyst assignments.

Two alternatives, which were certainly not mutually exclusive, were being considered: revising the full chargeback policy or reorganizing the system analyst function.

Each alternative could be implemented in a variety of ways. Describe some variations of each, and discuss their advantages and disadvantages.

NOTES

1. P. Ein-Dor and E. Segev, "Organizational Context and the Success of Management Information Systems," *Management Science* 24(1978):1064–77.

2. W. McFarlan, "Merging the Islands of Information Service," paper given at Second International Conference on Information Systems, Boston, Dec. 8, 1981.

3. R. W. Zmud, "Management of Large Software Development Efforts," *MIS Quarterly* 4(1980):45–55.

4. R. W. Zmud, "The Diffusion of Modern Software Practices: Influences of Centralization and Formalization," *Management Science*, in press.

5. G. Glazer, "The Centralization vs. Decentralization Issue: Arguments, Alternatives, and Guidelines," *Data Base* 2(1970):1–7.

6. M. H. Olson and N. L. Chervany, "The Relationship Between Organizational Characteristics and the Structure of the Information Services Function," *MIS Quarterly* 4(1980):57–68.

7. R. W. Zmud, "Toward an Understanding of the Computer Center/User Interface," unpublished Ph.D. dissertation, University of Arizona, 1974.

8. R. L. Nolan, "Effects of Chargeout of User/Manager Attitudes," *Communications of the ACM* 20(1977):177–84.

MIS STRATEGIES

This final set of MIS Strategies illustrates some major issues discussed in Part 3, as well as current trends in the way leading organizations are managing the information resource. The importance of both valid requirements and user involvement to CBIS implementation success is clearly seen with Hughes Aircraft. It is also quite evident that, even with advanced software methodologies and tools, many organizations are having difficulty meeting the increased demand for information services. Software, accordingly, is increasingly being acquired rather than developed, and considerable end-user computing is occurring. An important innovation in this regard is the "information center" mentioned in both the City of Chicago and Bechtel strategies. Such an organizational facility provides hardware (terminals, microcomputers), software (very high level languages, application generators), and human (consultants, technicians) resources directly to end-users, thus bypassing the traditional (and lengthy) CBIS implementation process.

The importance of effectively attending to CBIS planning (Bechtel and AMF), organization (City of Chicago, Bechtel, AMF, and Hughes), and control (MCA, Bechtel, and AMF) is evident in these strategies. The decentralization trend with CBIS decision making is shown, as is the desirability of maintaining a central policy group and a central technical service group. Finally, the importance of establishing a favorable CBIS climate (for both end-users and computer specialists) is seen with MCA and AMF. The closing comments by the MIS vice president of AMF suggest an appropriate role for the information function throughout the 1980's, to serve as a "liaison between the machines and management."

Inner Fraternity Builds Success at AMF

Ray Babayan will tell you that the most important contribution he's made at AMF Inc. is probably building an MIS fraternity among technologists and management within the large, decentralized corporation.

As MIS vice president for the White Plains, N.Y.-based conglomerate over the past 10 years, Babayan could easily point first to other, more tangible successes than that.

For example, he might mention that "over the years, we've saved over $6 million in hardware costs by being able to control the hardware environment."

He could also produce figures that would show a million-dollar-a-year (annualized) savings since 1974 when a Rolm Corp. telecommunications division computerized telephone system was installed at headquarters, replacing an AT&T system.

It is now also in place in most of AMF's 35 domestic and 25 foreign divisions. "No matter what Bell comes up with now," Babayan emphasizes, "we've gotten our money back and saved a lot in the process."

Another obvious success is in the Westbury, N.Y., corporate data center, which "has 14 fewer people than it did 10 years ago and does twice as much work—but the cost has remained the same."

The 31-person staff operates and maintains an IBM 370/145, which runs one of two centralized reporting systems (a corporate financial application), and also does cash management for the bowling division headquartered there.

Plus, the $18 million MIS budget (total corporation and divisions) is only 1.164 percent of corporate revenues, which Babayan claims is "low compared to decentralized corporations in general [based on a Diebold Inc. survey that comes out once every two years]."

Yet Babayan is convinced that none of this would have been possible without the "spirit of cooperation that began slowly but has been solid for the past five years."

In a rather unexpected way, Babayan's nontechnical background prepared him for his role as an MIS director, where he has to ride herd on a diverse collection of basically unrelated manufacturing operations that range from sports equipment to industrial products.

"I didn't know a thing about computers when I started. My background was in systems and controls," he remembers. He began as an accountant with AMF nearly 35 years ago, rising through the ranks of the corporate staff controller's office to director of internal audit, the post he held in 1970 when tapped for the MIS position.

His predecessors "were all technicians in charge; there had been five different MIS directors in each of the five years prior to my appointment," he says. "What turned out was that—luckily—what was needed was a businessman, an administrator."

But luck apparently had little to do with Babayan's subsequent successes. One of his first moves was to get the MIS section out from under the controller's office and into the administrative area.

"My own background and knowledge of the company said, 'Let's go where the money really is.' And," he continues, "since two thirds of the revenue is figured against manufacturing costs in this company, how we process paper—how we handle financial applications, the main interest of the controller's department—is secondary to manufacturing, marketing, and distribution applications."

Next, Babayan took the IBM executive training course and went around from division to division, educating himself. Then, with input from group and corporate executives, a strategy evolved.

That strategy, created in 1970, appears as relevant today as it proved to be then. It included:

• A budget control program, begun almost as soon as Babayan took over. "For the first time, this quantified the cost of our data processing operation," he notes.

• Three-year corporate and divisional plans were created, as well as group and divisional steering committees consisting of corporate MIS, divisional MIS and business unit managers.

• An educational program based on the IBM course Babayan attended was instituted for business-unit managers and corporate management.

• An MIS audit. "We called it a 'review' for psychological reasons, and set up the parameters for what are really operational audits—physically done in the factories—rather than financial audits, done by checking figures at headquarters."

• An application profile was created in 1971, listing all available applications company wide. Today that list comprises nearly 150 programs.

• "Most important," he says, "we instituted MIS conferences in 1970, including divisional MIS, corporate MIS, and business-unit managers. Here's where we began to create the fraternity, to exchange ideas and systems."

Babayan says today that the corporate MIS function is actually "centralized monitoring of our decentralized operations." Through the simple—in retrospect—creation of those MIS conferences in 1970, corporate MIS began to fulfill that definition.

A complete overview of the hardware and software applications environments at all divisions has resulted, enabling corporate MIS to administer them centrally. Corporate approval for all hardware and software expenditures is mandatory as well.

Babayan contends that the business knowledge could not have been effectively applied to the corporation without the confidence built up through close interaction of the corporate MIS staff and the divisions.

"It took years to build up the fraternity," he notes, "but now there is an open exchange of ideas between corporate MIS and the business unit MIS and group executives." Central to that communication is the corporate MIS consulting group—five men—who report to the several business unit heads they service, but who also have a strong dotted-line relationship to Babayan's office.

"They're always on the road, in constant touch with the business units they are responsible for," he says. "Each one has several of the 35 domestic business units and visits each unit about four times a year. They help with budgets, plans, and have complete knowledge of systems and hardware environments. That gives us continuing flexibility and control over equipment growth and selection, as well as the software environment.

The fraternity, Babayan believes, has made it easier to justify "taking a chance"—like going with Rolm equipment over Bell's, or buying a $20,000 software package from a one-man "garage" operation several years ago that today sells for over $250,000. "The trust is there, so we can try new things."

One of the newest things coming along for Babayan is office automation, and he appears to be taking a characteristically calm approach.

"Office automation, I believe, is another function of MIS, but it's still in the embryonic stage. Word processing applications are just the beginning.

"Each department has so far justified its own machines, according to their needs. And we've put out a letter to each department asking them to go slow, realizing there are no long-term answers yet.

"But it appears," Babayan says, "that equipment purchase should come after the decision-making process, and not the other way around. So we've got a project team together to figure out how office automation, telecommunications, and MIS will fit into the future."

That future appears strong for Babayan and AMF, even though he had his doubts about it 10 years ago. "We started out with a wealth of ignorance. But we've become translators, liaison between the machines and management."

Chicago's City MIS Effort: Bring Power to Users

The director of MIS operations for America's second largest city cites the programmer shortage as the major challenge facing corporate and municipal MIS departments alike, and the reason why the city has embarked on an effort to move computing power to users.

"The problem is more industry-wide than specific to government, and we are trying to find very-high-level software to allow non-DP personnel to use the software and set up their own systems," says Danielle Barcilon, director of the city of Chicago's data center.

"Perhaps companies can afford to pay more, and maybe the shortage hits governments a bit harder, but we all have to find ways to make people more productive."

"Many of our older systems still have big batch processes that we perform at night, but our newer systems have a larger on-line component," she says. For instance, a recently developed system to keep track of water bill collection is largely on-line, and a system to keep track of complaints against the sewer department is also transactional.

Another example of this variety is a system that supports the city's health department, which keeps track of services offered to the public and what drugs and pharmaceutical products were dispensed. "Each department is like a separate line of business, if you wish, and has very diversified needs," she says.

The city's police department has the most autonomous DP operation of the various agencies, yet Barcilon points to close links between it and her staff.

"They have unique needs and applications, but we jointly plan equipment purchases because we need a lot of input from them when we plan for capacity," she says.

One way to make programmers more productive is to use high-level software tools that can ease the pressure of application backlogs. Another way Barcilon spurs productivity in the data center is through the use of laser printing devices that help with the enormous output requirements sometimes generated by city jobs.

An example of such a job is the annual preparation of the city's budget, which requires the printing of 200 bound copies of the budget document within 48 hours of its release by the budget office. These copies, formerly produced by a professional printer, are now produced by Barcilon's department at a tremendous cost savings.

"Sometimes I wonder whether I am in the printing business or the DP business," she says. "We do a lot of things that are a combination of text and data processing, and the line between the two is increasingly gray, especially with the use of laser printers."

The creation of the city's budget was also eased by the use of an interactive budgeting system that allows Mayor Jane M. Byrne and her staff to look at the consequences of different courses of action.

"It makes a big difference if you can tell the effect of a different approach quickly and easily, especially in light of the current financial climate," Barcilon says.

"Funding is getting tight all the way around, and it is important for a city to know the impact of alternative plans. To some extent, that consideration affects our planning, but our emphasis on productivity is more a reflection of the continuing problem of finding good people."

Barcilon heads a staff of over 60 programmer/analysts, a staff she describes as lean, "when you consider how many city departments we serve." She estimates that the data center serves between 25 and 30 city agencies at any one time.

Some of these agencies have their own data processing personnel and development teams, but it is up to the data center to develop most city systems and to run them on its IBM 3081 Model D computer. Barcilon says the center runs more than a thousand applications at various times for the city's agencies.

"Most people who visit me have no idea what we do and suppose that we do only straight accounting applications," she says. "But we have an interesting variety of applications that support the different activities of the city government.

"A great many of our systems deal with the functions of the city government, such as building code enforcements, permit issuances, the collection of water bills, license fees, and taxes." Although most of these systems are batch-oriented, new development efforts are stressing on-line capability.

"Many of our older systems still have big batch processes that we perform at night, but our newer systems have a larger on-line component," she says. For instance, a recently developed system to keep track of water bill collection is largely on-line, and a system to keep track of complaints against the sewer department is also transactional.

Another example of this variety is a system that supports the city's health department, which keeps track of services offered to the public and what drugs and pharmaceutical products were dispensed. "Each department is like a separate line of business, if you wish, and has very diversified needs," she says.

The city's police department has the most autonomous DP operation of the various agencies, yet Barcilon points to close links between it and her staff.

"They have unique needs and applications, but we jointly plan equipment purchases because we need a lot of input from them when we plan for capacity," she says.

Barcilon explains that the use of productivity-enhancing software tools provides that flexibility and will prove a benefit to the city while relieving some of the pressure on the data center staff.

"We need to be able to provide services and to respond to requirements without a lot of lead time, and to do that you need flexibility.

"It's going to put the computer closer to the user, and often to let him make his own inquiry or report. If we can limit our involvement to ensuring up-to-date files, backups, etc., that is good use of our technical people. Making one-time reports is not."

Barcilon says the city follows classical programming and testing strategies when developing new systems that are "pretty much the same here as everywhere else." But the data center tries to use very-high-level programming aids whenever possible to speed up the development process.

For instance, the city has had "good success" developing systems with IBM's CICS transaction processing monitor, yet uses products that help put together CICS-oriented systems faster.

"In the cases where we've begun to use these things, we are very pleased with the results," she says.

Although the use of these software tools forces "a trade-off between hardware efficiency and getting things done," it helps the data center answer the city's need for a flexible DP response.

The customer services division of the data center's staff helps users develop their own information systems and reports.

She says this approach is borrowed from IBM's Information Center idea, which emphasized the importance of making data available quickly to managers.

"In terms of strategy, we are trying to go to the information center idea put forth by IBM, and have employed some of the concepts for our statistical jobs," Barcilon says.

By William P. Martorelli. From *Information Systems News,* May 3, 1982. Copyright © 1982 by CMP Publications, Inc. Reprinted by permission.

MCA Gets Results with Cost Justification

Keeping MIS costs under control is mostly a matter of knowing when to say "no" to users and "yes" to MIS department employees, according to Al Jerumanis, director of corporate data processing at MCA Inc.

Jerumanis' credentials as a cost controller are indisputable. In the eight years since he took over MCA's MIS operation in Universal City, Calif., the firm's revenues have grown at a 20 percent clip, while MIS costs have risen at a 9.5 percent rate. Adjusting for inflation, MCA spends less on MIS today than it did the day Jerumanis arrived.

Despite cost controls—or perhaps because of them—he notes that, in terms of users served and information processed, MCA is getting more out of the department now than it did then.

In just the last three years, Jerumanis has expanded the user base from corporate financial people and division controllers to a wide range of MCA divisions, by providing systems for hotel reservations at Yosemite, as well as an extra casting system, a studio call-sheet system, and a scheduling system for vehicles and teamster drivers.

The accomplishment takes on added luster when MCA's MIS expenditures as a percentage of revenues are compared to a dozen other firms in the entertainment business. In a study prepared from information provided by an outside consulting firm, Jerumanis found that the median expenditure level of competing firms was above 1 percent, with the highest at 1.45 percent. At MCA, the figure is 0.45 percent of revenue spent on MIS.

There is no simple explanation for his department's record, Jerumanis insists; instead, there are a variety of factors which, acting together, have produced a cost-effective MIS operation.

First and foremost, he said, is his absolute insistence on cost justification for all new systems development.

"Unless a responsible executive can translate the benefit into dollars, we won't touch it," Jerumanis said.

"We do feasibility studies. If the dollars won't come, if the payback is too far out—we won't do it. The payback can't be over three years."

The short payback horizon stems from the nature of the entertainment business, which provides three quarters of MCA's revenue, Jerumanis noted.

An industry tied so directly to the public taste, he said, must be "opportunistic" in the positive sense of the word, ready to shift resources rapidly from one area to another to meet sudden shifts in demand. Those frequent, sudden shifts mean a short life for many systems.

"If a system can't cut it in three years, we'll never see the dollars," he believes. "We'll have to make five changes in it, and the volume will either double or drop to one-quarter."

In fact, he added, most projects must offer a one-year payback because, "with 20 percent money, we can't afford to drag it out."

Marginal requests, unless they come with powerful backing from senior officials, are "put on the shelf."

Saying "no" to unprofitable work explains a large part of his department's efficiency, Jerumanis believes, but so does a satisfied work force. "We run a large shop with a small staff," he stated, with a management philosophy that says "yes" to professionals, who may be used to hearing "no" more often elsewhere when it comes to requests for odd working hours, high pay, or assignments that match their skills and interests.

Such freedoms might be difficult to grant in a typical MIS operation, but Jerumanis feels his insistence on hiring only "quality" people gives him more management latitude.

"We do not, as a rule, hire junior people in any category," he said. "We limit ourselves to hiring super programmers and gurus. It works well, and there is a tremendous payoff" in productivity.

On the flip side, he said, he and his managers are faced with the awesome task of riding herd on "45 prima donnas" when it comes to programmers and analysts.

He found it somewhat easier to describe what he does not do to manage his people than what he does do.

"I am not taking a close administrator's position. I don't stand out there with a stopwatch, checking to be sure the programmers are all here at 9 A.M. If they say they are going to be done by noon, I don't care if they come in at 7, 8, or 9, as long as the work is done."

There are some limits on management prerogatives, since data-entry clerks, computer operators, and programmers (but not analysts) are represented by the Office and Professional Employees International Union, Local 174. He said the union restricts arbitrary management actions, but no more so than a good manager would restrict them anyway.

Unionization has not been a problem, Jerumanis said, since it basically means, "if we bring someone in on Saturday that we'll have to pay double time to, we make sure it is someone who can earn their keep" by doing work twice as well.

Most important, Jerumanis tries to use good psychology to keep his staff happy. For analysts and programmers, this means "assessing their skills and our requirements" and looking for "a better match, a closer move to utopia."

Another technique is to recognize that most programmers and analysts "don't like to do grunt work"—specifically, maintenance of existing systems.

Although he disclaims having any particular secret for MIS cost control, Jerumanis proudly points to a single policy that he finds reduces maintenance work as well as reruns and pleases employees by freeing them for more interesting tasks: the originator of a system is permanently in charge of maintenance of that system.

"The best way to eliminate grunt work is to eliminate maintenance, to make sure old systems never come back to haunt you. The way you do that is to make sure you don't build yourself into the system."

Placing maintenance responsibility on the designer and creator of a system, he said, "causes some very creative things to happen."

For one thing, "production programs are sacred." Motivated by a desire not to be awakened at 3 A.M. by a problem with JCL, programmers and analysts create systems that "consistently require fewer than 1 percent reruns," according to Jerumanis.

Part of the creator's responsibility is to provide operator instructions so clear that "the recipient of the system knows how to run it flawlessly." The minimum standard for operating instructions is set by SDM 70, a product of Atlantic Software Inc., as modified by MCA, Jerumanis said.

But operating instructions almost always go beyond the minimum standard—in large part, Jerumanis believes, because of the built-in incentive of personal responsibility.

He takes that responsibility seriously, and makes sure his analysts do, too. The message for programmers: "I don't care if you are in Ohio on vacation. I paid good money for you to design this system. It doesn't work: Why?" Jerumanis concluded, "I don't let them off the hook."

Such a system might seem to be a surefire way to generate large turnover, but the benefits apparently outweigh the costs, he noted, since turnover in the time he has run the department has been under half the industry average of 30 percent per year.

At one time, Jerumanis said, he tried measuring lines of code produced, but discarded that as a measure of professional productivity, choosing instead to focus on whether, over time, programmers and analysts complete systems within the time budgeted.

Incentives for the clerical staff are based on directly measured productivity, he said, a system that has allowed MCA to reduce its data-entry clerk population from 56 in 1973 to 24 in 1981, while handling a triple volume of work.

The cost savings were not proportional to the reduction in staff, according to Jerumanis, because "our pay scales are excellent, with incentive pay on top of that."

He said MCA does not "hire any well-intentioned housewife that comes in," but instead limits itself to hiring "people who can do entry quickly, with both hands."

The incentive system is based on the productivity of the top 20 percent of the staff. While stringent, it has resulted in MCA retaining "the type of person who appreciates the challenge."

An outsider could easily imagine that working in the MIS department at MCA might be different from working in an MIS department at any other company. In some ways it is, but in some ways it is not. "The glamor wears off after three days, and isn't a factor in recruiting," Jerumanis believes.

His office, for example, like those of many MIS directors, is a windowless basement room near the computers. But his walls feature movie posters and paintings by movie art directors.

Finally, as a reporter was leaving the office recently, he asked about a blue binder, the likes of which he had not seen before in the office of any other MIS director. "It's a script they want me to read," said Jerumanis, one with a story centered around computer fraud.

By Paul E. Schindler, Jr. From *Information Systems News*, August 12, 1981. Copyright © 1981 by CMP Publications, Inc. Reprinted by permission.

Bechtel Disperses MIS Support

Last year Bechtel Group Inc., the largest privately held construction corporation in the world, was engaged in more than 100 major engineering and construction projects ($50 million and up) in 29 countries, and each required some form of MIS support.

Managing the information systems requirements for such a widely dispersed company calls not only for decentralized hardware and systems, but careful planning and—most important—a decentralized MIS organization, according to Donald E. Fowler, manager of information services at Bechtel Power Corp., the Bechtel unit that provides MIS services for the entire $11 billion (sales) organization.

Detailed strategic and tactical planning, moreover, is allowing for the smooth introduction of highly sophisticated communications networks, processing nodes, and special applications.

MIS at Bechtel has been distributed in recent years, according to Fowler, more accurately to reflect the distributed nature of the company. Nearly half his staff is now situated outside the headquarters complex in San Francisco.

Fowler has 1,500 DP professionals in his charge. "We position support directly with the users. We give them sufficient resources to meet their daily needs, including operating people, programmers, and system analysts," he said.

The typically small staff found in each division cannot develop expertise in all areas, he noted, so the technical support group at headquarters backs them up in specialized areas like networking and training.

Although each division effectively has its own DP shop, "the standards, guidelines, and procedures are developed centrally."

"Six years ago we were organized like most departments, with a COBOL group, a FORTRAN group, and an operating system group. Then we reorganized so that one group, say, supported personnel. In that group were people for the operating system, the language, and the hardware.

"Those groups were still located in the data center. Starting three years ago, we began to move them to the divisions. Then last year, we cemented the process with the designation of Division Information Services."

The Division Information Services organization was not deployed at user sites overnight, Carl D. Eben hastened to add. The manager of planning and research for information services said, "We have had small groups deployed for years," but the process was not pushed until three years ago.

Eben said the move toward deployment of support personnel was positive for MIS and users alike. "In general, it is hard for our MIS employees to see the product," especially when they are based in San Francisco.

Although placing MIS personnel in divisions does not mean they get to see every project, they do see many more than they did before, and the result is a greater sense of participation and a broader understanding of what the company does.

That, Eben added, has resulted in "reduced turnover among DP personnel."

From the user standpoint, the new arrangement allows them to "feel much more in control. They do not feel they are sending their requirements into some monolithic building, where we will do it when we get around to it."

There has been a pleasant side effect to that feeling, too, he said. "Before, when there was a conflict of priorities versus resources, they felt uninvolved. Now the user is in the middle, and he is much more realistic and understanding because he feels part of the process."

At Bechtel, planning stems from two functional strategies laid down in 1978: that the firm will have a worldwide communications network, and that processing will be decentralized when appropriate.

From these strategies flow annual corporate objectives, which are translated within the company into divisional objectives and then into divisional operating plans, which are integrated into the corporate MIS plan.

Planning and organization, he said, allow him to "forestall knee-jerk reactions to data processing problems."

The divisional operating plans are implemented by the division information services organization, comprising DP people who are nominally part of the MIS operation but take their daily marching orders from operational managers in the divisions.

The communications network strategy called for establishment of four major international nodes, Fowler said—in Hong Kong, San Francisco, London, and Bahrain. They are to be linked eventually by 56K-bit-per-second lines; at present the Hong Kong-to-San Francisco and San Francisco-to-London satellite links are on order.

The strategy also called for "upgrading the spaghetti communications network we developed over the years." A major step in that direction, according to Fowler, was the recent signing of a contract with Satellite Business Systems to link Bechtel's five major U.S. offices—in San Francisco; Ann Arbor; Gaithersburg, Md.; Los Angeles; and Houston—with a 1.544M-bit network.

"Although there will be some short-term savings in cost, that is not the main reason" for going to SBS, Eben said. "We will have more capability."

Once each of the five offices has its own satellite dish, it will be able to use that large, switchable bandwidth for voice and data communications as well as for teleconferencing and other communications.

The eventual goal is to provide lower-speed links from each job site to the nearest major node, where communications will be multiplexed for transmission to and from San Francisco, Fowler said.

The other major strategy developed in 1978 was to "establish a distributed processing system, with the bulk of the processing power remaining in a major data center." That center, now located in San Francisco, is slated to move soon to an as yet unselected suburban location.

The DDP strategy calls for "installation of computer power at local sites to solve their specific and unique problems," according to Fowler.

One location for distributed processing is at job sites, which Fowler said are often so large they can easily justify their own local processing for strictly local information, such as scheduling and payroll. Those sites formerly had IBM System 3 processors (as many as 56 at one time) and now use System/34 and System/38 processors.

Another type of system Bechtel is in the process of distributing is computer-aided drafting. There are 23 stand-alone systems in the company, made by Intergraph, Autotrol, Computervision, and Design Graphix.

Fowler wants to hook them to the network so they can interact with design and analysis programs on the mainframe and "become true computer-aided design systems, rather than just computer-aided drafting."

Also part of the distributed processing plan is Bechtel's increasing use of IBM's Information Center concept, a package of software programs that enables users to gain access to information without programmer assistance.

Eben noted that Bechtel has gotten "a foot in the door" of that concept through use of Univac's Mapper software to provide users with access to data bases maintained on the firm's large contingent of Univac mainframes.

As a result of emerging needs, Eben said, Bechtel has decided to continue to use Univac for engineering applications, which represent the bulk of its processing requirements, but to move administration and financial systems onto IBM computers over the next several years.

Thus, since most ad hoc queries are made against financial systems rather than engineering systems, he expects use of Mapper to wind down and use of the Information Center to increase as the programs are moved.

Fowler considers the two strategies to be essential to the planning process. "Given the strategies, we set goals. First, long-range goals, which contribute directly to fulfilling the strategies. Then, each year we set objectives." For example, the 1982 MIS department objectives include:

- Provide deployed information services functions.
- Establish services and productivity measures for information services.
- Establish and implement training programs for executives, managers, and professionals.
- Continue implementation of the integrated worldwide communications network.
- Evaluate and recommend new pricing, billing, and reporting methods more equitably to recover software costs and value-added features.
- Expand support of microcomputers.
- Minimize the number of vendors of duplicate products and services.
- Increase information services' coordination of outside service bureau use.

Once the MIS objectives are set, in June of the preceding year, they are sent out to user divisions with a package of information, according to Eben. These include historic data and instructions to aid divisions in developing their own objectives and operating plans.

The plans are due back in September, he said. Typically, a division will have 10 or 15 objectives, and perhaps 200 activities it expects to undertake to meet those objectives.

Although money is discussed, it is not the source of discord at Bechtel that it is at some companies, Eben said. The MIS department bills divisions for their use of shared MIS resources and the divisions bill customers for project-related DP costs.

"So, if a division manager says he needs 52 data-entry people next year instead of the 32 he had last year, fine. But he better have work for the 52, or his budget goes to pieces, and eventually so does ours."

Still, although MIS is run like a break-even service bureau, it still must integrate the departmental plans, Eben noted.

"We must ensure their objectives are consistent with ours. We must make sure the activities they plan will meet those objectives and are not either underkill or overkill. We must make sure the plans are consistent, that we are all pulling in the same direction."

The role of the planning and research section of MIS, Eben said, is to look for conflicts in the area he cited and bring them to management attention. It is assuredly not to dictate solutions.

"Divisions are interested in getting things done for their projects. They tend to look at their projects first and at standard needs second. We don't dictate—but we do try to anticipate their needs, so we can be there first, offering solutions before they have to ask for them."

Although Bechtel's highly autonomous structure contributes to the inability of the MIS department to dictate the kind of hardware a division will use, there is also the "customer is always right" factor.

Since virtually all of Bechtel's work is done for customers on a contract basis, if the customer insists a certain kind of computer hardware be used on the job site, that is the kind that will be used, Eben said.

In addition, if the division decides, even without customer pressure, to ignore the advice of the MIS department and buy an "Oddball 100" piece of hardware, MIS will still provide support, he noted.

"We don't know that hardware as well, so the support is not as deep as it could be for something we know better, but we'll still support it," he said.

Eben feels the planning process generally works pretty well, but sees the forecasting aspects as in need of improvement.

"Forecasting is very important but very difficult," he said. Division forecasts are used to predict the need for hardware and staff in the central MIS operation.

"Generally, they forecast flat demand. Yet for at least the last five years, actual demand shows a 40 percent annual growth rate." So, starting with the 1983 process this June, Eben plans to introduce some feedback into the system.

Simply put, when the packet goes out to the divisions, it will include last year's planned and actual figures. "Instead of coming up with a new plan each year, we will ask them to base their next plan on their previous plan."

Summing up the benefits of planning, Fowler said, "When a new requirement comes along, be it a new project or a new application, we have a mechanism to determine the proper response. We have a road map that provides us a context to place it into."

By Paul E. Schindler, Jr. From *Information Systems News*, March 8, 1982. Copyright © 1982 by CMP Publications, Inc. Reprinted by permission.

Hughes Unit Involves Users in Data Base Design

The Space and Communications Group of Hughes Aircraft Company has found that while data base technology is a blessing to corporate MIS, learning to employ it properly presents a complex management task in itself.

This lesson was learned during recent attempts to upgrade the systems that support construction of the group's primary product—communications satellites— and to prepare for a contract with Intelsat to build at least five spacecraft over the next several years, spacecraft that may be worth in excess of $1 billion in sales to the Culver City, Calif., firm.

"Data base management software has been around for 20 years, and we always knew it wouldn't solve all of our problems," says George Emmanuel, manager of data base information systems. "One of our fundamental lessons has been that data base technology is a useful tool, but if you use it as a hammer, you think everything is a nail," he says. "And not all our problems are nails."

Emmanuel says there are always three perspectives to data base development: that of the data processing department, that of management, and that of the actual user. The problem with most development efforts and commercially available data base systems, he says, is that they do not provide a combination of these three perspectives.

"In our view the English language itself is a limitation, because words vary so much in their meaning to different individuals."

Also, he says, "the business world in our environment is not a hierarchy, which is what many data base systems are geared for, but a network. And we wanted to move toward a network data relationship to reflect the real world. We selected IDMS from Cullinane Database Systems Inc. and have decided that it was the correct choice."

He has gleaned from his work another maxim—"the chief contributor to disaster is not what we don't know, but what we think we know that is not really so."

That view grew out of Hughes' recent attempts to provide data processing support for the construction of the firm's complex products, and the memory of a prior unsuccessful attempt to develop an automated manufacturing system without data base technology.

"Several years ago we attempted to design a manufacturing planning and control system, but when we completed it we had to discard our work," says Louis Kauffman, director of management systems. "We thought we heard what the user asked for, and we thought we delivered what the user wanted, but found out that it was inadequate."

The result was a "severe trauma" that led to the departure of many of the programmers and analysts who worked on the system. "They felt they were not rewarded for the good work they did, and they were right," Kauffman says.

The lessons Hughes learned in that episode are now applied to current development efforts. Chief among these are the importance of user involvement and the value of data base management, if used properly.

"We discovered we did not use the right technology. We were trying to work in the file management, not the data base world, and we also learned we had to have more user involvement," Kauffman says.

"We absolutely had to find a way to document as we went along. If you don't document when you install the system, the documentation will lag and you may never catch up."

A partial answer to Hughes' problem was Cullinane's IDMS system. However, the proper sequencing of activity and resisting the tendency to equate physical code with progress are also key considerations. "Several times we have delayed important milestones to get user participation and approval," Kauffman says.

Emmanuel says, "We disagree with the emphasis to get into physical coding as soon as possible, because the construction of network relational data bases is no longer a black art. It's getting easier and easier, and we prefer to spend our resources up front in the definition of the problem."

Kauffman explains that the Space and Communications Group's MIS operation has three major focuses—the administrative, financial, and product information systems areas. The last currently comprises the majority of the group's work.

"Our task is to provide systems for the management of our product, as well as to support the business functions of our organization," says Kauffman. "We do some of the administrative and financial systems, but not all of them.

"It is our long-range strategy to assume responsibility for all of those functions. However, since we are a group embedded within a corporation, many things that are the responsibility of the corporation are performed on the corporate level."

Carl Reynolds, staff vice-president for communications and data processing at Hughes corporate, says that last year Hughes spun off four separate business units out of what had been a completely centralized organization. That has provided little time for the firm's MIS arm to follow suit, he says.

"And we didn't want to rush hell-bent to get rid of all the systems that might more properly belong to the divisions. Instead, we try to evolve in a sensible way, and we're not rushing into it. Hughes' overall corporate philosophy is decentralization, and the firm's MIS activities have to support that philosophy."

Although Kauffman's group reports to its own group executives, and not to Reynolds' department, there is a "dotted line" relationship between the two groups that calls for regular interaction.

"We meet every month and try to work together as best we can," says Reynolds.

But it is more than the company's philosophy of decentralization that will bring added responsibility for financial and administrative systems to Kauffman's group.

"As we develop systems for the management of customer contracts, we have to depend on administrative and financial systems to interface with our product management systems, and they are becoming more and more entwined," he says. "We are not yet substantially into those types of systems—but we will be."

Until the firm's decentralization takes hold within MIS, Kauffman's primary role will be to manage development of the firm's products, a task heightened in importance since the firm won the Intelsat contract.

Kauffman explains that unlike many other aerospace companies, Hughes does a substantial amount of work for nongovernment customers, in addition to work for the federal government.

"We are not a typical aerospace company," he says. "The most substantial part of our business is fixed-price and commercial."

Because of the emphasis on cost control that fixed-price contracts bring, Hughes' Space and Communications Group has attempted to integrate engineering, manufacturing, and materials functions as a major component of its information processing activity.

"The product has to be extraordinarily integrated, since we are dealing with very high-tech stuff," he says. "There is a big overlap between engineering and manufacturing here, and since we only build a few of anything we make, we don't think the management of inventories is quite as critical."

Several years ago, Kauffman discovered that the existing systems designed to control engineering and manufacturing were not sufficient to the needs imposed by the firm's products. That discovery led to the ill-fated development effort.

"We found that we had some inadequate tools in the manufacturing and testing of our product, and it is primarily in this area that we are now emphasizing the data base philosophy that we hope will move us out of our 'dark ages'," he says.

Crucial to this philosophy is a data base methodology that truly reflects the relationships between data and provides for the extensive flexibility Hughes requires, while avoiding problems inherent in data base design.

The result has been a methodology that Kauffman calls "somewhere beyond the leading edge," that is primarily administered by Emmanuel.

"The reasons why we sometimes fail are the same reasons why business often has a low esteem for MIS. Because we are still too often concerned with establishing the inputs required first and then building our systems. However, inputs and outputs are dynamic, while we as MIS managers have largely built only for predictable problems," Emmanuel says.

"We now build data bases to reflect the true relationship of the data, and if we can link data sufficiently, we can answer any question."

By William P. Martorelli. From *Information Systems News,* May 17, 1982. Copyright © 1982 by CMP Publications, Inc. Reprinted by permission.

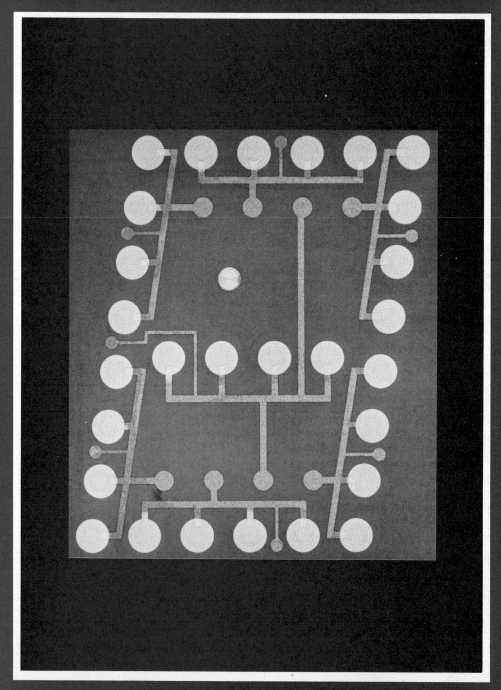

1970.
The industry's first monolithic planar numeric display. Appropriate segments of the 7-segment display illuminate to form numerals. Used in calculators and other digital readouts.

Cases 4

TOPIC: **Background on MTA and MIS Project**   November 10, 198_

FROM: Data Systems Branch Chief

TO: New Data Systems Team

Welcome aboard.

We are certainly happy to have you with us. I am sure that while you are on detail here, you will find this an enjoyable place to work.

I have had the attached background sheet prepared for you. Please read it immediately. I will be meeting with you to discuss these matters when you have finished.

Also, please note that a number of memoranda have been included in your materials. These are, of course, to be handled in a most confidential manner.

Enclosures: (1) Background Analysis
             (2) Memos dated Oct. 15, Nov. 3, Aug. 15, Nov. 4, Oct. 28,
                 Sept. 26, Sept. 29, Oct. 7, and Oct. 6, 198_

---

*Prepared by H. B. Lassiter and adapted by permission.

BACKGROUND ANALYSIS

Manpower Training Administration (MTA) is a training systems development agency that was organized as an independent agency four and one half years ago.

The agency reports to the President and is controlled by a Board of Governors consisting of ten members (five members appointed by the President, two members representing the management of the agency, and three members appointed by the President from industry, labor, and the general public). The agency also has a 21-member Technical Advisory Board consisting of internationally respected educators, psychologists, and business, labor, and social service leaders.

The major mission of the agency is to train persons who are difficult to train. This includes so-called culturally disadvantaged persons in the U.S.A., as well as persons in developing nations of Asia, Africa, and Latin America. The agency was established after it was recognized that private organizations alone could not afford to do the job required by this country and other nations.

The MTA has 500 field activities around the world (325 in the U.S.A. and 175 in foreign countries). These activities are divided into eight occupational areas:

- Butchering,
- Truck and auto mechanics,
- Computer repair and maintenance,
- Radio and communication equipment repair,
- Medical technology,
- Welding,
- Keypunch and key-driven tape-recording operations
- Computer programming.

There are five common features of these eight programs:

- Heavy use of audiovisual materials,
- Heavy use of advanced programmed-learning techniques,
- Use of role playing to teach job-related social skills,
- Use of tailored language programs (reading, listening, and writing),
- Some use of computer-assisted instruction.

Each program uses so much preprogrammed and pretested material that the role of the instructor is reduced to that of a monitor. The instructor-monitor observes the learners' progress through the training program, assists learners in lessons where necessary, and channels their attention to the appropriate sequences of preprogrammed materials.

The MTA has enjoyed some spectacular successes (e.g., training truck mechanics in Thailand within 4 months). Some programs have been moderately successful, while others have had high costs and have been installed behind schedule.

Typically, the training programs are operated by MTA for other government agencies and in cooperation with private firms and labor unions. The administrative and training systems development expenses are federally funded. Operational expenses of field activities are handled through a revolving fund to which participating agencies contribute. In most cases the staff for operating a local training site consists of 2–5 key MTA staff members, with a varying number (5–15) of locally hired instructor-monitors. The number of trainees per location varies from 25 to 2000.

The MTA has recently been directed by its Board of Governors to expand significantly. It is to develop 50 new training programs in the next 30 months and is to offer them in existing and new locations. The MTA is also adopting a policy of turning over its programs to industrial and government employers for operation.

In responding to these challenges, MTA management recognizes that it must do a better job of managing—particularly in the personnel area. It has relied pretty much on luck in recruiting, selecting, and assigning key people. It has a large number of temporary and contract workers, plus regular Civil Service employees. Some spectacular goof-ups have occurred (i.e., Spanish-speaking instructors were assigned to Hong Kong when projects in Chile were understaffed). The dedication and personal drive of the employees, however, have helped MTA handle new challenges.

The agency is organized as shown in Exhibits 1 and 2 and Table 1. In general, training programs are developed in the Training Systems Bureau and installed in pilot locations. The Operations Bureau operates the programs in the field once the pilots are successful. Conflicts have occurred in the past over the acceptability of pilots, but management feels these can be overcome through selection of more compatible personnel and the use of formal job descriptions.

EXHIBIT 1
MTA Organization Structure

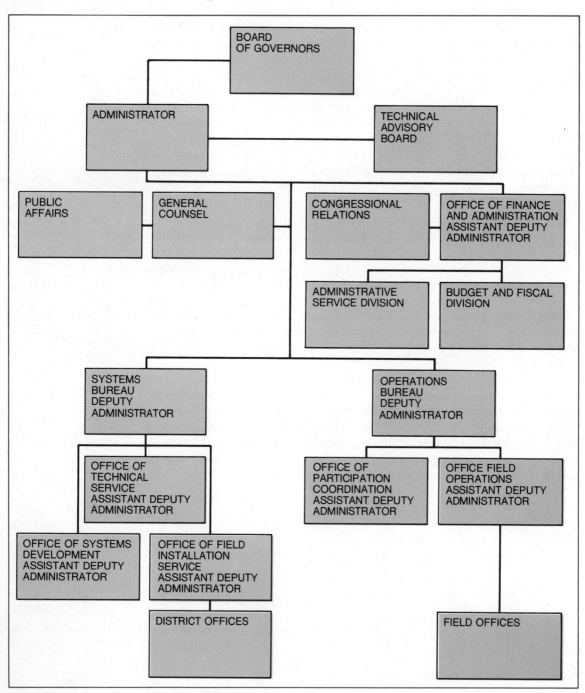

EXHIBIT 2
Organization of Budget and Fiscal Control

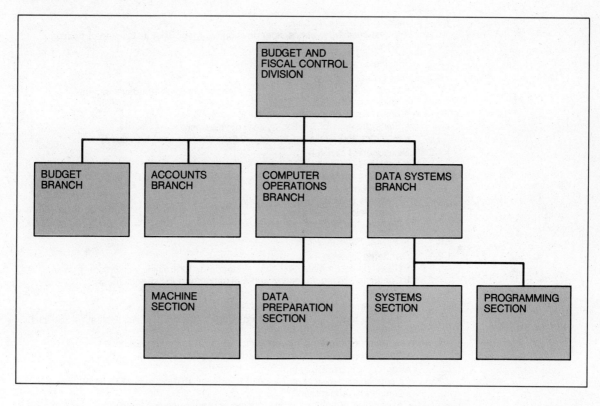

TABLE 1

Functions of MTA Bureaus, Offices, and Divisions

1.0   *Training Systems Bureau*
- Is responsible for conception, development, and pilot installation of training systems

1.1   *Training Systems Development Office*

1.1.1   Plans and Programs Division
- Provides liaison with participating agencies on program development
- Analyzes job market
- Analyzes training system feasibility
- Plans projects for training system development
- Monitors and evaluates training system development activities

1.1.2   Development Division
- Analyzes job market in detail
- Prepares job specifications
- Designs training system
- Prepares curriculum and materials
- Trains field installation staff
- Coordinates technical requirements

1.2   *Technical Service Office*

1.2.1   Standards Division
- Develops and maintains technical standards for training equipment
- Conducts continuing testing and evaluation of training equipment
- Monitors performance of equipment in field installations

1.2.2   Procurement Assistance Division
- Provides technical assistance to procurement activity in Administrative Services Division
- Helps monitor contract performance on equipment acquisition
- Helps develop technical equipment specifications

1.2.3   Assembly Control Division
- Controls configurations of acquired and available equipment to meet training equipment requirements
- Assembles prototypes of full training equipment components
- Coordinates assembly of course materials with Training Systems Development Office and Office of Field Installation Service

1.3   *Office of Field Installation Service*

1.3.1   Installation Planning Division
- Uses central staff to plan facilities for installation of training equipment, classrooms, etc., at local sites

1.3.2   Installation Control Division
- Controls 80 district installation offices (70 domestic, 10 foreign), which perform field installation of training programs
- Provides liaison with Operations Bureau's regional offices

1.3.2.1   District Office
- After appropriate orientation, installs training programs at site activities offices
- Trains instructor-monitors
- Evaluates initial training system performance

2.0   *Operations Bureau*
- Operates training programs developed by Training Systems Bureau

2.1   Participation Coordination Office
- Maintains liaison with participating agencies, business firms, and labor unions involved in field training activities
- Coordinates contacts between field activities and headquarters activities

2.2   Field Operations Division
- Provides line control and direction for all field training operations through 16 regional offices (12 domestic, 4 foreign)
- Conducts management training for site directors (managers of individual training activities)

2.2.1   Regional Offices
- Provides line management for training operations within the region
- Provides point of contact between headquarters activities and individual field activities
- Performs or controls field staff-type activities (e.g., personnel, local procurement, payroll processing)

2.2.1.1   Site Activity Office
- Manages one or more training programs at each site
- Performs required administration at local level
- Supervises senior instructor-monitor for each local program

TOPIC: Information Systems Project   October 15, 198_

FROM: Assistant Deputy Administrator
         Finance and Administration

TO: Data Systems Branch Chief

The recent dictates of the board require that we provide more sophisticated information services to our management. The fact that we have used computers effectively in computer-assisted instruction should enable us to expand quickly into management information systems.

I would like to see a system that will perform a variety of functions:

1. Allow us to determine the skills needed for our projects.
2. Keep tabs on personnel we have in house or on existing contacts who can staff new projects.
3. Determine whether or not someone is doing a job well.
4. Maintain better control of development people so we know what they are doing and when they will be finished.
5. Get our people to start more programs on time.
6. Improve our fiscal control of field operations.
7. Tell our board and Congress what our fiscal requirements will be as we increase our staff.
8. Tell where our people are so we can pay them on time and avoid morale problems.

I believe all these objectives can be reached.

Please let me know when you can get this show on the road. We've got 30 months to reach our targets, so don't tell me we have to wait that long for our information system.

TOPIC: Information Systems Project   November 3, 198_

FROM: Data Systems Branch Chief
            cc: Director Budget and Fiscal Control

TO: Assistant Deputy Administrator
            Finance and Administration

Enclosed please find a copy of a study report from our systems staff for a management information system to keep better control of our personnel. I believe this covers the points raised in your recent memo. I had not authorized a go-ahead on this project before now because I felt we were too small to justify it. With the growth we now anticipate, I feel the system is justified and respectfully request your approval.

The two analysts who prepared this report have since left the agency. However, with this report as a guide, I believe the new systems team on detail to us can move ahead immediately.

Enclosure: (1) Memo dated August 15, 198_

TOPIC: MIS—Personnel—Systems Planning Study   August 15, 198_

FROM: Special Systems Study Team Leader

TO: Data System Chief

SUMMARY OF FINDINGS

A.   Record Keeping and Record Maintenance

At present, personnel data are maintained in at least three and at some locations four separate files. There are files in the personnel branch, with personnel specialists in the principal divisions, at project offices, and at supervisory and division levels. As a result, there is much duplication of effort in handling and updating these records.

Almost every management representative interviewed felt that a basic improvement was needed in record maintenance and record-keeping procedures. The current system, although well designed to serve effectively up to now, can no longer meet the management information needs of the MTA. Some key points raised were these: long processing time of transactions, long management approval trail, and redundancy between records maintained by individual supervisors and those in personnel and payroll.

The following are representative management comments in this area:

> "There is a great deal of duplication of personnel records throughout the agency. They are scattered over many different units."

> "With all the record keeping we do, I still can't find out who knows how to do what."

The concept of a single set of computer-produced documents for both storage and change of information was readily accepted and considered extremely desirable.

B.   Reports and Management Information

Difficulty and a time lag in obtaining special reports were emphasized at both the Washington office and regional office levels. A system would have to recognize the unique needs of major groups in the MTA and meet them, while at the same time providing a central source in the main office for agency-wide information. In addition, all appropriate government regulations on personnel must be followed. A centralized body of knowledge and control could help avoid diverse policies and inconsistencies in personnel administration between the main office, the project offices, and other locations.

C.   Salary Administration

There is a broad need for rapid-access tools to assist in salary administration. Many areas for better control have been identified, but the present compensation record system cannot produce the required management information in the variety of ways needed to effect proper control. The new system should provide the ability to budget salary increases, show salary levels by grades, show correlations between pay and performance, and automatically signal when an individual is eligible for an increase or review.

D.   Skills Inventory and Management Development

A Skills Inventory System, coupled with key data on management and supervisory personnel and on employees in selected categories, is needed to identify candidates for promotional opportunities.

While there currently is some movement of key personnel within and between divisions, many of those interviewed felt this movement should be expanded. A similar need exists to identify promising candidates for management development and training. This is a current problem that is important to personnel's objectives. There was general agreement that a centralized inventory of skills should include all management personnel and certain other employees, such as lead instructors. The question of including temporary employees and consultants has not been resolved.

Following are some of the management comments on this subject:

> "Manpower planning is a key problem—particularly as it relates to an inventory of the skills of agency personnel. We need a system that will enable us to identify candidates to fill new positions as they become available."

> "We don't know who our capable people are or where they are. It's a sin that we can't get this information now."

"Selections are made on the basis of requests or personal knowledge. A record of skills and job preferences of employees would be extremely helpful."

Several management people saw a skills inventory as a tool for improving employee morale and suggested sending a printout to employees on an annual basis to show the data that had been maintained.

E.   Education and Training

A record of formal education attainment and all in-service and significant external training courses completed is needed. Some work has been done along this line, and the data already collected might be incorporated into the new system.

F.   Attendance Data

Some people felt absenteeism was a very costly problem. At present, data are kept manually. Key managers felt there was little value in those records and reports on absenteeism were misleading.

A system should be devised to record agency-wide attendance data for administration and control in this area.

RECOMMENDATIONS

The Systems Planning Study revealed areas in which application of the Personnel Data System concepts would alleviate immediate agency data-handling problems. These areas are described below. The study team recommends that the concept of an integrated Personnel Data System be adopted at MTA. The elements of the MTA PDS would include the following:

1. A comprehensive personnel data base that would incorporate all personnel information the MTA needs to know about its employees. This data base would be divided into four parts:
    a. A computerized Employee Personnel Record, which would store and maintain current statistical and confidential information about each employee and act as an updating change notice for all changes of information.
    b. A computerized Employee Skills Record, which would store and maintain data on work experiences, work preferences, and test scores for all management employees and certain other

employees. It would be given periodically to employees for review and updating.

    c. A computerized Attendance Record, which would store and maintain data on absences, tardiness, vacation time, and overtime.

    d. A computerized Education and Training Record, which would store and maintain data on educational attainment, objectives, and agency training for all employees. It would also record participation in community and professional activities.

2. The establishment of a personnel information center in the personnel branch, which would be the sole source of personnel information and eliminate the redundant handling and storage of data.

3. The establishment of advanced techniques of information retrieval, which would assure authorized personnel access to all stored information.

4. A systematic approach to handling employee information, which would strengthen MTA's personnel policies in the eyes of employees and the public.

Such a system would provide the Washington office with a base of information for operation and control over all MTA manpower resources.

INSTALLATION OBJECTIVES

The MTA Personnel Data System has been designed in modules so individual systems can be selected, programmed, and installed at different times, thereby avoiding massive commitments of manpower and programming support. In addition, the modular approach provides installation, data collection, and operating experience in smaller, easier-to-handle units than one total design and installation project. Each module, of course, will be computer-linked with the hub of the system, the Employee Personnel Record System, thereby affording the integrated system advantages of single additions, deletions control, automatic updating of certain data, etc.

Primary Installation Objective

The integrated systems design, by definition, establishes the Employee Personnel Record System as the first module to be programmed and installed. This module acts as the foundation for all other components to use for file creation and control. Therefore, the primary installation objective, within 10 months, is the Employee Personnel Record.

Secondary Installation Objectives

Each remaining module has been examined for priority on three bases: critical need, cost savings, and ease of installation, with each given a weight on the direction established during management interviews. Following is the study team's analysis of ranking for secondary installation objectives:

Module	Critical need ranking	Cost savings ranking	Ease of installation ranking
Skills inventory	1	2	2
Education	3	3	1
Attendance	2	1	3

The study team recommends the following priorities for secondary objectives:

1st priority	Skills inventory
2nd priority	Attendance
3rd priority	Education

Skills Inventory. Management comments consistently referred to the critical need to identify the skills and other capabilities of employees. Prerequisite for long-range planning for continued expansion is detailed knowledge of work experience, location preferences, special training, mobility, etc., of the work force. In addition, this module provides a base for identifying replacement needs resulting from normal turnover, attrition, and growth.

While the skills module does not represent a cost savings over present record-keeping methods (since no records are presently kept), the initial installation cost and annual recurring maintenance cost are reasonably low. This module, with its unique data collection and updating packages, can be installed with a minimum time and manpower commitment.

Attendance. Present costs of maintaining absentee, overtime, vacation, and tardiness data (presently estimated at $80,000 a year) and the need to have more usable information to control and reduce the estimated 80,000 worker days presently lost each year make the attendance module a high priority. Annual cost savings of the proposed system amount to 55 percent of what is presently being spent, a sufficient amount to amortize the development cost of the skills and attendance modules.

Education. Past data collection of education information gives this module the easiest installation ranking. Existing data can be formatted and easily converted.

TOPIC: Information Systems Project   November 4, 198_

FROM: Budget and Fiscal Control Director
          cc: Data Systems

TO: Assistant Deputy
          Finance and Administration

I want to endorse the personnel system suggested in the data systems memo. It looks like just what we need, and I urge you to fund it.

One of the MBA's who just joined my staff has prepared a memo outlining some features I would like to see added to the data systems proposal. In addition to the items in her memo, I would like to receive the following:

1.   Project budgets,
2.   Performance vs. budget statistics,
3.   Staffing projections by project,
4.   Predictions of slippage produced by the computer,
5.   Projected impact of changes in priorities on budget requirements.

If these things can be tied into the personnel system by something like PERT, I think we will really have a powerful management tool.

Enclosure: (1) memo dated October 28, 198_

TOPIC: **Recommendations on Project
and Output Control for MTA**   October 28, 198—

FROM: Ms. MBA—Management Intern

TO: Director
Budget and Fiscal Control

FOREWORD

This report covers three areas:

1. Recommendations on project control techniques and the reporting mechanism that would be used to accomplish project control,
2. Recommendations on quality control techniques and documentation standards that would be used to ensure quality control, and
3. Comments on the organization of MTA as related to its project activities.

INTRODUCTION

Project planning and control (and quality control) techniques are inherent in the management of any activity. The question is, which techniques should be implemented so as to support effective management of the agency and to facilitate a meaningful flow of information throughout the agency? A discussion of project and quality control must eventually result in an evolutionary system that can adjust to and reflect the growth of the agency. Therefore, despite the existence of prepackaged project management systems from software companies, we do not suggest that the agency do more than consider computerized control systems. These computer systems are believed to be unsuitable for MTA at this time.

The primary thesis of this report, then, is that personal management attention is the major element of any successful project and quality control system that truly contributes to the growth and mission fulfillment of MTA. It is this personal management commitment that is required at MTA: there is no mechanistic substitute for it.

PROJECT CONTROL RECOMMENDATIONS

The following actions are recommended as immediate steps in communicating and initiating project control activity at MTA:

1. Definition of a project, including phases of project activity and organizational responsibility for accomplishing tasks within phases,
2. Identification of project control mechanisms and the manner in which control will be effected and by whom, including a description of required reports and progress review requirements and actions, and
3. Specification of the roles of the project leader and team members during the developmental phases of a project.

These general recommendations are made more specific in the following section, although some organizational implications are also treated in the section entitled "Management Requirements." The most important recommendation for project control is enforcement of the rules for whatever approach is adopted.

PROJECT CONTROL TECHNIQUES AND MTA

Project Definition

This section presents guidelines for the control of MTA projects. The typical set of management standards for project control would begin with a broad categorization of project types for the organization under consideration. The purpose of describing, rather than defining, types of projects would be to provide a flexible but specific means of communicating the general character and relative amounts of resources normally required to accomplish that type of project. However, at this time it is possible to define MTA projects as follows:

> A project is a developmental activity to produce a prespecified result within a given period. An example of an MTA project is the conception, development, and installation of a training program. A project is considered complete when a training program can be field operated without assistance from developmental personnel.

Project Phases

A presentation of project phases, activities within phases, related documentation, and organization responsibility appears in Table 2. The primary purpose in assembling this table was to isolate those elements of control that could be used to monitor project progress. It is important to note that each phase has tangible outputs (e.g., documentation, equipment specs, hardware, etc.). Furthermore, each phase has an organiza-

TABLE 2
Project Phases, Activities, Documentation, and Responsibility

Phases	Activities	Output	Responsibility
Project selection	Confer with board and public policy representatives. Do initial surveys of trainee population, employers, and economic impact.	Conference minutes Proposals	Training Systems Bureau Administrator
System (project) scope	Survey trainee population and employers in detail.	Project plan and schedule General job descriptions Training options outline	Training Systems Bureau
Job analysis	Sample work and analyze tasks.	Detailed job descriptions	Training Systems Bureau
Systems specifications	Outline training system. Confer with potential users. Draft final cost estimates.	Functional systems specifications, revised budget and work plans Hardware specifications	Training Systems Bureau
Programming and assembly	Write course materials. Procure equipment.	Course materials Assembled training program	Training Systems Bureau
Testing and installation	Pilot test the system. Do initial evaluation and physical installation. Train instructors.	Documented and installed system (training program)	Training Systems Bureau
Operation and evaluation	Operate programs for one quarter. Conduct initial evaluation.	Evaluation report	Operations Bureau

tional component that has responsibility for both the progress of activities toward completion of the phase and the quality of the outputs of the phase.

Project Control Mechanisms—Reporting on Progress

The major control mechanism for any effective project control system is feedback, which is accomplished with two devices:

1. Progress reporting within phases, and
2. Management review at phase completion; depending on the phase, the management review might only be internal to MTA, or an internal review might be followed by a review by participating agency representatives.

Since we have some experience in developing training systems, certain general assumptions may be made:

- It should take 3-5 months from project selection to the development of functional specifications.
- It should take 6 months to prepare programmed instruction material and assemble and install the training system.
- No training system development project should exceed 12 months.

Since development activities are allegedly predictable, it is tempting to recommend that progress reporting be used only on completion of a phase. However, progress reporting should occur semimonthly within phases. These semimonthly reports can take the form shown in Exhibit 3.

EXHIBIT 3
Semimonthly Status
Report

Semimonthly Project Status

For Period Ending _____
Submitted By   Project No. & Name

PROJECT STATUS:
☐   Complete   Date _____

☐   On Schedule
     Est. Weeks to Complete _____

☐   Behind Schedule
     Weeks to Complete _____

COMMENTS:

RECOMMENDATIONS:

Reviewed by   Date   Approval

Semimonthly status reports should be submitted during all phases. These reports should be submitted to the responsible project leader. However, they require review by the relevant bureau-level managers when slippage exceeds the following limits:

Phase	Slippage requiring management review
Job analysis	4 weeks
System specification	2 weeks
Programming and assembly	4 weeks
Testing and installing	1 week
Operation and evaluation	2 weeks

QUALITY CONTROL RECOMMENDATIONS

The following actions are recommended as immediate steps in communicating and initiating quality control activity at MTA:

1. Establishment, agreement upon, and enforcement of control requirements,
2. Identification of quality control techniques and the manner in which control will be effected, including a description of review mechanisms and responsibility,
3. Specification of the responsibilities of the project leader and team members for exercising quality control.

MANAGEMENT REQUIREMENTS

The major management change will be to move from the present functional organization at the division level to a project-oriented organization in the Training Systems and Operation Bureau. Thus, the present division directors would become de facto project leaders. Project team members could come from any part of the agency and could remain on the team for one phase or the complete project.

TOPIC: Hiring Procedure   September 26, 198_

FROM: Director
         Budget and Fiscal Control
         cc: Assistant Deputy Administrator
             Finance and Administration

TO: Deputy Administrator
         Operations

Who the *heck* hired those 13 people in K.C.? Not only did we not know
about the people until they yelled about paychecks, we didn't even know
about the K.C. program. Are they temporaries, consultants, or what?

TOPIC: Hiring Procedure   September 29, 198_

FROM: Deputy Administrator
         cc: Operations Director
             Budget and Fiscal Control Deputy Administrator
             Training System

TO: Assistant Deputy Administrator
         Finance and Administration

I suggest you fire the Service Bureau that does your payroll or straighten
out your budget people. Those 13 folks in K.C. don't belong to me and
neither does that program. My project leader in north K.C. tells me that
the K.C. effort grew out of a Training System Bureau pilot test of a new
boat mechanic training system.
    Maybe your fancy new computer system will at least keep track of
what office should receive your inaccurate memos.

TOPIC: Hiring Procedure   October 7, 198_

FROM: Deputy Administrator
        cc: Training Systems
            Operations Bureau Administrator Director
            Budget and Fiscal Control

TO: Assistant Deputy Administrator
        Finance and Administration

I sympathize with the Budget and Fiscal Control people's problem in keeping their books straight, but I think we have to use reason. The Training System Bureau had surplus funds from a previous program and decided to use them to set up the K.C. pilot. It proved so successful we decided to make it a full-blown center.

As to why we didn't bring the Deputy Administrator of Operations into the picture: we expect to be modifying the system extensively for several years and didn't want to relinquish control. If it is used in other areas, his people could run it as long as they kept up with our changes—which would be difficult.

As I said in our meeting in the administrator's office, I will agree to any reasonable system of hiring people. Just don't hamstring my professional people with a lot of red tape. (Remember, we use a large number of temporaries who must be picked up when available.)

TOPIC: Recognition Awards   October 6, 198_

FROM: Administrator

TO: Assistant Deputy Administrator
        Finance and Administration

Two members of the Board have requested the names of individuals and projects deserving special recognition and attention. I am sure this sort of thing will become more important as we grow, and I hope your new computer system will provide this information.

Incidentally, we are going ahead with our plans to establish a planning staff reporting directly to me. I hope their needs will be satisfied in the new computer system.

CASE 2
Black Goose Uniform Corporation*

The apparel industry is one of the largest in the United States. It is also one of the lowest paying, with average hourly earnings in 1980 of $4.51. The industry is under siege from foreign companies. Imports accounted for 15 percent of total shipments in 1980, and this percentage is growing yearly. Trend analysis shows that the industry has had no real growth in the past six years.

The industry is made up of numerous subindustries, such as sportswear, women's high fashion, and uniforms. The professional uniform market is approximately $180 million annually, as seen by the following sales figures (in millions of dollars) for Black Goose and the industry:

	1978	1979	1980	1981	1982
Black Goose	11.1	12.6	14.4	15.8	18.0
Industry	124.7	135.0	149.0	164.0	180.0

As the figures make clear, Black Goose holds about a 10 percent market share. This stable, mature market, because of its utilitarian product, is not so subject to business cycle fluctuations as the rest of the industry.

The market is dominated by five manufacturers: White Swan (32 percent of the market), Crest (10 percent), Black Goose (10 percent), Whittington (4 percent), and Barton (38 percent). The competitors tend to be small, closely held corporations. None are publicly traded. Frequent attempts are made to steal management from another company. There are few, if any, real secrets in the industry, and there is plenty of gossip among both salespersons and suppliers.

BLACK GOOSE

Black Goose is a family-owned corporation with two principals, Harold Fein and Bob Blevlyn. It is closely associated with another uniform manufacturer, Chart, which specializes in lab coats and is jointly owned by Mr. Fein and Peter Wilson. While the companies maintain separate identities because of ownership structure, virtually all parts of the businesses with the exception of key account sales are integrated. Fixed expenses of the two firms are allocated on a cost-of-goods-sold basis; on average, Black Goose expenses account for 80 percent of all fixed costs. The fact that there are separate accounts causes many problems in maintaining accurate records. For example, customers frequently combine payments of Black Goose and Chart bills. Attributing these payments to appropriate invoices requires arbitrary decisions by the accounts receivable clerk.

*Prepared by Michael Horwith and adapted by permission.

EXHIBIT 1
Organization Chart

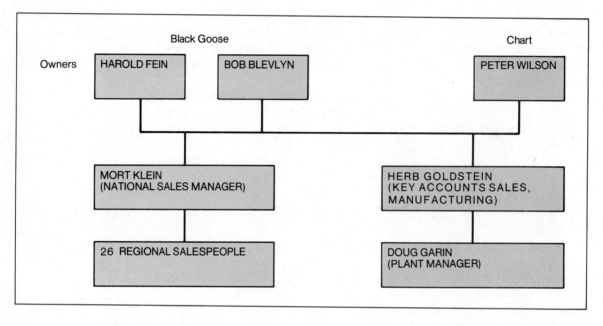

The organization chart in Exhibit 1 should be viewed solely as a formal outline—it does not represent true interactions between managers. Black Goose (as well as Chart) is an extremely informal company. No one wears a tie unless meeting clients, meetings are casual, and all communications tend to be oral or by memo, rather than by formal channels. Both firms' operations are run by Herb Goldstein, a 24-year veteran of the industry. Balance sheets for Black Goose are shown in Table 1.

Black Goose's factory is in Burkesville, Kentucky (population 1500), the county seat of Cumberland County. It is an isolated community on the Kentucky–Tennessee border, 90 miles from the nearest bar, 40 miles from a movie theater, and three hours from Nashville and Louisville. The factory is an efficient, well-run organization, the pride of the company. New York management makes frequent (at least monthly) trips south to keep in touch. Doug Garin is an excellent plant manager who, unlike many of his peers in the industry, gets along fine with "Yankees".

THE NEW YORK OFFICE

The only functional arm of the company located in Kentucky is manufacturing (along with associated materials and finished goods inventories). Sales, merchandising, finance, accounting, purchasing, production, and customer service are all located in New York. The Production Office, managed by Herb, is the hub of the company's operations. Herb forecasts demand (based on a six-week moving average of sales, combined with intuition and experience) and then issues cutting tickets based on the forecast. He purchases piece goods for the cuts from New York representatives of textile firms. Finishings (buttons, zippers, etc.) are also ordered by the Production Office. Design, pattern making, and sample making, all part of the production process, are also performed in New York. Naturally, each production activity requires its own form of information flow.

About 40 percent of Black Goose's revenues come from "Mom and Pop" stores nationwide. This has two effects on Black Goose's inventory. First, as "Mom and Pop" stores usually order fewer than a half dozen uniforms of any style and size, Black Goose must maintain a diversified, balanced finished goods inventory so it can pick sizes and styles from most active styles. This makes balancing the inventory and avoiding closeouts very difficult. Second, these stores are much more subject to regional influences than are national chains. A store in Ames, Iowa, is not going to order the same merchandise as one in southern California. Understandably, picking "hot items" also becomes difficult. Making the wrong decision results in closeouts, on which the company regularly loses 10–20 percent after fixed cost allocation.

TABLE 1
Black Goose Annual Balance Sheets (in thousands of dollars)

	1978	1979	1980	1981	1982
Cash	40	42	56	73	64
Accounts receivable	112	132	162	197	222
Inventory	2247	2663	2964	3833	3150
Other current assets	13	11	14	17	45
Total current assets	2412	2848	3196	4320	3481
Property, plant, & equip.	3046	3026	3006	3017	2999
Other fixed assets	41	37	33	29	41
Total fixed assets	3087	3063	3039	3046	3040
Total assets	5499	5911	6003	7366	6521
Accounts payable	367	351	642	1007	1194
Other current liabilities	803	961	1031	1186	1370
Short-term debt	1436	1221	843	1571	0
Total current liabilities	1170	1312	673	3764	2564
Common stock	600	600	600	600	600
Retained earnings	2693	2778	2887	3002	3357
Total stockholders' equity	1293	1378	1487	1602	1957
Total equity and liabilities	5499	5911	6003	7366	6521

THE MANUFACTURING PROCESS

Due to its maturity, the domestic apparel industry shares a very homogeneous manufacturing operation. The following description applies not only to Black Goose, but to almost all small garment manufacturers.

Cutting

The manufacturing process begins in the cutting room. A cutting ticket is sent south by Herb Goldstein to Doug Garin. This ticket lists styles, by dozens, with a priority code. Doug schedules the cuts according to these priority codes and the necessity to balance the work on the floor. He sends a cutting schedule to the cutting manager.

The actual cutting is an interesting procedure. Rolls of material, generally 80–100 yards long, are spread on a table. When the correct number of plys have been spread, a marker is laid on top and stapled to the cloth. An electric knife is used to trace the marker and cut out the patterns, after which a group of workers "bundle" the goods. These bundles form the basis of the internal bookkeeping system. Based on the marker and the amount of material spread for a particular cut, bundle tickets are made up. The actual "spread" may vary from the order sent over by Doug Garin because of inaccuracy, an end of roll, or imperfections in the materials. The bundle tickets carry the following information: piece, cut number, rate, style, and bundle number.

Stitching

Stitching is separated into two sections in the plant—parts and assembly. Young workers known as "bundlers" bring in the bundles from the cutting room and distribute them in sections by part, such as pocket, collar, front, back, cuff, etc. At this point something close to magic (at least to the uninitiated observer) happens. A single style with a cut of 120 dozen units is spread out on the floor among the mountains of white goods surrounding each operator. It is the bundler's job to see that style 123's cuffs don't get on style 132's sleeves. The cacophony of styles (all white) is directed by, in order of increasing authority, the bundlers, section supervisors, parts and assembly supervisors, expediter, and plant manager.

Although the bundle tickets theoretically provide a daily balance sheet, much of the control actually comes about through informal communications. As each operator finishes a bundle, a coupon is pulled off the bundle and attached to the operator's time card. Since all operators are paid on a piece-rate basis, these bundle coupons form the basis for payroll calculations.

A work-in-progress inventory is recorded as soon as goods have been cut, and an actual cutting record is produced by the cutting department. Goods are transformed from work in progress to finished goods as they pass through the finishing department into the warehouse. An employee at the end of the finishing line records each product sent to the warehouse on a "finishing sheet." After the finishing sheet and cutting schedule for any cut and style are compared to find the balance left in work in progress, this information is transferred to an inventory stock status report sent to the sales manager, operations manager, shipping manager, customer service, and top management in New York. This report is generally two to four weeks out of date when it reaches New York.

Billing

All billing of customers is done by the Shipping Department as goods are shipped. A copy of each invoice is enclosed in the shipping box and three copies go to New York—one for Customer Service, one for Accounts Receivable, and one "for the files." Exhibit 2 is a flowchart tracing Black Goose's paper flow.

INFORMATION FLOW

The following information is regularly sent by mail between the factory and the New York headquarters (it generally takes two to three days for mail to go in either direction):

New York to Kentucky	Cutting tickets, priority schedules, piece good orders, weekly factory profit and loss statement, paychecks, patterns, samples, financial statements
Kentucky to New York	Receiving report, raw material inventory, work-in-progress inventory, finished-goods inventory, cutting report, detailed work-in-progress report, invoices, shipping documents, payroll summary, efficiency reports, cost sheets

In many cases, multiple copies are needed. Additionally, 30 to 50 memos are sent each week. Since most of this mail is sent at bulk rates, postage costs are really not an issue.

Black Goose has approximately 450 employees, about 300 of whom are blue collar. At any time there are about 30 cuts of 20 styles in process. Each garment requires 15 to 25 operations, all of which must be recorded

EXHIBIT 2
Black Goose's Paper Flow

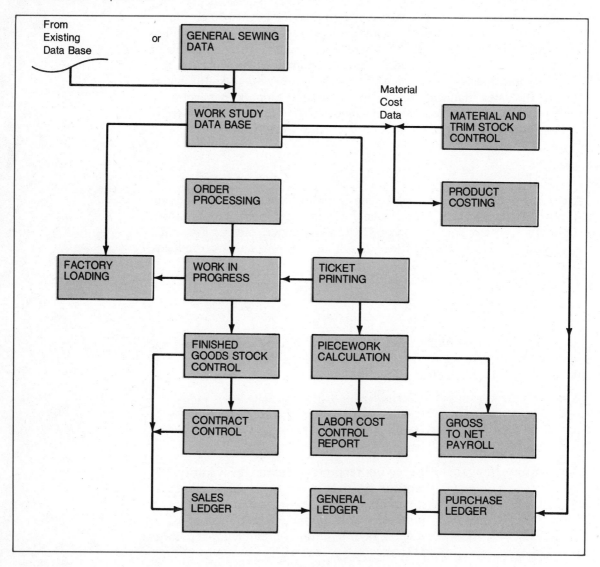

to maintain the piece-rate payroll system. The company produces about 80 styles each year, which are sold to about 12,000 customers ranging from "Mom and Pop" stores to J. C. Penney.

THE SYSTEM ACQUISITION DECISION

Herb Goldstein decided the time was ripe for Black Goose to enter the computer age: potential labor savings in both billing and accounting seemed clear, the efficiency gained should make Black Goose more profitable and competitive, a large amount of working capital was available (and had to be used before the owners decided to use it in other ways), inventory levels were low, the company had few debts, and everyone on 7th Avenue seemed to be getting a computer.

Herb was not that familiar with what computers had to offer, but he had some basic ideas about what Black Goose needed in a system. The hardware would be centered around a minicomputer at the Burkesville plant, along with several terminals and printers. A remote terminal and printer would be located at the New York office. Software packages would be acquired to replace most of the manual transaction processing systems currently in place—accounts receivable, accounts payable, payroll, inventory control, and sales commissions. With some of these manual systems, input data were prepared for use by a service bureau that produced various financial statements and reports; however, these reports lagged behind "real time" by about two weeks.

Herb believed an important area for improvement involved style coding: Black Goose ran hundreds of styles, many of which differed only by customer designation number. Herb believed there was also an opportunity to improve the current sales reporting system, although this was not a major factor in the contemplated acquisition.

Herb decided to consult three suppliers of information systems technology.

BMI

His visit to BMI headquarters in New York left Herb very impressed, for BMI was the industry giant, with well over $22 billion in sales in 1979. The sales representative's presentation had been very professional and had stressed the reliability of products and services offered by BMI. The company had an extensive assortment of hardware options and had developed generalized software packages for the apparel industry.

The sales representative estimated the cost of the required hardware at $82,000. Software packages would cost $20,940. Herb was looking for a two-year payback on his investment. He believed Black Goose would save $46,000 a year in labor costs and eliminate service bureau costs amounting to $40,000 yearly. Although many of the processing requirements were standard, Black Goose would require extensive software modifications to attain an exact fit between organizational needs and the capabilities of the software packages. For example, in the area of style coding, the estimated costs of necessary modifications and system installation was $32,500.

A major concern of Herb's was the service offered by each vendor. The BMI service contract cost $8,600 a year and guaranteed service within 24 hours. As additional insurance, BMI could arrange for a cooperative backup system between Black Goose and an apparel manufacturer in Glasgow, Kentucky, 34 miles away. If either system failed, the firm with the failed system could use the other firm's system between 6 PM and 6 AM. In addition to this service contract, Black Goose was told to expect regular programming maintenance expenses of $12,500 a year. The BMI representative said this cost was significantly lower than would otherwise be expected since extensive documentation was provided with the software. Herb recognized that the initial system costs were only a small part of the total costs and that, as time passed, maintenance could become the largest cost associated with the system.

Another benefit offered by BMI was an extensive training program for Black Goose employees. This involved both individuals who would be physically interacting with the system and those who would be using the system to make decisions. One of the largest obstacles Black Goose faced was the possibility of human resistance to this new approach to handling day-to-day tasks. The BMI representative assured Herb that BMI had overcome this problem before in other companies, and provided a list of firms to contact as references. Herb noticed that many names on the list were competitors or customers. This was particularly interesting as one of Black Goose's largest customers had recently suggested Black Goose adopt a computer system to enable both firms to electronically transmit order information to each other.

Diggs Corporation

Diggs Corporation was headquartered in Detroit. A Fortune 500 company, Diggs was a large competitor of BMI in the data processing field. It was well known in the industry that Diggs was very eager to enter the apparel systems market. Diggs' sales representative emphasized this fact when he said Diggs offered essentially the same system as the industry's major supplier at a substantially lower cost. This sales pitch was very technical, involving terms such as extra disk drives, ROM, and RAM; Herb had no idea what most of these terms meant.

Diggs offered a minicomputer comparable to BMI's for $60,000. While it had not developed any software packages specifically designed for the apparel industry, Herb was assured that program modifications would not be a problem. Herb was not exactly sure what might be involved, but he remembered that a competitor had recently spent $300,000 trying to develop an in-house system and finally had to acquire a system from an external supplier. The cost of Diggs' basic software packages was $21,000, but no estimate was given as to the cost of modifying these packages. Installation costs would amount to $7,500. Since extensive software modification was likely, the system would take longer to install than that proposed by BMI. The sales representative continued to stress that the hardware savings would amount to more than enough to cover any software modifications. Herb was well aware of the impact of this lower initial investment on Black Goose's 18 percent required rate of return.

Another savings offered by Diggs involved service. Service costs were estimated at $6,000 a year. This contract, however, did not guarantee 24-hour response. The nearest Diggs office was in Nashville, three hours away. However, Diggs did offer on-site training of personnel similar to that offered by BMI.

7th Avenue Systems

The office of 7th Avenue Systems was located in the heart of the garment district, in a building that also housed a pattern-making company and warehouse. 7th Avenue Systems was a subsidiary of a clothing group headquartered in Ireland. Dissatisfied with the cost and performance of outside systems, the group had brought together a team of programmers and clothing specialists to develop a system to match the specific needs of the apparel industry. As a result, its system provided a tight match between computer technology and the information processing requirements of apparel manufacturers.

The sales representative was much more customer oriented than those of BMI and Diggs, and seemed to know as much about the garment industry as about the computer industry. She told Herb that no hardware had ever been developed with the needs of the garment industry in mind, but that 7th Avenue Systems had located hardware components from a variety of vendors to create a computer system that was cost-efficient for the garment industry. Herb was quite pleasantly surprised to learn that 7th Avenue Systems could provide a hardware and software capability to meet 175 percent of Black Goose's current information processing needs at an installed cost of $30,000. This price included hardware, software, and any necessary software modifications. When asked how it was possible to provide a system at one-third the cost of comparable competing systems, the sales representative reiterated that these other systems were not industry specific; as a result, Black Goose would be paying for capabilities it would never use.

When asked about service, the sales representative said 7th Avenue Systems guaranteed 24-hour response and provided Herb with references to back up this claim. Herb noted all the firms on the list were within an hour's drive of New York City. He wondered how 7th Avenue Systems could guarantee service within 24 hours when a week earlier it had never heard of Burkesville, Kentucky. The cost of the service contract was comparable to that charged by BMI. Herb also reflected on the fact that it was unlikely any Black Goose customers would have computer systems compatible with the system offered by 7th Avenue Systems.

As Herb reflected on his meetings with the three sales representatives, he wondered how BMI had been so successful when firms such as 7th Avenue Systems offered so much.

HIRING A CONSULTANT

Herb Goldstein spent almost two months researching the purchase of a computer system for his company. With each visit from a vendor, he became more confused about the process of setting up an information system. He soon realized he needed outside help. On the advice of his accountant, Herb interviewed and hired Mr. Andy Teal as a consultant. Herb told Andy to take a few days to "meet the company." Once Andy had a feel for the firm and its managers, they could begin to work together and outline an information systems strategy.

After obtaining his MBA, Andy Teal had joined a Big Eight accounting firm as an MIS consultant. After a few years, the staid atmosphere of the accounting firm had begun to bother Andy and he had decided to consult on his own.

The first day, Andy studied the firm and its basic paper and materials flows. He learned that Black Goose was a sound company. It was more profitable than the average uniform company and turned out a high-quality product. The Burkesville plant was clearly an efficient operation.

The next stage consisted of a series of interviews with the firm's key management team. The following excerpts suggest the tone of each interview.

Bob Blevlyn

On the wall was a picture of the biggest fish Andy had ever seen, surrounded by all of Black Goose's top management. Long a lover of deep-sea fishing, Andy commented on the picture.

"Six-hundred-and-forty-pound black marlin," Bob explained. "Every year or two we get together and go fishing somewhere. We've been to the Caribbean, Mexico, Colombia. . . . This year we're going to Cabo San Lucas in the Baja."

They talked small talk for a while longer, and Andy was encouraged by Bob's apparent friendliness. Eventually, he turned the conversation to business.

"As you know, Herb has hired me to work with him on the MIS project. One of the major areas I'd like to explore is managerial decision making. Are there aspects of your work that would be easier or more efficient if you got better information?"

Andy noticed that, as he was talking, Bob's eyes had glazed over. The animation that had been present when the conversation was about fishing was totally gone.

"I don't know," Bob replied. "My job is really pretty cut and dried. I merchandise a few lines, I talk to my clients. I try to avoid having to leave New York too often, and I try to get free every day for an hour of tennis. My job is a people job—I've known my customers for so long that I sell by my personality, not by any numbers. If you really want to get involved in paperwork, you ought to talk to the women in customer service—they always seem buried in five inches of paper."

Andy tried various tactics to draw more informative statements from Bob about his use of company data, but soon found it was useless. Bob was friendly, nonconfrontational, confident of his abilities, and unwilling or unable to go into detail about his work.

Doug Garin

Next Andy flew to Burkesville to talk to Doug Garin. The plant manager's office had a glass wall on one side, which allowed him to watch the controlled bedlam created by so many machines and people. On the remaining walls were a style board and a scheduling board. The style board consisted of a sheet of paperboard with a small drawing of each garment. These were arranged by style numbers and there were at least 300 drawings on the board. The scheduling board was a massive chalkboard covered with what appeared to be secret codes. Andy couldn't see how anyone made sense of it, but Doug claimed it was quite easy to read once you knew the code. Doug's desk contained a number of manual reports on scheduling and efficiency in the plant.

"I've been looking forward to this meeting," Doug opened. "I really feel we have a good manual reporting system, but I would like to take advantage of any opportunities to improve on it or convert to a computer system."

Doug went on to describe the kinds of problems that an MIS might resolve. Of particular concern were last-minute changes in style design, quantities, or scheduling called in from Herb's office in New York.

"I understand," Doug said, "that we have got to be reasonable and flexible in our ability to respond to customer demands. But I don't think New York realizes the difficulties involved in changing a pre-engineered garment once it is in production. Even worse is the growing number of rush jobs. Everytime I get a call telling me to rush one cut or another, I can bet that the cost on the rush cut and whatever cut it displaces will rise 10 to 25 percent. However, I have no way of proving these numbers, because we don't have actual costs separated by cut.

"Another problem we've been encountering is a growing number of lost garments. Generally we expect to lose about .25 to .5 percent of all garments crossing the floor. Lately this number is reaching 1.5 percent. We produce up to 3000 dozen units a week. That means that we're currently losing about 540 garments a week. Someone is stealing large numbers of uniforms between cutting and finishing, and I have no way of tracking them down."

Mort Klein

Mort and Andy were sitting in Terrance's, a restaurant and bar in the middle of New York's garment district.

"The food here is mediocre," Mort confided, "but all the waitresses are out-of-work models. There is no better place in New York for a lunch to lift your heart while you down their spirits."

"I see my job as having two basic objectives," Mort went on. "The first and obvious one is to increase sales. The methods of doing this vary from offering our customers better products and services to going out and selling key accounts myself. The second objective of my job is to act as a buffer between Bob, Peter, and Herb on one side and the sales staff on the other. I want the sales staff to know I represent them to New York. If they are having trouble getting an order shipped or getting a commission check sent to them, I always take the time to intercede.

"On the other hand, I'd like to have stricter control over my sales force. Right now, the only performance measure I have is commissions earned. These figures are generally four to six weeks out of date. I also would like to see sales broken down by style. Currently the only sales report I get is a batch analysis of sales by accounts. This is anywhere from a month to a quarter late. If an account is slipping, I have to count on the sales representative to take action. In some cases this is no problem, but in areas with a weaker sales force, we may lose an important position in the retailer's stock because we react late. Even worse, I will have no idea why we have lost that position. Was it due to merchandising, shipping, poor sales-customer relations? We once lost a large account merely because the customer got angry over a prolonged bookkeeping error. This market is not a growth market. If we are ever to increase our sales, we have to do it by offering better service and better products than our competitors."

Herb Goldstein

Herb's office is the operational hub of Black Goose and Chart. During his forty-five-minute interview with Herb, Andy counted twelve interruptions. Herb cursed, kicked, stroked, and patted his people, but Andy was amazed to see the obvious affection the employees had for their boss. At one point a sales representative from a piece goods house came with a new style to show Herb. Herb screamed her out of the office, arguing over the quality of goods Black Goose had received on the last shipment. Andy had always heard about the dog-eat-dog world of Seventh Avenue, but now he felt like a Chihuahua in the kennel with a Great Dane.

"I take my job seriously," Herb began. "I act as if I'm an owner, which I'm not. I've been with Black Goose for over ten years. When I got here, manufacturing was telling New York what they were going to cut. It was the most screwed-up company I'd ever seen. On the other hand, these people are like family to me. Every top executive has been married two or three times. We keep changing wives but we never change our jobs. I'm being facetious, but there's a message for you in what I'm saying. This is a family company—don't try to make a Fortune 500 out of us.

"If you want to know why Black Goose is successful, I think you can look at a few major points. First, we produce a high-quality product. That is our image in the industry, and I make sure it doesn't get blemished. Second, we have the lowest turnover in the industry. We pay our people well and expect them to perform well. If they don't perform, I get rid of them—but that doesn't happen often. Third, and this is a key point, I stay on top of things. This is my company, and nothing is going to happen in it without my knowledge and input."

"As far as MIS goes, there are a few priorities I'd like to set. First of all, I want to get my receivables, payables, and general ledger on line. Let's go for labor savings and payback before we start hitting the "softer" issues. However, I'll leave all that up to you. I'd like a report from you next week on what we should do and why."

At this point another call came through and Herb waved Andy out of his office. Andy left thinking it was going to be a long week.

Appendix

Evaluating
Alternatives

SITUATIONS repeatedly arise in which, when scarce resources are allocated, comparisons are made of the extent to which various alternatives contribute to organizational purpose. The following CBIS activities produce such situations:

- Acquiring hardware or software resources,
- Selecting CBIS applications for inclusion within a master plan,
- Assessing the feasibility of a particular CBIS product,
- Specifying attributes of a sequence of versions that make up the CBIS product being implemented,
- Deciding among design alternatives for a CBIS product,
- Devising an implementation plan (determining time schedules and resource assignments).

Evaluation methods are also useful for assessing the effectiveness of CBIS implementations, CBIS products, or an organization's overall CBIS effort.

This appendix provides an overview of common evaluation methods. First, critical preanalysis issues are discussed. Then a selection of financial methods are presented. Finally, a few nonfinancial methods are introduced.

PREANALYSIS ISSUES

Three activities critical to any evaluation effort are clearly stating an evaluation objective, developing an evaluation framework, and identifying evaluation criteria. These activities must be addressed and agreed on prior to commencing an evaluation effort. Otherwise, participant biases may arise and not be recognized and counteracted.

The evaluation objectives guiding analysis vary with the decision addressed. Possible objectives include maximizing benefits given a cost limitation, minimizing costs given a set of requirements, maximizing early benefits, maximizing the cost/benefit ratio, and maximizing present value. This last objective—to be defined later—may be the soundest in general.[1] Studies with different objectives are likely to differ in both the set of alternatives considered and the resulting recommendations.

An evaluation framework consists of a listing of the major points to be addressed and a specification of an appropriate time horizon. This framework should be applied consistently to each alternative.

Evaluation criteria should not surface as evaluation proceeds; rather, they should be stipulated in advance. Otherwise, two behaviors can result. First, alternatives can be analyzed inconsistently. Second, and more important, criteria can be selected largely on the basis of what transpires during evaluation, instead of on the organizational purpose being served. If the need to include certain criteria is not recognized until after analysis has begun, all criteria should be reassessed and each alternative reanalyzed.

FINANCIAL METHODS

Financial analysis methods are important for at least three reasons. First, finance is the language of all organizations. While one department in an organization might not understand the purposes, activities, technologies, or terminologies of other departments, budgets and plans translated into dollar terms are meaningful. Second, a financial analysis tends to be objective. Third, a continuing problem in CBIS decision making is the multidimensional nature of CBIS objectives and impacts. By converting these into dollar terms, one can compare the overall contributions of various alternatives.

The financial methods presented fall into two groups: those that do not consider the time value of money and those that do. With both sets of methods, the focus is on streams of benefits and costs. Relevant benefits and costs are assumed to have been determined and expressed in dollar terms. The following notations are used in defining the various methods:

B_t The anticipated benefits to be attained in year t,
C_t The anticipated costs to be felt in year t,
C_o The anticipated initial investment,
n The anticipated time horizon in years.

Group I: No Consideration of the Time Value of Money

Cutoff Period.   If investment funds must be returned in a certain time period, the cutoff method may be appropriate. In this case, a time horizon is established by which anticipated benefits must surpass anticipated costs. For example, with a time horizon of three years, only alternatives meeting the following condition are considered:

$$\sum_{t=1}^{3} B_t \geq \sum_{t=0}^{3} C_t$$

The disadvantage of this method should be clear—benefits accruing after the selected time horizon are ignored. However, in some organizational situations an early return of investment funds is required.

Payback Period.   A related technique involves calculating the length of time required for an alternative to recover its costs. The following equation is solved for x:

$$\sum_{t=1}^{x} B_t = \sum_{t=0}^{x} C_t$$

By calculating the payback for each alternative, one can measure how soon investment funds are recovered for other uses. This can be important when there are cash flow problems or numerous equally attractive investment alternatives.

Average Rate of Return.   The average rate of return on the initial investment provides another means of comparing alternative uses of available investment funds. This is calculated as

$$\frac{\dfrac{\sum_{t=1}^{n} (B_t - C_t)}{n}}{C_o}$$

This measure is biased toward projects requiring smaller initial investments.

Group II: Consideration of the Time Value of Money

The major disadvantage of the preceding methods is that they do not consider the time value of money—future dollars are viewed as equal to current dollars. However, current dollars are more valuable than future dollars for several reasons:

- They have not felt the impact of inflation,
- They can be used to fund other investments and thus generate additional funds,
- They can be used to meet existing obligations and thus relieve the need to borrow funds.

Future costs and benefits thus, should be discounted to reflect their reduced value to the organization.

Exactly what should be used as the discount factor depends on a number of factors: the source of funds, the state of the economy, the financial health of the organization, the risk climate within the organization, the risk associated with a project, etc. Organizations differ significantly in their policies toward discount factors. Among the variables are the organizational cost of capital, the prevailing prime rate, the U.S. Government bond rate (a "risk-free" factor), the organization's average return on all investments, and a target level above the average return on investments. Clearly, a discount factor should be selected in a manner consistent with an organization's general investment policies. As the results of an analysis may be quite sensitive to the discount factor employed, all analyses should be performed with a range of discount factors, rather than a single factor. For the remainder of this section, r will represent the discount factor.

Present Value.   If a discount factor has been specified, it is possible to discount all future costs and benefits and arrive at the present value of an investment alternative. The calculations involved are

$$\sum_{t=0}^{n} \left(\frac{B_t - C_t}{(1 + r)^t} \right)$$

If the present value is greater than zero, a positive return on the investment is had. The rule to follow in comparing alternatives is to select the alternative with the highest present value.

Discounting future cost and benefit streams weights more heavily costs and benefits that accrue early in a project. As CBIS project costs tend to be felt sooner than benefits, employing a discount factor often makes it more difficult to justify a CBIS implementation effort. That CBIS managers have traditionally been reluctant to use discount factors should not be surprising.

Internal Rate of Return.   When an appropriate discount factor cannot be provided, a method analogous to determining an alternative's present value is to ascertain its internal rate of return. The purpose is to find the discount factor that equates the cost and benefit streams. Thus, the following equation is solved for r:

$$\sum_{t=0}^{n} \left(\frac{C_t}{(1 + r)^t} \right) = \sum_{t=1}^{n} \left(\frac{B_t}{(1 + r)^t} \right)$$

The alternative with the largest internal rate of return is most desirable.

The major deficiency of this technique relative to the present value method is the abstract nature of the discount factor. It does not convey as much information to individuals evaluating investment alternatives because a target rate of return is absent.

Relative Net Present Value.   An interesting companion to the present value method is the relative net present value.[2] This technique weights more heavily those investments requiring fewer overall investment funds—a characteristic that may prove important to organizations facing funding problems. The following calculations are performed:

$$\frac{\displaystyle\sum_{t=1}^{n} \left(\frac{B_t}{(1 + r)^t} \right)}{\displaystyle\sum_{t=0}^{n} \left(\frac{C_t}{(1 + r)^t} \right)}$$

An alternative with a present value of zero would have a relative net present value of one; alternatives with higher relative net present values are preferred.

NONFINANCIAL METHODS

Many CBIS evaluation criteria address issues that lose something when translated into financial terms. Others simply cannot be translated. And the financial methods invariably require subjectivity in estimating benefits and costs. Thus, it is necessary to employ nonfinancial (i.e., qualitative) methods in most CBIS assessments. Three nonfinancial methods are the weighting-scoring model, zero-based budgeting, and directed group assessment, as demonstrated by interacting groups, nominal groups, and the Delphi technique.

Weighting-Scoring Model

The procedure that follows is not meant to reflect a preferred approach, but simply to illustrate this type of nonfinancial analysis method. A two-stage process is involved. First, all alternatives are evaluated as to whether or not they meet a set of required criteria, *type A* criteria. This stage filters out clearly deficient alternatives. Second, the remaining alternatives are contrasted against a second set of criteria, *type B* criteria, leading to a preferential ranking of all the alternatives. The major tool that is employed in the second stage is the weighting-scoring model.

Type A criteria have two key features: they must be met by an alternative, and the extent to which an alternative meets the criteria must be assessed *unequivocally* (i.e., in a "yes–no" sense). Such criteria are usually present. By first screening out clearly inappropriate alternatives, one can greatly reduce the effort required to actually contrast alternatives.

The main activity in stage two is the construction of an appropriate weighting-scoring model, which is subsequently used to compare the alternatives that remain after filtering. The framework of a weighting-scoring model is shown in Figure A.1. The model components include criteria (C), weights (W), alternatives (A), scores (S), and ranks (R).

Criteria. Type B criteria include all factors believed to be important in comparing alternatives. Certain type A criteria may appear as well whenever the relative extent to which alternatives can meet a type A criterion varies.

Weights. The assignment of weights to criteria should reflect the relative importance of each criterion. Many forms of these weights are employed, the most common being the assignment of numbers between zero and one to criteria so the sum of all criterion weights equals one.

An effective way to assign such weights is to use a procedure known as "Q-sort". This involves the following steps:

1. Splitting all the criteria into two groups so the criteria in one subgroup are clearly preferred to those in the other,

---

FIGURE A.1
A General Weighting-Scoring Model

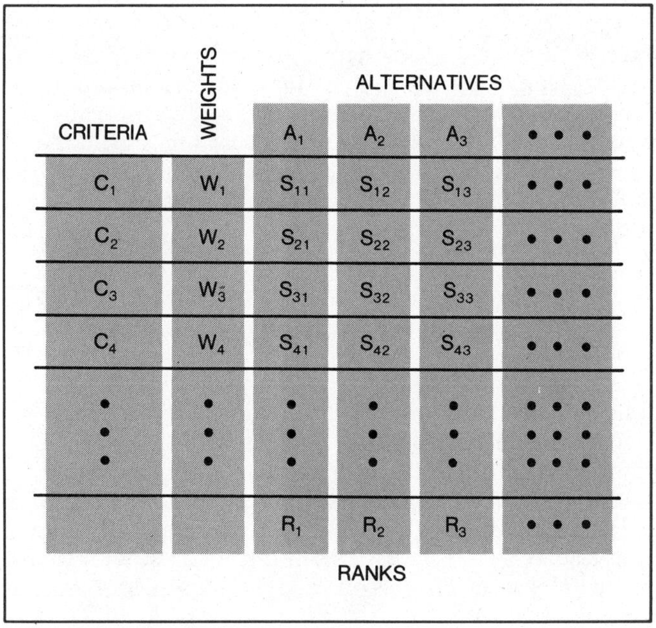

CRITERIA	WEIGHTS	ALTERNATIVES A_1	A_2	A_3	$\cdots$
C_1	W_1	S_{11}	S_{12}	S_{13}	$\bullet\ \bullet\ \bullet$
C_2	W_2	S_{21}	S_{22}	S_{23}	$\bullet\ \bullet\ \bullet$
C_3	W_3	S_{31}	S_{32}	S_{33}	$\bullet\ \bullet\ \bullet$
C_4	W_4	S_{41}	S_{42}	S_{43}	$\bullet\ \bullet\ \bullet$
$\bullet$	$\bullet$	$\bullet$	$\bullet$	$\bullet$	$\bullet\ \bullet\ \bullet$
		R_1	R_2	R_3	$\bullet\ \bullet\ \bullet$

RANKS

2. Continuing this splitting until further discriminations are impossible,
3. Assigning weights to the criteria.

Often a number of criteria are assigned very low weights (e.g., .01, .005, .02, etc.). It may be advantageous to simply drop such criteria from further analysis, as their impact will be minimal. In this case the entire weighting procedure should be redone with the reduced set of criteria.

Scores. Once weights are assigned to all criteria, the alternatives are rated according to the extent to which they meet each criterion. Such a rating may involve simply assigning each alternative a score from 1 to 10, with 10 indicating the alternative totally satisfies the criterion. More sophisticated scoring procedures might be employed to ensure consistency in scores. With one procedure, the *successive rating method*,[3] the following steps are taken for each criterion:

1. Assign a score of 100 to the best alternative and then rate the remaining alternatives accordingly,
2. Assign a score of 10 to the worst alternative and then rate the remaining alternatives accordingly,

FIGURE A.2
A Simple Weighting-
Scoring Example

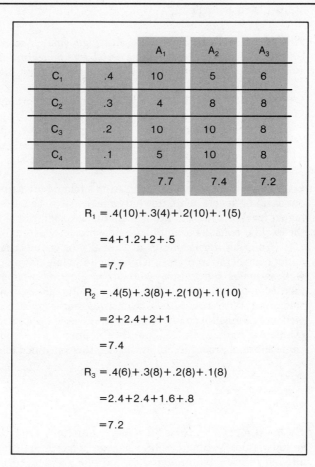

		A_1	A_2	A_3
C_1	.4	10	5	6
C_2	.3	4	8	8
C_3	.2	10	10	8
C_4	.1	5	10	8
		7.7	7.4	7.2

$$R_1 = .4(10) + .3(4) + .2(10) + .1(5)$$
$$= 4 + 1.2 + 2 + .5$$
$$= 7.7$$

$$R_2 = .4(5) + .3(8) + .2(10) + .1(10)$$
$$= 2 + 2.4 + 2 + 1$$
$$= 7.4$$

$$R_3 = .4(6) + .3(8) + .2(8) + .1(8)$$
$$= 2.4 + 2.4 + 1.6 + .8$$
$$= 7.2$$

3. Reconcile inconsistencies between these two sets of ratings, resulting in scores from 10 to 100 for all criteria.

Ranking of Alternatives.   Once scoring is completed, a total score for each alternative is calculated by multiplying each criterion score by the criterion's weight and adding all criteria (Figure A.2). These final totals for each alternative provide a means of ranking the alternatives.

The subjectivity of this type of analysis should be obvious. The superiority of any alternative over any other can be demonstrated, given a judicious assignment of weights and scores. Such evaluations should always be performed by groups, not individuals, preferably groups populated by participants with divergent perspectives and interests.

Zero-Based Budgeting[4]

When CBIS evaluation involves selecting a smaller set of items from a larger set because of a funding constraint, a zero-based budgeting approach can be appropriate. Two major features characterize this evaluation method:

• Each alternative is viewed in the context of both currently funded items and the items under funding consideration.
• All alternatives are viewed as a series of ventures (i.e., item attributes are specified at a number of levels, with higher levels containing less critical or more expensive attributes), rather than as a single venture.

Essentially, then, all of an organization's related investments are assessed at various funding levels. This not only makes item benefits more visible (i.e., each higher level provides additional benefits with additional funding), but also entails the explicit consideration of both new project ideas and those funded previously.

Consider, for example, an annual project selection activity. New projects under consideration might include the implementation of new CBIS products, as well as major and minor overhauls of existing products. All currently implemented applications would also be characterized as projects under funding consideration. With a zero-based budgeting approach, each project would be considered as a number of smaller projects and would be assessed according to the same evaluation framework. As a result, the project selection activity would also become a formal procedure for evaluating the continued relevance of CBIS products.

Directed Group Assessment

The need repeatedly arises in CBIS evaluations for groups of experts to assess various issues (estimate CBIS impacts, judge the relevance of vendor offerings, forecast future environments, etc.). There are a number of ways to direct such group assessment activities, but the three discussed here indicate the available options. Table A.1 summarizes the major attributes of these procedures.

Interacting Groups.   With interacting groups, participants congregate so they can hear and see each other. While a group leader directs group discussion, participants are encouraged to voice their views.

The major advantage of the interacting group is its freewheeling nature; a synergistic exchange of ideas ensues as participants introduce ideas, which are then immediately critiqued or extended. Its disadvantages lie in the tendencies for discussions to be dominated by participants with high status or strong personalities and for innovative or tangential ideas to be suppressed as participants are reluctant to associate themselves directly with such views.

Nominal Groups.   With a nominal group, participants again come together so they can see and hear each other. However, a group leader strictly directs the

TABLE A.1

Characteristics of the Three Directed Group Assessment Procedures

Procedure	Strengths	Weaknesses
Interacting group	Fast solution Conservative solution (focused on key issues as interpreted by dominant participants) Full capture of information (voice tones, facial expressions, etc.) Greatest likelihood for synergy	Failure to express certain ideas or views Domination by certain participants
Nominal group	Wider perspective Less influence by dominant participants	Slower procedure Failure to express some ideas or views Some loss of synergy
Delphi technique	Widest perspective Full range of ideas or views No chance for participant domination Highest likelihood of innovative solution	Slowest procedure Only partial capture of information No chance for synergy Difficulty in focusing or redirecting attention

discussion. Usually the group goes through a number of rounds. During each round the participants take turns expressing their views without interruption by the other participants. When all participants have expressed their views, the round concludes with a summarization by the group leader (an open discussion might be allowed as well). The session ends when agreement is reached or progress in bridging disparate views seems impossible.

The major advantage of the nominal group is that it increases the likelihood that the unique perspectives of each participant will be brought into the group discussion. The main disadvantages are some views may still not be voiced because of a fear of how others might react and the synergism associated with individuals' reacting to the ideas of others is lessened.

Delphi Technique. With the Delphi technique, participants are physically separated so they can neither hear nor see each other. All communication is accomplished through intermediaries (e.g., each participant may interact through a computer terminal). Again, the procedure involves a sequence of rounds. During each round, participants express their views in isolation. These views are then analyzed by the group leader and fed back to participants in summary form. The session ends, again, with agreement or stalemate.

The major advantage of the Delphi technique is the freedom of expression allowed isolated participants. *All* participants' views should be expressed, as participants know they will not be associated with their statements and are not influenced by the sources of other statements. This isolation, however, also creates the technique's main disadvantages: information exchanges among participants are incomplete (no voice tones are heard or facial expressions observed) and there is no opportunity for synergy.

CONCLUSION

In evaluating alternatives, one chooses not whether to employ financial or nonfinancial methods, but which collection of methods provides the most meaningful information, given the decision context. The immediate result of such analyses is not a solution, but at best a recommendation along with support for the recommendation. A second result is also achieved, which often proves more valuable than any recommendations offered. The processes of deciding on evaluation objectives and methods, identifying criteria, identifying costs and benefits, assessing the importance of criteria, and comparing alternatives all result in considerable participant learning that remains with the individual to be applied in other pursuits.

NOTES

1. J. L. King and E. L. Schrems, "Cost-Benefit Analysis in Information Systems Development and Operation," *Computing Surveys* 10(1978):19–34.

2. J. P. C. Kleignen, "The Investment Analysis of Data Processing Problems," working paper 80.98, Faculteit der Econonmische Wetenschappen, Katholieke Hogeschool, Tilburg, 1980.

3. W. E. Souder, *Management Decision Methods for Managers of Engineers and Research* (New York: Van Nostrand Reinhold, 1980).

4. J. C. Wetherbe, "A Zero-Based Approach to Allocating MIS Resources," *Proceedings of the 9th SMIS Annual Meeting* (Society for Management Information Systems, 1977), pp. 345–54.

Index

Centralization of information
systems, 362
Certified public accountants,
149–150
Charter, for master plans, 277
Chicago, City of, 374–375
Chief information executive, 37
Clerical tasks, conversion to
computer, 7
Closed systems, 66–67
Cognitive psychology, 59–60
COM. *See* Computer-output
microfilm.
Communication lines, 27
Communications devices, 27–28
Computer-based information
systems
decision making with, 191–193
effect of on organizations, 10
effect of on people, 340,
343–344
management of, 10
necessity for, 10
psychological climate of,
363–365
taxonomy of, 91–95
See also specific systems.
Computer crime, 146–148. *See
also* Security.
Computer graphics, 192
Computer operators, 35
Computer-output microfilm, 23,
24, 27
Computer services, in-house,
40–42
Computer security. *See* Computer
crime, Security.
Computer Software Management
Information Center, 46
Computer specialists, salaries of,
236

Computer systems,
configurations of, 37–39
Computer word size, 21
Computers, assessments of
attributes of, 88–89
Computervision Corp., 380
Concentrators, 28
Contract negotiation, 47
Control process, 165–166
anticipatory systems, 168–169
event-triggered systems, 169
exception principle, 169
indicators, 166
standards, 167–168
targets, 166
time-triggered systems, 169
Control unit, 20
Controllers, 68, 70
Conversion of systems, 255–257
Corporate war rooms, 206
Cost-benefit analysis, 291–294
CPU. *See* Central processing unit.
Crawling peg phenomenon, 167
Critical factors analysis, 325, 353
Cullinane Database Systems,
Inc., 383

D

Dallas Cowboys, 225–228
Data administration, 139
Data analyses, 164
Data base management system,
137–139, 197
Data bases, 135–140
access methods for, 111–114
currentness of, 116, 119
delays in updating, 116, 119
file structure, 108–111
indexed sequential access
method, 113–114

formal, 62, 64

informal, 62, 63

Organizational interfaces, 8–9

Organizational maturity, as
success factor, 359–360

Organizational planning, 157–158

and computer-based
information systems
master planning, 282–283

evaluation of, 161

goals in, 161, 162

implementation of, 162

monitoring of, 162

objectives of, 160–161

premises of, 162

strategies for, 162

Organizational size, as success
factor, 358

Organizational support systems,
54

Organizational suprasystems, 70

Organizational time frame, as
success factor, 359

Organizations

investments in information
processing, 8

nature of, 53–58

systems approach to, 67–74

Output devices, 26–27

P

Paine-Webber, Inc., 222–224

Paper, elimination of, 8, 124–125

Parallel conversion, in
computer-based information
system implementation, 256

Pattern matching, in decision
making, 189

Pattern recognition, in data
entry, 26

PDS. *See* Programmed decision
systems.

Performance indicators, in
control process, 166–167

Performance objectives, 340–341,
342–343

Performance standards, 167–168

Personnel

administrative, 18–19

for computer systems, 35–37

operations, 18

performance standards for,
167–168

for software development, 18,
36

Pidgin English, use of in
programming, 242

Pilot studies, for computer-based
information systems
implementation, 257

Planning, 172, 355. *See also*
Organizational planning,
Master plan.

Planning horizon, 278

Planning laboratory, 206–207

Portfolio Management System,
198–199

Primary memory, 20

Privacy, as a civil right, 148

Processing

modes

input, 17

interactive, 32

real-time, 32–33

time-sharing, 33

speeds, increase of, 7

validation of data, 18

Processors, 68, 70

Product efficiency, in computer-
based information systems,
345

Product utilization, 343
Program design language, 243
Programmed decision systems, 92–95, 207–208, 237
Programmers, 36
Programming, 239–241. *See also* Soft-ware development.
Project ideas, sources of, 284–285
Project inventory, 277
Project manuals, 259
Project review, 346–347
Project selection, 283–285
Protocol analysis, 315
Pseudocode, 242
Psychological climate, as success factor, 363–365
Psychology, cognitive, 59–60

Q
Quality assurance, in computer-based information systems, 341–342
Query language, 137

R
Random files, 109–110
Real-time processing, 32–33
Records, defined, 109
Redundancy, in distributed data processing, 144
Rental of hardware, 42–43
Report writer, for data base management system, 137
Reports
design, 173–177
dissemination methods, 177
Requirements analysis, 310–311, 355

for airline reservation system, 327–332
conceptual design for, 312
information collection tools for, 315–316
information sources for, 314–315
logical design in, 312
methods of, 318, 321–322
critical factors in, 325
future analysis of, 325–326
information analysis of, 323–324
operational modeling for, 322–323
variance analysis of, 324
strategies for, 313–314
validation of, 312–313
Requirements statement, 307–308, 308–310
Restructuring, of computer-based information system, 237
Rohm Corp., 371

S
Sabotage, 146
SADT. *See* Structured Analysis and Design.
Salaries, of computer specialists, 236
Schemata, 60–61
Security, 135, 147. *See also* Computer crime.
Security measures, 148–149
Sequential access, 23
Sequential files, 109–110, 117
Service centers, advantages and disadvantages of, 39–40
Short-term memory, 59
Software, 28–35

Time frame, in organizational
decision-making, 359
Time-phased diagrams, 278
Time-sharing systems, 39
Time-triggered systems, 169
Tools, for information collection,
315–316
Top-down modeling, 281
Top-down programming, 240,
247
Touch-tone telephones, 26
TPS. *See* Transaction processing
systems.
Training, for computer-based
information systems
implementation, 257
Transaction processing systems,
92, 94, 135, 237
Transmission facilities
band rate, 27
communication lines, 27
leased lines, 27
telephones, touch-tone, 26
Trends
in decision-support systems,
205–206
in hardware, 28
in software, 35

U
Updating, of computer-based
information systems, 237
User participation, in computer-
based information systems
implementation, 264–266,
356–357

User satisfaction, with
computer-based information
system products, 344–345
User's manuals, 258
Utility analysis, in requirements
analysis, 316

V
Validation, in requirements
analysis, 312–313
Variance analysis, in
requirements analysis, 324,
327
Vendors
bid evaluation, 46
bid solicitation, 45–46
contract negotiation with, 47
penalties for unmet conditions,
47
Virtual operating systems, 33
Voice grade communication lines,
27

W
Wang word processing systems,
79–81
Weltansicht, 60–61
Word processing, 79–81
Work stations, executive, 205–206
Work units, 54–58, 68, 87
Working memory, 60

Z
Zero-based budgeting, 432